658. 4012

Competence, Governance, and
Advances in Economic Stra

CW00435193

7000251321

WN
LIBRARY SERVICES

FR 10813/1

ML

UWE BRISTOL
WITHDRAWN
LIBRARY SERVICES

Competence, Governance, and Entrepreneurship

Advances in Economic Strategy Research

Edited by

NICOLAI FOSS
and
VOLKER MAHNKE

U.W.E.

20 OCT 2003

BUS
Library Services

UNIVERSITY PRESS

OXFORD
UNIVERSITY PRESS

Great Clarendon Street, Oxford OX2 6DP

Oxford University Press is a department of the University of Oxford.
It furthers the University's objective of excellence in research, scholarship,
and education by publishing worldwide in

Oxford New York

Auckland Bangkok Buenos Aires Cape Town Chennai
Dar es Salaam Delhi Hong Kong Istanbul Karachi Kolkata
Kuala Lumpur Madrid Melbourne Mexico City Mumbai Nairobi
São Paulo Shanghai Taipei Tokyo Toronto

Oxford is a registered trade mark of Oxford University Press
in the UK and in certain other countries

Published in the United States
by Oxford University Press Inc., New York

© The several contributors 2000

The moral rights of the author have been asserted
Database right Oxford University Press (maker)

First published 2000
Published new as paperback 2002

All rights reserved. No part of this publication may be reproduced,
stored in a retrieval system, or transmitted, in any form or by any means,
without the prior permission in writing of Oxford University Press,
or as expressly permitted by law, or under terms agreed with the appropriate
reprographics rights organization. Enquiries concerning reproduction
outside the scope of the above should be sent to the Rights Department,
Oxford University Press, at the address above

You must not circulate this book in any other binding or cover
and you must impose this same condition on any acquirer

British Library Cataloguing in Publication Data
Data available

Library of Congress Cataloging in Publication Data
Competence, governance, and entrepreneurship: advances in economic
strategy research/edited by Nicolai Foss and Volker Mahnke.
p. cm.
Includes bibliographical references and index.
1. Industrial organization (Economic theory) 2. Corporations—Growth. 3. Corporate
governance. 4. Entrepreneurship. I. Foss, Nicolai J., 1964- . II. Mahnke, Volker.
HD2326.C65 2000 658.4'012—dc21 00-025247
ISBN 0-19-829717-3 (hbk.)
ISBN 0-19-925981-X (pbk.)

1 3 5 7 9 10 8 6 4 2

Typeset in Garamond by
Cambrian Typesetters, Frimley, Surrey
Printed in Great Britain
on acid-free paper by
Biddles Ltd., Guildford and King's Lynn

Acknowledgements

Funding from the Danish Research Unit for Industrial Dynamics (DRUID) is gratefully acknowledged.

Oliver E. Williamson's chapter, 'Strategy Research: Competence and Governance Perspectives', was published in *Strategic Management Journal*, volume 20, no. 12, 1999, pp. 1087–1108. Copyright John Wiley & Sons Limited. Reproduced with permission.

Contents

Part C: The Dynamics of Governance

List of Figures

List of Tables

List of Contributors

Nicholas A. Argyres
Marshall School of Business
Department of Management and
Organisation
University of Southern California
USA

Jay B. Barney
Fisher College of Business
The Ohio State University
USA

Mark Casson
Department of Economics
University of Reading
UK

Patrick Cohendet
Université Louis Pasteur
Bureau d'Economie Théorique et
Appliquée
France

Rod Coombs
Professor of Technology Management
and Director of Centre for Research
on Innovation and Competition
(CRIC)
Manchester School of Management
UMIST
UK

Giovanni Dosi
Laboratorio di Economia e
Management
Scuola Superiore Sant'Anna
Italy

Kirsten Foss
Department of Industrial Economics
and Strategy
Copenhagen Business School
Denmark

Nicolai J. Foss
Department of Industrial Economics
and Strategy
Copenhagen Business School
Denmark

Paul A. Geroski
London Business School
UK

Sumantra Ghoshal
London Business School
UK

Martin Hahn
Massachusetts Institute of Technology
USA

Neil M. Kay
Department of Economics
University of Strathclyde
Scotland

Dr Woonghee Lee
Fisher College of Business
The Ohio State University
USA

Julia Porter Liebeskind
Marshall School of Business
University of Southern California
USA

Patrick Llerena
Université Louis Pasteur
Bureau d'Economie Théorique et
Appliquée
France

Anoop Madhok
Department of Management
David Eccles School of Business
USA

Volker Mahnke
Department of Industrial Economics
and Strategy
Copenhagen Business School
Denmark

Luigi Marengo
Department of Economics
University of Trento
Italy

J. Stanley Metcalfe
Department of Economics
University of Manchester
UK

Peter Moran
London Business School
UK

Eric Pfaffmann
Hohenheim University
Center for International
Management and Innovation
Germany

Ron Sanchez
International Institute for
Management Development (IMD)
Switzerland

Oliver E. Williamson
Haas School of Business
University of California at Berkeley
USA

1

Advancing Research on Competence, Governance, and Entrepreneurship

NICOLAI FOSS AND VOLKER MAHNKE

1. The Industrial Organization of the Theory of the Firm

It is hard to disagree with the proposition that after long neglect the theory of the firm, broadly conceived, has now become a significant growth industry. However, it is fair to say that the industry is also characterized by a substantial proliferation of diverse products. It is still very much in its 'fluid' phase, there are few signs of any shake-out of inferior intellectual products (indeed, there is little agreement on what constitutes inferior or superior products), the nature of competitive activity is not clear-cut, and there are few attempts at striking strategic alliances. Nevertheless, it is certainly possible to collect the diverse products and producers in a number of identifiable and distinct strategic groups.

Most obviously, the industry is populated by two major groups, namely those who espouse what are called in the present book the 'competence perspective' and the 'governance perspective' on the firm. In turn, both of these consist of several subgroups or, some may argue, they have several aliases. Thus, under the rubric of the 'competence perspective' we encounter the 'capabilities', 'core competence', 'knowledge-based', 'resource-based', and 'dynamic capabilities' perspectives, not to speak of the evolutionary theory of the firm. And under the rubric of the 'governance perspective'—at least as that term is used in this book—one encounters transaction cost economics, most notably associated with Oliver Williamson (1996*a*), as well as formal contract theory (agency theory and incomplete contract theory), and the measurement cost approach associated with Yoram Barzel (1997).[1]

To date, the barriers to mobility between the groups have been substantial, and there have been few attempts to pool resources to ascertain what may result from such innovative joint ventures. Furthermore, there has been a fair amount of consumer ignorance because of the presence of high switching costs and a

---

[1] Some may prefer to reserve the term 'governance perspective' for Williamson's brand of transaction cost economics alone, since his is the only approach that pays much attention to *ex post* governance. However, in the present context 'governance' is interpreted in a broad sense that encompasses governance through *ex ante* incentive alignment.

possibly excessive proliferation of products. Consequently, it has not been clear—either to incumbents or to consumers—how the groups relate to each other. Thus, it has lately been claimed by proponents of competence perspective insights that their product can accomplish what the products of the governance perspective can. Specifically, representatives of both groups claim that they are reaching for a 'strategic theory of the firm'—that is to say, a theory that not only is informative with respect to the traditional issues considered in the theory of the firm (why firms exist, what determines their boundaries and internal organization) but also is helpful for informing firm strategy issues, such as understanding the sources of competitive advantage, positioning in the market, strategic flexibility, etc.

Our motivation for organizing the conference on 'Competence, Governance and Entrepreneurship'—which took place from 9 to 11 June 1998 on the Danish island of Bornholm and gathered around 100 economists and business administration scholars—was to bring together the foremost representatives of competence and governance perspectives in order to compare products, reduce barriers to mobility, stimulate the formation of alliances, and reduce consumer ignorance. Particular emphasis was placed on the use of competence and governance perspectives in the context of business administration, particularly in the field of strategy. Hence, the subtitle of this volume. We think we were largely successful in stimulating conversation in the field, and we offer the present volume as partial evidence of this claim.

Thus, most of the chapters in this book make reference to both the competence and the governance perspective, and the critique that proponents of one perspective may launch against the other perspective is on the whole 'civilized, empirically attentive, and theoretically sophisticated', as Giovanni Dosi and Luigi Marengo (Chapter 4) note. For example, Oliver Williamson (Chapter 2) observes that the competence perspective contains many 'good ideas', and that in some respects it complements the governance perspective. In terms of actually building theory on the basis of both perspectives, Anoop Madhok (Chapter 13)—who has hitherto been a vocal critic of transaction cost economics (see, for example, Madhok 1996)—now suggests an integrative framework for analysing inter-firm relations that draws on ideas of both governance and competence.

Such observations and work may in themselves signal that the mutual ignorance and fixed stereotypes that have characterized much of the debate so far are disappearing. Indeed, the general tenor of the Bornholm conference was such as to encourage participants to engage in open and informed discussion, and the ethics of 'science as good conversation' was characterized by the mood of the gathering. However, this does not mean that critique was downplayed or that the perspectives were somehow accepted as being on an equal footing in terms of explanatory scope, precision, depth of insight, etc. Indeed, quite often the critique was very direct, and some of the chapters in the present book reflect this.

Thus, Williamson (Chapter 2) explicitly defends the governance perspective against what he takes to be misunderstandings on the part of writers who favour the competence perspective. As he points out, the governance perspective is in fact capable of incorporating, for example, path dependence. And Kirsten Foss and Nicolai Foss (Chapter 3) argue that although the competence and governance perspectives are indeed different, many key ideas of the competence perspective may be rendered compatible with the governance perspective by recasting these ideas in terms of the allocation of property rights inside firms. One may draw the provocative (and arguably too extreme) implication that certain, perhaps even most, competence perspective ideas are redundant, having already been stated in a superior manner within the governance perspective.

From the other end of the spectrum, Giovanni Dosi and Luigi Marengo 'forcefully disagree' with the proposition that much of the competence-based view can be 'reduced' to governance perspective insights. In actuality, they point out, the governance perspective largely neglects learning and problem solving. However, like Williamson, they also stress that the two perspectives are, at the same time, rivals and complements—a judgement that is amply confirmed by most of the chapters in the present volume. Thus, while some authors point out that the two perspectives are rivals in the sense that they provide conflicting explanations of the same phenomenon, others argue that because the domains of application of the two perspectives are not fully congruent, there is much scope for integrative work that begins from complementarities between the perspectives.

While Part A of the present volume deals with the meta-task of critical comparison and discussion, the chapters in the remaining two parts not only refer to and compare, but actually make constructive use of both perspectives. For example, Barney and Lee (Chapter 14), Neil Kay (Chapter 9), and Eric Pfaffmann (Chapter 12) all apply ideas from the competence as well as the governance perspective in the development of their own distinctive arguments. Such integrative views are very encouraging, since a commonly acknowledged source of scientific progress is indeed the integration (unification) of theories that have hitherto been taken to be opposed or unrelated.

In order to understand the background to the debates between competence and governance scholars, and why combining competence and governance ideas may be a worthwhile venture—in short, the background to the whole of this volume—the remainder of this chapter briefly presents and discusses the governance and competence perspectives, clarifies the differences between them, and suggests how the contributions to this volume help resolve some of the problems or suggest future points of contact, dialogue, and cross-fertilization. In particular, we focus on the use of the modern theory of the firm in the field of the strategy of the firm—a crucial issue that informs the discussion in the majority of the contributions to this volume.

2. 'Interesting Babble' or 'Tangled Discourse'?

More than a decade ago, at the conference arranged to celebrate the fifty years that had then passed since the publication of Coase (1937), Sidney Winter noted that:

[w]ithout demeaning the contributions that any of us have made, I think we must acknowledge that the present state is one of incoherence. If we ask, 'What does economics have to say about the role of the business firm in a market economy?,' the response will be silence followed by an interesting babble of significantly conflicting answers—an interesting babble, but a babble nonetheless. (Winter 1991: 179.)

Most observers of the present situation in the economics of organization (broadly conceived) would probably regard Winter's statement as still holding true, although it is also the case that in some dimensions, progress with respect to integrating diverse perspective has been made. As stated earlier, a number of the contributions to the present volume are instances of this. Thus, perhaps Dosi and Marengo's (Chapter 4) characterization of the present situation as one of 'tangled discourse' rather than 'interesting babble' is closer to the mark.

Nevertheless, as we have seen, the theory of the firm 'industry' is dominated by two very different groups, both with numerous precursors, aliases, and ramifications. They have only partly overlapping foundations, they approach theory building differently, and their institutional backgrounds and affiliations differ. Most importantly, they identify explanatory principles and mechanisms that seem to be very different indeed, so that they put forward rival explanations and predictions for the same phenomena. However, some differences are likely to be superficial, while others are more substantial. Table 1.1 is an attempt to capture the more substantial differences.[2]

It is important to stress that the characterizations in Table 1.1 admittedly border on the caricature. However, there is usually some truth to caricatures, and not all of the entries in the table are caricatures. For example, the claim that the governance perspective is in many respects a static (or functionalist) affair—dynamics entering at most through the 'fundamental transformation' (Williamson 1996a)—while the competence perspective aims at a more explicitly causal-genetic explanatory approach would probably be admitted even by proponents of the governance perspective. Indeed, a large number of the contributions to this volume have, in various ways, this schism at the heart of their reasoning. The attempts to provide room within the governance perspective for entrepreneurship (see, for example, Casson, Chapter 6), firm growth (Kay, Chapter 9), path dependence (Argyres and Liebeskind, Chapter 11), and real

---

[2] Foss and Foss (Chapter 2) and Dosi and Marengo (Chapter 4) present related tables; see also Winter (1991).

TABLE 1.1. Partial characterization of the competence and governance perspectives

The competence perspective	The governance perspective
• 'Production oriented' • 'Transaction *value*' • Knowledge building and knowledge utilization • Routines/competences are units of analysis • Differential cognition • Opportunism and other incentive conflicts relatively unimportant • Dynamic/evolutionary	• 'Exchange oriented' • 'Transaction *costs*' • Structuring incentives and allocating property rights • Transactions are units of analysis • Cognitive homogeneity • Incentive conflicts are central • Comparative statics

options (Sanchez, Chapter 15) are all evidence that the perspective is deficient in this respect.

However, other distinctions in Table 1.1 are close to the caricature. Consider, for example, what may be the most obvious caricature in the table, namely the distinction between the 'production oriented' competence perspective and the 'exchange oriented' governance perspective—a distinction that was probably first applied in the context of economic organization by Sidney Winter (1991) in a carefully guarded discussion. Indeed, it is necessary to exercise great care when invoking this distinction. This is because from a basic economic perspective, it may be difficult to see what the fuss is about. Thus, one normally thinks of efficient economic organization as maximizing joint surplus, given path dependencies, information asymmetries, and risk preferences. Clearly, production (relating to the size of the surplus) and exchange (relating to the sharing of the surplus) are both crucial elements of the process, so that the often invoked distinction is a misleading one.[3] Of course, we can conceptually make a distinction between production knowledge and organization knowledge, between knowledge about how to do things and knowledge about how to organize the 'doing'. However, as Nelson and Winter (1982) point out in their classic work, in actuality these bodies of knowledge are completely intertwined.

Still, there *is* something to the distinction. For if 'production oriented' is taken to mean that what is seen as distinctive about the firm lies in its determining what is produced and how, then this has undeniably not been the traditional turf of the governance perspective. Undeniably, too, this has served to limit the practical applicability of the governance perspective in the business administration field, since issues of positioning and manufacturing strategy have

---

[3] Strictly speaking, it is thus *not* true that, for example, the governance perspective neglects transaction benefits (as, for example, Zajac and Olsen 1993 assert).

been hard to conceptualize within this perspective. And it is to a large extent because of these limitations that the competence perspective has been able to obtain so much influence, both as a theory of the firm *per se* and as an approach to firm strategy. We consider this issue in the following sections.

3. The Governance Perspective and the Strategic Theory of the Firm

In the conventional reading, economists' interest in the firm as an institution in its own right began with Ronald Coase's 1937 paper on 'The nature of the firm'. Much later Coase (1972) observed that his 1937 essay had been 'much cited and little used'. Ironically, from about the time of this lamentation, the landscape of economic thought changed rather significantly, as a large body of literature—often referred to as 'the economics of organization'—quickly emerged that not only 'used' but in many ways sprang from Coase's paper (Alchian and Demsetz 1972; Williamson 1971; Arrow 1974).

There are many reasons for the strong growth of specialized research on the theory of the firm in economics during the last two decades. A trivial one is an increased division of labour as the number of academic economists has steadily grown. A more interesting explanation is that the theory of the firm stands out as one of the areas (industrial organization economics is another) in which the economist most obviously has had something to contribute to business administration, particularly in fields such as organization and strategy. In fact, perhaps the majority of the leading organizational economists are now employed (at least in the USA) by business schools.

There are good reasons for this. Organizational economics thinking on the structuring of incentives and property rights is immensely useful for addressing and understanding a host of management-related issues (see, for example, Milgrom and Roberts 1992; Miller 1992; Holmström and Milgrom 1991). Among these are issues such as incentive contracts, the make or buy decision, leveraged buy-outs, the use of profit centres, and much else of direct relevance for the strategy field.

Recognition of this contribution is not new. In 1980, Richard Caves (1980) argued that corporate strategy issues should be framed as constrained optimization problems, and that recent work in the economics of organization would be helpful in this regard. A little later Richard Rumelt (1984: 557) claimed that 'it appears obvious that the study of business strategy must rest on the bedrock foundations of the economist's model of the firm'. More specifically, he argued that by building on the work of Coase (1937) and Williamson (1975), the strategy field could arrive at a 'strategic theory of the firm' that would constitute the essential core of research.

The minimal requirement for a 'strategic theory of the firm' would seem to be that it is a theory that addresses the key issues of the modern economic theory of the firm and key issues of strategy. Addressing the following four issues would seem to meet this minimum requirement:

1. *The existence of the firm*—that is, why do firms exist as distinct mechanisms for resource allocation in a market economy (Coase 1937; Williamson 1996)?
2. *The boundaries of the firm*—that is, what explains why certain transactions are governed in-house while others are governed through market relations (Grossman and Hart 1986)?
3. *Internal organization*—that is, why do we observe different types of (formal and informal) organizational structure and accompanying phenomena, such as internal labour markets, job ladders, profit centres, etc. (Alchian and Demsetz 1972; Holmström 1982; Prendergast 1999)?
4. *Competitive advantage*—that is, which factors account for superior rent-earning capability (Wernerfelt 1984; Porter 1985; Barney 1991)?

These issues are clearly interdependent; for example, a given firm's internal organization may be a source of competitive advantage. Indeed, much of what is meant by terms such as 'capabilities', 'competences', and the like refer to organizational processes (as Foss and Foss point out in Chapter 3). Furthermore, where a firm places its boundaries may influence the sustainability of competitive advantage for reasons of appropriability. Or it may influence the gaining of competitive advantage because the boundary decision influences which real options are available to the firm, as Barney and Lee (Chapter 14) point out.

It may also be argued that the above list is incomplete, since it omits issues of, for example, entrepreneurship (cf. Casson, Chapter 6) and firm growth (cf. Kay, Chapter 9). However, once it is recognized that the issue of competitive advantage ultimately boils down to the issue of why firms are (persistently) heterogeneous, room may be made for entrepreneurship and growth issues also. The difficulties lie elsewhere.

To be more specific, the relevant difficulties have to do with the inability of the governance perspective, at least at its present stage of development, to come to grips with a number of issues that are relevant to the strategy field. Among these are issues relating to the accumulation of production and organization knowledge (that is, competences, organizational learning), market positioning, flexibility, and inertia, etc. As a recognition of this, leading organizational economists Bengt Holmström and John Roberts (1998: 90, our emphasis) recently noted that:

Information and knowledge are at the heart of organizational design, because they result in contractual and incentive problems that challenge both markets and firms . . . *In light of this, it is surprising that leading economic theories . . . have paid almost no attention to the role of organizational knowledge.*

A number of the chapters in this volume make related observations, which may be taken as an indication of the fact that while the governance perspective does indeed make room for management and strategy, it does not make sufficient room, to use Williamson's (Chapter 2) way of formulating it. Consider Rumelt, Schendel, and Teece's (1994: 9) discussion of strategic choices:

Because of competition, firms have choices to make if they are to survive. Those that are *strategic* include: the selection of goals; the choice of products and services to offer; the design and configuration of policies determining how the firm positions itself to compete in product markets (e.g., competitive strategy); the choice of an appropriate level of scope and diversity; and the design of organization structure, administrative systems, and policies used to define and coordinate work . . . It is the integration (or reinforcing pattern) among these choices that makes a set a strategy.

Note that the issues of where to draw the boundaries of the firm and how to design internal organization are explicitly seen as important strategic choices. More specifically, the issue of the boundaries of the firm, for example, relates to a number of strategic issues, such the firm's sourcing of resources (for example internal or external procurement of technology), supplier relations, the terms on which resources are acquired (for example, the firm may internalize activities if it can carry them out more cost efficiently), appropriation of rents (for example, internalization may be an appropriation strategy), etc. To put it briefly, virtually all issues of corporate strategy, and many of business strategy, involve the boundaries of the firm. Therefore, theory that illuminates the issue of the boundaries of the firm is also likely to be helpful for understanding strategic choices. Quite similar arguments may be put forward in connection with the issue of internal organization.

However, this is certainly not to say that all strategic choices can be neatly linked to the issues of existence, boundaries, and internal organization of the firm and interpreted using organizational economics insights. For example, it is difficult to link directly to these issues choices relating to the selection of goals and the choice of products and services to offer, as well as the issue of how to establish 'the integration (or reinforcing pattern) among these choices that makes a set a strategy'. Thus, it is difficult, if not impossible, to comprehend positioning and strategic co-ordination through the lens provided by the modern economics of organization. And, we may add, the same applies to issues that relate to entrepreneurship, growth, and competence building.

A number of the contributions to this volume recognize this situation and offer various remedies that are 'loyal', as it were, to the basic thrust of the governance perspective. For example, Nicholas Argyres and Julia Porter Liebeskind (Chapter 11) construct an argument that contractual commitments originally made to protect specific investments may prevent efficient adaptation in later periods, when the governance needs of a transaction has changed. Building on

the Riordan and Williamson (1985) model, Ron Sanchez (Chapter 15) integrates demand-side considerations into the governance perspective by incorporating options-theoretic representations of several potential forms of economic
value obtainable from flexible-use assets. Although his model may produce
results that are contradictory to those of Riordan and Williamson (1985),
Sanchez' chapter should be thought of as an extension of the governance perspective rather than a break with it. Mark Casson (Chapter 6) argues that any theory
of the firm should treat the role of the entrepreneur and the growth and diversification of the firm (see also Neil Kay, Chapter 9), thus striking a distinctly
Penrosian (Penrose 1959) chord. However, he argues forcefully that ideas on
economizing on the costs of gathering, collecting, synthesizing, and disseminat-
ing information are extremely useful for understanding these issues, when
combined with an explicitly entrepreneurial perspective.

4. The Competence Perspective and the Strategic Theory of the Firm

However, while many proponents of the governance perspective are thus aware
of its limitations, the advent of the competence perspective since the mid-1980s
should be seen against the background of the inability of the governance perspective to come to grips with many issues of fundamental strategic importance. To
theorists within the competence perspective, certain important features of the
governance perspective rendered highly implausible Rumelt's (1984) bold claim
that the governance perspective could serve as a foundation for strategy research.
To appreciate this view, consider some of the main features of the governance
perspective.

In spite of there being some variety among the contributions to this literature,
it is fair to say that the contributions that make up the governance perspective
are in agreement on the fundamentals. The basic insight is this: in explaining
institutions like the firm, one must also consider transaction costs, in addition to
production costs of the usual sort. Transacting is fraught with hazards, and the
problem of management and organization is one of creating governance structures and contracts that constrain the dissipation of wealth produced by 'hold-
up', 'moral hazard', and the like. Indeed, it is probably not unfair to say that the
heuristic driving this literature is to reduce virtually all problems of economic
organization to problems of misaligned incentives, usually, but not necessarily,
attendant on imperfect information (Langlois and Foss 1999).

While this research strategy has in many respects proved successful, it has also
led to the neglect of organization and management problems that are not so
obviously reducible to issues of incentive alignment. As Dosi and Marengo
(Chapter 4) point out, much of the activity going on inside a firm is problem
solving of all sorts and on all levels, ranging from mundane shoop-floor matters
to strategic decisions that may be determinative of the survival of the firm. Much

of this is not related in any meaningful way to misaligned incentives. Moreover, it relates to the production side of the firm, which—even taking Williamson's work (1975, 1985, 1996a) on asset specificity into account—has arguably been comparatively neglected within the governance perspective. Indeed, the case may be made (Langlois and Foss 1999) that there is an underlying assumption in the governance perspective that the standard neoclassical production function with its attendant assumptions tells us all that is worth knowing about production.

The attempt to consider the related issues of management and organization problems that do not turn on the alignment of incentives and the production side of firms as crucial ingredients of a theory of the firm, may be seen as the theme that unites a group of scholars from both economics and business administration, self-consciously working under the banners of 'the competence perspective', 'the capabilities approach', or 'the resource-based approach' (Conner 1991; Langlois 1992; Langlois and Robertson 1995; Kogut and Zander 1992; Dosi and Marengo 1994; Conner and Prahalad 1996; Madhok 1996).

According to a number of these writers (for example, Kogut and Zander 1992; Conner and Prahalad 1996), the competence perspective is reaching for a strategic theory of the firm, in the sense of a theory that can address all four of the issues discussed above. Since the competence-based strategic theory of the firm utilizes explanatory mechanisms that are different from those of the governance perspective—for example, its proponents claim that it is 'opportunism-independent'—it has often been seen as a theoretical rival to the governance perspective.

Although the opposite case—that the competence perspective is complementary, rather than rival, to the governance perspective—may also be made (cf. Foss and Foss, Chapter 3), there can be little doubt, of course, that the two perspectives are very different. The reasons for this are easily identifiable. To put it briefly, while the competence perspective has its background in business administration (strategy and organization) and various strands of heterodox economics and has been mainly cultivated in business schools, the economics of organization was originally developed in economics departments and stands directly in the mainstream economics tradition. And while the governance perspective is increasingly characterized by the formal, deductive approach to theory building characteristic of mainstream economics (cf. Dosi and Marengo, Chapter 4), the competence perspective is characterized by a verbal, non-formal discourse.

As Cohendet, Llerena, and Marengo (Chapter 5) explain, an important source of the competence perspective is evolutionary economics. Thus, the notion of competence is clearly related to the notion of routine, a cornerstone of the evolutionary theory of the firm (Nelson and Winter 1982). Another strong source of inspiration is Richardson (1972), as noted by both Williamson (Chapter 2) and Rod Coombs and Stan Metcalfe (Chapter 10). Richardson's notion of capabilities (or competence) and his argument that economic organization turns on the characteristics of such capabilities—specifically, their degree of complementarity and similarity—are real theoretical breakthroughs that arguably have not been satisfactorily conceptualized within the governance perspective. Coombs and Metcalfe's chapter (10) on the organization on the innovative process is a strong demonstration of the power of such Richardsonian reasoning, and also an indication of the explanatory limits of the governance perspective. In fact, Coombs and Metcalfe do not rely on governance perspective ideas at all when exploring the organization of the innovation process.

Although Richardson's paper does stand out as a landmark contribution, it also illustrates some of the general difficulties of the competence perspective. Thus, what *are* those capabilities? Or competences? Or *core* competences? Or *dynamic* capabilities? The lack of clear definitions of these key concepts is arguably symptomatic of a deeper difficulty in the competence perspective, namely that there is no agreement on the microfoundations of the knowledge-based view. What precisely is assumed about the motivation, cognition, and knowledge of agents in this perspective? To respond with, for example, 'bounded rationality' may not be very helpful, because that concept says more about what it is not (namely maximizing rationality) than what it actually is. Some implicitly decide to sidestep this issue, in favour of the empirical generalization that firms are simply constrained in what they know how to do well. Others think that it is necessary to draw on classic contributions to epistemology (for example Loasby 1991), while others again illustrate their points using mathematical computation theory (for example Dosi and Marengo 1994). Furthermore, it is seldom made clear how considerations of knowledge relate to issues of economic organization. This is because the micro-logic of the arguments is seldom spelled out, and connections to the relevant parts of economics not made clear. For example, to what extent may competence arguments be interpreted in terms of standard information costs? (Casson, in Chapter 6, provides relevant ideas here.)

5. Which Way to Go?

5.1. Research Strategies

To sum up, we are confronted with two imperfect bodies of theory—imperfect, that is, with respect to the role envisaged by early commentators (Rumelt 1984) of playing an integrative role in strategy research and perhaps business administration more generally. However, the theories in question are imperfect for very different reasons. While the governance perspective is of considerable relevance to business administration, and while—as explanation—it is characterized by relative elegance and simplicity, it may also misrepresent many issues because of its dominant heuristic of reducing virtually all problems of organization, management, and strategy as somehow turning on problems of aligning incentives. On the other hand, while the competence perspective may in some respects be truer to the traditional interests and concerns of the strategy field, it is at present rather undeveloped, comparatively speaking.

The extreme complexity of the issues involved partly helps us to understand why the two bodies of theory are imperfect in various ways. For example, the very framing of the issue of, say, the existence of firms is complex.[4] Therefore, claims that this or that theory is, for example, a 'strategic theory of the firm' should be looked upon with suspicion. The complexity of the relevant issues is overwhelming. Given this, what is necessary is that focused efforts be made that address selected issues, possibly using arguments that stem from both the competence and the governance perspective. On the other hand, because of the complexity, it may be that refining arguments rather than trying to integrate them with some fairly different perspective is a more viable strategy.

It is immediately apparent that two paths of development are possible: either the competence perspective and the governance perspective develop in isolation or integrative efforts are made. As already suggested, arguments may be advanced in favour of both paths. For example, purist strategies, in which one perspective is not permitted to be contaminated by the ideas of the other perspective, economize on the scarce mental resources of the relevant scholars and allow advantages of specialization to be exploited to their utmost. On the other hand, if the starting-point is that we are interested in assumptions and explanatory insights that better take us into 'the deep structure of economic organization' (Williamson 1996b: 49), it seems that it is possible to advance both methodological and substantive arguments in favour of a research strategy which considers both competence and governance ideas.

On the methodological level, one may argue that one problem with purist strategies is that they implicitly assert that 'the essence' of economic organization is either that it aligns incentives in an imperfect world, perhaps in a second- or third-best manner, or that it organizes and develops competences. There are, however, no objective criteria for determining what constitutes the immutable essence of the firm. Furthermore, what an appropriate conceptualization of economic organization is depends on the purpose at hand. For some purposes, a competence-based conceptualization may be the most appropriate one; for other purposes, it may be a governance perspective conceptualization; and for other purposes again, it may be a combined view that is appropriate.

---

[4] Thus, do we simply refer to explaining the presence of employment contracts in a market economy? To a specific pattern of property rights to assets? To the presence of low-powered incentives in institutions called 'firms'? Or do we refer to the presence of employment contracts *and* property rights to assets *and* low-powered incentives in a complementary way, so that what we really address are alternative three-tuples (cf. Holmström and Milgrom 1994)?

5.2. Challenging Phenomena

The latter purposes primarily have to do with the understanding of phenomena that are hard to comprehend through the lens provided by either the competence or the governance perspective, but which may be significantly illuminated by a combined view. In the now fashionable terminology, there may be 'complementarities' between the two perspectives when they are applied to the examination of certain phenomena. In fact, many of the chapters in the present volume identify and discuss such phenomena—phenomena that are particularly pertinent to some fields of business administration, such as strategy. Moreover, all of these ultimately boil down to the very meanings of 'governance' and 'competence'. We now briefly consider some of these phenomena.

5.2.1. Organizing competence

Ghoshal, Hahn, and Moran (Chapter 7) argue that the key to competitive success and sustainable growth is organizing competence (capability). By implication, what explains differential competitive success and growth is differential organizing competence. Organizing competence represents a challenge to both the governance perspective and the competence perspective. This is because the competence perspective has not so far paid much attention to organizational processes and issues of internal organization, essentially 'blackboxing' these through the use of rather aggregate concepts such as routines or competences (Foss and Foss, Chapter 3).[5] And although issues of internal organization may arguably be central in the governance perspective, little attention has been paid here to *differential* organizing competence.

If by 'organizing competence' we mean complicated problem-solving procedures that relate to determining what should be produced and how, it is, however, clear that both perspectives have something to contribute to the understanding and that the suppression of either cognitive issues or issues of incentive alignment can only be 'a first approximation, which is ripe time to overcome!' (Dosi and Marengo, Chapter 4). For example, the ability to write good contracts with employees or with outside suppliers is certainly an important competence—and this is another indication that the often invoked distinction between 'production' and 'exchange' approaches to economic organization is problematic. In fact, 'production' and 'exchange' should be linked more closely. As Claude Ménard (1994: 239) has rightly observed,

[t]he question of why firms decide 'to make rather than to buy', which is at the core of the transaction cost approach, cannot be answered in a satisfactory way without exploring the very process through which they produce goods or services.

The 'very process through which [firms] produce goods or services' is often taken to be the domain of the competence perspective (Langlois and Foss 1999), so

---

[5] This may be changing, however; see, for example, Conner and Prahalad (1996).

what Ménard essentially says is that the governance perspective needs to be infused with competence ideas. On the other hand, as Foss and Foss (Chapter 3) argue, ideas drawn from the governance perspective may actually be helpful for better understanding central ideas of the competence perspective, such as the very notion of competences and routines. Thus, there is room for continuous 'give and take' in a combined research effort. The phenomenon of inter-firm relations is another illustration of this.

5.2.2. Inter-firm relations   In their treatments of inter-firm relations, both Madhok (Chapter 13) and Coombs and Metcalfe (Chapter 10) focus on these relations as vehicles for knowledge building—a perspective that is arguably not well conceptualized by the governance perspective. Richardson (1972) argued— referring to Coase (1937)—that because the governance perspective pays little explicit attention to 'dissimilar' (yet complementary) competences, it has a hard time accounting convincingly for the existence of stable, long-term inter-firm relations. There is a genuine challenge here to the governance perspective, for much of the import of the notion of 'dissimilar' competences presumably refers to cognitive differences and differences in how problem solving is carried out in different firms—and this is a much neglected area within the governance perspective. Surely there is something to the position that cognitive differences matter for economic organization, a proposition with which any student of international business is likely to agree.

However, once one ponders the meaning of a notion such as 'dissimilar competences', it becomes clear how little we really understand about these cogni- tive issues in the context of the theory of economic organization (including the competence perspective). For example, what is the metric of 'dissimilarity'? What is the underlying theory? How exactly is it supposed to influence economic or- ganization? Which impediments to efficient transacting does it introduce? Here is an area where a combined research effort may be particularly worth while. Eric Pfaffmann (Chapter 12) goes some way towards this end.

5.2.3. The dynamics of governance choices   That the governance perspective is somewhat deficient in the dynamic dimension was noted earlier in this chapter. This is to a large extent a matter of neglect of issues of innovation and techno- logical change, as pointed out by Dosi and Marengo (Chapter 4). Furthermore, it is a matter of neglect of issues of strategic change, and neglect of how changing strategic requirements may necessitate changes in economic organization (Williamson, Chapter 2), or of how past contractual commitments impose constraints on which changes in economic organization are feasible at all (Argyres and Liebeskind, Chapter 11). But it is also a matter of over-simplifying of what is important for the economic viability of different governance structures—an issue clearly related to the growth theme of Part B. Thus, the transaction costs economizing properties of a governance structure is only one of a range of characteristics that influence the 'fitness' of the relevant governance structure. For example, learning capabilities and political relations that may not be reducible to transaction cost related problems are also relevant characteristics. Moreover, these characteristics (or 'traits') may interact; there may be 'epistatic effects', as Cohendet, Llerena, and Marengo (Chapter 5) suggest. Understanding such epistatic effects or complementarities requires a combined research effort.

5.2.4. Entrepreneurship Mark Casson (Chapter 6) boldly argues that the differences and conflicts between the governance perspective and the competence perspective 'can be traced to a common failure to take full account of the entrepreneur'. The point is that entrepreneurs, in Casson's view, are crucial information synthesizers and their decision making influences not only the founding, organization, and scope of firms, but also which types of information production and processing the firm specializes in. Hence, there is a direct link to the traditional concerns of both the governance and the competence perspectives. One may, of course, question whether Casson's specific story about the link between entrepreneurship and economic organization is the only such story possible, or the one that may unite competence and governance perspectives, but that entrepreneurship is a much neglected issue in both the governance and the competence perspective is evident (cf. also Cohendet, Llerena, and Marengo, Chapter 5).

The importance of entrepreneurship in the context of economic organization derives from issues of, for example, path dependence, corporate culture, and innovation, and other issues that relate to change. Thus, as much research has established, the founder/entrepreneur strongly conditions the future development path of 'his' firm through the 'constitution' that he defines for it. And for a broad understanding of issues of innovation, we often ultimately have to appeal to the superior foresight, instinct, or intelligence of certain enterprising individuals. One such individual was the businessman Rudolf Spreckels, whom Williamson (Chapter 2) quotes as explaining that '[w]henever I see something badly done, or not done at all, I see an opportunity to make a fortune'. And, as he argues, such entrepreneurial instincts 'ought to influence the theory of economic organization'.

6. Concluding Comments

Taken together, the chapters in this book do not offer a finely honed theory, such as *a* strategic theory of the firm. Neither do they offer any agreement on how integrative efforts should be carried out. What is offered is instead a snapshot of the conversation in an increasingly important field in both economics and business administration, and an offer to listen to some of the prominent voices in that conversation. Moreover, it is not merely a conversation; it is a *constructive* conversation that involves attempts to directly confront and, in some cases, to merge perspectives, based on the recognition that while governance requires requisite competences, competence needs an underlying structure of governance-related phenomena (co-ordination, incentives, order giving, etc.) to be effective.

However, the fact that proponents of the two perspectives are now openly engaging in discussion and in integrative work does not mean that if only all communicative difficulties could be eliminated, the two perspectives may be smoothly integrated for the benefit of both economics and business administration. The differences—for example, in terms of disciplinary and institutional backgrounds as well as mode of expression, terminological clarity, etc.—are still too significant for this to happen. The capabilities that competence and governance theorists possess are at present too dissimilar, to use competence perspective terminology (Richardson 1972), to warrant full integration. Moreover, as a number of the contributors to this volume make clear, both perspectives are in need of much more theoretical development and of confrontation with empirical reality (for example, Paul Geroski, Chapter 8). In the light of all this, the most that we may hope for, for a very long time to come, is that there will be focused collaborative ventures that approach selected problems, such as the ones listed in the previous section, in an incremental way. We should not expect a merger wave in the theory of the firm industry for a long time to come—but we may certainly expect a wave of joint ventures within the next decade.

References

ALCHIAN, ARMEN A., and HAROLD DEMSETZ 1972. 'Production, information costs, and economic organization', *American Economic Review* 62: 772–95.

ARROW, KENNETH A. 1974. *The Limits of Organization.* New York: Norton.

BARNEY, JAY B. 1991. 'Firm resources and sustained competitive advantage', *Journal of Management* 17: 99–120.

BARZEL, YORAM 1997. *Economic Analysis of Property Rights.* Cambridge: Cambridge University Press.

CAVES, RICHARD E. 1980. 'Industrial organization, corporate structure, and strategy', *Journal of Economic Literature* 18: 64–92.

COASE, RONALD H. 1937. 'The nature of the firm', *Economica* N.S. 4: 386–405. Reprinted in Oliver F. Williamson and Sidney Winter, eds., *The Nature of the Firm: Origins, Evolution, Development.* New York: Oxford University Press (1991).

—— 1972. 'Industrial organization: A proposal for research', in V. R. Fuchs, ed., *Policy Issues and Research Opportunities in Industrial Organization.* New York: National Bureau of Economic Research.

CONNER, KATHLEEN R. 1991. 'A historical comparison of resource-based theory and five schools of thought within industrial organization economics: Do we have a new theory of the firm?', *Journal of Management* 17: 121–54.

—— and C. K. PRAHALAD 1996. 'A resource-based theory of the firm: Knowledge versus opportunism,' *Organization Science* 7: 477–501.

DOSI, GIOVANNI, and LUIGI MARENGO 1994. 'Some elements of an evolutionary theory of organizational competences', in Richard W. Englander, ed., *Evolutionary Concepts in Contemporary Economics*. Ann Arbor, MI: University of Michigan Press.

GROSSMAN, STEPHEN, and OLIVER HART 1986. 'The costs and benefits of ownership: A theory of vertical integration', *Journal of Political Economy* 94: 691–719.

HOLMSTRÖM, BENGT 1982. 'Moral hazard in teams', *Bell Journal of Economics* 13: 324–40.

—— and PAUL MILGROM 1991. 'Multitask principal-agent analyses: Incentive contracts, asset ownership, and job design', *Journal of Law, Economics, and Organization* 7: 24–52.

—— —— 1994. 'The firm as an incentive system', *American Economic Review* 84: 972–91.

—— and JOHN ROBERTS 1998. 'The boundaries of the firm revisited', *Journal of Economic Perspectives* 12: 73–94.

KOGUT, BRUCE, and UDO ZANDER 1992. 'Knowledge of the firm, combinative capabilities, and the replication of technology', *Organization Science* 3: 383–97.

LANGLOIS, RICHARD N. 1992. 'Transaction-cost economics in real time', *Industrial and Corporate Change* 1(1): 99–127.

—— and NICOLAI J. FOSS 1999. 'Capabilities and governance: the rebirth of production in the theory of economic organization', *Kylos* 52: 201–8.

—— and PAUL L. ROBERTSON 1995. *Firms, Markets, and Economic Change: A Dynamic Theory of Business Institutions*. London: Routledge.

LOASBY, BRIAN J. 1991. *Equilibrium and Evolution*. Manchester: Manchester University Press.

MADHOK, ANOOP 1996. 'The organization of economic activity: Transaction costs, firm capabilities, and the nature of governance', *Organization Science* 7: 577–90.

MÉNARD, CLAUDE 1994. 'Organizations as coordinating devices', *Metroeconomica* 45: 224–47.

MILGROM, PAUL, and JOHN ROBERTS 1992. *Economics, Organization, and Management*. Englewood Cliffs, NJ: Prentice Hall.

MILLER, GARY 1992. *Managerial Dilemmas*. Cambridge: Cambridge University Press.

NELSON, RICHARD R, and SIDNEY G. WINTER 1982. *An Evolutionary Theory of Economic Change*. Cambridge, MA: The Belknap Press, Harvard University Press.

PENROSE, EDITH T. 1959. *The Theory of the Growth of the Firm*. Oxford: Basil Blackwell.

PORTER, MICHAEL E. 1985. *Competitive Advantage*. New York: Free Press.

PRENDERGAST, CANICE 1999. 'The provision of incentives in firms', *Journal of Economic Literature* 37: 7–63.

RICHARDSON, GEORGE B. 1972. 'The organisation of industry', *Economic Journal* 82: 883–96.

RIORDAN, MICHAEL, and OLIVER E. WILLIAMSON 1985. 'Asset specificity and economic organization', *International Journal of Industrial Organization* 3: 365–78.

RUMELT, RICHARD P. 1984. 'Towards a strategic theory of the firm', in Richard B. Lamb, (ed.), *Competitive Strategic Management*. Englewood Cliffs, NJ: Prentice Hall.

RUMELT, RICHARD P., DAN E. SCHENDEL, and DAVID J. TEECE 1994. 'Fundamental issues in strategy', in eid., eds., *Fundamental Issues in Strategy: A Research Agenda*. Boston, MA: Harvard Business School Press.

WERNERFELT, BIRGER 1984. 'A resource-based view of the firm', *Strategic Management Journal* 5: 171–80. Reprinted in Nicolai J. Foss, ed., *Resources, Firms, and Strategies: A Reader in the Resource-Based Perspective*. Oxford: Oxford University Press (1997).

WILLIAMSON, OLIVER E. 1971. 'The vertical integration of production: Market failure considerations', *American Economic Review* 61: 112–23.

—— 1975. *Markets and Hierarchies: Analysis and Antitrust Implications*. New York: Free Press.

—— 1985. *The Economic Institutions of Capitalism*. New York: Free Press.

—— 1996a. *The Mechanisms of Governance*. Oxford: Oxford University Press.

—— 1996b. 'Economic organization: The case for candor', *Academy of Management Review* 21: 48–57.

WINTER, SIDNEY 1991. 'On Coase, competence, and the corporation', in Oliver E. Williamson and Sidney G. Winter, eds., 1991. *The Nature of the Firm*. Oxford: Blackwell.

ZAJAC, EDWARD J., and C. P. OLSEN 1993. 'From transaction cost to transactional value analysis: Implications for the study of interorganizational strategies', *Journal of Management Studies* 30: 131–45.

Part A

Fundamental Perspectives

2

Strategy Research: Governance and Competence Perspectives

OLIVER E. WILLIAMSON

1. Introduction

Business strategy is an expansive enterprise. Not only do all of the functional areas in the business school relate, but strategy is, by nature, interdisciplinary. All of the social sciences—especially economics and organization theory—plus contract law are implicated. Indeed, in the high technology arena where some of the most difficult strategy issues reside, engineering and the law on intellectual property rights also have a bearing.

Of the various approaches to the study of strategy, this chapter focuses on the governance and competence perspectives. Both perspectives combine economic reasoning with organization theory. As between these two, the governance perspective gives greater prominence to economics, in that choice among alternative modes of governance is principally explained in transaction cost economizing terms, whereas the competence perspective gives greater prominence to organization theory, where the importance of process is especially featured.

Because the governance perspective got an earlier start and has been more fully operationalized, I begin with a sketch of the key moves out of which the governance perspective works. The long-awaited operationalization of competence is then examined with respect to the same six moves. Challenges posed by the competence perspective for governance—some of which I believe to be mistaken but the more important of which are wholly constructive—are addressed next. Concluding remarks follow.

2. The Governance Perspective

As I have discussed elsewhere (Williamson 1985, 1996, 1998), the governance perspective has been the beneficiary of distinguished antecedents. Prominent

This chapter was initially presented as a Keynote Address to the conference on 'Competences, Governance, and Entrepreneurship' on Bornholm Island in June 1998 and was later presented at the Institutional Analysis Workshop at the University of California, Berkeley. Comments from Fred Balderston, Glenn Carroll, Nicolai Juul Foss, Jeffrey Macher, Jackson Nickerson, the referees and, especially, Will Mitchell are gratefully acknowledged.

among these is Ronald Coase's classic article on 'The nature of the firm' (1937). Rather than describe the firm in technological terms (as a production function), he described firm and market as alternative modes of governance, the choice between which was principally decided by transaction cost differences. His later article on 'The problem of social cost' (1960) introduced the fiction of zero transaction costs but emphasized that choices, always and everywhere, had to be made between feasible alternatives. This emphasis on feasibility meant that the comparative institutional action turned on positive transaction cost features. John R. Commons likewise eschewed technology in favour of the economics of organization. According to Commons, 'The ultimate unit of activity . . . must contain in itself the three principles of conflict, mutuality, and order. This unit is a transaction' (1934: 4). Not only does transaction cost economics agree that the transaction is the basic unit of analysis, but it views governance as an economizing response to the Commons triple.

Chester Barnard's insistence that organization was important and undervalued was likewise prescient. Like Friedrich Hayek, Barnard held that adaptation was the central problem of economic organization. But whereas Hayek (1945) emphasized spontaneous adaptation realized through the market, Barnard emphasized co-operative adaptation of a 'conscious, deliberate, purposeful' kind (1938: 4), working through administration. Key elements in Barnard's theory of internal organization included: (1) a theory of authority, (2) the employment relation, (3) informal organization, and (4) economizing. Barnard's work was a turning-point for organization theory, as subsequently developed by Herbert Simon (1947, 1957) and related work at Carnegie (March and Simon 1958; Cyert and March 1963) as well as by Philip Selznick (1949).

The progressive development and refinement of the market failure literature led Kenneth Arrow to observe that 'market failure is not absolute; it is better to consider a broader category, that of transaction costs, which in general impede and in particular cases block the formation of markets' (1969: 49)—where by transaction cost Arrow had reference to the 'costs of running the economic system' (1969: 48).

These significant intellectual accomplishments and the intuitive appeal of transaction costs notwithstanding, the concept of transaction cost remained vague and elastic. There being too many degrees of freedom, any outcome could be rationalized after the fact by a suitable specification of transaction costs (Fischer 1977).

Awaiting operationalization, Coase's 1937 article was 'much cited and little used' (Coase 1972: 67). The operationalization of transaction costs finally got under way in the 1970s. Once begun, transaction cost economics has successively progressed from informal into preformal, semiformal, and fully formal modes of analysis (Williamson 1996: 18–20).

Armen Alchian and Harold Demsetz (1972) proposed that technological non-separabilities were the key factor in supplanting market by internal organization.

Such non-separabilities explain only small teams (Alchian and Demsetz 1972; Marx 1967, vol. 1: chap. 3), however, and do not engage contracting more generally.[1] How do we move beyond the employment relation to include complex contracting of other kinds? What explains the integration of techno-logically separable stages of activity? What explains non-standard forms of contracting, such as customer and territorial restrictions, exchange agreements, and franchising? What explains the choice between alternative modes of finance (debt and equity)? What explains corporate governance in the large corporation? What is the economic rationale for regulation/deregulation? How does gover-nance bear on the protection of intellectual property rights?

Directly or indirectly, these are all contractual issues—to which the lens of comparative contracting is well suited and in relation to which issues of organ-ization are salient. My first transaction cost article (Williamson 1971) dealt with vertical integration—or, in more mundane terms, with the make-or-buy deci-sion. That turned out to be a prototypical problem. Variations on a few key themes followed. With the benefit of hindsight, transaction cost economics has been implemented through the six key moves described below.

2.1. Human Actors

If 'Nothing is more fundamental in setting our research agenda and informing our research methods than our view of the nature of the human beings whose behaviour we are studying' (Simon 1985: 303), then social scientists should be prepared to name the key features of human actors to which their research project relates. Transaction cost economics names three.

Transaction cost economics eschews hyperrationality in favour of bounded rationality—according to which human actors are intendedly rational but only limitedly so (Simon 1961: xxiv). All complex contracts are unavoidably incom-plete by reason of bounded rationality. But there is more. Are human agents myopic, in the manner of the behavioural theory of the firm (Cyert and March 1963), or do they have the capacity for foresight, whereupon they look ahead and reposition? George Schultz's views on economics support the latter: 'my training in economics has had a major influence on the way I think about public policy tasks, even when they have no particular relationship to economics. Our discipline makes one think ahead, ask about indirect consequences, take note of variables that may not be directly under consideration' (1995: 1). The business-man Rudolf Spreckels knew this in his bones: 'Whenever I see something badly done, or not done at all, I see an opportunity to make a fortune.' Those instincts,

---

[1] Geoffrey Hodgson holds that the 'contractual approach' is preoccupied with monitoring and metering. That is more the focus of the agency perspective (Alchian and Demsetz 1972) rather than the governance perspective. For a comparison of these two, see Williamson (1975).

if widely operative, will influence the practice and ought to influence the theory of economic organization. Transaction cost economics ascribes foresight rather than myopia to human actors.

Another attribute of core importance is that of self-interest. Transaction cost economics goes beyond the orthodox description of simple self-interest seeking to include strategic behaviour—which manifests itself as adverse selection, moral hazard, and, more generally, as opportunism. Accordingly, human actors will not reliably disclose true conditions upon request or self-fulfil all promises. Contract as mere promise, unsupported by credible commitments, will not, therefore, be self-enforcing.

But for opportunism, the courts would simply ask witnesses to 'tell us what you know that is germane to our decision'. That is not, however, the way testimony is taken. Witnesses are required to take an oath to 'tell the truth, the whole truth, and nothing but the truth': don't lie, don't conceal, don't mislead. The temptation for witnesses to prevaricate is thus recognized and, because perjury in the courtroom carries severe penalties, actively deterred.

2.2. Unit of Analysis

Commons (1932) recommends that the transaction be made the basic unit of analysis. Transaction cost economics concurs.

To a first approximation, a transaction occurs when a good or service is transferred between technologically separable stages. Thus whereas there is a presumption that non-separable activities will be organized under unified ownership (perhaps a team of the Alchian and Demsetz (1972) kind), the possible joinder of separable stages is not driven by technology but needs to be derived.

A basic move in the operationalization of transaction cost economics is to name the principal dimensions with respect to which significant transaction cost consequences accrue. Three of these key attributes are the frequency with which transactions recur, the uncertainty (disturbances) to which transactions are subject, and the degree to which transactions are supported by transaction specific assets. A good deal of the explanatory power of transaction cost economics turns on this last.[2]

2.3. Describing the Firm

As Kenneth Arrow observes (1999: vii):

Any standard economic theory, not just neoclassical, starts from the existence of firms.

---

[2] As it turns out, asset specificity takes a variety of forms: physical, human, site specific, dedicated assets, brand name capital, and temporal. A condition of bilateral dependency is associated with all, but the governance structure responses differ with the asset specificity particulars (Williamson 1996).

Usually, the firm is a point or at any rate a black box ... But firms are palpably not points. They have internal structure. This internal structure must arise for some reason.

Transaction cost economics describes the firm not in technological terms (as a production function) but in organizational terms (as a governance structure). Indeed, firm and market are alternative modes of governance that differ in discrete structural ways. Chief among the attributes that describe a mode of governance are: (1) incentive intensity, (2) administrative controls, and (3) the legal rules regime (Williamson 1991). These in turn give rise to differential adaptive capacity—in both autonomous and co-operative adaptation respects. Alternative modes of governance are internally consistent syndromes of these attributes—which is to say each has distinctive strengths and weaknesses.

One of the important by-products of this exercise is that students of organization are forced to confront the Coasian puzzle: Why not organize everything in one big firm? Thus if firms enjoy advantages in relation to markets, and if there are no offsetting burdens, then net benefits will always accrue when a transaction is taken out of the market and organized internally. That is contradicted by the data: both the fact of many firms and the failures of socialism in Eastern Europe and the former Soviet Union speak to the limits of central planning. What explains the limits of firms/centralization?

Transaction cost economics addresses this puzzle by joining two hypothetical moves: replication and selective intervention. If two unified stages can always do as well as two independent stages by instructing each stage to conduct 'business as usual' when things go well (that is, by replication) and will intervene always but only when things get out of alignment (that is, will intervene selectively), then the unified firm can never do worse (by replication) and will sometimes do better (by selective intervention).

Transaction cost economics then examines the mechanisms of replication and selective intervention and finds that both experience problems of implementation (Williamson 1985: chap. 7). Accordingly, because of the added bureaucratic costs that unavoidably attend the decision to take a transaction out of the market and organize it internally, the firm is advised to integrate only for 'compelling reasons'.

2.4. Purposes Served

Transaction cost economics holds that economizing on transaction costs is the 'main case'—which is not to say the only case. The attributes of human actors are centrally implicated. Thus one productive way to think about economic organization is as a means by which to economize on bounded rationality and mitigate the hazards that accrue to opportunism. Cognitive specialization, within and between firms, is a means by which to economize on mind as a scarce resource (Williamson 1999b). And governance is an economizing response to the

Commons triple, in that governance is a means by which to infuse order in a relation where potential conflict threatens to undo or upset opportunities to realize mutual gains.

It is furthermore interesting that evolutionary biology proceeds similarly. As Richard Dawkins has observed, 'One unique feature of man . . . is his capacity for conscious foresight' (Dawkins 1976: 200). Indeed, it is the 'capacity to simulate the future in imagination . . . [that saves] us from the worst excesses of the blind replicators' (ibid.). The worse consequences to which Dawkins refers have their origins in selfishness: 'a predominant quality of a successful gene is ruthless selfishness' (1976: 2)—hence the title of his famous book, *The Selfish Gene*.

Credible contracting is very much an exercise in farsighted contracting, whereby the parties look ahead, recognize hazards, and devise hazard mitigating responses—thereby to realize mutual gain. These safeguards rarely take the form of pecuniary bonds but involve instead mechanisms of governance—information disclosure, discussion, dispute settlement of a private ordering kind (such as arbitration)—which permit the parties to work through their differences and get on with the job. Having the courts available for purposes of ultimate appeal nevertheless delimits threat positions, thereby providing support for private ordering. The efficacy of governance is thus jointly determined by local efforts (self-help to craft mechanisms) and as a function of the institutional environment (polity; judiciary; laws of property and contract).

More generally, transaction cost economics works out of the discriminating alignment hypothesis, according to which transactions, which differ in their attributes, are aligned with governance structures, which differ in their cost and competence, so as to effect an economizing result. The simple contractual schema shown in Figure 2.1 is illustrative.

Thus assume that there are two alternative technologies for producing a good or service. One is generic ($k = 0$), which leads to the ideal transaction in both law and economics at Node A. The second requires transaction specific investments ($k > 0$) that cannot be redeployed to alternative uses and users without loss of productive value. These transactions pose hazards of bilateral dependency. Lacking security features ($s = 0$), such transactions will pose considerable risk, which risk will be priced out at Node B. If instead safeguards are provided ($s > 0$), these can take either market forms (Node C) or unified ownership (Node D). Because internal organization experiences added bureaucratic costs, the firm (Node D) is usefully thought of as the organization form of last resort: try markets, try hybrids (long term contractual relations into which security features have been crafted), and resort to firms when all else fails (comparatively). Node D, the firm, thus comes in only as transactions have especially high degrees of asset specificity and as added uncertainty poses greater needs for co-operative adaptation. Problems of protecting intellectual property rights can also give rise to a Node D outcome (Teece 1986; Liebeskind 1996).

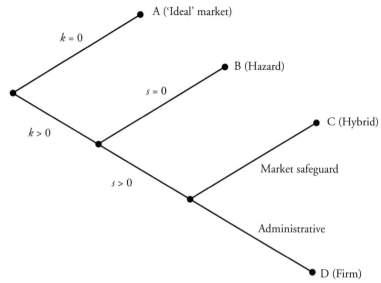

Figure 2.1. A simple contracting scheme

With appropriate interpretation, each class of transaction—intermediate product market, final product market, finance, labour market, knowledge, regulation, etc.—can be passed through variations on this same simple set-up and refutable implications derived. To repeat, transaction cost economics works out of a few key themes.

2.5. Empirical

Some theories of economic organization make little effort to advance refutable implications. Among those that do, few are empirically tested. Simon evidently believes that transaction cost economics is remiss in empirical respects: awaiting empirical testing, 'the new institutional economics and related approaches are acts of faith, or perhaps of piety' (Simon 1991: 27).

Coase had registered similar concerns about the dearth of empirical work on contract and organization twenty years earlier (Coase 1972), but that was before the operationalization of transaction cost economics had begun and predicted alignments were advanced. Empirical applications of transaction cost economics got under way in the USA in the 1980s and have grown exponentially since: the number of published studies exceeds 400 and involves scientists in Europe, Japan, India, Mexico, South America, New Zealand, and the list goes on.

It could have been otherwise, but the theory and evidence display a remarkable congruity (Masten 1995: xi). Recent empirical surveys include Howard Shelanski and Peter Klein (1995), Bruce Lyons (1996), Keith Crocker and Scott Masten (1996), and Aric Rindfleisch and Jan Heide (1997).

Not only has this research been broadly corroborative of the predictions of transaction cost economics, but the importance of risk aversion to commercial contracting has been placed in doubt. To be sure, transaction cost economics, like everything else, will benefit from more and better empirical work. I have no hesitation, however, in declaring that transaction cost economics is an empirical success story. Paul Joskow concurs: 'this empirical work is in much better shape than much of the empirical work in industrial organization generally' (1991: 81).

2.6. Efficiency Criterion

Whereas I would describe the five foregoing moves as essential to the operationalization of transaction cost economics, the efficiency criterion described here is more of a conceptual than an operational move. It is none the less a conceptual move with operational significance. Because all feasible forms of organization are flawed, and because choice must be made from the feasible set, hypothetical ideals are operationally irrelevant (Coase 1964; Demsetz 1969).

The remediableness criterion holds that an extant condition for which no *feasible* superior alternative can be described and *implemented* with expected net gains is *presumed* to be efficient. Consider each of the italicized features.

Proposed forms of organization that make impossible demands on limited rationality fail the test of feasibility. Marginal cost pricing, for example, is often infeasible because it makes impossible information demands. Even, however, if a proposed superior alternative is feasible, it may fail the test of implementation. Collective action, for example, may be needed to implement the change, but the requisite agreement may be impossible to reach and/or enforce (by reason of bounded rationality and opportunism). Note in this connection that a potential gain may fail to be realized if agreement requires the consent of those who currently enjoy an advantage (for example, the current beneficiaries of the US sugar programme). If current beneficiaries disbelieve implementation 'promises' that they will be made whole upon terminating a programme, then the requisite consent will be withheld. In that event, a preponderance of political support will be needed to override the status quo.

The presumed efficiency of an extant programme is nevertheless rebuttable. The issues are somewhat involved and are discussed elsewhere (Williamson 1996, 1999a). In the absence of rebuttal, remediableness stands as a reminder that it is impossible to be better than one's best.

3. The Competence Perspective

Richard Langlois and Nicolai Foss refer to a small but growing list of authors who have 'begun self-consciously referring to their work as lying within the confines of a "capabilities," "dynamic capabilities," or "competence" approach (Langlois, 1992; Langlois and Robertson, 1995; Kogut and Zander, 1992; Foss, 1993; Dosi and Marengo, 1994; Teece and Pisano, 1994)' (1997: 13). Albeit complementary to transaction cost economics (Langlois and Foss 1997: 4), this work is also different (Langlois and Foss 1997: 15):

> A key implication of the capabilities perspective as it relates to economic organization is that, in the terminology of G. B. Richardson (1972), the structure of complementarity and similarity among the various capabilities in the economy affects the pattern of organization (including the firm-market boundary) in ways not fully explicable in terms of the costs of transacting. Indeed, the ability to transact (and therefore the cost of transacting) is itself a capability (Winter 1988), which suggests a blurring of the boundary between production and exchange.

Much of this work draws inspiration from Edith Penrose's influential book on *The Theory of the Growth of the Firm* (1959) and Joseph Schumpeter's earlier work on *Capitalism, Socialism, and Democracy* (1942), especially as it relates to technical and organizational innovation. George Richardson's article on 'The organization of industry' (1972) is seminal. The book by Richard Cyert and James March on *A Behavioral Theory of the Firm* (1963) makes the case for a 'realism in process' approach to the study of organization. Richard Nelson and Sidney Winter's book, *An Evolutionary Theory of Economic Change* (1982), is in this same spirit and has had a significant influence on the strategy literature. In short, the capabilities/competence perspective has distinguished antecedents, the overarching theme of which is the importance of process. Common theme notwithstanding, it is not obvious how to bring the more important processes together in a coherent way. Not only is process analysis hard to do, but there are many important processes. What are the priorities?

Every stream of research—orthodoxy, transaction cost economics, agency theory—has strengths and weaknesses and stands to benefit from good critics and from taking stock. The competence perspective is no exception, yet competence research has been curiously exempted from sustained critique. I do not attempt a sustained critique here but do pose two related concerns: obscure and often tautological definitions of key terms; and failures of operationalization. To be sure, 'The early versions of most new paradigms are crude' (Kuhn 1970: 156). Eventually, however, all would-be contenders need to offer a positive research agenda (Kuhn 1970: 77). There being many good ideas in the competence perspective, what precludes operationalization?

As noted earlier, the concept of transaction costs, which is central to the study of governance, also suffered from a tautological reputation. Although Coase responded that a tautology is the 'criticism people make of a proposition that is clearly right' (1988: 19), that is not entirely satisfactory. Sooner or later, a would-be theory must be asked to show its hand.

The concept of competence is also important and it too has acquired a tautological reputation (Porter 1994; Mosakowski and McKelvey 1997). Its obvious importance and intuitive appeal notwithstanding, a relentless commitment to the operationalization of competence is needed lest the study of competence experience the fate of American Legal Realism and run itself 'into the sand' (Schlegel 1979: 459). Nicholas Georgescu-Roegen's view of the scientific enterprise applies: 'The purpose of science in general is not prediction, but knowledge for its own sake', yet prediction is 'the touchstone of scientific knowledge' (1971: 37). There being many would-be theories of the firm, there is a need to sort the wheat from the chaff. Predictions, data, and empirical tests provide the requisite screen.

Awaiting such developments, the competence perspective relies primarily on success stories to make its case. The influential article by C. K. Prahalad and Gary Hamel on 'The core competence of the corporation' (1990) helped to move the idea of core competence on to the agenda by ascribing greater core competence to Japanese than American corporations during the decade of the 1980s—especially contrasting the American firm GTE and its Japanese counterpart NEC. Whereas GTE plodded along, NEC moved ahead vigorously. More generally, Japanese firms were believed to be flourishing while their American counterparts were languishing (Prahalad and Hamel 1990: 81–5). Ironically, considering the Japanese success at subcontracting, Prahalad and Hamel conclude that 'too many [American] companies have unwittingly surrendered core competencies' by engaging in outsourcing (Prahalad and Hamel 1990: 84).

David Teece, Gary Pisano, and Amy Shuen 'define those competences that define a firm's fundamental business as core. Core competences must accordingly be derived by looking across the range of a firm's (and its competitors') products and services' (1997: 516). This is very nearly circular, in that it comes perilously close to saying that a core competence is a competence that is core. Teece and his co-authors add in a footnote that 'Eastman Kodak's core competence might be considered imaging, IBM's might be considered integrated data processing and service, and Motorola's untethered communication' (1997: 516, n. 4).

Both the Prahalad and Hamel and Teece *et al.* concepts of core competence are expansive and elastic. The ideas that firms possess both strengths (competences) and weaknesses (disabilities) and that they are engaged in intertemporal competence trade-offs (in relation to which the condition of competition plays an important role) are, to say the least, underdeveloped. There being no apparatus by which to advise firms on when and how to reconfigure their core competences, the argument relies on *ex post* rationalization: show me a success story and I will show you (uncover) a core competence.[3] (Or show me a failure and I will show you (uncover) a missing competence.)

Giovanni Dosi and Teece more recently describe the competence perspective as follows (1998: 284; emphasis in original):

a firm's *distinctive competence* needs to be understood as a reflection of distinctive organizational capabilities to coordinate and to learn. By 'organizational capabilities' we mean the capabilities of an enterprise to organize, manage, coordinate, or govern sets of activities. The set of activities that a firm can organize and coordinate better than other firms is its distinctive competencies. Posed differently, a distinctive competence is a differentiated set of skills, complementary assets, and organization routines which together allow a firm to coordinate a particular set of activities in a way that provides the basis for competitive advantage in a particular market or markets.

This is in the expansive tradition to which I refer above and covers a lot of ground: competence entails co-ordination and learning, is based on skill, assets, and routines, and is judged in comparison with rivals.

Big ideas often take a long time to take on definition. Thirty-five years passed between Coase's 1937 article and efforts to operationalize transaction costs in the early 1970s. Dating the origins of competence is arbitrary, but one candidate is Richardson's 1972 article in which 'capabilities' are introduced. If a 35-year gestation interval is added to 1972, the birth year for competence, after which operationalization will progress rapidly, will be 2007.[4] On the possibility that the six-part programme through which transaction cost economics works has relevance for competence, I examine how competence relates or could relate to these same six moves.[5]

3.1. Human Actors

The cognitive assumption out of which the competence approach works is that of bounded rationality, although that is sometimes implicit rather than explicit. Plainly, bounded rationality is featured in the behavioural theory of the firm

---

[3] More informative, often, than success stories are stories about failure—especially the failures of once successful enterprises to adapt to new circumstances. What is responsible for the inability to adapt? It being the case that firms have both competences *and* limitations, is the failure a predictable consequence of the limitations to which the firm is subject? Are those limitations remediable? If not, the 'failure' is the product of the syndrome of attributes that describe the firm. Having gone down a path to which highest expected net gains were projected at time t, the firm has to live with the (path-dependent) consequences at time $t + T$.

[4] The other obvious candidate is Penrose's 1959 book. In that event, the birth year of competence, given a 35-year gestation period, would be 1994.

[5] That could be an unfair comparison, in that competence is asked to play on transaction cost turf. I can understand, therefore, if competence scholars propose a different basis for comparison. A parallel comparison across these same six moves is none the less instructive.

(Cyert and March 1963), which is an important forerunner to the work on evolutionary economics by Nelson and Winter (1982). Competence-based research, moreover, ascribes great importance to learning and implicitly assumes incomplete contracting, both of which owe their origins to bounded rationality.

As between myopia and foresight, the competence perspective mainly emphasizes the former.[6] In the behavioural theory of the firm, for example, search is local and 'simple-minded', learning takes the form of trial and error, and adaptations are induced by crises (so the firm resembles a firefighting department more than a strategic actor). The literature from experimental psychology (Kahneman, Slovic, and Tversky 1982) is often cited in support of myopia, especially in relation to the learning and evolutionary literatures (Dosi, Marengo, and Fagiolo 1996).

The competence literature is chary on the subject of self-interest. Foss, Christian Knudsen, and Cynthia Montgomery make no mention of self-interest whatsoever in their examination of behavioural assumptions (1995: 12–13) and others treat it gingerly. Self-interest in the Carnegie set-up admits to subgoal pursuit, but Simon eschews opportunism in favour of 'frailties of motive' (1985: 304). Indeed, much of the competence literature displays an active aversion to opportunism and places emphasis on what Diego Gambetta has referred to as 'the elusive notion of trust' (1988: ix).

Whereas the competence perspective concedes the need to economize on mind as a scarce resource, it is curiously reluctant to treat trust in a calculative way. The concept of credible commitment, for example, which implies a calculative approach to contract and plays a crucial role in the economics literature, usually goes unmentioned. By contrast, both mind and trust (the absence of opportunism) are scarce resources under the transaction cost economics set-up, whence the cost-effective development and deployment of both mind and trust are projected.

3.2. Unit of Analysis

Foss *et al.* hold that the routine is the basic unit of analysis for evolutionary theory whereas the resource is the basic unit of analysis for resource-based theory (1995: 10). Sidney Winter evidently agrees and discusses resources and routines as follows (1995: 149; emphasis in original):

[According to] Wernerfelt (1984) . . . the term 'resources' embraces 'anything that could be termed a strength or weakness of a given firm . . . —(tangible and intangible) assets

---

[6] The resource-based approach associated with Penrose, however, views strategy as having a strongly intentional element (Foss, Knudsen, and Montgomery 1995: 12). As Sidney Winter puts it, 'The heart of the normative guidance offered by the resource-based view lies in the idea of leveraging the idiosyncratic profit opportunities in existing resource endowments' (1995: 148).

which are tied *semi-permanently* to the firm.' Subsequent discussion in the literature has emphasized the resources that underlie competitive advantage ('strengths'), and has sought to identify the characteristics such resources must have if success is to be sustained. The term 'routine' has been used in evolutionary economics in a similarly expansive fashion. Nelson and Winter (1982) say that '. . . most of what is *regular and predictable* about business behavior is plausibly subsumed under the heading "routine".'

Joseph Mahoney and Rajendran Pandian observe that 'The essential theoretical concept for explaining the sustainability of rents in the resource-based framework is "isolating mechanisms" ' (1992: 371). A list of eleven such mechanisms is then developed, to which they ask (1992: 371), 'what is the generalizeable insight?' Their response that 'isolating mechanisms exist because of *asset specificity* and *bounded rationality*' (1992: 373; emphasis in original) is very much in the spirit of transaction cost economics. Arguably, however, the concept of resources is more composite, in that it refers to a cluster of related transactions. In that event, the challenge is to define and dimensionalize clusters.

According to Nelson and Winter, 'routines play the role that genes play in biological evolutionary theory' (1982: 14). Routines are persistent, heritable, and selectable 'in the sense that organisms with certain routines may do better than others' and grow relatively (ibid.). Three kinds of routines are distinguished: short-run routines that determine the firm's operating characteristics; investment routines; and routines which 'modify over time various aspects of the operating characteristics' (Nelson and Winter 1982: 16–17). These routines inform 'the dynamic processes by which firm behavior patterns and market outcomes are jointly determined over time' (Nelson and Winter 1982: 18), which is the core concern of evolutionary theory.

If routines are to economic organization what genes are to biology, then we are evidently on to something very basic. As Dosi *et al.* put it, routines are 'foundational' (1996: 10). But how, then, does the routine get implemented? The department store pricing study by Cyert and March (1963: chap. 7) is the most fully developed illustration of the explanatory power of routines of which I am aware.

As against the orthodox prescription to set prices on the basis of marginal costs and demand elasticities, Cyert and March maintain that prices are set by simple routines. Exclusive items and import items excepted, the standard department store mark-up rule is simple: 'Divide each cost by 0.6 (1-mark-up) and move the result to the nearest $.95' (Cyert and March 1963: 138). Other (more extensive) routines apply to sale pricing and mark-downs (Cyert and March 1963: 140–5). The predictive powers of these three routines were thereafter tested with the following results (Cyert and March 1963: 147):

(1) normal pricing: from a random sample of 197 invoices, 188 were correctly predicted;

(2) sales pricing: from a random sample of 58 items, 56 were predicted correctly;
(3) mark-down pricing: from a sample of 159 items selected, 140 were correctly predicted.

The criterion for judging a successful prediction in all three cases is that prices must be correctly predicted 'to the exact penny'.

Although they contend that their computer model 'lends itself to further elaboration and testing' (Cyert and March 1963: 148), few organization theorists and almost no economists have followed that empirical lead.[7] Nelson nevertheless maintains that routines inform the idea of core competence (1991: 70):

The notion of a hierarchy of organizational routines is the key building block under our concept of core organizational routines. . . . If the lower-order routines for doing various tasks are absent, or if . . . there is no practical higher-order routine for invoking them [as needed] . . . then the capability to do that job lies outside the organization's extant core capabilities.

The pricing rules to which Cyert and March refer are presumably the lower-order routines in such a scheme of things, while the routines for switching among pricing rules are higher order. But while there is no disputing that department stores with better lower-order and higher-order pricing routines will perform better than those with worse, the possession of such a core competence does not take us very far in describing the overall competitiveness of this or any other department store. What are the questions to which the concept of routine is permitting us to give answers? What are the attributes with respect to which routines are described?

Implementing this last would be tantamount to treating the routine as the counterpart of the transaction. But there is another possibility: routines are a way by which we describe organization forms. Such a concept is suggested by Benjamin Coriat and Dosi, who distinguish between 'two archetypal sets of routines . . . namely "Tayloristic" and "Ohnistic" (loosely speaking, "Japanese") production methods' (1998: 116). It is their position that 'partic-

---

[7] Many potential units of analysis never take on sufficient definition to be broadly useful. Simon, for example, refers to the sociological concept of role as a potential unit of analysis, but observes that 'the term has never been given sufficiently precise definition' (1961: xxx). He thereafter goes on to nominate the decision premise as the unit of analysis: 'Behavior can be predicted . . . when the premises of the decision are known (or can be predicted) in sufficient detail' (1961: xxx). The decision premise as the unit of analysis for the study of organization has yet to be shown to have broad applicability.

The same applies to the concept of capabilities, which Richardson introduces with the observation that the functional activities in an industry need to be 'carried out by organizations with appropriate *capabilities*, or, in other words, with appropriate knowledge, experience, and skills' (1972: 888; emphasis in original). He subsequently concedes that the 'notion of capability is no doubt somewhat vague' (1972: 888) and refers to Penrose on how capabilities slowly evolve (Richardson 1972: 888). The operationalization of capabilities has also been slow to evolve, which may explain the replacement of the term capabilities by competence.

ular sets [clusters?] of routines can be traced back to the coevolution between corporate patterns of knowledge distribution and mechanisms of co-ordination and governance' (ibid.).

So conceived, routines are a much more composite concept than the pricing rules to which Cyert and March refer. Indeed, Taylorism and Ohnism are more akin to the organization form distinctions that I made when examining the organization of work (Williamson 1980). This latter entailed the comparison of six work modes—putting-out, federated, communal-emh, peer group, inside contracting, and authority relation—across product flow attributes, job assignment attributes, and incentive attributes. The Coriat and Dosi groupings (knowledge distribution; mechanisms of co-ordination; governance) are related but different. Might these be worked up in such a way as to operationalize the study of work organization more fully and effectively? Still another possibility is to operationalize the concept of routine by appealing to the cognitive science notion of 'script' (Nooteboom 1999).

3.3. Describing the Firm

The competence perspective also rejects the idea of the firm as a production function and emphasizes management and organization features instead. Starting from the basic unit of analysis, suppose that the firm is described as the aggregation of those basic units for which internal organization enjoys a comparative advantage. The firm then is a bundle of related resources (from the resource-based perspective), a bundle of routines (from the evolutionary perspective), and a bundle of transactions/contracts (from the transaction cost economics perspective).

According to Geoffrey Hodgson, the competence perspective can answer the same key questions of the existence, structure, and boundaries of the firm 'at least as well as the transaction cost and other contractarian theories' (1998: 181). He thereafter argues that the principal factor 'explaining the existence, boundaries, nature and development of the firm is the capacity of such an organization to protect and develop the competences of the groups and individuals contained within it, in a changing environment' (1998: 189). But while he follows this with a series of interesting remarks about formal and informal relations, tacit knowledge, mental models, organizational learning, trust, dynamic corporate culture, and the like, we are never told why these effects work better (or worse) in a unified firm (AB) than in two autonomous firms (A and B).

Furthermore, Hodgson (and the competence perspective) never address the issue of limits to firm size—except, perhaps, in the limits to growth to which Penrose (1959) refers. Thus although Hodgson avers that 'Firm competences have limits of scale and scope' (1998: 192), the supporting logic is not developed. The burdens of bureaucracy are curiously slighted by the competence literature.

This does not, however, mean that the competence perspective is unneeded. One possibility, which I discuss later, is that transaction cost economics informs the *generic* decision to make or buy while competence brings in *particulars*. That is broadly congruent with Dosi's view (quoted by Hodgson (1998: 195)) that 'the boundaries of the corporation need to be understood not only in terms of transaction cost considerations, but also in terms of learning, path dependencies, technological opportunities, selection, and complementary assets' (Dosi 1994: 231). Evidently composite transactions (clusters) and process considerations need to figure more prominently. I do not disagree but would urge that there is a need to breathe operational content into such competence features.

3.4. Purposes Served

According to Penrose, the distinctive competence of the firm resides in making better use of its resources (1959: 24). Sidney Winter similarly describes firms as 'repositories of productive knowledge' (1988: 175), to which Martin Fransman agrees (1994: 715). Differential learning within and between firms is evidently key: 'firms exist because they can more efficiently coordinate collective learning processes than market organization is able to' (Foss 1996a: 18). Hodgson concurs that firms enjoy efficiency advantages in relation to markets because of 'the relative intensity and longevity of interpersonal relations within the firm and the group and institution-based characteristic of much of the learning and knowledge within that organization' (1998: 193).

This line of argument finesses the question, however, of when to learn in a single, combined firm rather than in two or more autonomous firms. Thus the decision to buy in the market rather than make to one's own needs is not between zero firms (market) and a single firm (produce internally) but rather is between (at least) *two* firms (supplier and buyer) and *one* firm (produce internally). Given that all firms are repositories of knowledge and that all firms learn and develop interpersonal relations, the question is when is this best done in separate firms rather than in one. That issue is never addressed, much less worked through, in a comparative institutional way.

A related issue has, however, been posed by Teece (1986) and subsequently addressed by Julia Liebeskind (1996) in the context of weak property rights for knowledge. If inter-firm contracting exposes a firm to the leakage of proprietary knowledge (because the knowledge cannot be patented, possibly because the knowledge disclosed is much broader than that which can be patented, and/or patents cannot be effectively enforced), then a firm will take self-protective measures to reduce the leakage of such knowledge. Goods or services which, in a regime where proprietary knowledge is secure, would be contracted out will be undertaken by the firm instead (Teece 1986).

As Liebeskind points out, that implies that the mechanisms for protecting knowledge internally are superior to those that attend inter-firm contracting. Albeit intuitively 'obvious', that intuition needs to be worked through. What, precisely, are the mechanisms through which this differential protection is realized? As Liebeskind develops (1996), the comparative institutional action resides in inter-firm and intra-firm differences in the mechanisms of governance.

That, in effect, is a transaction cost argument. She particularizes it, however, by observing that 'not all firms may be equally competent at deploying their institutional capabilities to protect their knowledge' (Liebeskind 1996: 104). I agree and would urge that a second move be made: *Which* firms are more and which are less competent in deploying their institutional capabilities to protect their knowledge? If and as this question is addressed, we begin to operationalize the competence perspective.

3.5. Empirical

As discussed above, much of the competence perspective entails *ex post* rationalizations for success and has been remiss in predictive respects. Yasemin Kor and Joseph Mahoney nevertheless contend that 'resource-based theory has begun to generate a substantive stream of statistical data analysis' (1998: 28) and list nearly fifty articles of this kind. Many of the hypotheses to which they refer test for the 'importance of' various resources—of which unique resources, organizational factors, competences, and property rights are prominently included. The generic hypothesis is that 'more' of the resources named have a positive influence on the growth and performance of the firm. Whether, however, more resources are really better than less should be judged comparatively—in that some resources will be put to more productive use if the firm accesses them through outsourcing. No such comparative assessment is attempted.

That moves the issues on to transaction cost turf, but they can be returned to the more composite competence perspective by repeating the strategy referred to above: *Which* firms with what organizational attributes will deploy what types of resources to more productive advantage? Issues of an organization form kind, akin to those discussed earlier (Coriat and Dosi 1998; Williamson 1980), are implicated.

One way of looking at the research opportunity is to view transaction cost economics as feeding into the competence perspective in much the same way as organization theory is grist for the study of governance (where the latter is examined in Williamson (1996: chap. 9)). Albeit underdeveloped, the relation between governance and competence is beginning to take shape and would appear to hold promise.

3.6. Efficiency Criterion

The core competence literature frequently describes transaction cost economics as static and avers that competence deals with dynamic efficiency, where dynamic efficiency 'is essentially about learning and innovation' (Hodgson 1998: 188). This 'emphasis on dynamics and learning in an out-of-equilibrium context enables a more satisfactory accommodation of the real world of firm heterogeneity' (Hodgson 1998: 189). Path dependency is often implicated, sometimes with a claim that path dependency is responsible for inefficiency (where inefficiency is judged by comparing an actual condition with a hypothetical ideal). That is in the zero transaction cost tradition of Pigou to which Coase (1960) took vigorous exception. A feasible criterion for judging dynamic efficiency is never proposed. Remediableness considerations are never reached.

4. Challenges Posed by the Competence Perspective for Transaction Cost Economics

There are many respects in which the competence and transaction cost perspectives are congruent. Both take exception with orthodoxy, both are bounded rationality constructions, and both maintain that organization matters. Also, as discussed above, they deal with partly overlapping phenomena, often in complementary ways. But there are real differences and some tensions between the two. I deal here with competence challenges of two kinds: those that I regard as largely mistaken, and those which pose research opportunities.

4.1. Mistaken Critiques

Transaction cost economics needs good critics, but some of the criticisms that have been made are, I think, overdrawn or mistaken. The three criticisms on which I focus here are that: (1) opportunism does not have the organizational consequences that have been ascribed to it, (2) transaction cost is a static concept and needs to be made dynamic,[8] and (3) governance does not engage the issues of management. These are not new criticisms. That I have been 'misunderstood' on these matters is disconcerting. Authors have an obligation to make themselves clear.

---

[8] Another frequent criticism of transaction cost economics, which I do not address here, is that both production and transaction costs matter. I agree. My paper with Michael Riordan examines these issues and concludes that most, but not all, of the qualitative predictions that obtain when production costs are held constant survive when production cost differences are introduced (Riordan and Williamson 1985).

4.2. Opportunism

Opportunism is so familiar that we often fail to acknowledge it and its consequences when we see it.[9] The legal oath to which I referred earlier is one illustration, but there are many others. In the absence of opportunism, all of the following would vanish: moral hazard, adverse selection, shirking, filtering, undisclosed subgoal pursuit, distortions, and all other strategic deceits. If, moreover, as hitherto stated, governance arises (in part) to mitigate these hazards, then to assume the absence of opportunism will miss much of the action. Our understanding of economic organization would be needlessly impoverished as a consequence.

To concede opportunism is not, however, to celebrate it. Some economists have nevertheless been heard to say—often in jest, but not always—that 'avarice is the only reliable human motive'. That is a cynical and unhelpful construction. Many students of organization are understandably put off by opportunism (Ghoshal and Moran 1996; Kogut and Zander 1996; Hodgson 1998).

Kathleen Conner and C. K. Prahalad (1996), in an influential and thoughtful critique (to which, however, Foss (1966a, 1996b) takes exception), concede that opportunism has a massive influence on economic organization but insist that many interesting problems of organization are posed *even in the absence of opportunism*. They take the position that information asymmetry, in a world of bounded rationality/zero opportunism, is a candidate condition upon which to construct a 'knowledge-based theory of the firm' (Conner and Prahalad 1996: 484). A key part of their argument is that because 'some of each person's knowledge remains private' (1996: 483), 'honest persons may disagree as to the best allocation of individual responsibilities, or whether a particular arrangement of decision roles has the potential to generate net gains', whence markets may need to be supplanted by an authority relation, thereby to avoid disagreement, haggling, and discord (ibid.).

My main response to this argument is that removing opportunism has different and more pervasive organizational consequences than those Conner and Prahalad describe. The general effect of presuming the absence of opportunism is that we enter the world of what Frank Manuel and Fritzie Manuel describe as 'utopian fantasies' (1979: 1). As I have developed elsewhere (Williamson 1999b), the ideal forms of organization that will be observed under zero opportunism will take the form of a peer group (if every member has the same ability) or ideal merit assignment (if abilities differ). But a somewhat different and more operational way to put it is that the incentive, control, and contract law differences

---

[9] To deny or suppress opportunism in the study of economic organization is tantamount to staging Hamlet without the Prince of Denmark—which, however, is not to say that such a play/theory of organization could not be staged. (Team theory (Marschak and Radner 1972) is illustrative.)

that define alternative modes of governance (Williamson 1991) all vanish if opportunism is zeroed out. Thus (1) no incentive differences will appear among modes because all members of every group subscribe to the same 'general clause' (Williamson 1975: 237, 91–3; 1985: 64–7) and implement the same objective function in the same fully committed way; (2) all cost-effective regularities (practices and procedures) that are adopted by one group will also be adopted by another—whatever the nominal form of organization (private firm, public bureau, non-profit, autonomous market) from which they start; and (3) contract law differences serve no purpose among groups all of which share the same purpose and converge to the same form. Note, moreover, that the conflict and haggling to which Conner and Prahalad refer will never appear in opportunism-free groups, it being the case that every such group will work out its differences instrumentally.

There is, however, a caveat—especially to my argument that control differences vanish. The above argument assumes that initial conditions do not matter. If the organization form that is prescribed for a task is 'nearly optimal' for one group but far from optimal for another, then the second will need to undergo greater change, which will place it at an initial disadvantage—which disadvantage could be compounded by differential learning. But this does not imply that the firm is the superior form. Thus although Conner and Prahalad ascribe authority (centralization) benefits to firms, there will be other transactions for which markets (decentralization) will be the favoured form.

The possibility that initial conditions can be more consequential than they are usually treated by transaction cost economics is nevertheless well taken. I return to this issue in my discussion of strategy and learning, below.

4.3. Dynamic Transaction Costs

A common critique is that transaction cost economics is static because it works out of an equilibrium contracting set-up. Richard Langlois (1992) takes this position in his paper on 'Transaction-Cost Economics in Real Time'.[10] According to Langlois, dynamic transaction costs are 'the costs of persuading, negotiating, coordinating, and teaching outside suppliers' (1992: 113). So construed, dynamic transaction costs are 'the costs of not having the capabilities you need when you need them' (ibid.). More generally, 'these costs of persuasion . . . [are] costs of coordinating separate stages of production. David Teece encapsulates the argument nicely' (Langlois 1992: 115), whereupon Langlois quotes Teece as follows (ibid.):[11]

---

[10] The argument is repeated in his paper with Foss (Langlois and Foss 1999).
[11] The original appears in Teece (1976: 13).

If there is a high degree of interdependence among successive stages of production, and if occasions for adaptation are unpredictable yet common, coordinated responses may be difficult to secure if the separated stages are operated independently. Interdependence by itself does not cause difficulty if the pattern of interdependence is stable and fixed. Difficulties arise only if program execution rests on contingencies that cannot be predicted perfectly in advance. In this case, coordinated activity is required to secure agreement about the estimates that will be used as a basis for action. Vertical integration facilitates such co-ordination.

This argument also reduces, at least in some respects, to a contractual-incompleteness argument. Were it feasible to stipulate exhaustively the appropriate conditional responses, co-ordination could proceed by long-term contract. However, long-term contracts are unsatisfactory when most of the relevant contingencies cannot be delineated. Given these limitations, short-term contracts are likely to be considered instead. . . . Even if short-term contracts are defective neither on account of investment disincentives nor first-mover advantages, the costs of negotiations and the time required to bring the system into adjustment by exclusive reliance on market signals are apt to be greater than the costs of administrative processes under vertical integration.

I have no problem with the argument that vertical integration can arise in response to ex ante investment concerns as well as in anticipation of ex post contracting problems. Indeed, the explanation that Langlois ascribes to Teece is one that I had made previously. I see no reason, however, to refer to ex post contracting as a static construction and ex ante as dynamic. Both are intertemporal arguments and are consonant with the basic transaction cost economics thesis—namely, that problems of organization are not predominantly technological but have their origins in the attributes of transactions on the one hand and of human actors on the other.

As an examination of my original statement reveals,[12] incomplete long-term contracts will prospectively fail to anticipate and/or make correct provision for

---

[12] My initial treatment (since reproduced in *Markets and Hierarchies* (1975: 87–8)) is as follows (Williamson 1971: 120–1):

[I]f there is a high degree of interdependence among successive stages of production and if occasions for adaptation are unpredictable yet common, coordinated responses may be difficult to secure if the separate stages are operated independently. March and Simon (1958: 159) characterize the problem in the following terms: 'Interdependence by itself does not cause difficulty if the pattern of interdependence is stable and fixed. For, in this case, each subprogram can be designed to take account of all the subprograms with which it interacts. Difficulties arise only if program execution rests on contingencies that cannot be predicted perfectly in advance. In this case, coordinating activity is required to secure agreement about the estimates that will be used as the basis for action, or to provide information to each subprogram unit about the activities of the others.'

This reduces, in some respects, to a contractual incompleteness argument. Were it feasible exhaustively to stipulate the appropriate conditional responses, co-ordination could proceed by contract. This is ambitious, however; in the face of a highly variable and uncertain environment, . . . long-term contracts [can be expected to experience strain and] vertical integration may be indicated.

But what of the possibility of short-term contracts? It is here that the convergence of expectations argument is of special importance. Thus assume that short-term contracts are not defective on account either of investment disincentives or first-mover advantages. It is Malmgren's (1961) contention that such contracts may nevertheless be vitiated by the absence of structural constraints.

future contingencies (the March and Simon argument), while classical market contracting will not reliably effect convergent expectations (the Malmgren argument). The first of these has reference to timely adaptations (*ex post*), the second to timely convergence (*ex ante*). Both are intertemporal applications of transaction cost reasoning.

But my major point is this: intertemporal complications are not merely incidental but are *central to* the transaction cost economics project—which is hardly what one expects from what Langlois describes as a static construction. The most familiar of these is the fundamental transformation, which argument takes issue with the atemporal proposition that 'competition for the market' will assuredly yield an efficient outcome if large numbers of qualified bidders tender bids at the outset. What was missing but needed to be introduced was an examination of contracting in its entirety—to include contract execution and contract renewal. If, in effect, what had been a large numbers bidding condition at the outset is thereafter *transformed* into a small numbers supply relation (when the transaction in question is supported by non-trivial investments in durable, non-redeployable assets), then intertemporal contractual complications appear. More broadly, intertemporal considerations also enter into the transaction cost economics set-up in the following respects: governance structures are predominantly instruments for adaptation, it being the case that adaptation (of both autonomous and co-operative kinds) is the central problem of economic organization; organization has an intertemporal life of its own, which has special ramifications for bureaucracy; the efficacy of reputation effects are subject to intertemporal limits; the remediableness criterion casts a very different intertemporal interpretation upon path dependence; and disequilibrium contracting complications are posed by real-time events in the high technology arena.

That transaction cost economics engages these intertemporal issues is not to say that it has worked all of these out in a satisfactory way. I entirely agree that transaction cost economics stands to benefit from more fully dynamic constructions. But whereas saying dynamics is easy, doing dynamics is hard. Always and everywhere the need is to work through the mechanisms of economic organization in a 'modest, slow, molecular, definitive' way.[13]

4.4. Management

Coase contends that both production function and governance structure theories of the firm are remiss in management respects (1988 : 38):

The costs of negotiations and the time required to bring the system into adjustment by exclusive reliance on market (price) signals are apt to be great in relation to that which would obtain if successive stages were integrated and administrative processes employed as well or instead.

[13] The phrase 'modest, slow, molecular, definitive work' originates with Peguy. See Williamson (1996: 13, n. 9).

economists have tended to neglect the main activity of a firm, running a business. . . . [This neglect] has tended to submerge what to me is the key idea in 'The Nature of the Firm': the comparison of the costs of coordinating the activities of factors of production within the firm with the costs of bringing about the same result by market transactions or by means of operations taken within some other firm.

Although I do not claim that the firm-as-governance structure makes *adequate* provision for management, it certainly makes *significant* provision for management. For example, transaction cost economics took exception to the proposition that markets and hierarchies have identical access to fiat (Alchian and Demsetz 1972) from the very outset (Williamson 1975). Provision was also made for 'informal organization' (Barnard 1938) as a factor that supports added compliance and co-operation within firms as compared with markets (Williamson 1975, 1990) and for differential bureaucratic costs between markets and hierarchies (Williamson 1975: chap. 7; 1985: chap. 6). More generally, adaptation is taken to be the central problem of economic organization, in relation to which firms enjoy the advantage over markets in co-operative but not in autonomous adaptation respects. Indeed, the firm is described as a syndrome of 'managerial' attributes (Williamson 1991) in which (comparatively) low-powered incentives, extensive administrative controls, and its own dispute-settlement machinery are combined (specifically, courts will often refuse to hear intra-firm disputes, the effect of which is to make the firm its own court of ultimate appeal (which contributes to the differential access to fiat to which I refer above)). More recently, considerations of differential probity have been examined in the context of transactions where failures of loyalty and real-time responsiveness could undermine integrity (Williamson 1999*a*). And the importance of cognitive specialization has also been featured (Williamson 1999*b*).

To repeat, however, significant provision for management does not imply adequate provision for management. Cognitive specialization is underdeveloped. Our understanding of bureaucracy is still imperfect. Entrepreneurship continues to elude our understanding. Venture capital poses many puzzles. Knowledge-based and learning-based theories may have significant comparative institutional ramifications. As between focused critiques that deal with managerial particulars and sweeping critiques that are vague and unspecific, the former are much more useful.

4.5. Research Opportunities

Although I group the above critiques under the heading of mistaken, these are probably better described as 'unfocused' or 'overdrawn'. Plainly, research opportunities reside in all of them. My purpose here is to address three more constructive critiques that are raised by the competence perspective to which governance, in varying degrees, can respond.

4.5.1. Beyond piecemeal   Transaction cost economics is a microanalytic exercise in which transactions are aligned with alternative modes of governance so as to effect an economizing outcome. That can be illuminating but may also lead to incorrect predictions if interaction effects are missed or if holistic consequences are glossed over.

The practice of examining transactions 'as if' they were independent will not do if there are significant interaction effects between them (Nickerson 1997).[14] The neglect of technological non-separabilities means, in effect, that the transaction has been incorrectly specified. That applies also to contractual non-separabilities.

Such effects are easy to correct in principle: redefine the transaction to take these effects into account. In practice, that may require deeper knowledge of how the system actually works (Nickerson 1997) and/or a sensitivity to subtle but lurking strategic features (Williamson 1985: 318–19).

A more troublesome argument is that of aggregation. If we take a more holistic view, we see that the firm as a whole is different from and larger than the sum of the parts.[15] The economics of atmosphere is intended to reflect such considerations. That brings in informal organization and flags the limits of calculativeness (Williamson 1993). But there is more to it than that. Appealing to the Coriat and Dosi (1998) suggestion that organization form is the way we describe clusters of routines could well turn out to be an instructive way by which to uncover and better understand systems considerations. Inasmuch as transaction cost economics purports to be interested in all regularities whatsoever, it stands to benefit from research in the competence tradition on holistic consequences.

4.5.2. Beyond generic governance: Strategy   Richard Rumelt, Dan Schendel, and David Teece observe that, 'Of all the new fields of economics, the transaction cost branch of organizational economics has the greatest affinity with strategic

---

[14] The qualifier 'significant' is consequential. If the argument is that transaction cost economics has focused too much on the immediate effects of strong interactions to the neglect of weak interactions which, in the long run, are consequential, I would appeal to the two main theoretical findings of the literature on nearly decomposable systems (Simon 1962: 129):

(a) in a nearly decomposable system, the short-run behavior of each of the component subsystems is approximately independent of the short-run behavior of the other components; (b) in the long-run, the behavior of any one of the components depends in only an aggregative way on the behavior of the other subcomponents.

Near decomposability is a widely observed design principle in complex social systems and reflects respect for the cognitive overload (bounded rationality) and the ability to shrug off responsibility (opportunism) that beset fully connected systems.

[15] For example, if the bureaucratic costs of managing a transaction internally vary with the size and complexity of the firm, then whether the firm should integrate transaction $N+1$ will not be independent of the fact that $N-Q$ transactions have already been internalized (where Q is the number of outsourced transactions). I conjecture that such aggregation effects are of second-order importance, but others could be more consequential.

management' (1991: 14). They also observe that 'strategic management is about co-ordination and resource allocation *inside the firm*' (1991: 19; emphasis in original). And they challenge strategy scholars to supply 'a coherent theory of effective internal co-ordination and resource allocation, of entrepreneurship and technical progress' (ibid.).

That is a tall order. One way in which transaction cost economics can participate in this project is to push beyond the generic level at which it now operates to consider resource/capability/endowment particulars. Rather, therefore, than ask the question, 'What is the best generic mode (market, hybrid, firm, or bureau) to organize X?', which is the traditional transaction cost query, the question to be put instead is, 'How should firm A—which has pre-existing strengths *and* weaknesses (core competences *and* disabilities)—organize X?'

In effect, the traditional transaction cost query assumes that the specialized investments needed to support a transaction (or related set of transactions) have not yet been made—either by the firm or by potential outside suppliers. If, however, either the firm or potential outside suppliers have made *pre-existing investments*, of a (largely) non-redeployable kind, that are well suited to support the transaction in question, then the alignment calculus will be tilted in favour of the form that possesses such specialized, underutilized capacity—at least temporarily (until the investment renewal decision comes up for consideration) and possibly longer. Path dependency considerations thus arise in this way.

Taking an inventory of pre-existing investments, by the firm and its potential suppliers, is tantamount to including previously omitted variables. Such should help to reduce the unexplained variance in simple tests of the generic alignment hypothesis. Considerations of learning (see below) are also implicated.

Yet another move would be to make allowance for competition, taking the market niche to be served (say α_1) as given. The question here is: How do the pre-existing strengths and weaknesses of firm A compare with those of its extant rivals with respect to market niche α_1?

Still further moves can be contemplated. The firm and its extant and potential rivals can be examined in relation to a variety of niches: How do the pre-existing strengths and weaknesses of firm A compare with those of extant and potential rivals with respect to market niches described by $(\alpha_1, \alpha_2; \beta_1, \beta_2, \beta_3; \gamma)$?

An even more ambitious move would be to reposition the firm, to build up core competences and/or relieve disabilities (Shapiro and Varian 1998). The question at this level is: How should firm A, with its pre-existing strengths and weaknesses, reposition for the future in relation to the strategic situation (actual and potential rivalry; actual and potential market niches) of which it is a part or to which it can relate?

A sixth move would be to go beyond value realization to include strategizing, where the object is to deter and discipline actual and potential rivals. This introduces issues with which game theory is especially concerned.

TABLE 2.1. Transaction cost economics and strategy

Level	Strategy issue
1: Generic	How do alternative generic modes (markets, hybrids, firms, bureaux) compare for purposes of organizing transaction X?
2: Particular	How should firm A, with its pre-existing strengths and weaknesses (core competences and disabilities), organize transaction X?
3: Fixed niche	How do the pre-existing strengths and weaknesses of firm A compare with those of its extant rivals with respect to market niche α_1?
4: Variable niche	How do the pre-existing strengths and weaknesses of firm A compare with those of its extant and potential rivals with respect to niches described by $(\alpha_1, \alpha_2; \beta_1, \beta_2, \beta_3; \gamma)$?
5: Repositioning	How should firm A, with its pre-existing strengths and weaknesses, reposition for the future in relation to the strategic situation (actual and potential rivalry; actual and potential market niches) of which it is a part or to which it can relate?
6: Strategizing	If firm A possesses monopoly power, how can it best deter and discipline actual and potential rivals?

Each of the foregoing moves is summarized in Table 2.1. Transaction cost economics relates productively to all, the first three being the easiest to implement. That is gratifying in that, although many strategy scholars aspire to push out the time horizon to work on problems of the last three kinds, a huge number of interesting strategy issues surface at levels 1 to 3.[16]

This exercise nevertheless operates at a very high level of generality. At best I offer added perspective. While we await operationalization of competences (where I expect that asset specificity will continue to play an important role) and of niches (where marketing and population ecology have a lot to offer), there are no refutable implications.

4.5.3. Learning   Although transaction cost economics made early provision for the difference between explicit and tacit knowledge (Williamson 1971) and thereafter developed the contractual/organizational ramifications of firm-specific human capital, in that both worker and firm have incentives to craft added contractual safeguards as human asset specificity builds up (Williamson 1975: chap. 4), it makes only limited contact with the subject of learning. Learning being a large subject, it is not possible to relieve this lapse here. I will, however,

---

[16] I conjecture that level 5 will often be implemented piecemeal rather than as a comprehensive plan (in which mergers and acquisitions, investments, contracting, finance, marketing, etc. are all considered simultaneously). Be that as it may, transaction cost economics could have an important role to play in taking an inventory of a firm's assets (and those of its rivals) and in assessing the hazards associated with alternative planning scenarios. Jackson Nickerson describes such an undertaking in his dissertation (1997).

relate learning to foresight and examine the ramifications for some of the myopic biases to which learning is subject.

As stated at the outset, transaction cost economics assumes that economic actors have the capacity to look ahead and recognize contractual hazards and investment opportunities. Often, however, the requisite recognition will come as a product of experience. Whether positive or negative, the basic proposition is that, once the relevant features have been disclosed, the firm will react to such knowledge by taking actions that mitigate future hazards and more fully realize future gains. Learning through experience—by discovering more about the environment and suppliers and rivalry, after which appropriate adaptations are worked out—is more ambitious than merely trial-and-error learning but is less ambitious than the idea of farsighted contracting to which I referred earlier.

Consider the issue of level 2 strategy, where both the firm and its suppliers have pre-existing strengths and weaknesses for producing a good or service. Assume, in particular, that the firm has not yet made the requisite specialized investments itself and that outside suppliers are partly qualified in this respect. Out of considerations of timeliness and the costs of self-learning, the firm decides to procure from one of these outsiders. A contract of medium duration is agreed to.

The parties are then faced with unanticipated disturbances during contract execution to which adaptations are required. Both parties learn better about the nature of the contractual hazards and of their abilities to communicate and their propensities to co-operate. Learning also takes place with respect to the nature of the specialized investments needed to support the transaction.

Such learning will have a bearing on contract renewal. Are the disturbances and associated hazards greater or less than projected? Are the communication needs great or little? Are the bilateral mechanisms for working through the problems adequate? Serious dissatisfaction on the part of either buyer or seller could result in non-renewal. Even if, moreover, the parties are satisfied in these respects but the requisite *new* investments in non-redeployable assets are especially great, reaching a new agreement for continuing outside supply could be difficult. More generally, the point is this: a predictive theory of economic organization will be enriched by making more prominent provision for the many ways in which learning influences the intertemporal governance choice calculus.

Transaction cost economics also has a bearing on the 'biased learning' issues that are dealt with in articles by James March (1991) and by Daniel Levinthal and March (1993). I will put emphasis on the latter (which builds upon the former). Both articles illustrate how the lens of organization theory can and should apprise economists about important phenomena that are ignored or undervalued in the usual economic approach to economic organization.

Levinthal and March begin with the proposition that 'The effectiveness of learning in the short run and in the near neighborhood of current experience interferes with learning in the long run and at a distance' (1993: 97). They then go on to describe the major learning mechanisms that organizations employ, the problems of myopia that arise, and the trade-offs that are posed. They observe with reference to the first that (1993: 97; emphasis in original):

Organizations use two major mechanisms to facilitate learning from experience. The first is *simplification*. Learning processes seek to simplify experience, to minimize interactions and restrict effects to the spatial and temporal neighborhood of actions. The second mechanism is *specialization*. Learning processes tend to focus attention and narrow competence. Unsurprisingly, these learning mechanisms come at a cost, of which myopia is salient.

Three myopic tendencies are distinguished: (1) ignore the long run, (2) ignore the larger picture, and (3) overlook failures. Regarding the first, 'normally sensible forms of specialized adaptation' sometimes produce 'dysfunctional second-order effects . . . A strategic problem is created by the fact that learning in one domain is likely to be rewarding in the short run, but it leads to a longer-run potential decay of adaptive capability in other domains' (Levinthal and March 1993: 102). Also, organizational power that is used to exercise control over an environment, which yields short-run advantage, can come at the cost of 'atrophy of capabilities to respond to change' (Levinthal and March 1993: 102).

As with all unanticipated consequences, transaction cost economics responds by (1) making note of these previously unrecognized regularities and (2) asking what lessons for more efficient organizational design reside therein. Once disclosed, dysfunctional consequences and other long-run propensities will not be mindlessly repeated or ignored. Upon being apprised of costly biases, lapses, or distortions, the object is to mitigate the effects in question *in cost-effective degree*.

Myopia of the second kind involves subgoal pursuit at the expense of the larger picture. The incentive to free-ride on the efforts of others is an example (Levinthal and March 1993: 104):

the best strategy for any individual organization is often to emphasize the successful explorations of others. Such a strategy, if followed by all, produces no innovations to imitate and a downward spiral of refining existing technologies and strategies. The system as a whole underinvests in exploration.

Overcoming failures of a systems kind normally involves collective action. Albeit the 'obvious' move, such action is sometimes prohibitively expensive (Arrow 1969). In the event that it is too costly to effect a merger among the autonomous parts, if co-operation is too costly to effect through contract, and if corrective public policy is beset with problems of its own, then the fact that the 'system as a whole underinvests in exploration' is simply a condition with which we need to come to terms.

The propensity to overlook failures arises because 'Organizational learning produces . . . a biased history. . . . As learners settle into those domains in which they have competence and accumulate experience in them, they experience fewer and fewer failures. Insofar as they generalize that experience to other domains, they are likely to exaggerate considerably the likelihood of success' (Levinthal and March 1993: 104). Inasmuch as 'organizations promote successful people to positions of power and authority, rather than unsuccessful ones, it is the biases of success that are particularly relevant to decision making' (Levinthal and March 1993: 105). As with underinvestments in exploration, however, whether such promotion biases are remediable turns on whether a superior alternative can be devised.

The upshot is that while competence research on learning and path dependency is especially good at uncovering biases, the lens of transaction cost economics (with special emphasis on the remediableness criterion) affords comparative institutional perspective. Both are needed.

5. Conclusions

The competence perspective is attuned to good issues and challenges both orthodoxy and the governance perspective to be responsive. As developed herein, I see the relation between competence and governance as both rival and complementary—more the latter than the former, since some of the differences turn out to be more apparent than real.

I begin with a statement of the six key moves out of which the governance perspective works and has been progressively operationalized. Having in mind the possibility that this sequence has lessons for the long-awaited operationalization of competence, I next take the competence perspective through these same six moves. I then address challenges posed by competence for the governance perspective—some of which I believe to be mistaken, but others of which are constructive.

Given that both governance and competence are bounded rationality constructions and hold that organization matters, both share a lot of common ground. To be sure, there are differences. Governance is more microanalytic (the transaction is the basic unit of analysis) and adopts an economizing approach to assessing comparative economic organization, whereas competence is more composite (is the routine the unit of analysis?) and is more concerned with processes (especially learning) and the lessons for strategy. Healthy tensions are posed between them. Both are needed in our efforts to understand complex economic phenomena as we build towards a science of organization.

References

ALCHIAN, ARMEN, and H. DEMSETZ 1972. 'Production, information costs, and economic organization', *American Economic Review* 62 (December): 777–95.

ARROW, KENNETH 1969. 'The organization of economic activity: Issues pertinent to the choice of market versus nonmarket allocation', in *The Analysis and Evaluation of Public Expenditure: The PPB System.* Vol. 1. U.S. Joint Economic Committee, 91st Congress, 1st Session. Washington, DC: US Government Printing Office, 47–73.

—— 1999. 'Foreword' in Glenn Carroll and David Teece, eds., *Firms, Markets, and Hierarchies.* New York: Oxford University Press, vi–vii.

BARNARD, CHESTER 1938. *The Functions of the Executive.* Cambridge, MA: Harvard University Press (fifteenth printing, 1962).

COASE, RONALD H. 1937. 'The nature of the firm', *Economica* N.S. 4: 386–405. Reprinted in Oliver E. Williamson and Sidney Winter, eds., *The Nature of the Firm: Origins, Evolution, Development.* New York: Oxford University Press (1991).

—— 1960. 'The problem of social cost', *Journal of Law and Economics*, 3 (October): 1–44.

—— 1964. 'The regulated industries: Discussion', *American Economic Review* 54 (May): 194–7.

—— 1972. 'Industrial organization: A proposal for research', in V. R. Fuchs, ed., *Policy Issues and Research Opportunities in Industrial Organization.* New York: National Bureau of Economic Research, 59–73.

—— 1988. 'The nature of the firm: Meaning', *Journal of Law, Economics, and Organization* 4 (Spring): 19–32.

COMMONS, JOHN R. 1932. 'The problem of correlating law, economics, and ethics', *Wisconsin Law Review* 8: 3–26.

—— 1934. *Institutional Economics.* Madison: University of Wisconsin Press.

CONNER, KATHLEEN, and C. K. PRAHALAD 1996. 'A resource-based theory of the firm: Knowledge versus opportunism', *Organization Science* 7 (September–October): 477–501.

CORIAT, BENJAMIN, and GIOVANNI DOSI 1998. 'Learning how to govern and learning how to solve problems: On the co-evolution of competences, conflicts, and organizational routines', in Alfred Chandler Jr., Peter Hagström, and Örjan Solvell, eds., *The Dynamic Firm.* Oxford: Oxford University Press, 103–33.

CROCKER, KEITH, and SCOTT MASTEN 1996. 'Regulation and administered contracts revisited: Lessons from transaction-cost economics for public utility regulation', *Journal of Regulatory Economics* 8: 5–39.

CYERT, RICHARD, and JAMES MARCH 1963. *A Behavioral Theory of the Firm.* Englewood Cliffs, NJ: Prentice Hall.

DAWKINS, RICHARD 1976. *The Selfish Gene.* New York: Oxford University Press.

DEMSETZ, HAROLD 1969. 'Information and efficiency: Another viewpoint', *Journal of Law and Economics* 12 (April): 1–22.

DOSI, GIOVANNI 1994. 'Boundaries of the firm', in Geoffrey Hodgson, Warren Samuels, and Marc Tool, eds., *The Elgar Companion to Institutional and Evolutionary Economics, Vol. 1.* Aldershot: Edward Elgar, 229–37.

—— and LUIGI MARENGO 1994. 'Some elements of an evolutionary theory of organizational competences', in Richard England, ed., *Evolutionary Concepts in Contemporary Economics*. Ann Arbor, MI: University of Michigan Press, 157–78.

—— and DAVID TEECE 1998. 'Organizational competencies and the boundaries of the firm', in Richard Arena and Christian Longhi, eds., *Markets and Organization*. New York: Springer-Verlag, 281–301.

—— LUIGI MARENGO, and GIORGIO FAGIOLO 1996. 'Learning in evolutionary environments', unpublished manuscript.

FISCHER, STANLEY 1977. 'Long-term contracting, sticky prices, and monetary policy: Comment', *Journal of Monetary Economics* 3: 317–24.

FOSS, NICOLAI J. 1993. 'Theories of the firm: Contractual and competence perspectives', *Journal of Evolutionary Economics* 3: 127–44.

—— 1996*a*. 'Knowledge-based approaches to the theory of the firm: Some critical comments', *Organization Science* 7 (September–October): 470–6.

—— 1996*b*. 'More critical comments on knowledge-based theories of the firm', *Organization Science* 7 (September–October): 519–23.

—— CHRISTIAN KNUDSEN, and CYNTHIA MONTGOMERY 1995. 'An exploration of common ground: Integrating evolutionary and strategic theories of the firm', in Cynthia Montgomery, ed., *Resource-Based and Evolutionary Theories of the Firm*. Boston: Kluwer, 117.

FRANSMAN, MARTIN 1994. 'Information, knowledge, vision and theories of the firm', *Industrial and Corporate Change* 3(3): 713–57.

GAMBETTA, DIEGO 1988. *Trust: Making and Breaking Cooperative Relations*. Oxford: Basil Blackwell.

GEORGESCU-ROEGEN, NICHOLAS 1971. *The Entropy Law and Economic Process*. Cambridge, MA: Harvard University Press.

GHOSHAL, SUMANTRA, and PETER MORAN 1996. 'Bad for practice: A critique of the transaction cost theory', *Academy of Management Review* 21(1): 13–47.

HAYEK, FRIEDRICH A. VON 1945. 'The use of knowledge in society', *American Economic Review* 35 (September): 519–30. Reprinted in Friedrich A. von Hayek, *Individualism and Economic Order*. Chicago: University Press (1948).

HODGSON, GEOFFREY 1998. 'Competence and contract in the theory of the firm', *Journal of Economic Behavior and Organization* 35 (April): 179–201.

JOSKOW, PAUL L. 1991. 'The role of transaction cost economics in antitrust and public utility regulatory policies', *Journal of Law, Economics, and Organization* 7 (Special Issue): 53–83.

KAHNEMAN, DANIEL, PAUL SLOVIC, and AMOS TVERSKY, eds. 1982. *Judgment Under Uncertainty: Heuristics and Biases*. Cambridge: Cambridge University Press.

KOGUT, BRUCE, and UDO ZANDER 1992. 'Knowledge of the firm, combinative capabilities, and the replication of technology', *Organization Science* 3: 383–97.

—— 1996. 'What do firms do? Coordination, identity, and learning', *Organization Science* 7 (September–October): 502–17.

KOR, YASEMIN, and JOSEPH MAHONEY 1998. 'Penrose's resource-based approach', Working Paper Number 98-0126, University of Illinois.

KUHN, THOMAS S. 1970. *The Structure of Scientific Revolutions*. Chicago: University of Chicago Press.

LANGLOIS, RICHARD N. 1992. 'Transaction-cost economics in real time', *Industrial and Corporate Change* 1(1): 99–127.

—— and NICOLAI FOSS 1997. 'Capabilities and governance: The rebirth of production in the theory of economic organization', DRUID working paper.

—— —— 1999. 'Capabilities and governance: The rebirth of production in the theory of economic organization', *Kyklos* 52: 201–18.

—— and PAUL L. ROBERTSON 1995. *Firms, Markets, and Economic Change: A Dynamic Theory of Business Institutions*. London: Routledge.

LEVINTHAL, DANIEL, and JAMES MARCH 1993. 'The myopia of learning', *Strategic Management Journal* 14: 95–112.

LIEBESKIND, JULIA 1996. 'Knowledge, strategy, and the theory of the firm', *Strategic Management Journal* 17 (Winter, Special Issue): 93–107.

LYONS, BRUCE 1996. 'Empirical relevance of efficient contract theory: Inter-firm contracts', *Oxford Review of Economic Policy* 12: 27–52.

MAHONEY, JOSEPH, and J. R. PANDIAN 1992. 'The resource-based view within the conversation of strategic management,' *Strategic Management Journal* 13: 363–80.

MALMGREN, H. 1961. 'Information, expectations and the theory of the firm', *Quarterly Journal of Economics* 75 (August): 399–421.

MANUEL, FRANK, and FRITZIE MANUEL 1979. *Utopian Thought in the Western World*. Cambridge, MA: Harvard University Press.

MARCH, JAMES 1991. 'Exploration and exploitation in organizational learning', *Organization Science* 2 (February): 71–87.

—— and HERBERT A. SIMON 1958. *Organizations*. New York: John Wiley & Sons.

MARSCHAK, JACOB, and ROY RADNER 1972. *The Theory of Teams*. New Haven, CT: Yale University Press.

MARX, KARL 1967. *Capital*, Vol. 1. New York: International Publishers.

MASTEN, SCOTT 1995. 'Introduction to Vol. II', in Oliver Williamson and Scott Masten, eds., *Transaction Cost Economics*. Brookfield, VT: Edward Elgar, xi–xxii.

MOSAKOWSKI, ELAINE, and BILL MCKELVEY 1997. 'Predicting rent generation in competence-based competition', in Aime Heene and Ron Sanchez, eds., *Competence-Based Strategic Management*. Chichester: John Wiley, 65–85.

NELSON, RICHARD 1991. 'Why do firms differ, and how does it matter?', *Strategic Management Journal* 12 (Winter): 61–74.

—— and SIDNEY WINTER 1982. *An Evolutionary Theory of Economic Change*. Cambridge, MA: The Belknap Press, Harvard University Press.

NICKERSON, JACK 1997. 'Toward an economizing theory of strategy: The choice of strategic position, assets, and organizational form', unpublished Ph.D. dissertation, University of California, Berkeley.

—— 1999*b*. 'Innovation, learning, and industrial organization', *Cambridge Journal of Economics* 23 (March): 127–50.

PENROSE, EDITH 1959. *The Theory of Growth of the Firm*. New York: John Wiley & Sons.

PORTER, MICHAEL 1994. 'Toward a dynamic theory of strategy', in Richard Rumelt, Dan

Schendel, and David Teece, eds., *Fundamental Issues in Strategy Research*. Boston: Harvard Business School Press, 423–61.

PRAHALAD, C. K., and GARY HAMEL 1990. 'The core competence of the corporation', *Harvard Business Review*, May–June: 79–91.

RICHARDSON, GEORGE 1972. 'The organisation of industry', *Economic Journal* 82 (September): 883–96.

RINDFLEISCH, ARIC, and JAN HEIDE 1997. 'Transaction cost analysis: Past, present, and future applications', *Journal of Marketing* 61 (October): 30–54.

RIORDAN, MICHAEL, and OLIVER WILLIAMSON 1985. 'Asset specificity and economic organization', *International Journal of Industrial Organization* 3: 365–78.

RUMELT, RICHARD, DAN SCHENDEL, and DAVID TEECE. 1991. 'Strategic management and economics', *Strategic Management Journal* 12: 5–29.

SCHLEGEL, JOHN HENRY 1979. 'American legal realism and empirical science: From the Yale experience', *Buffalo Law Review* 29 (Spring): 195–323.

SCHULTZ, GEORGE 1995. 'Economics in action: Ideas, institutions, policies', *American Economic Review, Papers and Proceedings* 85 (May): 1–8.

SCHUMPETER, J. A. 1942. *Capitalism, Socialism, and Democracy*. New York: Harper & Row.

SELZNICK, PHILIP 1949. *TVA and the Grass Roots*. Berkeley: University of California Press.

SHAPIRO, CARL, and HAL VARIAN 1998. *Information Rules*. Boston: Harvard Business School Press.

SHELANSKI, HOWARD, and PETER KLEIN 1995. 'Empirical research in transaction cost economics: A review and assessment', *Journal of Law, Economics, and Organization* 11 (October): 335–61.

SIMON, HERBERT 1947. *Administrative Behavior*. New York: Macmillan.

—— 1957. *Models of Man*. New York: John Wiley & Sons.

—— 1961. *Administrative Behavior*, 2nd edn. New York: Macmillan (originally published 1947).

—— 1962. 'The architecture of complexity', *Proceedings of the American Philosophical Society* 106 (December): 467–82.

—— 1985. 'Human nature in politics: The dialogue of psychology with political science', *American Political Science Review* 79: 293–304.

—— 1991. 'Organizations and markets', *Journal of Economic Perspective* 5 (Spring): 25–44.

TEECE, DAVID 1976. *Vertical Integration and Vertical Divestiture in the U.S. Oil Industry*. Stanford: Institute for Energy Studies.

—— 1986. 'Profiting from technological innovation: Implications for integration, collaboration, licensing and public policy', *Research Policy* 15 (December): 285–305.

—— and GARY PISANO 1994. 'The dynamic capabilities of firms: An introduction', *Industrial and Corporate Change* 3(3): 537–56.

—— GARY PISANO, and AMY SHUEN 1997. 'Dynamic capabilities and strategic management', *Strategic Management Journal* 18(7): 509–33.

WERNERFELT, BIRGER 1984. 'A resource-based view of the firm', *Strategic Management Journal* 5: 171–80. Reprinted in Nicolai J. Foss, ed., *Resources, Firms, and Strategies: A Reader in the Resource-Based Perspective*. Oxford: Oxford University Press (1997).

WILLIAMSON, OLIVER E. 1971. 'The vertical integration of production: Market failure considerations', *American Economic Review* 61 (May): 112–23.

—— 1975. *Markets and Hierarchies: Analysis and Antitrust Implications*. New York: Free Press.

—— 1980. 'The organization of work', *Journal of Economic Behavior and Organization* 1 (March): 5–38.

—— 1985. *The Economic Institutions of Capitalism*. New York: Free Press.

—— 1990. 'Chester Barnard and the incipient science of organization', in Oliver E. Williamson, ed., *Organization Theory: From Chester Barnard to the Present and Beyond* New York: Oxford University Press, 172–206.

—— 1991. 'Comparative economic organization: The analysis of discrete structural alternatives', *Administrative Science Quarterly* 36 (June): 269–96.

—— 1993. 'Calculativeness, trust, and economic organization', *Journal of Law and Economics* 36 (April): 453–86.

—— 1996. *The Mechanisms of Governance*. New York: Oxford University Press.

—— 1998. 'Transaction cost economics: How it works; Where it is going,' *De Economist* 146 (April): 23–58.

—— 1999*a*. 'Public and private bureaucracies', *Journal of Law, Economics, and Organization*, forthcoming.

—— 1999*b*. 'Human actors and economic organization', unpublished manuscript.

WINTER, SIDNEY 1988. 'On Coase, competence, and the corporation', *Journal of Law, Economics, and Organization* 4 (Spring): 181–97.

—— 1995. 'Four Rs of profitability: Rents, Resources, Routines, and Replication,' in Cynthia Montgomery, ed., *Resource-Based and Evolutionary Theories of the Firm*. Boston: Kluwer, pp. 147–58.

3

The Knowledge-Based Approach and Organizational Economics: How much do they really Differ? And how does it Matter?

Kirsten Foss and Nicolai Foss

1. Introduction

The knowledge-based (competence-based) approach (henceforth, the 'KBA') and organizational economics (the governance approach) (henceforth, 'OE') are often seen as offering rival explanations of organizational phenomena such as the existence, boundaries, and internal organization of the firm. The main differences between the two perspectives would appear to turn on how the firm is conceptualized, the explanatory variables that are used, and behavioural assumptions. But how different are the KBA and the OE? And how does it matter in terms of research strategies?

To date, there has been little dialogue between proponents of OE and the KBA, communication being limited to KBA writers criticizing OE. There may be many reasons for this, one possible reason being that different disciplinary and institutional backgrounds (economics and universities as opposed to business administration and business schools) are involved. However, we do believe that dialogue is necessary to clarify differences and similarities, so that it can become clearer in what ways the two theories can complement each other in the understanding of organizational phenomena. Notably, there is the possibility that KBA writers have pointed to phenomena and insights that, while crucial to economic organization, have been neglected by proponents of OE (or vice versa). However, there is also the opposite possibility that what KBA writers are saying is not at all in conflict with OE, but is merely expressing insights about economic organization in a different theoretical language. Or it may be the case that some differences are only apparent, while others are real. These possibilities need to be explored in detail—an exercise we believe to be conducive for a more fruitful dialogue between proponents of the two theories.

In principle, there are two potentially complementary ways of resolving differences with respect to the explanations provided by rival theories, namely empirical tests and conceptual analysis. In the choice between these two research strategies, conceptual analysis takes logical priority. This is because if a conceptual analysis reveals that there are few or no real differences between the relevant theories, there is no need to carry out empirical tests of which one offers the better explanation. However, so far little analysis of the similarities and differences between the KBA and OE has been undertaken. Our aim is to fill the lacunae. In fact, we believe this to be the first rigorous analysis of its kind. Specifically, we argue that an analysis of the basic assumptions and insights of the KBA reveals that many of these are not fundamentally in conflict with basic OE assumptions and insights. In fact, it is possible to cast many of the KBA insights in OE 'language'. However, not everything in the KBA may be 'translated' into OE; there is an important residual left.

The analysis is organized around four questions, which are reflected in the structure of the chapter. First, we ask how relations between theories can best be analysed and put forward a framework for handling this. Second, we ask if there is a shared language in which OE insights can be phrased, and argue that property rights economics (for example Barzel 1989) is such a shared language. The third question is: Are the KBA and the OE really so different? We address this question using the language of property rights economics, and conclude that there is a huge overlap between the KBA and OE. However, the overlap is not complete. Specifically, what is distinctive about the KBA is its stress on cognitive limitations, while OE puts much less explanatory weight on this. In contrast to a prevalent position among KBA writers (for example Conner and Prahalad 1996), we do not consider the issue of opportunism to be truly distinguishing. We finally discuss how this matters for OE and the KBA. For example, would they be more complete theories if they adopted the basic assumptions of the other approach?

2. A Framework for Analysing Relations between Theories

As already stated, the relation between the KBA and OE is often seen as one of rivalry. To quote two proponents of the KBA:

Our view differs radically from that of the firm as a bundle of contracts that serves to allocate efficiently property rights [i.e., OE] . . . Rather, we suggest that organizations are social communities in which individual and social expertise is transformed into economically useful products and services . . . Firms exist because they provide a social community of voluntaristic action structured by organizing principles that are not reducible to individuals (Kogut and Zander 1992: 384).

One would perhaps expect conflicts between the KBA and OE to be settled through empirical tests. However, work here has been very meagre, so far being limited to one tentative study (Poppo and Zenger 1995). Empirical work that aims at testing the predictions of the KBA (Kogut and Zander 1993) does not control for a possible competing OE explanation, and vice versa (Klein and

Shelanski 1995). Indeed, empirical work in this area is bound to be fraught with severe difficulties of operationalization of key concepts such as capabilities, difficulties of separating, for example, asset specificity from the specific human capital embodied in capabilities, etc. We therefore believe that much more conceptually oriented analysis of the relations between these theories should be undertaken. The question then is how to proceed with such an analysis.

In order to be able to discuss the relation between the KBA and OE in a more precise manner, we rely on Krajewski (1977). He suggested a useful framework for classifying and discussing relations between different theories. The taxonomy in Table 3.1 reflects this framework. We use Krajewski's framework and taxonomy as a heuristic tool. Our aim is not to place KBA and OE unambiguously in one of the categories of Table 3.1. Rather, the taxonomy provides useful insights with respect to the dimensions in which theories may differ.

The taxonomy maps possible relations between two theories, T_1 and T_2, in terms of their domain of application (D) (that is, their *explanandum*) and their theoretical language (V) (that is, their *explanans*). The domain of application refers to what the theory is designed to explain. For example, OE is designed to explain the existence, boundaries, and internal organization of firms (cf. Alchian and Demsetz 1972; Barzel 1989; Coase 1937; Hart 1995; Williamson 1985, 1996). Initially, the KBA was developed to address competitive advantage

TABLE 3.1.   A taxonomy of relations between theories

Type	Domain	Theoretical language	Relation
Commensurabilty	$D_1 \cap D_2 \neq \varnothing$		
Equivalence	$D_1 = D_2$	$V_1 \leftrightarrow V_2$	$T_1 = L_1 (T_2)$
			$T_2 = L_2 (T_1)$
Reduction:			
—Homogeneous	$D_1 \subset D_2$	$V_1 \subset V_2$	$T_1 \wedge A \Rightarrow T_2$
—Heterogeneous	$D_1 \subset D_2$	$V_1 \rightarrow V_2$	$T_1 \wedge A \wedge S \Rightarrow T_2$
Contradiction	$D_1 = D_2$	$V_1 \neq V_2$	$T_1 \Rightarrow \neg T_2$
			$T_2 \Rightarrow \neg T_1$
Correspondence:			
—Homogeneous	$D_1 \subset D_2$	$V_1 = V_2$	$T_2 \Rightarrow a T_1$ in D_1
			$T_2 \Rightarrow \neg a T_1$ in $D_2 - D_1$
—Heterogeneous	$D_1 \subset D_2$	$V_1 \rightarrow V_2$	Same as above

Note: The notation is standard set notation; however, some of the expressions used deserve explanation. '$\leftrightarrow$' means that there is a one-to-one correspondence (so that double translation between two theories is possible). 'L' is a translation operator (metaphorically speaking, a sort of 'dictionary'). '$\rightarrow$' is used to indicate a one-sided correspondence (so that double translation is not possible). '$\Rightarrow$' refers to implications of a theory (e.g., '$T_1 \Rightarrow \neg T_2$' means that the negation of T_2 follows from T_1). 'A' refers to supplementary hypotheses. 'S' are bridging principles (e.g., principles of aggregation). Finally, 'a' means 'approximates'.

Source: Reproduced from Krajewski (1977: 67) with modifications.

(Barney 1986; Wernerfelt 1984), but has increasingly expanded its *explananda* phenomena to include also those traditionally considered in OE, see Table 3.2.

Table 3.2 reveals that the KBA and the OE have overlapping domains of application ($D_1 \cap D_2 \neq \emptyset$). They are therefore commensurable, which is a precondition for comparing them. Given commensurability, there are then several possible relations between the KBA and OE, of which the extreme possibilities are equivalence and contradiction. The possible relations between the theories all intimately involve the issue of what the relation is between the respective theoretical languages. The concept of theoretical language refers to the explanatory framework of the theory, including terminology, explanatory variables, behavioural assumptions, and type of explanation. For example, while OE relies on an explanatory framework largely derived from mainstream economics, the KBA relies instead on a framework drawn from strategy and organizational and behavioural research, and emphasizes bounded rationality, routines, capabilities, and the like rather than incentives, asymmetric information, property rights, and contracts. A key question then is what the relation is between these theoretical languages. For example, can equivalence be established through translation of KBA language into OE language or vice versa? If this cannot be done, this still leaves us with numerous other possibilities. For example the theories may be contradictory, as is asserted by some proponents of the KBA (for example, Kogut

TABLE 3.2. The knowledge-based approach and organizational economics: *Explananda* and key contributions

Explanandum phenomenon	Knowledge-based contributions	Organizational economics contributions
Why do firms exist?	Conner (1991), Conner and Prahalad (1996), Grant (1996), Kogut and Zander (1996)	Alchian and Demsetz (1972), Coase (1937)
What factors determine firms' boundaries relative to the market?	Kogut and Zander (1992, 1993), Madhok (1996), Penrose (1959), Richardson (1972), Winter (1988)	Hart (1995), Hart and Moore (1990), Williamson (1985, 1996)
What determines firms' internal organization?	Dosi and Marengo (1994), Ghoshal, Moran, and Almeida-Costa (1995), Ghoshal and Moran (1996)	Barzel (1989), Holmström (1982), Holmström and Milgrom (1991), Putterman (1995)
What determines competitive advantage?	Barney (1986, 1991), Peteraf (1993), Wernerfelt (1984)	Kreps (1990), Williamson (1994)

Note: Some of the contributions address more than one of the *explanandum* phenomena. However, they have been classified according to their main thrust.

and Zander 1992; Madhok 1996). In terms of Table 3.1, this means that while the domain of application (D) of the theories is the same, the theories work with different untranslatable languages (V), and their implications with respect to the domain of application contradict each other (that is, $T_2 \Rightarrow \neg\, T_1$ and $T_1 \Rightarrow \neg\, T_2$).

We shall argue that the relation between OE and KBA is neither one of equivalence, nor one of contradiction. In order to find out what the true relation is between the KBA and OE, we begin by examining to what extent it is possible to arrive at the same insights by trying to translate the theoretical language of the KBA into OE language. This allows us to find out what is not just 'semantic' differences, but genuine theoretical differences. However, for that purpose we need a 'translation operator' ('L' in Table 3.1). We argue that property rights economics (Barzel 1989; Furubotn and Richter 1998) is one such possible translation operator. In other words, we try to state concepts such as routines and capabilities in terms of property rights economics. If this can be done successfully, we infer the conclusion that the KBA can indeed be translated into OE. If this is only partially successful, other possibilities must be examined.

We may begin by asking whether a *reduction* is possible. Two general types of reduction may be distinguished. First, a homogeneous reduction is obtained if it is possible to show that the KBA is a special case theory of OE (or vice versa), in the sense that one can obtain OE by adding hypotheses (A) to the KBA, and that the theoretical language of the KBA is a subset of OE. Second, in the case of a heterogeneous reduction we also need bridging principles (S), which generally refer to how one moves from one level of analysis to another. For example, there may be principles that explain how the notion of 'routine' is obtained from aggregating individual actions. Finally, there is the possibility of *correspondence*. In a homogeneous relation of correspondence, the two theories apply identical explanatory apparatuses, and T_1 is an adequate approximation to T_2 within D_1, while the more general theory T_2 corrects T_1 in $D_2 - D_1$ by taking into account new variables, assumptions, etc. A final possibility is the heterogeneous relation of correspondence, which differs from the homogeneous relation by taking into account differences in theoretical languages. We shall make reference to these possibilities in the course of the discussion, although we wish to restate that it is not our aim to place the KBA or OE unambiguously in one of the categories of Table 3.1.

3. The Property Rights Approach: A Shared Organizational Economics Language

Organizational economics is a collection of theories, including the transaction cost (Coase 1937; Williamson 1985, 1996), the agency (Holmström 1982; Holmström and Milgrom 1991; Jensen and Meckling 1992), the measurement cost (Barzel 1989), the information cost (Casson 1994), the team (Marschak and Radner 1972), and the incomplete contracts (Hart 1995) perspectives. To be sure, the languages of these theories differ. For example, one may distinguish between OE models that make use of the assumption of incentive conflicts (for example, opportunism) and those that do not (for example, team theory). Moreover, there is an overall distinction between models founded on the notion of incomplete contracts, and models founded on the notion of complete contracts, such as agency theory. The incomplete contract approach stresses the importance of the high cost of drafting complete contracts, while complete contract theories stress the high cost of monitoring contractual compliance.

While assumptions about the information that agents possess, the incentives they confront, and their cost of drafting and monitoring contracts are important for explaining different kinds of institutional arrangements, they do not fundamentally distinguish the theories. Our position therefore is that these differences simply reflect dialects of the same overall theoretical language—one with a vocabulary consisting of self-interested behaviour, economic equilibrium, transaction costs, and property rights (Furubotn and Richter 1998). This overall language is the property rights approach (Alchian 1965; Barzel 1989; Coase 1960; Demsetz 1964; Eggertson 1990; Jones 1983; Libecap 1989; North 1990). In fact, most OE approaches can be subsumed under the property rights approach, because these all look at different costs of specifying, exchanging and enforcing property rights. Thus, in order to focus on the more fundamental differences in the language between OE and the KBA, we can use the overarching language of the property rights approach as a translation operator.

3.1. Characteristics of Property Rights

There are numerous characteristics of property rights that are salient to the present discussion. We present these in the following paragraphs.

3.1.1. Types of rights   Property rights are the rights people hold over assets, such as physical, human, financial, and intellectual property assets. More specifically, they include the following kinds of rights (Alchian 1965; Eggertson 1990):

1. *Use rights*, which define the potential uses of an asset.
2. *Income rights*, or the right to consume an asset.
3. *Rights to exclude* non-owners from access to assets.
4. *Rights to transfer* permanently to another party all the above-mentioned rights over an asset—that is to alienate or sell an asset.

3.1.2. Rights and relationships   Property rights define the *relationships* among individuals with respect to scarce assets. Therefore, property rights are social institutions. However, it is important to observe that property rights systems may exist at several levels, among which there is a hierarchical relation. Thus, on the societal level, the law, norms, and mores of society define and delimit the range of privileges granted to individuals to assets. The combination of property rights and their institutional support is a 'property rights system'. However, property rights systems also exist on lower levels than the societal level, notably inside firms (Williamson 1985). For example, the system of property rights existing in a firm 'is the set of economic and social relations that define the position of each individual with respect to other team members and with respect to the use of resources (Demsetz 1964)' (Jones 1983: 456). However, property rights systems inside firms are still constrained by the law and customs of society, as partially defined and enforced by the state (North 1990).

3.1.3. Preciseness   An important characteristic of property rights is the degree of preciseness with which they are delineated. For example, one may distinguish between *specific* and *residual* rights (Barzel 1989; Hart 1995). Specific rights are those rights that are specified in contracts and allocated between the transacting parties before any transaction takes place. Residual rights are those rights that are not constrained by stipulations in contracts or by the law. Both user and income rights can be either specific or residual. Residual income rights (or residual claims) are the non-specified income or pleasure a person can enjoy from using or alienating an asset (including his or her labour). In firms rights and obligations may be more or less clearly defined. For example, if all rights are truly perfectly defined, according to the so-called 'Coase theorem' (Coase 1960), this literally means that:

- all possible uses of assets are fully known;
- all returns from all uses of all assets are perfectly known;
- all legitimate and illegitimate uses of assets are perfectly specified;
- all this is perfectly enforceable.

If all rights are completely defined in this way, there cannot, by definition, arise any conflicts over the use of scarce resources or the returns from assets, because individuals do not have any discretion in the use of resources. For example, intra-firm conflicts cannot arise. Indeed, it would be hard to explain why there should be firms in such a world (Coase 1937). Of course, this is a highly unrealistic situation. In actuality, all rights are far from perfectly defined, and this opens the door for organizational phenomena. From a property rights perspective, the reason for such lack of preciseness is to be found in the existence of *transaction costs*.

3.1.4. Delegation   Rights to decide between uses of assets may be delegated to others (Jensen and Meckling 1992). The person who has the rights to determine the set of possible uses as well as the right to decide on delegating decision rights

is said to possess residual rights. Legal rights to specify specific rights over physical assets, and to delegate and otherwise transfer rights over assets, follow from
legal ownership over assets, and in the case of labour from voluntary agreements
to transfer these rights (Hart 1995).

3.2. Property Rights, Contracts, and Transaction Costs

Historically, the property rights approach emerged from the insight that what is
exchanged are not assets *per se*, but rather the rights to those assets (Coase 1960).
Contracts, whether formal or informal, are used to define the terms of transfer
of rights. However, the exchange of rights is not costless. For example, often
physical and human assets have different properties and may sometimes yield a
number of different services depending on how the assets are used. In principle,
each one of the properties and different uses of assets can be specified and be
subject to negotiations between parties to a transaction. Moreover, use rights
over different properties or uses of assets may be shared between individuals
(Barzel 1989). For example, a copying machine can be used in different time
periods and for many different types of copying work.

To specify and to contract over the different possible uses of assets are clearly
costly actions—more precisely, they involve transaction costs. In the property
rights framework, transaction costs are conceptualized as the costs due to the
'transfer, capture and protection of rights' (Barzel 1989: 2). When such costs
exist, not everything will be specified in contracts. Notably, the employment
contract is left partly open because of prohibitively high costs of specifying in
detail all rights and obligations of the employee in all future conceivable situations. Related to this, the authority relation arises from the presence of transaction costs, because in the presence of such costs, incomplete contracts will give
rise to conflicts and disagreements over the uses of assets. Assigning the right to
decide how assets should be used in situations that are not covered by the
contract is often a low-cost way of resolving this problem. However, the extent
to which authority is necessary depends on the nature of the property rights
system of the firm, more specifically, the norms and social values existing inside
it.

We shall use these ideas to restate and reinterpret fundamental ideas and
insights in the KBA. However, before we can do this, we need to state briefly the
main ideas and insights of the KBA.

4. The Knowledge-Based Approach

The knowledge-based approach reflects a number of diverse influences, and
arguably exists in somewhat different versions. In this section, we shall briefly restate
what we believe are the main insights associated with the KBA. In particular, we

focus our attention on how the KBA addresses the *explananda* of competitive advantage, the boundaries of firms, the existence of firms, and the internal organization. Briefly, the theoretical language that is used to address these *explananda* consists of concepts as resources, routines, capabilities, learning, and bounded rationality, and insights relating to these (see Figure 3. 1).

4.1. Main Insights and Propositions of the Knowledge-Based Approach

4.1.1. Competitive advantage   Conventionally, the KBA is seen as beginning with the work of Edith Penrose (1959). Although the main concern of Penrose was to discuss the limits to firm growth, insights have been further refined by modern proponents of the KBA to develop a theory of the competitive advantage of firms. They begin from the same premise as Penrose did, namely, the essential notion of the firm as a bundle of heterogeneous resources. Because resources mesh with each other in a team-like manner, they are worth more to the firm than to the market (meaning other firms). They therefore yield rents.

Although resources can be any asset that may be a strength to a firm (Wernerfelt 1984; Barney 1991), most interest has centred on internally accumulated resources, such as routines and capabilities, rather than on those that can be purchased on factor markets (Dierickx and Cool 1989). Routines are an important aspect of what allows 'multiple individuals [to] integrate their specialist

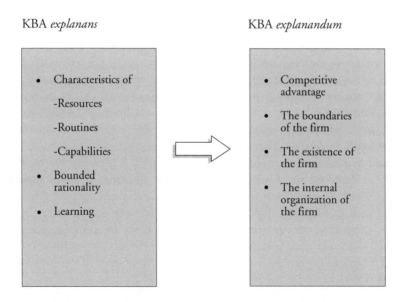

Figure 3.1. The *explanans* and *explanandum* of the knowledge-based approach

knowledge' (Grant 1996: 112). Indeed, some argue that '[r]outines are the skills of an organization' (Nelson and Winter 1982: 84). This is because they embody the knowledge needed for repeatedly implementing the (specialized) services of resources in some specific context. Much of this knowledge is tacit and routines may themselves be partially tacit (Nelson and Winter 1982). This implies that there is a conservative quality to routines. However, often firms are confronted with tasks that go beyond what pre-programmed routines are capable of handling. For example, activating a new productive task, or undertaking an organizational restructuring, or trying to duplicate or modify an existing routine, etc. require conscious action on the part of management. The capacity to do this effectively represents the firm's capability, the possession of which is often seen as necessary for sustained competitive advantage in dynamic environments.

The KBA analysis of competitive advantage is founded on these basic insights (Barney 1986, 1991; Dierickx and Cool 1989; Peteraf 1993; Wernerfelt 1984). The primary contribution of this work consists of an analysis of the conditions under which resources yield rents. To sum up this now fairly well-known analysis, only heterogeneous, rare, and hard-to-imitate resources that are, moreover, acquired in imperfect factor markets (Barney 1986) can be rent-yielding strategic assets to firms.

4.1.2. The boundaries of the firm   Path-dependencies and tacit knowledge are important in the application of the KBA to issues relating to economic organization, such as the boundaries of the firm. A starting-point is that the creation of a productive organization is a time-consuming process of learning about how to utilize and co-ordinate productive assets. This results in the creation of routines and capabilities. These change as they are applied to new problems, as new personnel come into the firm, etc.; however, the development of knowledge is steered by strong inertial forces that narrowly circumscribe learning domains (Dosi, Winter, and Teece 1992). This in itself suggests knowledge-based limits to how far the firm may efficiently diversify its activities, that is, its path-dependent process of growth places limits on where its boundaries are placed. For example, excess management capabilities may be created as a natural by-product of the firm's activities (Penrose 1959), but may only be deployed in closely related industries. In general, firms may avoid undertaking activities that require dissimilar capabilities. Instead, the services from such capabilities may be acquired through markets or inter-firm relations, depending on the degree of complementarity of activities (Richardson 1972). Typically, very specific and strategically important routines and capabilities have to be deployed internally, due to the absence of markets for these assets (Dierickx and Cool 1989).

To sum up, in the KBA the boundaries of the firm are seen as determined by knowledge-based considerations. Specifically, knowledge assets that are hard to trade and idiosyncratic are governed inside the boundaries of the firm, while firms generally avoid integrating knowledge assets that are strongly dissimilar from the ones they already control. It is important to note that this is claimed to hold quite independently of considerations of incentive conflicts stemming from opportunism, etc.

4.1.3. The existence of the firm   According to KBA writers, the issue of the existence of the firm can be addressed in terms of knowledge-based reasoning rather than in terms of opportunism, etc. Thus, according to Kogut and Zander (1992), firms can—because of their function as moral communities and bodies of what they call 'higher-order organizing principles'—cultivate learning processes and achieve co-ordination that are inaccessible under market relations. Grant (1996) also argues that firms can develop and utilize knowledge more efficiently than markets are capable of. And Conner and Prahalad (1996) construct a stylized setting, in which they try to demonstrate that what they call the 'knowledge-substitution' and 'flexibility' effects may take place more efficiently under hierarchy than under market. While the former effect relates to direction, where, in a sense, the knowledge of the hierarchical superior at least partly 'substitutes' for that of the inferior (Demsetz 1988), the latter effect refers to the ease with which the parties' obligations and duties are changed during a contractual relationship (Coase 1937). These different KBA ideas can be summed up thus: Firms exist because they more efficiently than markets produce, store, and utilize knowledge, particularly tacit knowledge. Rational agents will choose firm organization in the expectation of knowledge-based benefits.

4.1.4. Internal organization   Finally, some writers claim that the KBA has implications for understanding internal organization that are completely different from OE (Ghoshal and Moran, 1996; Ghoshal, Moran, and Almeida-Costa 1995). According to them, empirical evidence from big companies suggests that they do not fundamentally use the kind of control and incentive mechanisms in the workings of their internal organization that an OE perspective (purportedly) would lead one to recommend. Rather, these companies try hard to construct a 'shared context', that is, an internal institutional context that not only acts as a co-ordinating device, but more fundamentally influences the values and ambitions of employees. This assists 'the development and utilization of local knowledge for local initiatives' (Ghoshal, Moran, and Almeida-Costa 1995: 752). In contrast, OE is claimed to be 'bad for practice' (Ghoshal and Moran 1996), because it operates with an overly cynical view of human nature. Thus, to follow the prescriptions flowing from OE will result in perverse psychological responses and impede the development and utilization of local knowledge for local initiatives.

5. Translating the Knowledge-Based Approach

According to KBA scholars (for example Kogut and Zander 1992; Ghoshal and Moran 1992), the ideas that we have tried to summarize in the above section are either in conflict with OE or simply outside its domain. Because the economics of organization does not conceptualize economic organization in knowledge-based terms, it cannot come to grips with either the analysis of competitive advantage or the knowledge-based determinants of economic organization (for example Madhok 1996). This is essentially the claim that will be examined in this section. As we shall argue, many of the explanatory concepts and insights of the KBA can *themselves* be interpreted in terms of OE (using the language of property rights economics). Thus, in a sense we take the theoretical language of the KBA as our *explanandum*. Figure 3.2 illustrates our reasoning.

5.1. Resource Heterogeneity

Arguably, the key dimension of resources in the KBA is their heterogeneity, both within and across firms. Ultimately, it is heterogeneity that explains performance differences between firms and why, for example, different firms organize different activities. What has OE to say about the issue of heterogeneity?

5.1.1. Consequences of heterogeneity   Proponents of the property rights approach have always perceived valuable assets as heterogeneous (for example Alchian and Demsetz 1972; Barzel 1982). Not only do different assets have

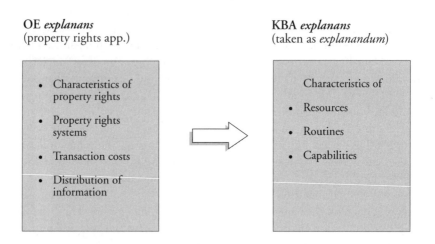

Figure 3.2. Translating the knowledge-based approach

many and different uses, but even assets of the same type are heterogeneous. From this, theorists have drawn conclusions that are actually remarkably close to those of the KBA. For example, property rights theorist Harold Demsetz long ago pointed out that in the presence of uncertainty, less-than-fully-mobile factors, and private information about the cost or benefits of realizing different plans, 'a differential advantage in expanding output develops in some firms' (Demsetz 1973: 1). Thus, heterogeneity is clearly tied to competitive advantage. Demsetz also argued that superior private information about the true value of heterogeneous resources, or luck in obtaining rights to these assets at a price below value, was a necessary condition for competitive advantage—a key conclusion in the knowledge-based analysis of competitive advantage (Barney 1986). However, even in Demsetz's work, heterogeneity is asserted, rather than explained. In the next section, we try to develop an economic approach to heterogeneity and link it to the analysis of competitive advantage.

5.1.2. Causes of heterogeneous market assets   According to KBA writers (Dierickx and Cool 1989), two types of resources are particularly likely to generate long-lasting rents. These are internally accumulated market assets and organizational assets, such as routines and capabilities. Examples of the former category are brand names and reputations. However, KBA writers do not give an account of why these resources are heterogeneous and why they are valuable. We believe that OE is uniquely positioned to provide such an explanation. It may proceed along several possible lines.

A possible starting-point is that variability in the quality of the attributes and services from products entails waste from, for example, search and screening activities, that is, activities aiming at capturing rights to unspecified attributes of products (Barzel 1982). By reducing such variability, some of this waste may be eliminated by setting up different institutional solutions, such as product guarantees, long-term service contracts, and protected brand names (Akerlof 1970). The differential accumulation of a reputation for honesty across firms depends on their historic records of being able to keep a uniform quality of products. In this case, they have accumulated heterogeneous brand-name capital that reflects differences in their reputations among consumers (Barzel 1982). A good reputation is valuable to a firm because when buyers believe that sellers will not misrepresent product quality, they will spend less on ascertaining the quality of the products on offer, and firms may therefore raise the prices of their products.

5.1.3. Causes of heterogeneous organizational assets   Of course, competitive advantage is not just a matter of such market-oriented resources as reputations. One possible point of departure for an understanding of valuable organizational assets is Alchian and Demsetz (1972). They argue (1972: 75) that sometimes 'gains from specialization and cooperative production may better be obtained within an organization like the firm', because continuity of association among resource owners and specialized monitoring services reduce the costs of ascertaining quality differences across heterogeneous resources. Both depend on the specific allocation of property rights inside firms. First, continuity among resource owners is a matter of the duration of contracts. Second, the manager is in a unique position to acquire superior information about the diverse services that can be extracted from heterogeneous resources of variable quality because he has the right to monitor employees. Based on this information he is also able to specify property rights—that is, specify the rights and obligations of employees—in ways which will yield the highest returns. Given this, efficiency differences between firms are 'a result not of having *better* resources but in *knowing more accurately* the relative productive performances of those resources' (Alchian and Demsetz 1972: 94; emphasis in original). Thus, an important source of competitive advantage lies in what may roughly be called 'organizational factors'.

This line of reasoning may be extended to the issue of sustainability of competitive advantage. Thus, it may be claimed that an important source of sustainability of competitive advantage is having and maintaining a lead in terms of reducing the measurement costs of learning about specific inputs and about how the characteristics of inputs may be combined in productive processes. Since costs of detecting shirking, and also of detecting productive talents, within a given team is lower for the monitor within the firm than for anyone else, competition for superior resources will be imperfect. This reasoning adds a dimension to the KBA approach that is oddly absent in its present version—namely the actual organization and application of various resources in production. This process of application is made effective through contractual devices (implicit as well as explicit) and monitoring and enforcement arrangements (including bonding and the like)—in other words, the property rights system of the firm.

5.1.4. Causes of heterogeneous routines   According to the KBA, firm-specific assets, such as routines and capabilities, are particularly difficult to imitate. The reasons normally given are that these assets are particularly likely to encapsulate knowledge that is (a) tacit, (b) firm-specific, and (c) path dependent. But what are the economics of this? And what are routines and capabilities from an OE perspective?

We suggest that—as a first abstract approximation—routines are sequences of activities that are carried out as individuals exercise their use rights over assets. As we argued earlier, if there are no transaction costs, all rights will be perfectly specified. In such a world, all activities will be pre-planned, and routines will simply be the execution of a fully specified programme. This means that the skill-like, partly unconscious character of routines (Nelson and Winter 1982) will not obtain, which is inconsistent with the KBA. In order to explain routines as conceptualized in the KBA, we have to introduce transaction costs. Given transaction costs, we may explain routines as solutions to recurrent co-ordination problems among individuals in situations where rights are not perfectly defined. As we explained earlier, imperfect definition of rights implies that individuals have discretion with respect to the use of scarce assets. Of course, discretion may be useful, for example for gaining knowledge from experimenting with different ways of using assets, but discretion may also cause problems of shirking and problems of misallocation due to lack of co-ordination of complementary activities carried out by different agents. However, with repeated interaction in recurrent situations, a convention may emerge as a solution to co-ordination problems (Sugden 1986).

In property rights terminology, such a convention is a self-inflicted restriction on the exercise of use rights where the restrictions are in accordance with the interests of the holder of the rights. These restrictions make the behaviour of each individual more predictable relative to a situation without the convention, and establish a stable pattern of behaviour, that is, a routine. The firm-specific element of routines can be interpreted as a consequence of different historic circumstances under which a convention emerges (Sugden 1986). Such circumstances include different players, the physical layout of the firm, and the organizational structure as defined by the formal allocation of use and income rights. They are therefore not generally transferable to other settings. Since routines are responses to imperfect information, it may be difficult and costly to try to augment routines in order to reach more efficient outcomes. This accounts for persistent heterogeneity of routines across firms. From an economic perspective the path-dependent aspects of routines may be translated into a proposition about sunk costs of developing conventions.

5.1.5. Causes of heterogeneous capabilities   Consistent with the KBA, we take capabilities to reside on the level of management. More specifically, we interpret capabilities as management's skills with respect to the exercise of their residual rights to control the uses of human and physical assets. By exercising this control, management may influence the development of routines. First, conventions do not emerge in a vacuum; for example, managers may create environments that are more or less conducive to the evolution of co-operative solutions. Second, managers may voluntarily restrain their exercise of rights in order to 'convince' employees to truthfully reveal private information and co-operate rather than act on the basis of short-term self-interest (Miller 1992). In property rights terminology, management creates favourable expectations with respect to the value of the property rights granted to employees. The ability of management to create shared expectations of co-operative behaviour among team members or between employees and superiors may in turn strongly depend on the history of the firm with respect to honouring co-operative behaviour (Kreps 1990; Miller 1992). Therein lies some of the firm-specific quality of a capability.

5.2. Implications for the Knowledge-Based Approach to Economic Organization

A key knowledge-based idea is that the issues of the existence, boundaries, and internal organization of firms should be cast in knowledge-based terms. However, we have argued that many of these knowledge-based terms are themselves given to explanation in terms of OE reasoning. In this section we examine what this implies for KBA explanations of economic organization.

5.2.1. The boundaries of the firm
According to KBA theorists, the boundaries of the firm should be explained in terms of the specificity and non-tradeability of knowledge assets, such as routines and capabilities. This is not in contrast to OE reasoning (for example Williamson 1985). On the contrary, OE identifies the causes of the transaction costs that make some assets hard to trade in markets.

Some KBA theorists (for example Kogut and Zander 1992) have argued that what ultimately sets the KBA apart from OE is that the KBA is much more explicit about productive knowledge that cannot be specified in blueprints (that is, tacit, skill-like knowledge). Such knowledge, they argue, holds the key to understanding the boundaries of the firm. However, it is not made clear why the co-ordination mechanisms characterizing firms are more efficient than markets in making use of tacit, skill-like knowledge. In order to understand this, we can make use of property rights arguments. Thus, we may associate tacit, skill-like knowledge with imperfectly specified rights to valuable attributes of assets, notably the human capital of employees. Given the high costs of writing explicit contracts over such knowledge, the firm may have advantages relative to market contracting, because its property rights system allows it to make less costly use of the services that tacit human capital may yield. This is because the continuous association between the employee and the firm allows the manager to extract information about the true skills of employees. Finally, the firm is particularly efficient in enforcing the implicit elements of contracts (Williamson 1996) such as the norms and conventions that emerge from the continued interaction among employees. This leads directly to the issue of the existence of the firm.

5.2.2. The existence of the firm
Knowledge-based theorists generally assert that firms exist because they, more efficiently than markets, produce and utilize knowledge, particularly tacit knowledge, not because they provide efficient responses to incentive conflicts (Conner and Prahalad 1996). A problem is that exactly the same has been claimed on behalf of markets (Hayek 1945). This is not to deny that such knowledge-based explanations of the existence of the firm may be developed. However, we need discriminating principles that allow us to tell when markets will do the job and when firms will, and unfortunately only very few knowledge-based contributions try to supply the relevant

discriminating principles (for example Conner and Prahalad 1996) or are even aware that there is a problem.

In the light of OE, the discriminating principles turn on the transaction costs involved in the co-ordination of productive activities (Alchian and Demsetz 1972; Coase 1937; Foss 1996*a* and 1996*b*; Putterman 1995). As we have repeatedly argued, firms may reduce contracting, monitoring, and enforcement costs and thereby maximize the rents that a productive team may create relative to market organization of the same team.

From the perspective of KBA writers, these may at best be limited stories, since they do not take into account the important aspects of firms as 'cultural entities' (Kogut and Zander 1996). However, in our view it is not clear how being a cultural entity can be an argument for the existence of the firm, unless this quality reflects the characteristics of a specific property right. For example, industrial districts, firm networks, and other extended forms of governance may also be cultural entities.

The OE perspective on firm-specific norms and conventions is that they are part of the property rights system of a firm. Thereby, OE provides a more thorough understanding of the conditions under which routines and capabilities are efficiency-enhancing aspects of such a system. Specifically, the property rights perspective provides a frame in which it is possible to enquire into how the allocation of rights influences the evolution of informal norms and conventions which are constraints on behaviour, that is, routines (Jones 1983). In our view, therefore, existing KBA explanations of the existence of firms are either consistent with OE or simply not convincing.

5.2.3. Internal organization   Knowledge-based writers have argued that internal organization is better understood in terms of the creation of a shared context and an avoidance of 'blunt incentives' (for example Ghoshal and Moran, 1996; Ghoshal, Moran, and Almeida-Costa 1995). However, this is not in contradiction to OE. For example, in a property rights interpretation, a shared context means that it is not necessary to expend many resources on specifying rights, since there is a shared understanding of the allocation and definition of rights. More to the point, perhaps, the issue of avoiding 'blunt incentives' has been treated in recent OE work (for example Barzel 1989; Holmström and Milgrom 1991) in terms of property rights, specifically as a matter of explaining why internal organization is normally characterized by 'low-powered incentives'. The explanation is that some vital activities are very costly to measure and that tying specific income rights to measurable activities may produce a bias away from activities that are hard to measure, but vital to the firm. This is an explanation that has particular force in connection with knowledge-related activities, such as research and development, because these are clearly hard to measure and specify in contracts.

5.3. Summing Up: Relations between OE and the KBA

So far, we have tried to demonstrate how key insights of the KBA may be refor-
mulated in terms of OE insights, using the property rights language. This raises
the question of how we may use the taxonomy in Table 3.1 to cast light over the
relation between OE and the KBA.

To begin with, note that OE and the KBA attempt to address the same
domain of application (the same *explananda*) (cf. Table 3.2). However, we have
argued that the KBA does not provide convincing independent explanations of
the existence and internal organization of firms, because KBA arguments here
can be directly recast as OE arguments. This effectively means that the true
domain of application of the KBA is a subset of the domain of application of
OE. It is more complicated to sort out the relations between the KBA and OE
with respect to how they explain the boundaries of the firm and competitive
advantage. Note that the KBA explanation of these relies on concepts—such as
routines and capabilities—that are not part of the OE language (*explanans*). This
then raises the issue of what the relation is between the languages used in OE
and the KBA.

Essentially, we have argued that the language of the KBA (V_1) may to a large
extent be translated into the language of OE (V_2) (cf. Figure 3.2). This is because
concepts such as routines, capabilities, and heterogeneity could to a large extent
be given an OE interpretation. Therefore, the KBA explanation of the boundaries of the firm and competitive advantage may be translated into OE insights,
but only after first translating insights about routines and capabilities into OE
insights. More specifically, OE provided a sort of 'micro-foundation' for these
more aggregate concepts. Note that in order to build up from OE insights to
KBA insights one needs bridging principles (S) that help us to come from one
level of analysis to another level. For example, routines may be seen as emergent
properties of interaction between agents constrained by transaction costs and the
property rights system of the firm. On the other hand, we do not believe that it
is possible to translate the other way around, that is, translate OE language into
KBA language. This is because there are no bridging principles that will allow us
to go from routines and capabilities to property rights, asymmetric information,
transaction costs, etc. As a first approximation, this means that there is a 'one-
sided correspondence' between the two languages ($V_1 \rightarrow V_2$).

Our reasoning so far points to either a heterogeneous reduction or a heterogeneous correspondence (cf. Table 3.1) as the 'true' relation between the KBA
and OE. In the case of the heterogeneous reduction, the theories have the same
implications ($T_2 \wedge A \wedge S \Rightarrow T_1$), provided one of them is supplemented with
additional hypotheses (A) and bridging principles (S). In the case of the heterogeneous correspondence, one of the theories approximates the other one in the
latter's domain of application ($T_2 \Rightarrow a\ T_1$ in D_1), while adding some new

implications that cannot be reached by the latter theory ($T_2 \Rightarrow \neg\, a\, T_1$ in $D_2 -$ D_1). In our view, the true relation between OE and KBA comes closest to that of the heterogeneous correspondence, because OE has implications with respect to competitive advantage, and the existence, boundaries, and internal organization that cannot be reached by the KBA. However, it may be argued that we have only been able to reach these conclusions by implicitly side-stepping issues such as bounded rationality, learning, and (differential) cognition—in short, ideas that relate to the endogenous creation of heterogeneity. Can these ideas be reduced to OE insights? And are they important to the KBA? We discuss this in the following section.

6. Challenges to the Economics of Organization?

In the previous section, we have tried to 'cut to the bone' of the KBA, as it were. One purpose of this exercise is to find out what is genuinely different in the KBA relative to the OE. In fact, we do believe that there are important concepts and insights in the KBA that cannot be reduced to OE insights, and that may in fact challenge OE. We discuss some of these in the following paragraphs.

6.1. Bounded rationality and learning

According to KBA writers (for example Conner and Prahalad 1996; Ghoshal, Moran, and Almeida-Costa 1995; Grant 1996; Spender 1996) one strength of the KBA relative to the OE is its more explicit treatment of bounded rationality and learning. The treatment of bounded rationality in OE (Williamson 1985, 1996) is arguably narrow, since it only figures as a constraint on a decision problem. Changing bounds of rationality through, for example, satisficing search activities is not inquired into. And learning only appears in OE as changes in human asset specificity ('the fundamental transformation') (Williamson 1985, 1996), while the learning process itself is largely neglected. All this may rightly be criticized, particularly because the emergence and change of firms and property rights systems in firms become hard to comprehend without a more sophisticated theory of learning (Denzau and North 1994).

However, OE is not inherently cut off from treating learning and bounded rationality. For example, learning by doing requires the exercise of use rights over assets. One may even suggest that the more well specified and easily monitored use rights are, the less can asset users experiment, and the more constrained will their learning be. Experimentation is important as a way of finding solutions to co-ordination problems (for example, finding the optimal sequence of activities). Managers holding residual use rights over assets are able to conduct controlled experiments without continuously having to renegotiate contracts and it is by exercising residual rights that managers change the conditions under which skills, conventions, norms, and other types of socially shared knowledge emerge. This suggests one way in which OE may better come to grips with processes of building routines and capabilities. But obviously much more needs to be done here.

6.2. Cognition

In contrast to the narrow view of learning in OE, learning in firms also is a social process of cognitive development in which cognitive categories (such as business conceptions) arise and are adopted and possibly changed (Bandura 1977; Dosi and Marengo 1994; Penrose 1959). This goes significantly beyond both the information-processing view and conventional views on bounded rationality. If this is what is meant by learning in the KBA, then we acknowledge that here is a genuine challenge to OE. However, so far KBA writers do not appear to have incorporated this cognitive perspective into their reasoning to any great extent: thus, it may also be just as much a challenge to the KBA.

More specifically, it is possible that a cognitive view may have important implications for the understanding of the main *explananda* of OE and the KBA, namely competitive advantage, and the existence, boundaries, and internal organization of the firm. For example, we may think of the distribution of competitive advantages in an industry as stemming from both the resources that firms control and the cognition of managers, for example with respect to how resources should be deployed (cf. Penrose 1959) and how elements in the external environment should be categorized. Moreover, it may be conjectured that a cognitive perspective has implications also for the remaining *explananda*. For example, internal organization may be understood in terms of conflicts and disagreements stemming from different cognitive categories, and a major organizational design problem may actually be to create shared cognitive categories. It should be noted that such a cognitive perspective may both further OE (Williamson 1998) and itself be furthered by OE insights. Thus, on the one hand, the property rights system of the firm may, by defining the social relations and positions of individuals, crucially influence the processes of interaction that may lead to shared cognitive categories. On the other hand, problems stemming from the delegation of rights may arise from differential cognition inside the firm, as well as from transaction costs (Miller 1992). In practice, it may be difficult to separate organizational problems stemming from differential cognition from those stemming from opportunism (a problem with which courts are all too familiar).

6.3. Opportunism

It has been argued that a main difference between the KBA and OE lies in the KBA not being dependent upon the assumption of opportunism (Conner and

Prahalad 1996; Madhok 1996). It is true that much of the modern economics of organization builds on this assumption, and that it is often held within this approach that it is not possible to explain much of observed economic organization without this concept (Foss 1996a and 1996b; Williamson 1996). It is also true that the assumption has served theorists well, and that many new insights have been produced building on this assumption. Nevertheless, KBA critics are right in asserting that aspects of economic organization that do not turn on incentive conflicts have been overly neglected. For example, Hart (1995) argues that in the absence of incentive conflicts, the optimal outcome can always be realized. But this claim requires the theorist to abstract from misallocation due to misunderstandings, communication costs, different cognition, etc. Opportunism is not the sole cause of management problems!

However, it should be noted that many contributors to OE are actually uncomfortable with the notion of opportunism, because it is not precisely defined compared to the ordinary assumption of self-interest (for example Barzel 1989; Hart 1995). And Williamson (1985, 1996), who is the inventor of the concept of opportunism, tends to use it in connection with the hold-up situation only. Moreover, not all contributors to OE have made the assumption of opportunism. Instead, they have focused attention on opportunism-independent costs, such as measurement costs (Barzel 1989), costs of communicating (Segal 1996; Wernerfelt 1997), search costs (Casson 1994), and costs of storing, retrieving, and processing information (Bolton and Dewatripont 1994; Marschak and Radner 1972). As these OE theorists point out, it is possible to say a good deal about economic organization without relying on the assumption of opportunism. For example, Casson (1994) argues that decision rights within firms will be distributed according to who has important ('decisive') tacit knowledge and the costs of communicating this knowledge. And Segal (1996) argues that understanding the managerial task requires that we take account of communication costs: if all computations and observations can be communicated without any cost, it will never pay to concentrate managerial effort (that is, to appoint a manager). Finally, Wernerfelt (1997) argues that the choice between markets, hierarchies, and intermediate forms also reflects economizing on costs of communication.

These are indeed promising avenues that help to correct a strong bias in OE. Moreover, in various ways they link up with the KBA. For example, an emphasis on communication costs fits naturally with the KBA. This is because it is largely specific and tacit knowledge that gives rise to communication costs which, in turn, produce co-ordination problems (Langlois and Robertson 1995). This, we believe, is one way to interpret the KBA theory of the boundaries of the firm (see, for example, Kogut and Zander 1992; Richardson 1972): because of firm-specific and tacit knowledge in firms, it may be more costly to communicate across the boundaries of the firm than inside the firm. Efficient boundary choice may therefore reflect communication costs.

7. Conclusion

In this chapter, we have critically compared the KBA and OE for the purpose of establishing what is genuinely different in the KBA relative to the OE and in the hope that this will facilitate critical dialogue. Thus, we put forward an overarching methodological framework for comparing the two theories. We next suggested that property rights economics allows us to see that many KBA insights may be translated into OE insights. We found that while there are many overlaps, the two theories are different. Specifically, we argued that ideas on bounded rationality, differential cognition, and learning can be singled out as genuinely different elements in the KBA, whereas opportunism-independent determinants of economic organization are not. We fully acknowledge that on the one hand KBA writers have developed important concepts and insights, such as routines and capabilities, but that these need a micro-foundation. On the other hand, OE writers have also developed important concepts, such as transaction costs and property rights systems, that are helpful for establishing these micro-foundations; however, we also agree that OE may stand to gain from incorporating ideas on differential cognition, learning, and so on (cf. Williamson 1998). Similarly, OE may benefit from a better understanding of how formal and informal elements of the property rights system interact, and here research is likely to be furthered by attention to what KBA writers have said about norms, social relations, etc. in firms.

Thus, the overall message that flows from this chapter is to not overestimate differences. However, what will this mean for research in organizational phenomena? There are several possibilities. For example, the proponents of the KBA and OE could join forces or they could continue to pursue independent research strategies while maintaining a critical dialogue. What makes the first research strategy problematic is that, at least in some manifestations, the KBA is a process-oriented theory (cf. the stress put on learning, cognition, etc.), whereas OE is a more static and structure-oriented theory. Such theories are hard to align. However, as indicated earlier (in different terms), a process-oriented theory stands to gain from a structure-oriented theory and vice versa. This is how the differences between KBA and OE matter. Therefore, future dialogue is highly recommended.

References

AKERLOF, GEORGE 1970. 'The market for "lemons": Quality uncertainty and the market mechanism', *Quarterly Journal of Economics* 84: 488–500.

ALCHIAN, ARMEN A. 1965. 'Some economics of property rights'. Reproduced in Armen A. Alchian, *Economic Forces at Work*. Indianapolis: Liberty Press (1977).

—— and HAROLD DEMSETZ 1972. 'Production, information costs, and economic organization', *American Economic Review* 62: 772–95.

BANDURA, ALBERT 1977. *Social Learning Theory*. Englewood Cliffs, NJ: Prentice Hall.

BARNEY, JAY B. 1986. 'Strategic factor markets', *Management Science* 32: 1231–41.

—— 1991. 'Firm resources and sustained competitive advantage', *Journal of Management* 17: 99–120.

BARZEL, YORAM 1982. 'Measurement costs and the organization of markets', *Journal of Law and Economics* 25: 27–48.

—— 1989. *Economic Analysis of Property Rights*. Cambridge: Cambridge University Press.

BOLTON, PATRICK, and MATHIAS DEWATRIPONT 1994. 'The firm as a communication network', *Quarterly Journal of Economics* 115: 809–39.

CASSON, MARK 1994. 'Why are firms hierarchical?', *Journal of the Economics of Business*, 1: 47–76.

COASE, RONALD H. 1937. 'The nature of the firm'. *Economica* N.S. 4: 386–405. Reprinted in Oliver E. Williamson and Sidney Winter, eds., *The Nature of the Firm: Origins, Evolution, Development*. New York: Oxford University Press (1991).

—— 1960. 'The problem of social cost', *Journal of Law and Economics* 3: 1–44.

CONNER, KATHLEEN R. 1991. 'A historical comparison of resource-based theory and five schools of thought within industrial organization economics: Do we have a new theory of the firm?', *Journal of Management* 17: 121–54.

—— and C. K. PRAHALAD 1996. 'A resource-based theory of the firm: knowledge versus opportunism', *Organization Science* 7: 477–501.

DEMSETZ, HAROLD 1964. 'The exchange and enforcement of property rights', *Journal of Law and Economics* 7: 11–26.

—— 1973. 'Industrial structure, market rivalry, and public policy', *Journal of Law and Economics* 16: 1–10.

—— 1988. 'The theory of the firm revisited', In Harold Demsetz, ed., *Ownership, Control and the Organization of Economic Activity*. Oxford: Basil Blackwell (1990).

DENZAU, ARTHUR, and DOUGLASS C. NORTH 1994. 'Shared mental models: ideologies and institutions', *Kyklos* 47: 3–33.

DIERICKX, I., and K. COOL 1989. 'Asset stock accumulation and sustainability of competitive advantage', *Management Science* 35: 1504–11.

DOSI, GIOVANNI, and LUIGI MARENGO 1994. 'Some elements of an evolutionary theory of organizational competences', in Richard W. England, ed., *Evolutionary Concepts in Contemporary Economics*. Ann Arbor, MI: University of Michigan Press.

—— SIDNEY G. WINTER, and DAVID J. TEECE 1992. 'Towards a theory of corporate coherence', in Giovanni Dosi, Roberto Giannetti, and Pier-Angelo Toninelli, eds., *Technology and Enterprise in a Historical Perspective*. Oxford: Clarendon Press.

EGGERTSON, THÁINN 1990. *Economic Behaviour and Institutions*. Cambridge: Cambridge University Press.

FOSS, NICOLAI J. 1996*a*. 'Knowledge-based approaches to the theory of the firm: Some critical comments', *Organization Science* 7: 470–6.

—— 1996*b*. 'More critical comments on knowledge-based theories of the firm', *Organization Science* 7: 519–23.

FURUBOTN, EIRIK G., and RUDOLF RICHTER 1998. *Institutions and Economic Theory*. Ann Arbor, MI: Michigan University Press.

GHOSHAL, SUMANTRA, and PETER MORAN 1996. 'Bad for practice: A critique of the transaction cost theory', *Academy of Management Review* 21(1): 13–47.

―――― and LUIS ALMEIDA-COSTA 1995. 'The essence of the megacorporation: Shared context, not structural hierarchy', *Journal of Institutional and Theoretical Economics* 151: 748–59.

GRANT, ROBERT A. 1996. 'Toward a knowledge-based theory of the firm', *Strategic Management Journal* 17: 109–22.

HART, OLIVER 1995. *Firms, Contracts and Financial Structure*. Oxford: Oxford University Press.

―― and J. MOORE 1990. 'Property rights and the nature of the firm', *Journal of Political Economy*: 1119–58.

HAYEK, FRIEDRICH A. VON 1945. 'The use of knowledge in society', *American Economic Review* 35 (September): 519–30. Reprinted in Friedrich A. von Hayek, *Individualism and Economic Order*. Chicago: University of Chicago Press (1948).

HOLMSTRÖM, BENGT 1982. 'Moral hazard in teams', *Bell Journal of Economics*, 13: 324–40.

―― and PAUL MILGROM 1991. 'Multitask principal-agent analyses: incentive contracts, asset ownership, and job design', *Journal of Law, Economics, and Organization* 7: 24–52.

JENSEN, MICHAEL, and WILLIAM MECKLING 1992. 'Specific and general knowledge and organizational structure', in Lars Werin and Hans Wijkander, eds., *Contract Economics*. Oxford: Blackwell.

JONES, GARETH R. 1983. 'Transaction costs, property rights, and organizational culture: An exchange perspective', *Administrative Science Quarterly* 28: 454–67.

KLEIN, PETER, and HOWARD A. SHELANSKI 1995. 'Empirical research in transaction cost economics: A review and assessment', *Journal of Law, Economics and Organization* 11: 335–61.

KOGUT, BRUCE, and UDO ZANDER 1992. 'Knowledge of the firm, combinative capabilities, and the replication of technology', *Organization Science* 3: 383–97.

―― 1993. 'Knowledge of the firm and the evolutionary theory of the multinational corporation', *Journal of International Business Studies* 24: 625–45.

―― 1996. 'What do firms do? Coordination, identity, and learning', *Organization Science* 7: 502–18.

KRAJEWSKI, WLADYSLAW 1977. *Correspondence Principle and Growth of Science*. Dordrecht: Reidel.

KREPS, DAVID. 1990. 'Corporate culture and economic theory', in James Alt and Kenneth Shepsle, eds., *Positive Political Economy*. Cambridge: Cambridge University Press.

LANGLOIS, RICHARD N., and PAUL L. ROBERTSON 1995. *Firms, Markets, and Economic Change*. London: Routledge.

LIBECAP, GARY 1989. *Contracting for Property Rights*. Cambridge: Cambridge University Press.

MADHOK, ANOOP 1996. 'The organization of economic activity: transaction costs, firm capabilities, and the nature of governance', *Organization Science* 7: 577–90.

MARSCHAK, JAKOB, and ROY RADNER 1972. *The Theory of Teams*. New Haven, CT: Yale University Press.

MILLER, GARY 1992. *Managerial Dilemmas*. Cambridge: Cambridge University Press.

NELSON, RICHARD R., and SIDNEY G. WINTER 1982. *An Evolutionary Theory of Economic Growth*. Cambridge, MA: The Belknap Press, Harvard University Press.

NORTH, D. C. 1990. *Institutions, Institutional Change and Economic Performance*. Cambridge: Cambridge University Press.

PENROSE, EDITH T. 1959. *The Theory of the Growth of the Firm*. Oxford: Basil Blackwell.

PETERAF, MARGARET A. 1993. 'The cornerstones of competitive advantage: A resource-based view', *Strategic Management Journal* 14: 179–91.

POPPO, LAURA, and TODD ZENGER 1995. 'Opportunism, routines and boundary choices: A comparative test of transaction cost and resource-based explanations for make-or-buy decisions', *Academy of Management Best Paper Proceedings*.

PUTTERMAN, LOUIS 1995. 'Markets, hierarchies, and information: On a paradox in the economics of organization', *Journal of Economic Behavior and Organization* 26: 373–90.

RICHARDSON, GEORGE B. 1972. 'The organisation of industry', *Economic Journal* 82: 883–96.

SEGAL, ILYA 1996. 'Modelling the managerial task', *Working Paper*, Department of Economics, UCLA.

SPENDER, J.-C. 1996. 'Making knowledge the basis of a dynamic theory of the firm', *Strategic Management Journal* 17: 45–62.

SUGDEN, ROBERT 1986. *The Economics of Rights, Cooperation and Welfare*. Oxford: Blackwell.

WERNERFELT, BIRGER 1984. 'A resource-based view of the firm', *Strategic Management Journal* 5: 171–80. Reprinted in Nicolai J Foss, ed., *Resources, Firms, and Strategies: A Reader in the Resource-Based Perspective*. Oxford: Oxford University Press (1997).

—— 1997. 'On the nature and scope of the firm: An adjustment-cost theory', *Journal of Business* 70: 489–514.

WILLIAMSON, OLIVER E. 1985. *The Economic Institutions of Capitalism*. New York: Free Press.

—— 1994. 'Strategizing, economizing, and economic organization', in Richard P. Rumelt, Dan E. Schendel, and David J. Teece , eds., *Fundamental Issues in Strategy: A Research Agenda*. Boston: Harvard Business School Press.

—— 1996. *The Mechanisms of Governance*. Oxford: Oxford University Press.

—— 1998. 'Human actors and economic organization'. Manuscript.

WINTER, S. G. 1988. 'On Coase, competence, and the corporation', *Journal of Law, Economics, and Organization* 4: 163–80.

On the Tangled Discourse between Transaction Cost Economics and Competence-Based Views of the Firm: Some Comments

GIOVANNI DOSI AND LUIGI MARENGO

1. Introduction

The insightful and thorough (albeit, in our view, somehow 'imperialist') comparative discussion by Oliver Williamson of the governance and competence views of economic organizations (Williamson, 1999a), as well as the daring 'counter-reformation manifesto' by Foss and Foss, trying to reinterpret most views on organization in terms of property rights (Foss and Foss this volume, Chapter 3), provide a valuable background for an overall assessment of similarities, convergence, controversies, and unexplored issues in one of the most lively fields of current socio-economic theory.

It is in this spirit that we contribute the rather sketchy remarks that follow. We begin by briefly recalling some basic elements of the competence perspective (henceforth CP) as we see it (section 2). Next, we offer a short comparison with equally basic tenets of the 'orthodox' view—which for brevity we equate to the 'orthodox' agency theory (henceforth OA)—and the transaction costs economics (henceforth TCE) (section 3). Finally, in section 4 we try to mimic some of the 'moves' suggested by Williamson, stressing possible convergence but also potential controversy between TCE and CP.

2. The Competence View of Organizations: A Telegraphic Overview

Given the growing number of detailed and rich accounts of CP and germane views[1]—such as 'resource-based' theories—of organizations, we can afford to be

The views presented here have greatly benefited from discussions with the participants at the DRUID Summer 1998 Conference, 'Competences, Governance and Entrepreneurship', Bornholm, Denmark, June 1998 and in particular with Nicolai Foss, Oliver Williamson, and Sidney Winter. Support to the research by the European Union (TSER, DG XII, projects Dynacom and Essy) is gratefully acknowledged.

[1] We consider the resource-based perspective as a theory of the firm which is largely germane to CP, though it presents some important differences. In particular, it is very much an equilibrium

particularly brief and refer the reader to the other works for details (for example Dosi, Nelson, and Winter 1999; Dosi and Marengo 1994; Kogut and Zander 1992, 1996; Nelson and Winter 1982; Nelson 1991; Marengo *et al.* 1999; Teece, Pisano, and Shuen 1994; Teece *et al.* 1994; Madhok 1996; Conner and Prahalad 1996; Leonard-Barton 1995; Winter 1988).

The phenomena the theory addresses include, first, heterogeneity among firms and the sources of persistent competitive advantage. For this primary purpose, it elaborates a theory of the nature of the firm whose perspective departs quite significantly from the Coasian one. First of all, firms are not seen exclusively as *loci* of co-ordination, but also and more importantly as *loci* of creation, implementation, storage, and diffusion of productive knowledge (cf. Winter 1982). Second, and relatedly, the very existence of firms is considered not in terms of a departure from the original state of nature in which co-ordination is carried out entirely by competitive markets, but in terms of their being the primary *loci* of the process of division of labour, that is, of the creation of those separable units which competitive markets might (or might not) co-ordinate efficiently. Equivalence between markets and organizations might well hold (lacking transaction and bureaucratic costs) for a given state of division of knowledge and labour, but it does not hold if the latter are themselves dependent upon the organizational structure. (There is more on this 'anti-Coasian' perspective in Marengo 1999 and Marengo *et al.* 1999.)

In addition to this enquiry into the sources and consequences of heterogeneity, CP attempts to interpret both the vertical and horizontal boundaries of the firm (cf. Teece *et al.* 1994); it investigates the properties of different forms of internal organization; it tries to establish the sources of differential performance among firms; it analyses the processes by which particular organizations became what they are (that is, the underlying evolutionary processes).

As a first approximation, and notwithstanding the limitations discussed in Coriat and Dosi (1998), it tries to accomplish the above tasks by focusing on organizations as repositories of problem-solving knowledge and by studying some salient properties of knowledge accumulation and the ways the latter co-evolve with organizational structures and practices (including, of course, routines but also managerial heuristics and strategies).

Organizational specificities and persistently different revealed performances are interpreted also on the grounds of path dependence in knowledge accumulation and inertial persistence of organizational traits. Bounded rationality, in its broadest meaning, is the norm. Its general sources include the 'complexity' and procedural uncertainty associated with problem-solving procedures (cf. Dosi and Egidi 1991, Marengo *et al.* 1999) and the intrinsic 'opaqueness' of the relationship

---

theory rather than a disequilibrium one, and it is centred on the issue of having control of an asset rather than having the knowledge of how to make use of it.

between actions and environmental feedback, so that it is seldom obvious, even *ex post*, to state how well one did and why (cf. March 1994).

The analysis is, or ought to be, undertaken in terms of both comparative properties of different organizational forms (a methodology intrinsically shared with TCE) and modal learning processes, properly accounting for initial conditions and for their embeddedness in broader institutional set-ups, such as those governing the markets for labour, finance, and products).

The above provides the briefest of summaries of some basic features of CP. In the next section we sketch some of its relations with the other major perspectives on the political economy of organizations.

3. Knowledge, Incentives, and Organizational Forms: Theoretical Similarities and Divides

Before making a detailed comparison between TCE and CP, let us start with a more general comparative assessment in which we look also at the orthodox view of agency (OA). By OA we mean the whole class of interpretations grounded on equilibrium contracting with completely rational far-sighted agents in possession of asymmetric/incomplete information. (This is also not very different from the archetype Foss and Foss have in mind when in Chapter 3, this volume, they describe what they call 'organizational economics'.) Table 4.1 highlights some major distinguishing features.

In order to emphasize the differences, consider first a major divide concerning the primary dimensions of analysis. Both OA and TCE concentrate essentially on incentive governance, while CP focuses on the problem-solving dimensions of organizations. In a nutshell, CP's 'primitive story', which has antecedents in the work of Herbert Simon as well as multiple streams of organization theory, bears considerable 'cognitive' emphasis, but tends to neglect all governance issues that arise from potentially conflicting interests, opportunism, etc. Williamson (Chapter 2, this volume, and 1999) is right to remind us that, taken at face value, that 'primitive story' implies a Utopian view of actors as benevolent co-operators. On the other hand, the same epistemological status can be also attributed to the 'primitive story' implied by both OA and TCE, whereby one censors the fact that organizations essentially conduct complicated procedures to carry out complicated tasks such as producing aircraft, shoes, transportation services for people and goods, etc. and that they do it more or less well for reasons which are partly divorced from incentive alignment issues. Thus, in the OA and TCE 'Utopia', the implicit *ceteris paribus* assumption is that organizations naturally possess, in its optimal form, the knowledge required to carry out such complex tasks and, moreover, that this optimal knowledge in itself is independent of the organizational structure. The members of the 'Utopian' organization depicted by OA and TCE are not themselves engaged in acquiring

TABLE 4.1. Orthodox agency, transaction costs economics, and competence perspectives: A comparative appraisal

Dimensions of analysis and theoretical building blocks	Orthodox agency	Transaction costs economics	Competence (and evolutionary) perspectives
1. Problem solving/ cognition/knowledge	No	Not so far (but see Williamson 1999*a* and 1999*b*)	Yes (central dimension of analysis)
2. Incentive governance	Yes (central dimension of analysis) via equilibrium contracting	Yes, possibly via organizations as substitutes for equilibrium contracting	Not so far (but see Coriat and Dosi 1998)
3. Behavioural microfoundations	Perfect, far-sighted rationality	Bounded rationality with far-sightedness	Bounded rationality (usually, with 'myopic' attributes)
4. Organizational behaviour	Strategic (in the game-theoretic sense)	Cost-economizing	Driven by routines, heuristics, etc.
5. Learning	No	Not so far	Yes (central dimension of analysis)
6. Unit(s) of analysis	• Strategies • Allocation of information • Allocation of property rights	Transactions	• Elementary 'bits' of knowledge • Routines and other elementary behavioural traits
7. Non-economic dimensions of organizations	Not as original dimensions	No	Power, trust, identity building, etc.

and implementing the knowledge necessary to carry out the complex tasks real organizations perform, but are only engaged in playing among themselves devious games of cheating, hiding, double-crossing, etc.

Needless to say, the crucial issue beyond the caricature is what kind of empirically robust propositions each view is able to generate. In this respect, Foss and Foss (see Chapter 3, this volume) assert that many of the propositions that have been made about organizations can be accounted for within the OA framework, and in particular and even more pertinently, by the property rights framework.[2] We would like to disagree strongly. One of the basic tenets of CP is that the

---

[2] Foss and Foss (1999) focus on the theory of property rights rather than agency models. However we believe that, at least in terms of relevance for the present discussion, property rights and agency theories are basically equivalent, at least as regards complete markets and in the absence of slavery.

domain of accumulation and social distribution of knowledge cannot be reduced simply to either incentives or property rights allocation. As witness to that, consider the voluminous literature on the economics of innovation and organizational learning (cf., among others, Freeman 1982; Dosi 1988; Pavitt 1999; Dosi, Nelson, and Winter 1999) which tries to establish a few 'stylised facts' on the patterns of learning at the level of firms, industries, and countries. These can hardly be interpreted as equilibrium responses to distributions of property rights . This general proposition can, however, be refuted empirically: in that case the challenge would be for the proponents of OA to derive non-trivial propositions on inter-firm, intersectoral, and international differences in technological and organizational innovation from their own 'primitive story' and its refinements. This is of course different from exercises of *ex post* rationalization which Foss and Foss seem at times inclined to undertake in their 'counter-reformist' urge to bring everything back into the same fold. Imagine, if you will, somebody asking why Manchester United won the 1998–99 European Champions League, which is just the same as asking why Intel is the world leader in microprocessors or why Toyota responds swiftly to changes in demand. CP analysts would build their answer on both the individual skills of Manchester United players and, even more important, how such skills blend and complement each other in the team, giving rise to collective routines, tactics, automatic reactions, plus the 'strategic' skills of the team's coach; finally they would acknowledge the important role of chance and random events (and chance certainly had a major role in many of United's wins). On the other hand, OA analysts would give an answer along more or less the following lines: 'Manchester United won because they made optimal use of the property rights on the services provided by the legs (and heads) of their players.'

In fact, OA investigations entail a very important research endeavour, aimed—as we see it—at exploring possible robust features for a wide class of notional, incentive-compatible, organizational designs, which may be derived from a very meagre (and admittedly unrealistic) set of assumptions. This is how we interpret Laffont and Tirole (1993) and a few other works of this genre. It would be unfair to the most sophisticated contributors to that approach to make 'imperialist' empirical claims, which actually they never (perhaps with a few exceptions) make.

Indeed, it does not do justice to TCE to group it within the catch-all OA camp. In fact TCE does share with OA roughly the same theoretical primitives (see above) and also an inclination to emphasize the explanatory properties of equilibria which CP practitioners usually consider unwarrantedly excessive. However, if there is some truth in the checklist of Table 4.1, the points of departure are at least equally important. Let us examine two of them.

First, the bounded rationality perspective on microfoundations is a major distinguishing feature (and a major point of overlap with CP). It is a matter not of religious commitment but of looking for behavioural assumptions that are in some way disciplined by empirical and, especially, psychological evidence: how much rationality agents should be attributed is largely a pragmatic matter, depending on the context, the complexity of the problems they face, etc. Rather, bounded rationality might loosen the control—roughly speaking—on the 'lower bound' of what agents may do and achieve (so that it may allow highly suboptimal outcomes to be empirically feasible or even likely) but it also firmly controls the 'upper bound' on what one may theorize as being empirically plausible. (Thus, for example, one excises, as figments of the imagination, all collective outcomes which depend on agents working out transversality conditions, solving Bellman equations, etc.)

Second, as we read Williamson's main contribution to TCE, organizations are institutional entities with a 'syndrome of attributes' that differ neatly from sheer bundles of contracts. This is another major distinguishing feature between TCE and OA. It is true that TCE has not done much to date to open up the organizational 'blackbox', but it does hint at an intraorganizational *modus operandi* displaying behavioural patterns akin to those identified by sociology and organization theories—at least in so far as they entail abandoning sophisticated calculations and general intrahierarchical 'acts of forbearedness'. The opposite interpretation is that TCE organizations may be fully interpreted as bundles of incomplete contracts. The degree to which Williamson sees, for example, Grossman and Hart (1986) or the relevant parts of Hart (1995) as genuine 'reduced forms' of his own theory of organization is for him to say. (For an insightful assessment of the achievement of and limitations to reducing TCE to an OA game-theoretic framework, see Kreps (1996).)

However, the much broader issues here are (a) whether organizations are behavioural entities to be studied in their own right, quite apart from the possible contractual acts of which they are comprised; and (b) whether that makes a difference for both theory and empirical predictions. Clearly, CP gives a clearcut affirmative answer to both questions. In a sense, CP takes for granted the massive 'ontological' incompleteness of most contracts one empirically encounters, and it studies the arrangements by which different organizational archetypes master co-ordination of boundedly rational learning agents. This route is admittedly difficult to explore and requires much attention to empirical—sociological, organizational, and cognitive—detail. In the best scenario, it is also likely to nurture novel syntheses between TCE and CP. Conversely, the 'incomplete contract reduction' promises quicker formal rewards: incompleteness happens to be more respectable than bounded rationality and gives more freedom to the imaginative modeller.

Finally, we would like to point to some caveats in relation to TCE. First, we believe that founding organization theory on equilibrium incomplete contracting requires that escalating demands be made either on agents' rationality and/or on the optimality properties of market-selection mechanisms. As to the former, there is a growing literature which is trying to extend the standard model of rationality and decision making not in the direction of more empirically grounded behavioural foundations, but in the opposite one, of more and more demanding assumptions on rationality, in order to embody in the model some treatment of unforeseen contingencies. (Good examples of this view are Maskin and Tirole (1999) and Tirole (1999), in whose analysis incompleteness and transaction costs themselves become irrelevant if agents have unbiased priors on their future pay-offs and correctly perform dynamic programming; see also Dekel *et al.* (1998) for a survey of recent research on models of unforeseen contingencies.) As to the latter, TCE has not yet developed sufficient in-depth investigation into how efficient governance structures can emerge spontaneously. The topic is a problematic one, and the 'optimistic' views explicitly, or more often only implicitly, embraced by much TCE research seem somehow unwarranted. At least two problems arise in this respect: (a) one is dealing here with a problem of selection of selection mechanisms (governance structures are in fact selection mechanisms themselves), a problem whose implications are largely ignored and where one should very likely observe multiple equilibria and path dependence; (b) governance structures are 'complex' entities made of many interdependent elements, and we know now that when the units of selection possess this kind of property, selective forces tend to lose their power to drive a population to optimality (cf. Levinthal 1997; Marengo 1999).

Finally, we also see a danger that some TCE research may lose its predictive power in an ever-expanding, incomplete contracting position (a situation somewhat similar to that when there were empirically undisciplined applications of OA to organizational research or of game theory to industrial organization).

4. Competence-Based Views: Mimicking some TCE 'Moves'

One of the most valuable contributions made by Williamson (see Chapter 2, this volume) is a sequence of 'theoretical moves' that may structure the comparison between TCE and CP. Let us follow some of them.

4.1. Human Actors

As already mentioned, both TCE and CP emphasize some form of bounded rationality. There are, however, at least two important differences worth mentioning.

First, bounded rationality in TCE has to date been taken to mean bounds on the strategic sophistication by which agents may behave opportunistically and by which they can anticipate other agents' opportunistic behaviour. Conversely, in CP bounded rationality has largely stood for individual and, especially, collective bounds to problem-solving competences. This difference might be a fruitful source of complementarity in so far as it pushes CP to take cognizance of the incentive/conflict governance dimension (cf. Coriat and Dosi 1998) and TCE to account for the knowledge dimension of organizations. Incidentally, note that Williamson (1999) begins to offer a taxonomy of organizational arrangements based on combinations of different means and variances in cognitive abilities and conditions of opportunism. This is a welcome move, but is possibly not suffi-cient to meet the requirements of CP, which sees competence also as a collective property of organizational procedures, irreducible to intrinsic individual skills.

Second, TCE emphasizes bounded rationality with foresightedness, while CP—Williamson stresses—is much more inclined to see its myopic aspects. Again, how myopic or foresighted agents are supposed to be is a question which should be settled essentially on empirical grounds. The only case CP would normally find hard to accept is 'bounded rationality with rational expecta-tions'—in effect an oxymoron—with forward-looking agents who know the damaging effects of their pursuit of 'self-interest with guile' and thus design insti-tutions which purposefully exploit at best bounded rationality in order to tie their own hands (a sort of institutional Ulysses expecting the sirens to come out of his own soul).

4.2. Unit(s) of Analysis

As is well known, transactions, with their characteristics, are the basic unit of analysis of TCE; for CP, we suggest, the basic units of analysis are the elemen-tary (physical or 'cognitive') problem-solving procedures. However, for many purposes CP analyses take a broader perspective and study the properties of collections of elementary procedures (such as organizational routines).

Since the unit of analysis issue is clearly fundamental in assessing differences and possible complementarities between the two approaches, we shall discuss it at greater length in the following pages.

4.3. On Transacting versus Problem-Solving Procedures

The TCE 'primitive story' deals with the efficiency of different governance struc-tures in managing transactions across given technologically separable interfaces: technology and the division of labour, which constitute the solution to the productive problem at hand, are taken as being already in place in their optimal form. Behind this story lies an implicit assumption that organizations merely perform tasks of co-ordination and that what is being co-ordinated (that is, the pieces of 'productive knowledge', cf. Winter 1982) is independent of the organ-izational arrangement.

CP approaches tend to emphasize the opposite view, that organizations are primarily responsible for designing and implementing solutions to productive problems and that specific organizational arrangements are essential parts of such a design process, and determine which solutions can be generated and tested. (This arguement is developed at greater length in Marengo *et al.* 1999.)

Probably the most promising, and yet almost entirely unexplored, research area in which TCE and CP can meet lies in trade-offs, balances, and co-evolution between transaction-coordinating and problem-solving organizational procedures and arrangements. Multiple 'organizational equilibria' and path dependence are likely to weaken the explicative power of the principle of transaction costs minimization: one could in fact imagine a multiplicity of organizational solutions with similar overall efficiency but very different arrangements for co-ordination and problem solving, ranging from organizational arrangements with very effective problem-solving procedures but possibly high transaction costs to the opposite case of low transaction costs with low problem-solving efficiency (from which emerges another source of heterogeneity among organizations).

4.4. On the Nature of the Firm

As regards the nature of the firm, CP basically subscribes to the description offered by Williamson (Chapter 2, this volume) but it adds the organizational attributes associated with the intraorganizational distribution of: (a) information (roughly speaking who speaks to whom about what); (b) authority (not a theoretical specificity of CP, but a domain where our interpretation of CP is in line with more sociological theories of organization); and (c) problem-solving tasks (cf. Dosi and Marengo 1994, Coriat and Dosi 1998).

4.5. Refutable Interpretative Implications

We have already mentioned the main interpretative purposes of CP in terms of the nature and internal characteristics of organizations, their horizontal/vertical boundaries, their comparative performances, and their origins. These purposes largely overlap with TCE's research programme, although the lines of explanation and also the predictions are likely to differ in part. The operationalization of CP is admittedly at an earlier stage than that of TCE, but one ideal line of investigation runs as follows:

1. Identify the salient characteristics of particular problem-solving activities (that is, of particular 'technological paradigms', to use the terminology of Dosi 1982).
2. Derive the organizational implications of the above (admittedly not an easy task, but one that is achievable, on the grounds of what we increasingly know from both the economics of innovation and micro-organizational studies).

3. Check the empirical robustness of the predictions.
4. Test, both cross-sectionally and longitudinally, whether specific organizational forms—conditional on specific 'learning regimes'—sustain differential corporate performances.

Another more qualitative but equally important line of investigation uses the theory, so to speak, 'heuristically', as a diagnostic guide. (For example, it may ask where the distinguishing competences of a given firm reside. Or how they relate to underlying differences in organizational routines *vis-à-vis* other firms.)

Of course, empirical observations of organizational forms and performances are likely to be influenced by both transaction cost- and competence-related factors. However, the observational non-equivalence of the two 'pure' theories is likely to derive precisely from what we could call the learning ineffectiveness of complete incentive alignment, as against the incomplete incentive alignment of pure problem solving. Let us elaborate on the idea. The advantage of having one theory—CP—which 'pushes the fiction of zero-opportunism to completion' (Conner and Prahalad 1996) and another one—TCE—'exploring the fiction of homogeneous problem-solving abilities across organizations' might provide valuable clues to how empirical organizations trade off problem-solving exploration against economizing governance and how that affects corporate performance. (For an interesting, albeit preliminary, investigation of CP as opposed to TCE factors in technology acquisition see Delmas 1999.) The evidence so far is too weak to disentangle first- and second-order effects, for example, whether one should call upon TCE for generic make-or-buy decisions and CP for the particular, as Williamson (Chapter 2, this volume) suggests, or the other way round. In any case it is a fundamental question in its own right, the answer to which is likely to depend also on specific technologies, stages of the industry life cycle, and country-specific institutions.

4.6. *From Individual Organizations to Competitive Advantages*

Note that CP also allows an easy link between the theory of organization and a (testable) theory of competitive performance, in so far as it predicts persistent heterogeneity in problem-solving competences (which are also due to path-dependent idiosyncratic learning). Conversely, the more TCE relies on equilibrium and considerations of optimality to account for particular organizational forms, the less it can interpret the observed empirical variance in corporate performance (which also occurs across firms mastering rather similar transactions). TCE would in fact predict (through 'economizing' and 'remediableness' arguments) that in equilibrium all transactions of a given class (that is, transactions across similar technological interfaces and characterized by similar degrees of asset specificity, frequency, and uncertainty) should be subject to the same governance structure and have the same efficiency properties.

4.7. Processes versus Outcomes

One of the problems with full operationalization of CP—as Williamson rightly points out—stems from the fact that it is to a large extent a theory of organizational processes, in both senses—that it aims to become a theory of organizational learning and also in the more humble sense that even incumbent competences are largely revealed through their exercise. (The same argument applies to individuals, who might not know how good they are at doing something unless they do it, and applies even more to organizations.) However, in our view, the qualitative understanding—and eventually also the formalization—of the processes of organizational exploration, learning, and adaptation is one of the central challenges of organization theory. It also provides the crucial link between exercises conducted in a comparatively static mode and the dynamics of organizational innovation (or, for that matter, the appreciation of the determinants of organizational inertia). Leaving aside the general difficulty of the task, dynamics could and ought to assume a more central position in TCE analyses, in the sense that: (a) considerations of dynamic adaptability ought to enter the comparative assessment of different organizational forms (as advocated by Langlois 1992), and also that (b) it does not appear at all inconsistent with TCE to assume some competitive dynamics exercising selection over different organizational arrangements. These are areas where a dialogue between TCE and CP (especially in its more 'evolutionary' forms) theories could be more fruitful. But, especially with regard to the issue of evolutionary dynamics, we find little response in current research.

On the contrary, Williamson (1999) seems to suggest a purely purposeful equilibrium design of organizational arrangements, which is further strengthened by a stand against path dependence on the grounds of a 'remediableness' argument. The underlying criteria of the latter are that feasible (observed) organizations must not be compared with unfeasible (ideal) ones—a very sound point indeed—and that the observed organizations are the 'best' of the feasible ones because all achievable cost-minimizing opportunities are always exploited. The latter point makes a much more dubious and problematic assumption, and carries TCE unnecessarily near the Panglossian territory where one always lives in the best of all possible worlds.

5. Some Conclusions on Research Opportunities

Given the arguments sketched in the preceeding pages, our conclusion is bound to be very similar to that adduced by Williamson: that TCE and CP are at the same time rival and complementary. Explorations of the two ways in which they could fit into a more comprehensive theory of organization and of their observational non-equivalence are only the beginning. In the process, some (moderate) imperialistic drives are perfectly understandable. So, while Williamson seems to suggest CP refinements over the basic TCE framework, our inclination is to suggest the full development of a 'second generation' of CP theories accounting for the co-evolution of problem-solving and governance functions in organizational arrangements, crystallizing and operationalizing the conjectures sketched in Coriat and Dosi (1998). In any case, a civilized, empirically attentive, and theoretically sophisticated dialogue is beginning to emerge.

References

CONNER, K. R., and C. K. PRAHALAD 1996. 'A resource-based theory of the firm: Knowledge vs. opportunism', *Organization Science* 7: 477–501.

CORIAT, B., and G. DOSI 1998. 'Learning how to govern and learning how to solve problems', in A.D. Chandler, P. Hagstrom, and O. Solvell, eds., *The Dynamic Firm. The Role of Technology, Strategy, Organization and Regions.* Oxford: Oxford University Press.

DEKEL, E., B. L. LIPMAN, and A. RUSTICHINI 1998. 'Recent developments in modeling unforeseen contingencies', *European Economic Review* 42: 523–42.

DELMAS, M. A. 1999. 'Exposing strategic assets to create new competences: The case of technological acquisitions in the waste management industry in Europe and in the United States', *Industrial and Corporate Change* 8(4): 635–71.

DOSI, G. 1982. 'Technological paradigms and technological trajectories', *Research Policy* 2: 147–62.

—— 1988. 'Sources, Procedures and Microeconomic Effects of Innovation', *Journal of Economic Literature* 26: 1120–71.

—— and M. EGIDI 1991. 'Substantive and procedural uncertainty. An exploration of economic behaviours in complex and changing environments', *Journal of Evolutionary Economics* 1: 145–68.

—— and L. MARENGO 1994. 'Toward a theory of organizational competences', in R. W. England, ed., *Evolutionary Concepts in Contemporary Economics*: Ann Arbor, MI: Michigan University Press, 157–78.

—— R. NELSON, and S. G. WINTER, eds., 1999. *The Nature and Dynamics of Organizational Capabilities.* Oxford: Oxford University Press.

FREEMAN, C. 1982. *The Economics of Industrial Innovation*, 2nd edn. London: Frances Pinter.

GROSSMAN, S., and D. HART 1986. 'The costs and benefits of ownership: A theory of lateral and vertical integration', *Journal of Political Economy* 94: 691–719.

HART, D. 1995. *Firms, Contracts and Financial Structure.* Oxford: Oxford University Press.

KOGUT, B., and U. ZANDER 1992. 'Knowledge of the firm, combinative capabilities and the replication of technology', *Organization Science* 3: 383–97.

—— —— 1996. 'What do firms do? Co-ordination, identity and learning', *Organization Science* 7: 502–17.

KREPS, D. M. 1996. 'Markets and hierarchies and (mathematical) economic theory', *Industrial and Corporate Change* 5: 561–96.

LAFFONT, J. J. and J. TIROLE 1993. *A Theory of Incentives in Procurement and Regulation.* Cambridge, MA: MIT Press.

LANGLOIS, R. N. 1992. 'Transaction-cost economics in real time', *Industrial and Corporate Change* 1: 99–127.

LEONARD-BARTON, D. 1995. *Wellsprings of Knowledge: Building and Sustaining the Sources of Innovation.* Boston: Harvard Business School Press.

LEVINTHAL, D. 1997. 'Adaptation on rugged landscapes', *Management Science* 43: 934–50.

MADHOK, A. 1996. 'The organization of economic activity: Transaction costs, firm capabilities and the nature of governance', *Organization Science* 7: 577–90.

MARCH, J. G. 1994. *A Primer on Decision Making. How Decisions Happen.* New York: Free Press.

MARENGO, L. 1999. 'Decentralisation and market mechanisms in collective problem-solving', mimeo.

—— G. DOSI, P. LEGRENZI, and C. PASQUALI 1999. 'The structure of problem-solving knowledge and the structure of organizations', mimeo.

MASKIN, E., and J. TIROLE 1999. 'Unforeseen contingencies and incomplete contracts', *Review of Economic Studies* 66: 83–114.

NELSON, R. R. 1991. 'How do firms differ, and how does it matter?', *Strategic Management Journal* 12: 61–74.

—— and S. G. WINTER 1982. *An Evolutionary Theory of Economic Change.* Cambridge, MA: Harvard University Press.

PAVITT, K. 1999. *Technology, Management and Systems of Innovation.* Cheltenham: Edward Elgar.

SIMON, H. A. 1991. 'Organizations and markets', *Journal of Economic Perspectives* 5: 25–44.

TEECE, D. J., G. PISANO, and A. SHUEN 1994. 'Dynamic capabilities and strategic management', CCC Working Paper No.94-9. Berkeley: University of California.

—— R. RUMELT, G. DOSI, and S. G. WINTER 1994. 'Understanding corporate coherence: theory and evidence', *Journal of Economic Behavior and Organization* 23: 1–30.

TIROLE, J. 1999. 'Incomplete contracts: Where do we stand?', *Econometrica* 67: 741–81.

WILLIAMSON, O. 1975. *Markets and Hierarchies: Analysis and Antitrust Implications.* New York: Free Press.

—— 1985. *The Economic Institutions of Capitalism.* New York: Free Press.

—— 1999. 'Human actors and economic organization'. Berkeley: University of California, mimeo.

WINTER, S. G. 1982. 'An essay on the theory of production', in H. Hymans, ed., *Economics and the World around It.* Ann Arbor, MI: University of Michigan Press, 55–93.

—— 1988. 'On Coase, competence and the corporation', *Journal of Law, Economics and Organization* 4: 181–97.

Part B

Firm Growth and Entrepreneurship

5

Is there a Pilot in the Evolutionary Firm?

PATRICK COHENDET, PATRICK LLERENA, AND LUIGI MARENGO

1. Introduction

Since the seminal work by Nelson and Winter (1982), the evolutionary approach to the theory of the firm has made significant progress. As Coriat and Weinstein (1995) pointed out, this approach to the theory of the firm offers the unique advantage, compared with other competing theories, of providing an explanation of three key issues that are crucially important for a theoretical understanding of the firm. Thus, the evolutionary approach explains:

- how one can *define* a firm—namely, in terms of the set of competences that the firm controls;
- why firms *differ*—namely, because they rely on different routines and competences that are specific and that cannot be transferred (at low cost);
- the *dynamics* of firms—namely, through the combined mechanisms of selection and variation that work on the body of existing routines, considered as the possibility of transforming a set of secondary routines into a new core competence.

However the evolutionary theory of the firm still has very little to say on some key characteristics of the firm, such as the resolution of conflicts within firms and of potential conflicts that could emerge between shareholders and managers. Most importantly, there is a major element missing from the evolutionary theory of the firm: the role of the entrepreneur. Only very recently have some contributions to the literature (Teece and Pisano 1994; Witt 1998; Foss 1996, 1999) started to investigate the role of the entrepreneur in an evolutionary context. It is in many ways paradoxical that the neo-Schumpeterian theoretical developments pay so little attention to the key actor in Schumpeter's writings.

The aim of this chapter is not only to show that there is room for introducing the role of the entrepreneur into the evolutionary approach, but moreover to

The authors are very grateful for comments made by the participants in the DRUID Conference 1998, 'Competences, Governance and Entrepreneurship', in particular Keith Pavitt, Dominique Foray, and Nicolai Foss. They are also grateful to Monique Flasaquier for her assistance in translation.

support the idea that the presence of the entrepreneur on the evolutionary scene brings more coherence and explanatory power to the evolutionary theory of the firm. As Casson suggests (Chapter 6, this volume), we cannot conceive of a modern theory of the firm that does not address the issue of the role of the entrepreneur. The main argument of our contribution will thus be that the evolutionary theory of the firm, in order to be consistent, needs the entrepreneur to play a major role in some specific functions, namely, matching the internal environment of the firm with the external one, shaping the learning processes at stake, and selecting the core competence of the organization. These functions emerge in an evolutionary environment, and are additional to the traditional function played by the entrepreneur in the classical approaches. Moreover, in an evolutionary perspective, since the process of creation of resources always interferes with the process of allocation of resources, the traditional distinction between entrepreneurs (those agents in charge of the process of creation of resources) and managers (those agents in charge of the process of allocation of resources) no longer holds. We shall argue for a conception of a 'manager/entrepreneur' as a specific result of the evolutionary vision of the firm.

In the first part of this chapter, we present the main elements of the evolutionary theory of the firm, as suggested by the existing literature. The second part is devoted to a discussion of the consequences of the evolutionary theory on the co-ordination and incentive mechanisms of the firm. In this synthesis of the literature we draw attention to the neglect of the role of the entrepreneur. The third part shows the relevance of and the key role played by the entrepreneur in an evolutionay context. We then focus on the consequences of introducing the entrepreneur/manager into the theory of the firm. In the conclusion, we compare the evolutionary entrepreneur with other representations of the role of the entrepreneur in more traditional theoretical approaches to the firm.

2. On the Evolutionary Theory of the Firm

The evolutionary theory of the firm is hybrid, and results from the integration of two main theoretical approaches. These are surveyed in the following pages.

2.1. The Building Blocks of the Evolutionary Theory of the Firm

The first building block relies on pure evolutionary principles. The first is the principle of heredity, which considers routines as the 'genes' of the organization. Routines are programmes or models of repetitive activities that ensure the coherence between individual and collective behaviour, and allow the predictability of behaviours within the firm. The second is the principle of mutation (the generation of diversity), which is initiated by the searching behaviours of firms that consist of exploring and testing new routines. The third is the principle of selection, which shapes the routines or mutations. A given firm can face different mechanisms of selection, such as markets or imitation.

The second building block relies on the existence of the cognitive mechanisms of individual agents. These cognitive mechanisms involve the development of a collective knowledge base that encompasses the establishment of rules, habits, norms, and codes. What matters in this conception is the set of mental processes through which agents shape their interpretation of the environment. The functioning of these cognitive mechanisms through which routines are progessively built and modified over time occupies, within the evolutionary approach, a place equivalent to the one occupied by substantive rationality in the traditional approaches of economic theory.

From these theoretical premises, we may deduce some major characteristics of the evolutionary theory of the firm. It is noticeable that the role of the entrepreneur is entirely neglected in the literature. We will return to this issue later.

2.2. The Main Characteristics of the Evolutionary Theory of the Firm

2.2.1. Diversity Evolutionary models stress the importance of heterogeneity among agents. Diversity is seen not only as a realistic assumption, but also as a major driving force for evolutionary dynamics. In evolutionary models of industrial dynamics there emerges a need for microfoundations which accounts for persistent heterogeneity across firms both in their characteristics (their size, technology, and behavioural traits) and in their performance (their competitiveness, profitability, etc.). At this point it is worth pointing out the existence, in the evolutionary literature on the theory of the firm, as Foss (1996: 5) suggested, 'an overall distinction between firms in phylogenetic theories of the economic evolution, that is, theories that are concerned with the evolution of a population of firms, and ontogenetic theories of the firm, that is, theories of the evolution of the individual firms'.

2.2.2. Variation and selection Evolutionary models suppose that collective adaptation and learning require persistent diversity, generated by mechanisms of variation which always introduce new traits into the characteristics of firms (that is, mutation), but also mechanisms that guarantee the necessary global coherence: the selection mechanisms. Ultimately, each economic organization can be considered as an evolutionary system which implements a particular balance, between mechanisms of variation and mechanisms of selection, in what constitutes the organizational knowledge basis. Mechanisms of variation are both internal (as, for instance, incentive and co-ordination mechanisms that act as selection and variety-stabilizing devices) and external (competitive pressures on the market) to the firm. In a sense the traditional debate on markets and hierarchies can be recast in evolutionary terms as the interplay between different selection forces (market mechanisms versus internal mechanisms) which might well show different dynamic properties, not necessarily in line with the static allocative properties analysed for instance by transaction costs economics.

In organizations, this trade-off between commonality and diversity of knowledge is also strictly connected to the trade-off between exploitation and exploration (cf. March 1991): both exploitation and exploration are necessary for the survival of an organization. Without exploration of new possibilities, the organization would find itself trapped in suboptimal states and would eventually become ill adapted to changing environmental conditions. But organizations that devote all their resources to the exploration of new possibilities will face too high a degree of risk, and even in the case of successful discoveries they will fail to exploit the knowledge they acquire and will systematically perform worse than followers and imitators.

2.2.3. Search for better performance   Evolutionary models suppose that the learning process is driven by the search for better performance. This search is focused on some specific targets which require evaluation procedures. One must note a clear difference from the pure Darwinian hypothesis of selection by mutation. Firms have, in their logic of adaptation, the ability not only to learn and to transmit knowledge, but also to focus on specific targets, to expose the system to some specific mechanisms of selection, and to orientate the mechanisms of generation of diversity.

2.2.4. The firm as a processor of knowledge   The evolutionary approach to the firm belongs to a family of approaches which consider the firm as 'a processor of knowledge' (Fransman 1994). On this point, the evolutionary approach differentiates itself from more traditional theories which see the firm as 'an information processor'. In this latter case, the behaviour of the firm can be understood as an optimal reaction to the environmental signals which are detected by the firm. In the former case, the firm is considered as the *locus* for setting up, construction, selection, usage, and development of knowledge. It is more sensitive to the sharing and distribution of knowledge than to the distribution of information. 'It is not so much the saturation of its abilities to deal with information which concerns the firm, as the risk of becoming too confined by inefficient routines' (Cohendet *et al.* 1997). In other words, the governance of the firm is focused not on the resolution of informational asymmetries, but on the co-ordination of diverse pieces of knowledge and different learning processes.

When we consider the firm as a processor of knowledge, the main concept at stake is the 'competence' of the firm. It has recently been suggested that this is one of the main explanatory variables for diversity and its persistence (Dosi and Marengo 1994). The concept of competence, which relies on that of routines and rules, refers to a view of the firm as a social institution, the main characteristic of which is to 'know [well] how to do' certain things. These competences are coherent sets of knowledge and capabilities to use them in an efficient way. Some of these competences are strategic ('core competences', according to Teece (1988)) and constitute the main sources of the competitiveness of a firm. They are the results of a selection process both internal and external to the firm. The management, the construction, and the combination of these competences are critical in order to understand the limits of the firm and the co-ordination of as well as the incentive structure of the firm.

3. Consequences of the Co-ordination and Incentive Mechanisms

The above theoretical foundations of the evolutionary theory of the firm have some important economic consequences. In particular, they suggest the need for a reconsideration of the two main categories of mechanisms that shape the organization of the firm: the co-ordination mechanisms and the incentive mechanisms. We emphasize the importance of these mechanisms because we believe that the role of the entrepreneur in the evolutionary firm should be understood in terms of ensuring the efficiency of these mechanisms and also of allowing the global coherence of the firm.

3.1. Co-ordination Mechanisms

Co-ordination mechanisms *stricto sensu* are those mechanisms that make it possible to bring together both individual actions to meet a defined set of objectives, and local and decentralized learning processes to drive organizational change in a given direction (Cohendet and Llerena 1991; Avadykian, Cohendet, and Llerena 1995). Co-ordination mechanisms are not the main focal point of traditional theories of the firm. These theories often consider them as given. However, as Langlois and Foss (1999) noted, 'Coase's explanation of the theory of the firm is ultimately a co-ordination one: the firm is an institution that lowers the cost of qualitative co-ordination in a world of uncertainty'.

When considering the co-ordination mechanisms, the evolutionary approach emphasizes the tension between centralization and decentralization in the organizational learning process. Firms require both centralization and decentralization to operate successfully in a changing environment. Decentralization in the acquisition of knowledge is a source of diversity, of experimentation, and ultimately of learning. But, eventually, knowledge has to be made available for exploitation by the entire organization.

When agents differ with regard to their representations of the environment and their cognitive capabilities, a body of common (or collective) knowledge must exist, within the organization, which guarantees the coherence of the various learning processes. This is a prerequisite for efficient management of the competences. In order to cope with changing environments, the process of generation and modification of such a body of common knowledge, although fed by decentralized learning processes, has to undergo some forms of centralization, even if it is basically maintained by decentralized learning processes (Cohendet and Llerena 1991). Thus a tension inevitably arises between the forces that maintain the coherence of the organization, that is, the common knowledge and the forces that promote decentralized learning. The balance will depend on the characteristics of the learning processes and those of the environment in which the firm operates.

This cognitive perspective on the study of the firm has been taken by, among others, Cyert and March (1963), Cohen, March, and Olsen (1972), Cohen (1991), Loasby (1976, 1983), Eliasson (1990), Dosi and Marengo (1994) and Marengo (1996, 1994). Simulation exercises (Marengo 1994) have shown that, when flexibility and fine-tuning of the environment are required, local learning processes can be effective, provided higher hierarchical levels have the capability of pulling them together. Effective decentralization seems therefore to be based on bottom-up knowledge and information flows more than on horizontal information flows, as Aoki (1988) emphasized. Aoki's analysis tends to overestimate the importance of horizontal information flows: if learning receives its due emphasis, the main issue of decentralization becomes the possibility that operational units can influence such a process, but this depends on the organizational use of *ex post* information flows coming from such units, that is, on vertical, bottom-up information flows.[1]

In fact, these information-processing characteristics of the hierarchical and non-hierarchical modes of co-ordination have logical consequences for their efficiency in different environmental conditions; these results seem to provide support to the previously mentioned stylized facts about the Japanese economy. Aoki's (1986, 1990) and Itoh's (1987) main conclusions are (as expressed by Aoki):

When environments for planning (e.g. markets, engineering process, development opportunity) are stable, learning at the operational level may not add much information value to prior planning, and the sacrifice of economies of specialisation in operational activities may not be worthwhile. On the other hand, if environments are extremely volatile or uncertain, decentralised adaptation to environmental changes may yield highly unstable results. In both these two contrasting cases, the hierarchical mode may be superior in achieving the organizational goal. In the intermediate situation, however, where external environments are continually—but not too drastically—changing, the J-mode is superior. In this case, the information value created by learning and horizontal co-ordination at the operational level may more than compensate for the loss of efficiency due to the sacrifice of operational specialization. (Aoki 1990: 8–9)

---

[1] See Cohendet, Llerena, and Marengo (1994) for a detailed discussion of this point.

Thus, if the environment is stable, economies of specialization become essential and the hierarchical structure of co-ordination is likely to be the one that fosters the exploitation of such economies. If the environment is radically changing, the need for overall planning and broad resource reallocation might again require strict hierarchical co-ordination. On the other hand, if the environment is gradually changing and adjustment to varying consumer tastes becomes crucial, decentralized information processing might speed up the process of adaptation.

From a theoretical point of view, there are basically two divergent positions in the analysis of co-ordination mechanisms, depending on the nature of the cognitive behaviours of agents: at one extreme we can assume that agents' models of the world can differ, at the other extreme we can assume that one model of the world is shared by all the members of the organization. If the models of the world differ, *ex post* information coming from subordinates might necessitate a revision of the model maintained by the superordinate, but such a revision cannot be carried out within a Bayesian framework. This revision would imply a modification of the superordinate's state of knowledge, that is, a process of learning. For this reason, most neoclassical models which allow for some heterogeneity among agents are limited to the consideration of *ex ante* information flows, represented by the top-down transmission of plans. In this perspective diversity of representations of the world has only negative implications: it generates a chain of misinterpretation of the plans and loss of control and efficiency. The fact that diversity of representations could also have the positive effect of improving the process of plan revision, by making use of the *ex post* information coming from subordinates, is not taken into consideration. The team-theoretical tradition admits the use of *ex post* information, but it has to assume a perfect alignment of preferences, which are shared by the entire organization.

On the one hand, the 'loss of control' tradition ignores the problem of co-ordination, while the team-theoretical literature postulates co-ordination. From this viewpoint Aoki tried to move forward and examine the issue of co-ordination, by allowing horizontal information flows at the operational level, which can improve on the execution of plans. But learning is still ruled out, as was noted earlier.

3.2. Incentive Mechanisms

Incentive mechanisms are those mechanisms which provide a 'pay-off structure' in order to guide actions in a certain direction. They include control/monitoring mechanisms, which instead exert a direct check on actions and their results.

Over the past few decades, the theory of the firm has been dominated by the principal-agent theory and the transaction cost approach. These approaches have been increasingly preoccupied with the determination of incentive schemes in order to keep opportunism under control and to constrain the unproductive rent-seeking behaviour of economic agents, allowed by imperfect and asymmetric information. According to these theories, the divergence of preferences and objectives between principal and agent implies inefficient solutions. Asymmetries of information and conflicts of interests lead mainly to opportunistic behaviour (hidden actions, hidden information, free-riding, etc.).

If we adopt the point of view of the evolutionary theory of the firm, the optimal incentive schemes proposed by the principal–agent theory are not completely satisfactory. In a dynamic learning environment, the divergence of preferences can imply other effects than those generated by the strategic use of informational asymmetries. Cohen (1984) shows that unresolved diversity concerning preferences and objectives is conducive to higher performance in a disturbed environment where learning and creation of novelty are the main factors of success. The collective advantage of this aspect of diversity is also pointed out by Schelling (1978) in the prisoner's dilemma with n players. But to exploit the potential sources of performance, specific co-ordination mechanisms have to appear. The cross-fertilization of local learning processes should find an appropriate co-ordination scheme.

The main point in the standard principal–agent theory is the optimal allocation of efforts among tasks. This theory is in general reluctant to allow for co-operation between agents, or even for some local or horizontal co-ordination mechanisms. Furthermore, the objective is static efficiency. The information structure in such cases allows *ex ante* decisions and makes any co-ordination useless. But when the interest lies in organizational learning, the main objective is dynamic flexibility. Incentive schemes should therefore allow the organization to respond, continuously and in a satisfactory and co-ordinated way, to a turbulent environment. This necessity means that there must be an in-depth reconsideration of the setting-up of incentive schemes, asking, for example, how to stimulate local learning and diversity while maintaining co-ordination inside the firm; how to allow for trials and errors without diminishing the accountability of the final results; and how to ensure that the incentive scheme fosters co-ordination among actions and processes.

There are several dimensions along which the evolutionary theory of the firm considers incentive schemes: incentive schemes are one of the main driving forces of any learning process in so far as they provide an evaluation of the performance of trials in trial-and-error and more generally in all adaptive processes and thus they select the direction in which the learning process can or cannot move.[2]

---

[2] In learning models in artificial intelligence, providing appropriate incentive/reward mechanisms to intermediate steps in complex learning problems is one of the most difficult and delicate issues. For instance in programmes which teach how to play chess (but also in humans learning to

The overall picture is much more complicated than economists usually suggest in their models. First of all, there is not a single set of incentive mechanisms, but several which act at different levels of the organization, with different timings and with different intensity. Moreover, some of these incentives are strictly intraorganizational, whereas others are interorganizational and are implemented by market or quasi-market mechanisms.

This complex system of incentive mechanisms is one of the most important determinants of the evolutionary dynamics of firms, industries, and economic systems, but the comprehension of their dynamic properties is still largely underdeveloped.

A first point which certainly deserves more attention concerns the issue of the timing of selection and its balance with the intensity of the selection forces. Very tight and high-frequency selection forces have effective short-term systemic optimization properties, but are easily caught in local optima and allow for very little individual learning. We submit that one of the fundamental properties of intrafirm incentive mechanisms—which needs investigation—is the protection of parts of the organization from or the modulation exposure to market selection forces, as some form of relief from tight market selection is necessary to promote learning.

A second, and related, point concerns the role of internal incentive mechanisms in successfully managing change in such a complex system of closely interrelated elements as a modern organization. It is now well known in biology (cf. Kauffman 1993) that in systems characterized by high degrees of interrelatedness among components, the mere action of selection forces is very likely—all the more so as selection forces become tighter—to determine lock-in into local optima. Intraorganizational incentive schemes, which may be at least partly divorced from those implemented by decentralized markets, may be seen as more appropriate devices to drive search, adaptation, and learning in such systems (see, for very preliminary investigations along these lines, Levinthal 1997 and Marengo 1998).

Finally, this latter consideration impinges upon the issue of division of labour and the role of market and organizational incentive mechanisms in promoting it (for a similar argument see Pavitt 1997). Industry dynamics studies in the evolutionary tradition, and especially those within the so-called industry life cycle literature (cf. the survey in Klepper 1997) should more directly address the fundamental 'structural' issue of the division of labour between markets and hierarchies in the course of the evolution of industries and technologies (cf. Andersen 1998). Again some room is left for the entrepreneur to have an active role, defining his 'business conception' (Witt 1998: 166).

---

play chess) an 'objective' evaluation of a strategy comes only at the end of the game and is therefore of little use in guiding learning: temporary systems for evaluating moves and positions during the development of a game are necessary, but they are unavoidably imperfect, biased, and subject themselves to learning.

Furthermore the central question remains: what incentive mechanisms are the most effective in promoting which kind of learning? (It is quite feasible for effective incentives for learning not necessarily to coincide with effective incentives for resource allocation.) It then becomes important to differentiate between types of routines and rules. In this respect we might mention the work by Favereau (1993, 1995) on salary rules. He distinguishes between two types of rules and routines: the first type of rule is very precise, leaving no room for interpretation, while the second entails ambiguities ('interpretative ambiguity': Fransman 1994) and allows for interpretation, and, in fact, allows for the emergence of learning processes. Some persistent imperfection in the alignment of information and incentives is the main driving force behind the organizational learning process. Ambiguity, persistent information and knowledge asymmetries, and unresolved conflict: all of these phenomena hinder short-term efficiency but are vital elements for long-term learning performance. A world where all incentives are perfectly aligned and information asymmetries and conflicts are optimally resolved by appropriate contractual arrangements is a world where the organization has lost all opportunities for learning.

Finally, routines and rules possess another characteristic, through the implementation of mechanisms of incentive and authority. As Cohen *et al.* (1996: 670) point out, 'A crucial step when trying to bridge the evidence from cognitive psychology with organizational routines, involves an explicit account of the double nature of routines, both as problem-solving actions patterns and as mechanisms of governance and control'. Coriat and Dosi (1998: 121) discuss this issue in the case of Taylorism and 'Ohnism':

The set of 'Japanese' (or 'Ohnist') production routines does not only embody different channels of information processing but also distributes knowledge within the organization in ways remarkably different from the 'Tayloristic'/'Chandlerian' enterprise. And, at the same time, on the governance side, individual incentives to perform efficiently and learn are sustained (in the Japanese firm) by company-specific rank-hierarchies, delinked from functional assignments (Aoki, 1990).

On the other hand, it is clear that incentive schemes are themselves routines (or conventions) and are themselves subject to learning and adaptation. This 'learning the incentives' line of enquiry has been the object of some preliminary exploration in Coriat and Dosi (1998).

4. The Role of the Entrepreneur in the Evolutionary Theory of the Firm

As stated in the introduction to this chapter, when considering the Schumpeterian antecedents of the evolutionary approach, it is paradoxical that the entrepreneur is missing in the evolutionary literature on the firm. The reasons for this absence may be twofold.

First, it is common to distinguish Schumpeter I, author of *The Theory of Economic Development* (1934), from Schumpeter II, author of *Capitalism, Socialism and Democracy* (1942), the former using the 'entrepreneur':

as the innovative agent, breaking the equilibrium of the circular flows and the latter concerned by large firms where the economic development gradually becomes deperson-alized and automatized. Consequently, 'innovation is being reduced to routine. Technological progress is increasingly becoming the business of trained specialists who turn out what is required and make it work in predictable ways' (Schumpeter 1942: 132). (Hagedoorn 1996: 890.)

The entrepreneur as a change-agent had disappeared and innovation became a routine activity of large firms. At the same time, the link between the way these innovation activities were organized in the firm and their relevance for the external environment was lost.

The second reason can be found in the willingness to draw a strong parallel between the economic vision of evolution and other evolutionary disciplines: for the latter there is by definition no specific agent and no hierarchy responsible for regulating the evolutionary process. However, the economic version of evolutionary theory is not a pure one. The problem is, as mentioned earlier, that the economic evolutionary vision is founded on pure evolutionary principles, but also requires (at least in its ontogenic perspective) specific hypotheses about the cognitive capabilities of agents. That is the price to pay for founding the evolutionary theory of the firm on the concept of routines. Thus, within this hybrid theory, if we do not accept the idea that a specific agent is responsible for ensuring coherence between the evolutionary forces and the cognitive evolution of the agents within the firm, we are forced to confront many problems of indeterminacy. This situation will in turn prevent the theory from leading to relevant explanations of behaviour of firms and useful applications in real business life. The main types of indeterminacy that result from the evolutionary theory of the firm without an entrepreneur are discussed in the following pages.

4.1. Indeterminacy in Degree of Diversity

There is indeterminacy in the degree of diversity that a firm can afford. Since diversity not a free good, there should be an internal selection mechanism, in addition to the external ones, to shape the relevant routines. Let us imagine, for instance, that from a pure evolutionary perspective, all the routines of the organization were equally successful, with the result that the external environment did not reveal the hierarchy of choice between routines: in the absence of a specific agent in the firm responsible for selecting efficient routines where there are limited resources, the theory will lead to complete indeterminacy. Moreover, there is a need to delimit the efficient routines that the selection mechanisms have detected, that is, those that will be part of the core competence of the organization. External selection mechanisms cannot reveal what the core competences of an organization are. They can select an efficient basket of routines, each of them being a potential component of the core competence of the firm. But the domain of core competence has to be shaped according to a long-term strategy and a vision. The core domain is not simply a juxtaposition of efficient routines. It is the result of a coherent and patient process of building up of specific knowledge, which requires some idiosyncratic connections between different routines and bodies of knowledge. And such a building process requires a specific agent to be in charge of directing the process of creating and accumulating the resources of the firm.

4.2. 'Exploration' and 'Exploitation' Indeterminacy

There is a key distinction in the evolutionary theory of the firm between 'exploration' and 'exploitation' indeterminacy. As stated earlier, organizations always face the dilemma of concentrating their resources on the exploitation of the knowledge which is already available to them and the exploration of new possibilities. The theory calls for some internal agent to be in charge of tackling the problem of trade-off between exploration and exploitation, for there is no means within the sole routine conception of the firm for solving the indeterminacy. Another way to put this is to say that the dynamic capabilities of the firm should not become critical rigidities as time goes on. But as well as the need for the trade-off between exploitation and exploration, there is a specific need to 'allocate the intensity of learning' within the firm to the learning processes that appear strategic. As far as learning is concerned, as Cyert and March (1963) noticed, attention is a scarce resource within the firm. External selection mechanisms tell us nothing about where to focus the intensity of learning. There is critical room there for an agent to be in charge of controlling resources by allocating the intensity of learning processes according to the 'vision' of the firm defined by this agent. Cyert and March indicate, for instance, the process of 'sequential attention to goals' as one of the mechanisms for driving participants of the firm towards adopting a problem-solving perspective. But there could be many mechanisms.

4.3. Indeterminacy in Speed of Evolution

There could be some time discrepancies between the speed of evolution of the external environment (and in particular the speed with which external selection mechanisms function), and the speed of evolution of the cognitive processes at stake in the organization. It could take too long for the external environment to reveal if a given routine is to be successful, just as it could require too short a time for a firm to allocate the required resources and stimulate the learning processes that are needed to keep a given efficient routine active: without a specific agent in charge of 'tuning' the balance between different speeds of evolution, there are strong risks of indeterminacy.

As a consequence of the above indeterminacy in speed of evolution, a specific agent, responsible for creating resources, has to be reintroduced, to provide the missing link between the internal and the external environment of the firm. The introduction of this specific agent is in no way an artificial one: it follows logically from the theoretical premises of the evolutionary firm. This agent, which we call the 'entrepreneur', has to be an active element of the interaction between the environments, designing the internal organization and being proactive towards the external environment. Of course, this agent may be a collective one: the 'entrepreneur' is in fact the repository of the 'entrepreneurial spirits' of the organization. In one of his last works, Schumpeter (1949) considered an 'entrepreneurial function', saying of this:

the entrepreneurial function need not be embodied in a physical person and in particular in a single person. Every social environment has its own ways of filling the entrepreneurial function . . . Again the entrepreneurial function may be and often is filled cooperatively. With the development of the largest-scale corporations this has evidently become of major importance: aptitudes that no single individual combines can thus be built into a corporate personality; on the other hand, the constituent physical personalities must inevitably to some extent, and very often to a serious extent, interfere with each other. In many cases, therefore, it is difficult or even impossible to name an individual that acts as 'the entrepreneur' in a concern.   (Schumpeter 1949: 71–2; quoted by Hagedoorn 1996: 891.)[3]

In the context of this evolutionary perspective, we can now try to define more precisely the characteristics of this entrepreneurial function.

First, the entrepreneurial function has to be characterized by a specific 'asset', namely its 'dynamic capabilities' (Teece and Pisano 1994), that is, the ability to manage strategically the adaptation, the integration and the re-configuration of internal and external organizational skills, resources and functional competences towards changing environment; where time to market and timing is critical, the pace of innovation is accelerating, and the nature of future competition and markets is difficult to determine. This capability means that, in particular, the entrepreneur has a representation, not only of the possible evolution of his external environment, but also of the corresponding internal configuration, that is relevant for meeting the requirements of the external environment. In other words, the key entrepreneurial function in an evolutionary approach is to organize the process of matching the internal and the external environment.

---

[3] Schumpeter (1949: 71) even mentions the possible innovative role for organizations other than companies e.g. the role of state agencies, as 'collective entrepreneurial change-agents' (Hagedoorn 1996: 891).

Secondly, to be an active interface between the internal and external environments of the firm, the entrepreneur has to develop and diffuse a specific 'vision' of the firm's context and future. The vision of a firm is defined as the dominant set of beliefs in the firm regarding the firm's internal and external circumstances, the shape of things to come in the future, and, in the light of these factors, how the firm should 'play its cards'. Since vision depends on the particular construction of particular beliefs, vision is by definition always bounded. Bounded vision and the possibility of vision failure are, therefore, logical implications of the concept of vision (Fransman 1994). It is in accordance with this vision that the entrepreneur will position the firm in its environment, defining both its strategy and its internal structure.

It should be emphasized that when we say the entrepreneur should take an active position towards the external environment, we mean that he is able to influence the competitive context in which he evolves. Innovations of a different nature will allow him to determine, at least partially, the selection mechanisms at work outside the firm. In fact, he might endogenize the external environment, and build a flexible initiative (Amendola and Bruno 1990). This capacity for shaping the external environment is also a means to influence the evolution of industry. Expectations and visions are of major importance for understanding not only the evolution of firms, but also the evolution of industries.

Thirdly, the vision or the business conception, which is a primary entrepreneurial input (Witt 1998: 162), will affect the organization of the firm itself. In fact, we would argue at this point that there is, in this respect, room in the evolutionary approach for a hierarchy and a managerial component. Some authors (Loasby 1991; Witt 1998) have already reappraised the role of entrepreneurs, and underlined the role of leadership as setting out provision and enforcement frames in an evolutionary context.

Cognitive commonalities, that is, socially shared tacit knowledge including knowledge about social models of behavior, may emerge spontaneously from intense communication as an unintended collective outcome and may, as such, be difficult to influence.

Sometimes, however, the institutional set-up of the interactions assigns certain individuals a position in which they get a chance to shape the communication processes and thus to exert an influence on the collective outcome. The firm organization is a case in point. Indeed, the social-cognitive implications of bounded rationality are the key to the understanding why firms, as organizations, are able to achieve internal consistency and co-ordination of individual efforts.   (Witt 1998: 166.)

In the perspective of the firm as processor of knowledge, as proposed by the evolutionary approach, the role of the entrepreneur and the role of the manager tend to overlap to a large extent. This convergence of the role of entrepreneur and the role of manager is suggested in the literature (Philipsen 1998; Drucker 1995). In the case of evolutionary entrepreneurship, the very reason for convergence is that managing knowledge cannot be distinguished from conducting the process of creating of resources. There are in fact two main specific contexts in which the overlap is extreme.

In relation to the core competences of the firm, the role of entrepreneur and the role of manager overlap totally. The focus of the firm is entirely on the process of management of knowledge. The remainder of the activities of the firm (those that are not part of the core competences) seem to require a classical type of management which is independent of any entrepreneurial consideration. However, it has been shown (Cohendet and Llerena 1999; Amin and Cohendet 1999) that, in this case, there is a specific problem for the firm of coherence between the management of activities that are part of the core competences, and the other activities. This risk of incoherence supposes that the manager finds ways to diffuse his vision throughout the firm, so that there is at least partial overlap with the entrepreneurial role.

When the environment is constantly changing, the process of allocating resources cannot be separated from the process of creating resources. Thus the role of the entrepreneur and the role of the manager also converge in such turbulent cases.

If we accept the hypothesis that, in the evolutionary approach, the roles of entrepreneur and manager merge, we can then call the key actor in the evolutionary firm the 'entrepreneur/manager'. This central actor, as well as having the classical attributes of entrepreneur and manager that exist in the traditional theories of the firm, is able, under the evolutionary approach, to shape cognitive commonalities and socially shared patterns and frames of interpretation. By introducing the manager/entrepreneur as the key agent responsible for the process of creating resources in the evolutionary firm, we are now in a position to rethink the two main mechanisms, the co-ordination mechanisms and the incentive mechanisms, that we investigated earlier.

As far as co-ordination mechanisms are concerned, the introduction of the entrepreneur/manager clarifies how the process of centralization/decentralization takes place at the level of the firm. If he cannot by himself modify or change a given routine, the entrepreneur/manager may (directly or/and indirectly) influence routines at all levels of the firm. More precisely, he may shape the learning processes at stake within a given routine, or in different routines, by focusing attention on certain characteristics of these processes (by rewarding, for instance, exploration instead of exploitation). By developing common frames of representation he may obtain a certain degree of internal coherence, in particular in the sets of routines and rules that govern the internal structure of the firm. In this case the business conception plays the role of a shared pool of 'common knowledge', which Foss (1999: 1) saw as the founding element of leadership, defining the latter as 'the ability to resolve social dilemmas by influencing beliefs'. The building of a pool of common knowledge within the firm is one of the key tools

UWE LIBRARY SERVICES

that the entrepreneur/manager can control. Not only can he define the depth of the common knowledge, he can also orient the form the common knowledge takes in the enterprise. (The common knowledge could be wholly identified with the 'culture of the firm', or rather through the type of structure of information that is implemented in the firm.) However, as he contributes to shaping the common knowledge of the firm, he also implicitly defines *a contrario* what remain 'ambiguous' in the firm, in the sense used by March and Olsen (1978). The degree of ambiguity of the organization is, in the dynamic perspective, associated with the margin of interpretation of the members of the firm. This which is to a certain extent associated (as noted earlier), with the firm's potential for creativity (provided that the pool of common knowledge is sufficiently strong). The efficiency of the entrepreneur/manager in relation to the co-ordination mechanisms will thus to a large extent result in fine-tuning common knowledge and ambiguity.

When we turn to incentive mechanisms, we see that the explicit introduction of a hierarchy in the evolutionary theory of the firm helps to clarify how incentive schemes are set up. These additional characteristics of entrepreneurs/ managers demand more comprehensive incentives than those provided for in the pure transaction and incentive-oriented approaches.[4] What becomes clear when we take into account the role of the entrepreneur/manager, as detailed above, is that this actor brings with him—besides the classical incentive mechanisms— another type of incentive mechanism: one that has to do with the ways in which the entrepreneur/manager may diffuse his vision through the firm. The leadership quality (or 'business conception') of the entrepreneur/manager 'may induce the employees to believe in the success of the entire venture in which they are participating. It may also promise to be personally rewarding in terms of qualification enhancements, working conditions, career options and remuneration' (Witt 1998: 168).

When we first consider the coherence between co-ordination and incentive mechanisms, the incentive-based and transaction costs approaches appear to have significant advantages over evolutionary ones, if we apply them to real-life situations such as relationships between shareholders and managers on the one hand, and managers and employees on the other. They make explicit who, in a given context, sets the incentive schemes and for what reasons, and the extent to

---

[4] It can also be argued, although this is beyond the scope of this chapter, that there is room for shareholders in the evolutionary scene. From this perspective, it must be realized that shareholders do not generally comprise a multitude of small investors interested only in maximizing their returns. (If this were the case the evolutionary approach would be meaningless.) For the majority of shares, shareholders comprise a small nucleus of quite stable companies, each of which seeks a firm that designs its core competences in such a way that they are compatible with (if not complementary to) its own core competences. From this perspective, each member of the nucleus can be considered as a specific kind of 'principal' *vis-à-vis* an 'agent'-manager who is responsible for shaping the core competences of the firm.

which the firm is centralized or decentralized. In the evolutionary approach, on the other hand, it is often said that the role of hierarchy is generally hidden by the emphasis put on routines, and the influence of shareholders is not even mentioned. This emphasis constitutes *a priori* a major obstacle to the integration of incentive mechanisms in the framework of the evolutionary approach. We have tried to show that this is not the case: the introduction of the evolutionary entrepreneur leads to a detailed reconsideration of the main characteristics of the firm, including the key question of incentive mechanisms.

5. Conclusions

In this exploratory chapter, we have tried to show that, in an evolutionary perspective of the firm, not only is there room for the entrepreneur, but the entrepreneur plays the central role as an agent of change. This agent of change has some traits in common with the agent Schumpeter introduced in his theory of innovation. However, the evolutionary entrepreneur also differs from the Schumpeterian one. While the Schumpeterian entrepreneur introduces novelty by breaking the circular flow, the entrepreneur in the evolutionary theory of the firm prepares and shapes the cognitive process leading to novelty, by building (or imagining) new business conceptions, managing the evolution of the knowledge base of the firm, and shaping its internal and external environments according to his vision.[5]

If we go beyond the comparison with the Schumpeterian conception, we see that the entrepreneur in the evolutionary theory of the firm has some specific and original traits not found in other theoretical approaches.

Knight (1921) conceived of the entrepreneur as being inherently associated with the existence of uncertainty. For Knight, in a context of uncertainty, if the role of producers is to take responsibility for forecasting the consumer's wants, 'in a second place, the work of forecasting and at the same time a large part of the technological direction of control and production are still further concentrated upon a very narrow class of the producers, and will meet a new economic function, the entrepreneur' (Knight 1921: 268). Even if Schumpeter was right to criticize Knight for not having distinguished between the role of the entrepreneur and that of the resource owner of the firm, it seems that Knight's conception suggests some overlapping between the roles of entrepreneur and manager. The Knightian entrepreneur, who is focused on facing uncertainty, has no vision and no sense of knowledge management; however he shares with the evolutionary

---

[5] In this respect, the evolutionary approach to the firm does not limit the 'firm as an organization dedicated to the planning of markets. The firm's planning is based upon a synthesis of information. An initial synthesis of the information improvised by its entrepreneurial founder is followed by recurrent syntheses effected more routinely by its managerial organization' (Casson 1997: 5). It places 'knowledge processing' at the core of the analysis.

entrepreneur the characteristic of being an interface between the internal organization and the external environment. As Kirzner wrote:

Now I choose . . . to label that element of alertness to possible newly worthwhile goals
and to possible newly available resources . . . the entrepreneurial element in decision
making. It is this entrepreneurial element that is responsible for our understanding of
human action as active, creative, and human rather than as passive, automatic and
mechanical   (Kirzner 1973: 35).

The pursuing of opportunities through alertness is a trait that the evolutionary
entrepreneur shares with the Kirznerian entrepreneur. However, Kirzner focuses
only on the imperfect distribution of information, whereas the evolutionary
entrepreneur is mainly concerned with the distribution and creation of knowledge.

   Other similarities can be found between the evolutionary entrepreneur and
Casson's conception of the entrepreneur (as 'someone who specializes in making
judgemental decisions about the co-ordination of scarce resources', Casson 1982:
23), or Leibenstein's conception (1968), which views the entrepreneur as an
agent who solves the problems caused by X-inefficiencies. However, as
mentioned earlier, our view of the entrepreneur has very close similarities with
the recent stream of literature investigating the overlap between the entrepreneur
and the manager (Philipsen 1998; Witt 1998). But our specific conviction,
which we have tried to demonstrate in this chapter, is that the very nature of the
evolutionary entrepreneur, as the 'agent of change', results from the specific need
to deal with knowledge and not just with pure information.

References

AMENDOLA, M., and S. BRUNO 1990. 'The behaviour of the innovative firms: relations
   to the environment', *Research Policy* 19: 419–33.
AMIN, A., and P. COHENDET 1999. 'Leaning and adaptation in decentralized business
   networks', *Space and Society* July (forthcoming).
ANDERSEN, E. S. 1998. 'The evolution of the organization of industry', Aalborg
   University, DRUID Working Paper 98-13.
AOKI, M. 1986. 'Horizontal vs. vertical information structure of the firm', *American
   Economic Review* 76: 971–83.
—— 1988. *Information, Incentives and Bargaining in the Japanese Economy*. Cambridge:
   Cambridge University Press.
—— 1990. 'Toward an economic model of the Japanese firm', *Journal of Economic
   Literature* 28: 1–27.
AVADIKYAN, A., P. COHENDET, and P. LLERENA 1995. 'Coherence, diversity of asset:
   Towards an evolutionary approach', *Revue International de Systémique* 7(5): 505–31.
CASSON, M. 1982. '*The Entrepreneur. An Economic Theory*. Oxford: Martin Robertson.
—— 1997. *Information and Organization: A New Perspective on the Theory of the Firm*.
   Oxford: Oxford University Press.

COHEN, M. D. 1984. 'Conflict and complexity: Goal diversity and organizational search effectiveness', *American Political Science Review* 78: 435–51.

—— 1991. 'Individual learning and organizational routine: Emerging connections', *Organization Science* 2: 135–9.

—— J. G. MARCH, and J. P. OLSEN 1972. 'A garbage can model of organizational choice', *Administrative Sciences Quarterly* 17: 1–25.

—— R. BURKHART, G. DOSI, M. EGIDI, L. MARENGO, M. WARGLIEN, and S. WINTER 1996. 'Routines and other recurring action patterns of organizations: contemporary research issues', *Industrial and Corporate Change* 5(3): 653–98.

COHENDET, P., and P. LLERENA 1991. 'Integration and learning processes', in P. Bourgine and B. Walliser, eds. *Economics and Artificial Intelligence*. Oxford: Pergamon Press.

—— 1999. 'La conception de la firme comme processeur de connaissances', *Revue d'Economie Industrielle* 88(2): 211–36.

—— and M. MARENGO 1994. 'Learning and organizational structure in evolutionary models of the firm', Paper presented to EUNETIC Conference, European Parliament, Strasbourg, October.

—— F. KERN, B. MEHMANPAZIR, and F. MUNIER 1997. 'Routines, structures of governance and knowledge-creating processes', BETA, Strasbourg, mimeo.

CORIAT, B., and G. DOSI 1998. 'Learning how to govern and learning how to solve problems: on the coevolution of competences, conflicts and organizational routines', in A. D. Chandler Jr., P. Hagström, and Ö. Sölvell, eds., *The Dynamic Firm: The Role of Technology, Strategy, Organization and Regions*. Oxford: Oxford University Press, 103–33.

—— and O. WEINSTEIN 1995. *Les nouvelles théories de l'entreprise*. Paris: Le Livre de Poche.

CRÉMER, J. 1993. 'Corporate culture and shared knowledge', *Industrial and Corporate Change* 2(3): 351–86.

CYERT, R. M., and J. G. MARCH 1963. *A Behavioural Theory of the Firm*. Englewood Cliffs, NJ: Prentice Hall.

DOSI, G., and L. MARENGO 1994. 'Toward a theory of organizational competences', in R. W. England, ed., *Evolutionary Concepts in Contemporary Economics*. Ann Abor, MI: Michigan University Press.

DRUCKER, PETER F. 1995. *Managing in a Time of Great Change*. Oxford: Butterworth Heinemann.

ELIASSON, G. 1990. 'The firm as a competent team', *Journal of Economic Behaviour and Organization* 13: 275–98.

FAVEREAU, O. 1993. 'Suggestions pour reconstruire la théorie du salaire sur une théorie des règles', WP Laetix, University of Paris X, April.

—— 1995. 'Apprentissage collectif et co-ordination par les règles: application à la théorie des salaires', in N. Lazaric and J. M. Monnier, eds., *Co-ordination économique et apprentissage des firmes*. Paris: Economica, 23–38.

FOSS N. J. 1996. 'Evolutionary theories of the firm: reconstruction and relations to contractual theories', forthcoming in K. Dodfer, ed., *Foundations of Evolutionary Economics*. Boston: Kluwer, 1999.

—— 1999. 'Understanding leadership: a co-ordination theory', DRUID Working Paper 99-3, March.

FRANSMAN, M. 1994. 'Information, knowledge, vision and theories of the firm', *Industrial and Corporate Change* 3(3): 713–57.

HAGEDOORN, J. 1996. 'Innovation and entrepreneurship: Schumpeter revisited', *Industrial and Corporate Change* 5(3): 883–96.

ITOH, H. 1987. 'Information processing capacities of the firm', *Journal of the Japanese and International Economies* 1: 299–326.

KAUFFMAN, S. A. 1993. *The Origins of Order. Self-Organization and Selection in Evolution.* New York and Oxford: Oxford University Press.

KIRZNER, I. 1973. *Competition and Entrepreneurship.* Chicago: Chicago University Press.

KLEPPER, S. 1997. 'Industry life cycles', *Industrial and Corporate Change* 6: 145–81.

KNIGHT, F. 1921, 1985. *Risk, Uncertainty and Profit.* Chicago: University of Chicago Press.

KREPS, D. 1992. 'Corporate culture and economic theory', in J. Alt and K. Shepsle, eds., *Positive Perspectives on Political Economy.* Cambridge: Cambridge University Press.

LANGLOIS, R., and N. FOSS 1996. 'Capabilities and governance: The rebirth of production in the theory of economic organization', *Kyklos* 52(2): 201–18.

LEIBENSTEIN, H. 1968. 'Entrepreneurship and development', *American Economic Review* 58: 72–83.

LEVINTHAL, D. 1997. 'Adaptation on rugged landscapes', *Management Science* 43: 934–50.

LOASBY, B. J. 1976. *Choice, Complexity and Ignorance.* Cambridge: Cambridge University Press.

—— 1983. 'Knowledge, learning and the enterprise', in J. Wiseman, ed., *Beyond Positive Economics?* London: Macmillan, 104–21.

—— 1991. *Equilibrium and Evolution: An Exploration of Connecting Principles in Economics.* Manchester: Manchester University Press.

MARCH, J. G. 1991. 'Exploration and exploitation in organizational learning', *Organization Science* 10(1): 71–87.

—— and J. P. OLSEN 1978. *Ambiguity and Choice in Organizations.* Bergen: Universitetsforlaget.

MARENGO, L. 1994. 'Knowledge distribution and co-ordination in organizations: On some social aspects of the exploration vs. exploitation trade-off', *Revue Internationale de Systémique* 7: 553–71.

—— 1996. 'Structure, competence and learning in an adaptive model of the firm', in G. Dosi and F. Malerba, eds., *Organization and Strategy in the Evolution of the Enterprise.* London: Macmillan, 124–54.

—— 1998. 'Interdependencies and division of labour in problem-solving technologies', paper presented at the DRUID Conference, 'Competences, Governance and Entrepreneurship', Bornholm, 9–11 June.

NELSON, R. R. and S. G. WINTER 1982. *An Evolutionary Theory of Economic Change.* Cambridge, MA: Harvard University Press.

PAVITT, K. 1997. 'Technologies, products and organization in the innovative firm: what Adam Smith tells us and Joseph Schumpeter doesn't', mimeo, SPRU, September, presented at the DRUID Conference, 'Competences, Governance and Entrepreneurship', Bornholm, 9–11 June 1998.

PHILIPSEN, KRISTIAN 1998. 'Entrepreneurship as organizing', presented at the DRUID Conference, 'Competences, Governance and Entrepreneurship', Bornholm, 9–11 June.

SCHELLING, T. 1978. *Micromotives and Macrobehavior*, New York: W. W. Norton.

SCHUMPETER, J. A. 1934, 1980. *The Theory of Economic Development*. London: Oxford University Press.

—— 1942, 1975. *Capitalism, Socialism and Democracy*. New York: Harper & Row.

—— 1949. *Economic Theory and Entrepreneurial History—Change and the Entrepreneur; Postulates and Patterns for Entrepreneurial History*. Cambridge, MA: Harvard University Press.

TEECE, D. J. 1988. 'Technological change and the nature of the firm', in G. Dosi, C. Freeman, R. Nelson, G. Silverberg, and L. Soete, eds., *Technical Change and Economic Theory*. London: Pinter, 256–81.

—— and PISANO, G. 1994. 'The dynamic capabilities of firms: an introduction', *Industrial and Corporate Change* 3: 537–56.

WITT, U. 1998. 'Imagination and leadership: The neglected dimension of the evolutionary theory of the firm', *Journal of Economic Behaviour and Organization* 35: 161–77.

6

An Entrepreneurial Theory of the Firm

MARK CASSON

1. Information and Co-ordination

The modern theory of the firm addresses four main issues; they concern:

- the boundaries of the firm;
- the internal organization of the firm;
- the formation, growth, and diversification of the firm; and
- the role of the entrepreneur.

These issues are all related, but the relationships between them are not always clear. This chapter argues that the fourth issue—the role of the entrepreneur—is the most fundamental. The theory of the entrepreneur has a distinguished pedigree in the work of Cantillon (1755), Say (1803), and Knight (1921), but its contribution to the theory of the firm has often been ignored. This is unfortunate, because theories that neglect the entrepreneurial dimension can offer only a partial explanation of the behaviour of the firm. Apparent conflicts between some of the more recent theories of the firm—such as transaction cost theories (Williamson 1985; North 1981) and resource-based theories (Foss 1997)—can be traced to a common failure to take full account of the entrepreneur. In providing a modern exposition of the entrepreneurial theory of the firm, therefore, this chapter also contributes to the debate over the relative merits of other theories.

The conventional view of the real economy is highly materialistic, and the legacy of this view is still reflected in the theory of the firm. It emphasizes the flow of tangible resources such as physical products, rather than intangible resources such as information. It fails to emphasize sufficiently that the co-ordination of tangible flows requires major flows of information to support it (Granovetter 1985). A substantial proportion of the output of an advanced economy is intangible, and most of this is accounted for by information in its various forms (Eliasson, Folster, Lindberg, Pousette, and Taymaz 1990). Some information is consumed directly—as entertainment for example—but most of the information used in business has purely instrumental value. It is not a final product, but an intermediate product—for example technological know-how generated by research and development. It is often supposed that information is ultimately factual, but this is not so. Theories as well as facts are informative, for without a theory to interpret it a fact has no meaning. Values are an important form of information too (Casson 1991).

The principal instrumental use of information is for co-ordination. A high proportion of clerical and administrative workers are involved, directly or indirectly, in co-ordination. This includes professionals working in the service sector, and managers in manufacturing firms responsible for marketing, purchasing, personnel, and accounting. Tangible assets are involved in co-ordination as well. Offices are used to accommodate clerical workers, paper-based filing systems aid memory, while computers support not only memory, but communication and decision making too. Industries such as banking, advertising, and travel agencies are almost entirely devoted to co-ordination of one kind or another.

Information resembles an ordinary product in some ways, but is crucially different in others, as indicated in Table 6.1. Like ordinary products, it flows across space and time along channels created for this purpose. These channels have a network structure. Like an ordinary durable good, information is both a stock (when stored in memory) and a flow (when communicated as news to other people).

Co-ordination may be defined as an improvement in the allocation of resources. It is assumed that co-ordination is normally effected by a specialist co-ordinator. Under certain conditions this specialist co-ordinator can be identified as an entrepreneur (Casson 1982). If no attempt were made at co-ordination then the allocation of resources would remain unchanged. Co-ordination is therefore a 'pro-active' form of decision making in which the decision maker rejects the passive option of maintaining the status quo. A change in the use of any one resource will normally require an accommodating change in the use of some other resource. Thus if one resource produces less of one output and more of another, then some other resource will have to substitute in favour of the more abundant resource and against the scarcer one. On this view, co-ordination consists of interrelated substitutions.

A market is a web of potential linkages between alternative sources of supply and demand. Because of transport costs and transaction costs, these alternatives are not perfect substitutes for each other. Co-ordination alters the volume of trade along each linkage. By reducing some volumes to zero, and increasing others from zero, it replaces one set of linkages with another. This means that the interrelated substitutions consist of pairs of individuals switching from one linkage to another.

Co-ordination can raise and lower the volume of trade in a quite dramatic way. New markets are brought into existence by raising volumes to positive levels for the first time, while existing markets are eliminated by reducing volumes to zero. Co-ordination does not therefore merely adjust the volume of trade within a given set of markets; it brings new markets to life through innovation, and eliminates other markets through obsolescence.

TABLE 6.1. Key characteristics of information

Type of information	Characteristics
Public good	Access to information can be extended without limit (though communication costs will be incurred in the process—see below).
Discretionary exclusion	Unlike some public goods, such as defence, information does not have to be shared with everyone. Thus information can, in principle, be privately appropriated.
Property rights difficult to enforce	Appropriation is difficult because legal rights to the exploitation of information (e.g. patents) are difficult to enforce. This means that markets in information are difficult to operate. Indeed, the concept of a market in information seems strange to many people precisely because so few markets of this type actually exist.
Quality assurance problems are acute	Information can be kept secret, but selling secrets is difficult because it is difficult for the purchaser to assess their quality. Information can be either true or false. Corroborative evidence is often difficult to obtain because such evidence would give the seller's secret away.
Information is very heterogeneous	A vast amount of information is required to specify all the spatial, temporal, and personal details of an economic situation. If every item of information had a separate market then the number of markets would be enormous.
Communication is costly	Communication costs increase with geographical distance, psychic distance, and the speed required. Some modes have high fixed costs and low variable costs (e.g. broadcasting) while others have low fixed costs and high variable costs (e.g. face-to-face conversation).
Access to information is unequal	Primary sources of information are widely dispersed, and people cannot be in several places at the same time. Communication costs impede the dissemination of information from one place to another. Thus everyone tends to have a unique set of information at their disposal.
How produced	Information is produced by observation and interpretation, rather than by the physical transformation of raw materials. Since the costs of discovery cannot be recovered from direct sales, they have to be appropriated in other ways instead. This appropriation problem is a crucial building-block for a comprehensive theory of the firm.

2. Volatility

Why is co-ordination a continuing activity, rather than just a once-for-all activity required to set the economy up? The answer lies in volatility. In the absence of volatility, co-ordination would eventually shift the economy into a state of equilibrium, where it would remain indefinitely. No new information would need to be collected because everything would remain exactly the same as before. By contrast, volatility brings change, which means that any allocation of resources will in time become obsolete. Attempts to maintain the status quo in the face of changing conditions will cause the system to degenerate into anarchy.

Because co-ordination needs to be continuous, information flow has to be continuous as well.

Because co-ordination involves interrelated substitutions, a single observation is normally insufficient to identify a co-ordination opportunity. Several items of information are normally required, one relating to each substitution. These observations need to be synthesized in order to identify a co-ordination opportunity. Synthesis is more than just aggregation. To effect a meaningful synthesis, some kind of theory or mental model of the environment is required. Without some sort of theory it is difficult to decide what sort of observations need to be made. Since theories require imagination, however, there may sometimes be no theory available for this purpose. In other cases, theories may proliferate. On many topics, the set of historical and experimental observations so far accumulated is insufficient to determine which of several theories is correct. Indeed, the less factual evidence there is available, the greater is the scope for proliferation of theory.

Observations are costly. Some observation that could be made may not be made, simply because the cost is too high. This has two effects. The first is that some co-ordination plans may be developed on the basis of very limited information. The benefits of wider synthesis are traded off against savings in observation costs. The second is that observations become less frequent, so that the information used in co-ordination becomes, on average, more out of date. In addition, the desire to economize on costs of synthesis means that co-ordination plans are produced less frequently too. Less attempt is made to change the status quo.

The information used in co-ordination is often highly subjective. It is not only theories that can be in error, but observations too. What is usually observed is a symptom of an underlying situation which cannot itself be directly observed. While symptoms are correlated with the underlying situation, the correlation is not perfect, and mistakes can therefore be made. Moreover, since no one can observe the true situation, but only different symptoms of it, disagreements over interpretation of an observation are difficult to resolve.

Not all the errors that are made are unavoidable, though. Some may be the result of the incompetence of the observer. Others may be a consequence of deliberate negligence. These problems can be tackled through appropriate selection and motivation, but only partial solutions can normally be found.

An individual co-ordinator can obtain information not only at first hand, by direct observation, but also at second hand, through communication with other people. Communication can result in delays and in misunderstanding. It also provides opportunities for deceit. Embedding communication within an institutional framework helps to speed up communication, reduce misunderstandings, and provide moral checks on deceit.

Errors in observation, communication, and synthesis show that a co-ordination plan can be far from perfect. A mistaken co-ordination plan can make matters worse. In a volatile economy there are thus two main reasons for co-ordination failure. One is that new co-ordination plans are developed only intermittently, so that the status quo is preserved after changes have occurred. The other is that new co-ordination plans are imperfect, and may even be so misconceived as to make the situation worse. The slower the development of plans, and the greater the risk of error in them, the lower is the degree of co-ordination that prevails, on average, at any given time, and the more inefficiently the economy performs as a result.

3. Observation and Synthesis: A Flexible Division of Labour Applied to Co-ordination

The trade-off between information cost and co-ordination error can be improved by implementing a division of labour in which people specialize in those aspects of information processing which they do best. Thus some people are more accurate observers than others, whereas synthesizing ability is often quite scarce. Specialization incurs additional communication costs, however. Figure 6.1 illustrates a combination of a vertical specialization between observation and synthesis and horizontal specialization between different observers. Each observer monitors a different source of information. The sources are embedded in the economy, and are differentiated by location, subject-matter, and so on. There is two-way communication between the observers and the synthesizer—the observers report their findings to the synthesizer and the synthesizer passes down instructions about how to implement his co-ordination plan (see the discussion of authority relations in section 9 below).

The centralization of decision making on a single synthesizer creates problems,

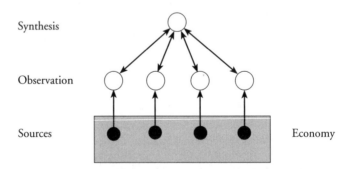

Figure 6.1. Centralized synthesis with vertical division of labour between observation and synthesis and horizontal division of labour in observation

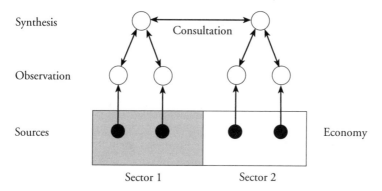

Figure 6.2. Rigid sectoral division of labour in synthesis

however. Communication costs are very high, and the synthesizer is likely to be 'overloaded' by a mass of detail, and unable to filter out the really important information.

A division of labour can also be implemented between synthesizers. This can be effected in either a rigid or a flexible way. A rigid system of specialization is illustrated in Figure 6.2. Each synthesizer is given responsibility for a particular sector of the economy. On this basis, each monitors separate sources of information. Each synthesizer uses local information sources, and so avoids the use of the distant sources which a single synthesizer must employ.

Decentralization creates its own set of problems. The different sectors of the economy are not totally isolated from each other, but are linked by product flows, so that each sectoral co-ordination plan has knock-on effects on the other. One solution is to buffer the different sectors against each other by investing in inventories and idle capacity. Buffers do not separate different sectors on a permanent basis, however; they only 'buy time' before the 'knock-on' effects of a change in any given sector are felt elsewhere. The alternative solution is for the synthesizers to share provisional plans with one another, as indicated in the figure. These plans are reconciled through a process of revision. However, the plans communicated between the synthesizers are complex, and so communication costs may quickly escalate as the revision process iterates.

While a combination of buffering and revision goes a long way to eliminating inconsistencies between different partial plans, it is inefficient to try to eliminate them altogether. Inconsistencies will remain, which create future opportunities for co-ordination. The process of co-ordination is therefore myopic, but in the long run it is myopic to an optimal degree. It trades off the risk of co-ordination failure against inventory costs, capacity costs, and the costs of communication.

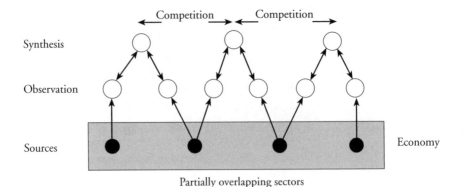

Figure 6.3. Flexible decentralization

Partial planning does not have to be implemented rigidly on a sectoral basis, however. Partial plans can be allowed to overlap. Indeed, rival plans can be produced for the same sector. The obvious weakness is that a large amount of duplication of synthesis is tolerated. A synthesis is a bundle of information, and information, as noted in Table 6.1, is a public good. A single synthesis can therefore be shared without limit. This suggests that replication of synthesis is wasteful. Replication would seem to be warranted only when distance-related communication costs are high, and even then only if the replicators are suitably dispersed.

This objection loses much of its force, however, when synthesis is liable to error. Not every synthesizer has access to the same information, and so each synthesis is likely to be different. Even where the information is the same, the interpretation of it may be different because different synthesizers use different theories and no one knows which theory is right. This is the situation illustrated in Figure 6.3. Each synthesizer uses a distinctive information set, which is incomplete. He must make a judgement about what the missing information would be like. Different synthesizers formulate different plans because they use different information, and because they hold different theories about what the information they are missing is likely to be. The co-ordination plan that they devise will normally apply to some subset of the economy. The same synthesizer may develop plans relating to different sectors, or different groups of activities, on different occasions, depending upon what his information sources suggest to him.

4. Recruitment and Motivation of Synthesizers

Synthesis requires considerable time and effort, but the potential rewards—both social and private—are high. Attracting the right sort of person to synthesis is crucial for the performance of the economy.

Under rigid decentralization, each synthesizer is assigned a monopoly of co-ordination within a certain sector by the state authorities. It is undesirable to allow him to appropriate large monopoly rents for himself. He is therefore likely to be paid a fixed salary. Potential candidates compete for these posts. The higher the salary, the larger the field is likely to be. The number of competent applicants is likely to be higher as well, but screening them out from the others is difficult because the relevant qualities are often hidden. It requires considerable judgement to pick the best applicant.

Under flexible decentralization, synthesizers are not selected by other people and appointed to predetermined roles. Rather, synthesizers volunteer for their role. Indeed, they are free to set-up and define their role for themselves. Each synthesizer can back his own judgement if he wishes. Each individual has an initial endowment of resources, and if these are not sufficient then the individual can borrow the use of more resources from other people. Synthesizers exchange these resources for the resources required to implement their co-ordination plan.

If different synthesizers plan to use the same resources in different ways then they must compete. Prices will be bid up until all but one of the synthesizers drop out because their plans are no longer profitable. The maximum reward that can be appropriated by the successful co-ordinator is equal to the excess of the value of his plan over the value of the next best plan being promoted at the same time. (This refers, of course, to the value of the plan as anticipated by the co-ordinator, which may be different from what the value actually turns out to be.) If no new plans are being promoted, then the reward is equal to the excess of the value of the plan over the value of the status quo. The profit accruing to the successful synthesizer provides a natural method of reward. This is the basis of the free enterprise system.

Flexible decentralization works better than rigid decentralization when there is a high probability that any given co-ordination plan will be mistaken. When there is general recognition that mistakes are likely then it is best to have several alternatives to choose from. All the entrepreneurs who promote rival plans believe that they are right and the others are wrong. Other things being equal, it is the most optimistic and self-confident entrepreneur who will prevail. This entrepreneur takes a more favourable view of the economic environment than others, and is therefore prepared to pay more for the resources for which they are all competing. Being self-confident, the entrepreneur does not discount these valuations—because it is possible that he may be wrong. Because his firm actually pays for the resources it uses, the successful entrepreneur insures the less optimistic against his own misjudgement, for if he is wrong then his firm bears the loss. Competition therefore forces entrepreneurs to gamble on their own optimistic judgements by insuring others against the possibility that they are wrong.

5. Prospecting for Opportunities under Flexible Decentralization

To avoid wasteful duplication of discovery, and losing out through competition, different synthesizers need to focus their search for co-ordination opportunities in different regions of 'information space' (Boisot 1995). Unfortunately, however, this space is not 'mapped out' in the same way as geographical space. This means that agreements to divide up the space between different searchers are difficult to specify (let alone enforce—see the discussion of patents in section 10 below). The best that can be expected is for individuals to recognize their neighbours and 'keep their distance' from them. If opportunities are equally likely to be discovered anywhere in information space then this generates a tendency to an equilibrium in which searchers are uniformly distributed over this space. In practice, there are likely to be widely held beliefs that potential discoveries are particularly dense in certain areas. Beliefs of this kind, which are common to most members of a group, are part of its culture. The most successful searchers are likely to be competent 'deviants' who correctly recognize mistakes in these beliefs, and search in other areas instead. The majority believe that the deviants know less than they do about where discoveries are likely to be made, and this acts as a natural 'barrier to entry' into the deviants' fields of search. In fact, the competent deviants may know more than the average person does. Once the deviants succeed, and the average people become aware of their own mistake, the deviants have more difficulty maintaining their lead because they have become leaders of the new majority, and face competition from others as a result.

The threat of competition is intensified by the fact that the field is likely to be too crowded in the first place. This is a special case of the 'tragedy of the commons' applied to undiscovered opportunities as an unappropriated resource. The expected number of opportunities discovered in any period increases with the number of prospectors, but at a diminishing rate. Marginal returns to the number of prospectors eventually fall to zero. But average returns remain positive at this point. When a new entrant goes prospecting for a synthesis, the incumbents crowd together more closely in order to keep the same distance from the incumbent as they do from each other. Even if the new entrant adds nothing to the expected number of discoveries, therefore, he still receives a positive return. Because he is treated the same as everyone else, he receives the average return. His entry is subsidized by the redistribution of territory from incumbent searchers.

The problem is not quite so serious as this suggests because searchers differ in their comparative and absolute advantage. Many people stay out because their expected earnings are higher in other work, so the average return never falls to zero. Those who are very good at search snap up opportunities before others, and earn a reward that is well above the average. The ablest synthesizers continue to be attracted to the field, therefore, but there may be a surplus of less able synthe-sizers who are not very good at anything at all.

6. Transaction Costs and Market Institutions

The system of flexible decentralization described above relies heavily on volun-tary transactions. Transactions need to be easy for this system to work well. But in practice, transactions can be costly. An efficient economy minimizes the trans-action costs of supporting a given set of transactions. Devices for reducing trans-action costs are a prominent feature of the market economy, and a significant influence on the behaviour of the firms within it. Transaction costs are of two main kinds: information cost and appropriation cost. Appropriation costs are incurred as a consequence of strategic behaviour by the other party—notably, bluffing in negotiations before the contract is made, and default in delivery after the contract has been made. Bluffing results in the other party appropriating more of the 'gains from trade' than would otherwise be the case. Default is a form of theft, whereby the other party fails to honour their side of the deal.

Information costs are incurred in making contact with the other party to begin with, specifying the property rights to be exchanged, carrying on the nego-tiations, and arranging the logistics of delivery. Additional costs of investigation may be incurred in order to reduce appropriation costs. Thus alternative trading opportunities available to the other party may be investigated in order to assess whether they are bluffing, and the reputation of the other party may be investi-gated to discover whether they are likely to default.

Communication costs can be reduced by the co-ordinator acting as an infor-mation hub. Because many different transactors are involved in the implemen-tation of a typical co-ordination plan, it is uneconomic to set-up the plan through multilateral negotiations involving all the parties. The co-ordinator transacts separately with each party instead. Bilateral negotiations economize on communication costs. A firm may be established for this purpose. It becomes a nexus of contracts. The contracts can be negotiated sequentially, to avoid an information overload for the co-ordinator, although a co-ordinator following such a procedure runs the risk that a deal negotiated early on may be regretted later. Use of a firm as a legal shell means that the nexus does not disintegrate when the co-ordinator dies.

If contracts involve barter then the co-ordinator will be involved in handling many different goods in order to achieve the requisite 'double coincidence of wants' with each party. Money is therefore useful as a medium of exchange, and the state can help by providing a stable supply of currency in suitable denom-inations. The co-ordinator can then concentrate on handling only those goods in which he has an information advantage. He can reduce information costs by using money as a unit of account as well.

The bundling of rights is another important strategy for reducing transaction costs. Because co-ordination consists of interrelated substitutions, a co-ordination plan creates a set of demands and supplies for specific services. The specificity of the services expresses the definiteness of the plan proposed. The degree of specificity is increased by the fact that most co-ordination plans involve a significant time dimension, so that all the services involved must be dated. Indeed, most co-ordination plans might be better described as 'co-ordination projects'. Lags in production and distribution mean that inputs usually occur before outputs are generated, so that even the simplest plan may involve an element of intertemporal substitution.

In principle, the natural way to set-up a co-ordination project in a market economy is to use forward contracts. A comprehensive set of forward contracts would telescope all decisions about the future into the present, binding all parties to a predetermined course of action. Because of volatility, contingent forward contracts are required—an ordinary contract would remove the opportunity to respond to information received later on. When contracts are contingent, an organization is required to monitor the environment in order to decide what to do at each stage. The decision rules embodied in the organizational procedures are, however, entirely dictated by the contractual arrangements made at the time the organization was set up. Thus although decision making is continuous, contracting is not. Contracting is a once-for-all affair. Each transaction consists of two separate parts: the negotiation of the terms at the outset, and its implementation and enforcement later on.

The problem with this approach is that the transaction costs are prohibitive. Each contract must specify the service, the time of its delivery, and the circumstances under which delivery has to be made. The further forward a contract runs, the greater its memory cost. Memory is more than storage; it involves making records, storing them in the proper order, and retrieving them at the appropriate time. It is only memory that links the negotiation of the contract to its subsequent enforcement, and there is scope for disagreement if the memory of one or other of the parties is flawed. Because of these problems, the state is reluctant to invest in enforcement mechanisms for contracts of this kind. This means that for individual transactors, the risk of default is increased.

To tackle this problem, the element of specificity must be reduced. One approach is to replace rights to specific services with general rights to goods instead. The simplest general right to specify is one that includes all possible specific rights. Instead of being specified by inclusion—listing all the specific rights involved—it is specified by exclusion—namely by what is left out—which is nothing at all. This is the classic form in which the 'ownership' of a good is expressed. Replacing specific rights with comprehensive general rights like 'ownership' effects enormous economies in communication costs.

Since a single general right replaces an entire set of specific rights, a small number of markets in general rights can replace an enormous number of markets in specific rights. Many transaction costs are fixed costs, specific to the market and independent of the number of trades. For this reason, reducing the number of markets effects an additional economy in transaction costs.

When ownership is traded, the allocation of resources takes place in two stages rather than one. To acquire a service, an individual first acquires the good and then allocates it to the appropriate use. The seller does not therefore have to be told the specific use to which the good is to be put. Indeed no one else is told at all—this is entirely private information. This arrangement incurs no penalty so long as no one else cares how the good is used. But if others do care, because they experience negative 'externalities' such as pollution, for example, then it may be more efficient to revert to trading specific rights instead. The benefit of the ownership system is greatest when the use of a resource affects only the owner himself. The ownership system is therefore particularly suitable for mobile resources that are utilized inside buildings, because the owner can carry the goods off and use them in private, without disturbing anyone else. It is less suitable for immobile resources utilized out of doors, where others are more likely to be unavoidably affected by the way in which the goods are used.

Ownership also has implications for the time dimension. Because services are perishable, they have to be dated. Thus an intertemporal co-ordination plan must specify 'appointments' when deliveries of particular services are to be made. But goods are more durable than services, and it is therefore more natural to define rights over them in perpetuity. 'Ownership' of a good therefore confers a perpetual right. This right is particularly easy to enforce because it corresponds to the bundle of *de facto* rights conferred by uninterrupted physical possession of the good.

The perpetual nature of ownership means that the ownership of durable goods can be used as a substitute for forward contracts in specific services. Instead of acquiring a dated claim for the delivery of a service, an individual can purchase ownership of the good which generates the service instead. This extends the principle of multi-stage allocation of resources, explained above, from the present to the future.

Durable goods are sometimes rented out. Not all co-ordination plans require the perpetual use of the same assets, and it is often economic to limit commitments to only a short period of time, with an option to negotiate a renewal later on. Like ownership, rental affords a substantial degree of control. But it does not include the right to consume or sell the good. Rented goods must be returned to the owner in the same condition they were received in, after normal allowance for wear and tear. Rental agreements are more costly to make than outright sales because of the additional information on dates that is required. Nevertheless, rental is extremely useful for the utilization of specialized but versatile machinery. Because it is specialized, most users require the machinery only on an intermittent basis, and not in perpetuity. Because it is versatile, many different people can use it, and each of them may wish to put it to a different use. It is uneconomic to specify every use in detail. It is therefore more efficient to rent it out than to sell the specific services it provides.

The contingent aspect of a contract also contributes materially to transaction cost. This component of cost can be reduced through the standardization of contracts on simple contingencies that apply to everyone. Choosing contingencies that can be objectively specified and publicly observed can reduce the costs of enforcement. These are the principles on which the insurance industry operates.

Insurance can also be effected indirectly, by investing in the ownership of very versatile goods instead of more inflexible ones. The more different uses there are for the good, the more likely it is that an adequate response can be made to unfavourable circumstances. In a market economy the ultimate versatile good is money. Money can be quickly and easily converted into any other good through trade. Holding a stock of money therefore supports a flexible multi-stage resource-allocation mechanism, in which money is first converted into ownership of goods, and the goods are then used to generate the services required. The intermediating role of money in this multi-stage strategy means that access to money is crucial to the implementation of co-ordination plans.

7. Transitory and Persistent Change

Some of the factors driving change are transitory and others are persistent. The role of co-ordination in response to transitory change is to restore the original situation as quickly as possible. Persistent changes cannot be reversed, however, and so co-ordination adjusts other factors to accommodate them. The factors driving transitory change tend to be small in number, but they change fairly frequently. By contrast, the factors driving persistent change are more varied, but change only intermittently.

There are two main kinds of response to volatility. One is to anticipate change and plan in advance how to deal with it. This is the appropriate way of handling transitory change. The other is not to anticipate change, but simply to deal with it as and when it occurs. This is the appropriate way of handling persistent change.

Because of the small number of factors involved, the situations generated by transitory changes tend to be of a limited number of types. Because each factor changes frequently, the same situation tends to recur regularly. The relevant sources of information are fairly easy to identify in advance. It is therefore feasible to employ specialists to monitor each of these sources on a regular basis. This means that it is economic to plan in advance how to deal with these situations. The set-up costs of planning can be spread over a large number of subsequent situations. Situations are dealt with using rules which relate the action to be taken to the observations that have been made. These rules are codified, and routinely applied whenever changes occur.

There is often a division of labour between rule making and rule implementation. Rule making is an entrepreneurial activity which calls for some improvisation, whereas rule implementation is routine, and is characteristic of purely managerial and administrative work. The division of labour can be applied to the implementation of rules as well. Some people collect information, some communicate it, others store it and retrieve it, and some use it to take decisions.

The rules that are used in an organization typically have a procedural quality to them. This is because the processing of information normally benefits from being carried out in a sequential manner. A sequential process allows the processing of information at later stages to be conditioned on the outcomes of earlier stages. This applies to the processing of information on both persistent and transitory factors, but its implications are greater for transitory factors because of the recurrent nature of decision making. The advantage of sequential information processing is that the later stages of a procedure can be modified in the light of the results obtained at earlier stages. If the early steps yield decisive results then the later steps need not be carried out. Indeed, the different stages can be sequenced to maximize the probability that a decisive result is obtained early on. This last step is a refinement of the 'optimal stopping rules' employed in the conventional theory of search (Lippman and McCall 1979).

Procedures need to be fairly simple to reduce the cost of memorizing them. However, if using a procedure 'refreshes' the memory, so that its memory cost falls the more frequently it is used, then quite complex procedures may be used to handle the more common situations (Nelson and Winter 1982).

By contrast, the proliferation of factors, and the intermittent nature of change, means that the situations created by persistent factors recur very infrequently indeed. For any given situation, the average lag between recurrences is very long. This makes it uneconomic to plan in advance how to deal with a persistent change. It is better to wait until the change occurs and improvise a response instead. It may not be worth remembering this response either, because it is cheaper to repeat the improvisation later. Such improvisation is characteristic of the entrepreneur.

It is difficult to identify in advance the relevant sources of information on persistent changes. People who specialize in the identification of persistent change may therefore rove around, working on the basis of hunches as to where the relevant information is likely to be found. This makes it difficult for them to employ specialists on a regular basis, although they may do in a casual way.

Because transitory situations recur regularly, it is easy to learn how to deal with them, and so over time fewer mistakes are likely to be made in responding to them. It is unnecessary to routinely seek a 'second opinion' on each situation, because the symptoms associated with each possible situation are well understood. This does not apply to persistent changes, however, which only infrequently recur. Even if they do recur, they may impinge upon a later generation that has forgotten 'the lessons of history'. Mistakes are much more likely in the response to persistent change. What is even more significant, opinions may well differ about what the appropriate response should be. Opinions may even differ about what change has occurred, whether it is persistent or transitory, or whether any change has in fact occurred at all. This means that multiple responses, based on different interpretations of events, may well be efficient. Indeed, the greater the risks involved, the more important it is to encourage diversity of response, so that the probability of experimenting with the right response is as high as possible.

A rigid division of labour is inappropriate for identifying and responding to changes of this kind. A market system which provides freedom of entry into prospecting for information tends to work better than a formal organization which rigidly demarcates areas of search and allocates exclusive rights in each of them to particular people. Because the sources of transitory changes are more predictable, co-ordination of response benefits more from organization. Thus persistent changes favour market co-ordination and transitory changes favour organization.

An organization is different from an institution. An organization is dedicated to the processing of information through the routine application of official procedures. An organization must be part of an institution, because otherwise it cannot make the implementation of its decision secure. Most institutions have an organization, because there are certain routine matters that need to be decided about the resources under its control. But institutions do not have to have organizations—thus the market is an institution, but not an organization, in the sense defined above.

8. Organizational Innovation in Response to Persistent Change: The Market-Making Firm

A persistent change may change the pattern of transitory volatility. For example, a new cult of 'healthy living' may increase the demand for 'alternative medicines' on those transitory occasions when a person falls ill. A change in the pattern of transitory volatility may in turn lead to a new type of co-ordination opportunity occurring on a regular basis—for example, the opportunity to sell a new kind of medical drug.

Changes can be general or specific. Very general changes affect the entire economy, but most changes are specific to particular industries, particular locations, or particular people. Firms specialize in responding to product-specific changes. Some of these may be specific to customers too (where products are 'bespoke') but many—such as fashion—are common to everyone.

A particularly important type of opportunity is to establish a market for an entirely new type of good. This kind of opportunity is often associated with the foundation of a new firm. The geographical scope of the firm will depend on the nature of the persistent factor that is driving the change. It might be local, regional, or national, although if it is based on a new technology then it is likely to be global instead. The recognition of such opportunities requires a distinctive type of information synthesis. The sources of information tend to be widely dispersed, and a sophisticated mental model may be required to interpret the information. Improvisation based on outstanding judgement is often needed to effect a synthesis of this kind. By contrast, one-off opportunities can often be identified by repeatedly scanning the same small set of local information sources. Synthesis can be effected without judgement just by following simple procedures.

The establishment of a market-making firm thus typically involves two distinct types of synthesis. The first identifies a persistent change and the second involves recurrent syntheses relating to transitory changes. The impossibility of organizing the first type of synthesis makes it a highly individual task. The second type of synthesis, by contrast, normally benefits from systematic organization.

A firm contributes to the continuing smooth operation of a market through the supply of intermediating services. These services reduce the transaction costs encountered by its customers.

- *Contact making*. In the absence of intermediation, consumers may be unable to identify suitable sources of supply. This can be addressed by locating retail premises at a suitable central place, and by advertising the product through the media.
- *Specification*. Consumers may be unsure of how the product addresses their specific needs. Advertising entices customers to visit showrooms which display the product, and where salespeople demonstrate how it performs. Where goods need to be customized, the firm can establish a protocol whereby consumer and producer can share the knowledge in order to compromise on a suitable specification.
- *Negotiation*. The intermediator can avoid protracted negotiations by publicizing a non-negotiable price. The fact that he sells to many people, and that a concession to one customer would soon be discovered by others, gives credibility to this stance. Also, by agglomerating together to facilitate comparison shopping, intermediators can invoke local competition to back their claim that they are setting the lowest possible price.
- *Enforcement*. The intermediator can use his reputation to assure customers about quality, and to assure producers that they will get paid.

An intermediating firm can simplify the administration and the logistics of the physical distribution of the product too. To economize on memory costs, orders may be fulfilled on a spot basis. Because consumers normally demand products in smaller batches than those in which producers manufacture them, inventory is held for break-bulk purposes. To minimize the risk of stock-out, precautionary inventory is also held. This means that orders to replenish inventory are placed before levels get too low. To minimize transport costs, the warehouse is sited at the hub of a freight transport network. Speed of transport is determined by the trade-off between energy costs and the cost of financing stock in transit. Processing of payment is streamlined by substituting cash for credit wherever possible, though credit cards are accepted if the increased information cost is offset by the greater convenience and security afforded to the customer.

To cover his costs, the intermediator needs to extract a reward for this service. This can be done in two main ways. The first is to charge a fee, and the second is to buy and resell the product. The first approach may be identified with brokerage. It is most commonly used for trading in heterogeneous secondhand durable goods. Brokerage is not entirely risk-free, because most brokers operate on a no sale–no fee basis. It involves less risk than buying and reselling the product, however, because there is normally a lag between purchase and resale, during which time the price may change unexpectedly.

9. Pyramids and Authority Relations

Organizations are sometimes referred to as 'hierarchies', suggesting that their structure is like a pyramid, and that the relation between adjacent levels is one of authority and subordination. However, it can be questioned how far organizations really are like this. Recently it has been suggested that organizations can dispense with the hierarchical principle altogether, and substitute internal 'networking' instead (Hedlund 1993).

The logic of volatility and information costs suggests that most large organizations will tend to have a pyramid form, and that many internal relationships will be based on authority, but that there is plenty of scope for variation. Unusual environments may call for unusual organizations.

Consider the pyramid principle first. Transitory changes are initially monitored at the lowest level of the organization and reported to the next level above, where a preliminary synthesis takes place. The most commonly occurring situations are dealt with at this level using simple procedures, whereas the 'exceptions' are passed up to a still higher level. The specialists at this level know procedures which allow them to distinguish between different types of unusual situation, and to resolve each type. Extremely rare situations are referred to the specialist synthesizer at the top of the organization for a solution to be improvised.

While this explains the emergence of a pyramid of competence, it does not directly predict a hierarchy of authority. It is also necessary to explain why the person who has the knowledge of what needs to be done tells someone else what to do. If a person is in the best position to implement his own solution then no authority relation is involved. The person who receives instructions is often the person who collected the information in the first place. This is because observation is often cheapest when it is a by-product of implementation. Thus a production worker is in the best position to observe the production conditions, and a salesperson is in the best position to observe local demand. It is because the observer was implementing the previous decision taken by the synthesizer that he was able to collect the information that has been fed into the current synthesis.

The synthesizer could, of course, simply pass back his synthesis to the observers, leaving them to work out the strategy for themselves. Because the synthesis is 'tacit', whereas instructions are explicit, however, communication costs are lower when the synthesizer acts, not as adviser, but as 'the boss'.

This explanation of hierarchy differs radically from 'principal-agent' theory, which emphasizes supervision instead (Milgrom and Roberts 1992). Hierarchies exist, it is said, because superiors are needed to monitor subordinates. According to this view, the ratio between the numbers of people at successive layers of the pyramid is governed by the 'span of control'. The problem with this approach is that it does not really explain why superiors need to give orders, since it does not even consider the kind of orders that need to be given. The only information collected by superiors, according to this view, is about how their subordinates behave. The obvious objection to this view is that since the superiors do not collect or process information about the firm's environment, they cannot know what orders need to be given.

Once it has been established that a hierarchy of competence exists, however, it is easy to show that the synthesizers who take the most difficult decisions will normally take responsibility for recruiting and motivating the observers as well. The structure of supervision can only be properly understood as an adjunct to organization of synthesis.

This account of hierarchy explains, in turn, the employment relation that is so characteristic of the firm. A firm typically 'rents' the services of its employees in the same way that it rents the services of machinery. The main difference is that employees care about the tasks to which they are assigned whereas machines do not. This applies both to information processing and to the implementation of decisions. Employees usually need to be in place before the information becomes available that determines what they have to do, so they cannot be hired to perform specific tasks. They could be compensated, using a contingent contract, for being asked to perform unpleasant tasks, but the information costs of formalizing this arrangement are very high. Employees must therefore take a risk when accepting employment. This is a calculated risk, however, so long as they can estimate the probability that they will be assigned to any given task.

When the organization is driven by standard procedures which respond to volatility in a predetermined way then it is possible, in principle, to calculate the probability that an employee in any given role will be assigned to a given task. Even if the employee cannot do this, the employer can. Provided that the the employee can trust the employer to give an honest description of the job, he can make a fully rational choice of occupation. Thus the contract of employment emerges as a rational response to the problems of running an organization. To make it work successfully, however, it is necessary for law, society, and morals to encourage the employer to describe each job in an honest way.

10. The Market for Information: The Appropriation Problem

The formation of a market-making firm requires a combination of skills in identifying a market opportunity and then establishing an organization to exploit it. People who are good at identifying changes may not be good at building an organization, and vice versa. It is therefore advantageous, in principle, to establish a division of labour between the discovery of a market opportunity on the one hand and its exploitation on the other. Given the advantage of flexibility, this division of labour would be effected by the creation of a market in entrepreneurial ideas, in which opportunities for co-ordination discovered by one person could be sold to another for exploitation.

In practice, this arrangement is rarely observed. The explanation lies in one of the most important features of the market economy—namely that the transaction costs of trading information about co-ordination opportunities are exceptionally high (Casson 1982). To begin with, the market system rewards the co-ordinator only if his synthesis is unique. This is related to the public good property of information emphasized in Table 6.1. People will not pay for information they can discover easily for themselves or obtain more cheaply elsewhere. Competition from a rival synthesizer selling the same idea will bid down the payment towards zero, because once a synthesis has been effected, the costs are sunk. Unless the synthesizers collude, they will lose out. Even if there is no current competitor, prospective buyers of the information may believe that competition will shortly emerge and so delay their purchase.

If the initial synthesizer could obtain a patent then he would be better protected against competition. But patents are difficult for the state to define and enforce. The complexity and specificity of a synthesis make the cost of communication with prospective buyers very high. Evidence of priority may be difficult to supply to the patent authority. Simple variations may be patented by rivals.

There is a bargaining problem too. If one of the resources required to exploit the patent is monopolized, then the patent may alert the monopolist to the enhanced value of the resource he controls. This may shift the outcome of bilateral monopoly bargaining against the patentee. An alternative is to have recourse to secrecy. Secrecy is a substitute exclusion mechanism: the ignorance of others replaces an unworkable patent right. Secrets are difficult to sell, however. When a secret is advertised for sale, the buyer needs to know what it can do for him in order to value it. But in describing what it can do, the seller may give the secret away. In any case, if the buyer does know what the secret is, he cannot know that he does not know it already. Neither can he check out whether it is true. Checking is advisable because, given that a synthesis can be very valuable, there is an incentive for those who have no information to make it up and pretend that it is true. But if the buyer knows the secret before he pays for it, then he does not need to pay in order to obtain it. He simply remembers what he has already been told.

If the co-ordinator cannot sell his synthesis then he has to appropriate returns in some other way. Two main alternatives are available. One is to take up a speculative position, and the other is to exploit the idea himself. A speculator's strategy is to analyse the consequences of his plan being adopted by other people. Suppose that he published his plan and in consequence a number of people competed to implement it. Are there certain resources that would increase in value? Any resource which would be used more intensively as a result of the plan, and the supply of which is less than perfectly elastic, would appreciate in value. The co-ordinator can therefore benefit by acquiring all such resources. Once the purchases have been made, he announces his secret, and he sells out to the imitators. Because of competition between them, and his own monopoly position, the co-ordinator reaps all the profit. If 'short sales' are possible (because their transaction costs are not too high) then the co-ordinator also profit from resources that will fall in value. He can sell them forward and buy them more cheaply later. Indeed, if there is anyone whose judgement differs from his then he can profit by betting with them on those aspects of his plan where their differences lie. The transaction costs involved in this ploy are, however, normally prohibitive. Indeed, the whole speculative approach, though ingenious, is rather limited in its potential. It requires an enormous outlay of funds, far in excess of what the co-ordinator is likely to have at his disposal (see below). It also depends on key resources being in inelastic supply, which certainly cannot be guaranteed, especially when the scope of the plan is relatively small.

The most promising approach is the second—for the co-ordinator to implement the plan himself. He internalizes the market for the right to exploit the opportunity. To do this effectively, though, he must pre-empt others in the field. As soon as he begins to trade, his secret may leak out. One way to avoid this problem is to tie in all the customers and suppliers using forward contracts. The difficulties of doing this have already been explained. It has also been explained that a simple alternative is to acquire the ownership of assets instead. In this sense speculation can come to his aid. If he buys up the assets required by his plan then he loses nothing if he sells their services back to himself, but he gains if he sells them to imitators that he has failed to stop.

It is interesting to compare the strategic significance of ownership and rental in this context. Physical implementation of a co-ordination plan normally requires only the rental of the assets required. Rental gives sufficient control to reallocate the assets to an alternative use, while the ability to renew rental agreements fairly easily provides a useful element of flexibility. By contrast, ownership of assets is most valuable as part of an appropriation strategy. Using secret information about the value of the plan to purchase undervalued assets, the co-ordinator appropriates profit in a pre-emptive way. On this view, the only link between ownership and physical operations is that ownership may sometimes be a cheaper way of obtaining control because it is more easily specified and more readily enforced.

Practical confirmation of the significance of this point comes from the way that many firms do not use the assets they own, but rent them out, often to potential rivals. Conversely, these same firms often rent assets of the same type that they own, because they are in a more convenient location for their use. A prime example concerns integration by trading companies into shipping, where the company's ships are chartered out, and the company's goods are carried on independent vessels.

There are other means of pre-emption too. The exploitation of an opportunity usually benefits from organization, as noted above. An organization represents an investment, in which fixed costs are incurred at the outset in order to reduce variable costs later on through the application of a routine. By sinking substantial funds in an organization, the co-ordinator raises the stakes for imitators, who must make similar investments if they are to match his variable costs. If they do not match them then they can expect that if they enter he will initiate a price war to drive them out. It is important, though, for the co-ordinator to avoid the use of fixed interest bonds to finance the investment, because otherwise he could be forced into bankruptcy by a fall in price, and potential entrants would be encouraged by this prospect.

The main problem with this second approach is that the synthesizer has to become an organizer too. He can, of course, hire an organizer, but then he has to select the right person and motivate them too. Requiring a synthesizer to be an organizer reduces the effective supply of synthesizers. The problem should not be exaggerated, however. In many cases the information gained through the process of synthesis is crucial to the design of an efficient organization. This information may be tacit, in the sense that it is costly to communicate to other people. Just as before, high communication costs discourage a division of labour in information processing, and in this case encourage the synthesizer to give up his role when he makes a successful synthesis and turn his attention to organization instead. Only when appropriate procedures have been designed, and routines are working smoothly, does he return to synthesis again.

11. Internalization

This emphasis on the internalization of information runs counter to much of the transaction cost literature on the theory of the firm, which focuses instead on vertical integration based on material flow (Williamson 1975). Many transaction cost issues are, of course, common to both types of flow, and are simply more acute in the case of information. Thus the question of whether secret information is genuine or not has a parallel in the way that quality control applied to components and raw materials stimulates backward integration (Casson 1987).

On the other hand, the concept of 'asset specificity' (Klein, Crawford, and Alchian 1978; Williamson 1985) translates rather poorly from the material domain to the information domain. At an intuitive level, there is nothing specific about the use of a public good like information—particularly information about a product innovation opportunity that can be exploited in any part of the world (Kay 1993). Indeed, many of the assets used to exploit a product innovation, such as distribution facilities and computer information systems, are extremely versatile and not specific to the product at all. The only relevance of asset specificity lies in the fact that the costs of discovering an opportunity are sunk at the time the opportunity comes to be exploited, so that if there were just a single potential licensee or franchisee then they would be able to bid down the price very low.

The question of whether transaction costs apply first and foremost to information flow or material flow has important implications for the theory of the firm. Emphasis on the transaction costs of trading information leads directly to a theory of the multinational enterprise in a way that theories of asset specificity do not. The concentration of multinationality in high-technology, advertising-intensive industries is most naturally explained by the costs of licensing product innovations (Buckley and Casson 1976). Extending this idea to the exploitation of more general co-ordination opportunities suggests that the boundaries of the firm are determined by the scope of the co-ordination plan that has been developed by the entrepreneur (Casson 1985). The industrial scope of a firm's operations reflects the range of vision of the entrepreneur. An entrepreneur who plans a radical innovation which, he believes, will rationalize and restructure an entire industrial sector has a strong incentive to acquire control of resources in all the industries within this sector in order to maximize the appropriation of rents, for the reasons given above. Similarly, an entrepreneur whose vision of an industry encompasses every activity between raw material input and the distribution of the finished product has a strong incentive to integrate all the stages of production, in comparison with an entrepreneur with more limited vision, who may integrate just a single vertical linkage instead.

This point re-emphasizes the importance of the holistic perspective introduced at the outset. Modern transaction cost theories tend to work with a partial equilibrium view of the firm, which emphasizes just a single linkage involving material flow, whereas the holistic approach affords a vision of an entire network of such flows, co-ordinated by another network of information flows. As Schumpeter (1934) suggests, élite entrepreneurs promoting radical innovations in a leading sector have a vision of an industrial network they plan to create, rather than just a single linkage they plan to make, and this is reflected in the scope of the co-ordination plan that they propose. The economics of internalizing any given linkage will certainly influence their plans, but the importance of internalizing all the activities encompassed by their vision is the main driving force. It is, therefore, in the appropriation of rents from entrepreneurial vision that the key to the boundaries of the entrepreneurial firm are to be found.

12. Diversification and the Evolution of the Firm

It may seem improbable that a large-scale sectoral co-ordination plan could spring from nowhere into the mind of an entrepreneur. Ambitious plans of this kind are more likely to be unworkable schemes devised by populist politicians to be carried out at public expense. It is possible, though, that such a plan could

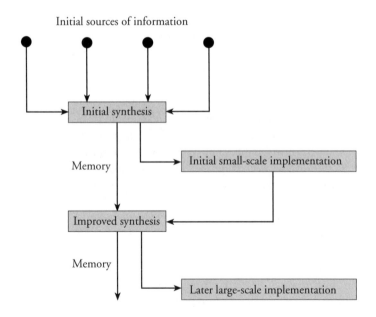

Figure 6.4. Incremental synthesis though learning from experience

evolve from the accumulated practical experience of a successful entrepreneur. By continually feeding back information from his recent operations the entrepreneur may be able to augment the scope of his synthesis, as indicated in Figure 6.4. Because he is accumulating information on persistent changes, his initial information is unlikely to obsolesce while additional information is being collected. He can therefore evolve a large scheme from a sequence of increasingly ambitious smaller schemes.

There is a problem, however. As his schemes are progressively refined, the organizational procedures required to implement them will become increasingly complex. As the organizational division of labour becomes more elaborate, the links between individual managerial performance and individual managerial reward are weakened. In addition, jobs are increasingly delegated to people who are not personally known to the entrepreneur. Furthermore, every modification of procedures disrupts existing ones. Continuous growth means that no sooner has one set of procedures been stabilized than it is time to change them again. New recruits have to be trained as the organization expands, increasing the pressures on experienced employees (Penrose 1959). Naturally, growth brings opportunities for promotion for those who are able to 'grow with the job'. But, on the other hand, long-serving staff who are unwilling or unable to take greater responsibility may become resentful as they 'get left behind in the promotion stakes'.

One solution is to structure the organization in a modular fashion. The procedures in each module can remain largely unchanged while new modules are added elsewhere. Each module is led by an internal entrepreneur, who 'networks' with other internal entrepreneurs to negotiate intermodular relations. The effects of change are focused as far as possible on the intermodular relations, leaving intramodular relations stable for as long as possible. This goes some way towards introducing the principle of flexible specialization to the organization, making the organization less intrinsically rigid than it was before. It is similar to the process of divisionalization, but not identical to it, since unlike divisionalization, it is specifically geared to the problem of maintaining organizational flexibility in a fast-growing firm. (The same principle, incidentally, can be applied to smooth out the running-down of a firm through modular divestment, but this issue cannot be pursued further here.)

It could, of course, be argued that it is a mistake to incorporate new activities within an existing organization, and that it is better to establish entirely new firms for this purpose. The advantages of integrating the new activities into an existing organization are greatest when the same administrative procedures are applicable to both (Teece, Rumelt, Dosi, and Winter 1994). Where the activities face the same pattern of transitory volatility, there are economies of scope in applying existing procedures to the new activity. If the demands for two different consumer products are driven by similar kinds of fashion, for example, then

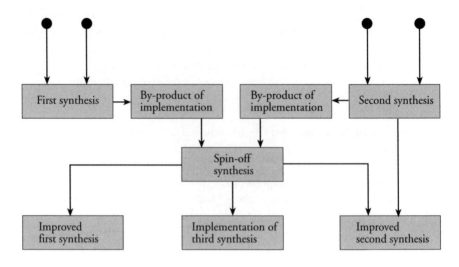

Figure 6.5. A distributed information synthesis with two-way information spill-overs

it may pay for them to share the same market research and distribution procedures. Conversely, if the patterns of transitory volatility are unrelated, it will normally pay the entrepreneur to establish a new organization instead.

Not all incremental synthesis follows the pattern represented in Figure 6.4, however. Figure 6.5 illustrates a more complex situation, exemplified by 'technological convergence', in which two distinct activities generate information spill-overs for each other. These spill-overs not only afford improvement to the existing activities, but offer scope for the innovation of a new activity too. If both of the original entrepreneurs recognize the new opportunity simultaneously then it will pay them to collaborate rather than to compete in its exploitation (Langlois and Robertson 1995). Although one entrepreneur could, in principle, buy out the other, they could not be certain that the other would not later re-enter the field. Since the new activity is likely to benefit from information feedback from the original activities, economies of internalization mean that the speed of improvement of the new activity is maximized when both the entrepreneurs hold a continuing equity stake.

Figure 6.5 represents just one of the many forms that incremental information synthesis can take. Some other possibilities are listed in Table 6.2. This table indicates in the right-hand column the type of corporate growth and diversification strategy that is favoured by each type of synthesis. The correspondence indicated by the two columns underlines the importance of the logic of information synthesis as a factor in the evolution of the boundaries of the firm.

TABLE 6.2. Some types of information synthesis and their implications for the boundary of the firm

Type of synthesis	Probable institutional response
Singular synthesis	New firm formation
Distributed synthesis	Partnership formation
Combinatorial synthesis	Merger
Incremental synthesis	Diversification
Improved synthesis	Growth through learning
Spin-off synthesis	Inter-firm joint venture

13. Financing the Firm

It was noted earlier that inputs normally precede outputs in a co-ordination plan. It has been shown that the entrepreneur must normally assume responsibility for implementing his own plan. He must obtain inputs by owning or renting the relevant resources. Such rights are acquired through the payment of money. If his vision is very broad then many different resources may be required. Conversely, the entrepreneur normally supplies his output to consumers in the form of goods and services which are sold in return for money. It follows immediately that co-ordination requires financing in terms of money.

It is possible that the entrepreneur may have sufficient funds of his own for this purpose, particularly if he possesses good collateral (such as a house) to secure a loan. If he does not, then he is dependent on others. He cannot guarantee the repayment of additional loans because he cannot sell his output forward. The only way to guarantee such loans is to obtain insurance for them. This insurance is provided by equity shareholders. By accepting an uncertain and potentially volatile income stream, the equity holders guarantee a certain and stable income to other parties—not only to fixed-interest lenders, but to waged and salaried employees as well. The simplicity of the equity contract arises from the fact that the equity holder supplies insurance against every kind of risk. It is specified, not by the contingencies it includes, but by those it excludes, which is basically none at all.

The question is why anyone would become an equity shareholder in a firm that is run by another entrepreneur. The problem is not that the firm's environment is uncertain, because the insurance principle can deal with this. If different firms face different local market environments, then the risks can be pooled using a diversified equity portfolio. Furthermore, because the entrepreneur cannot influence the environment, moral hazard is unimportant in this respect. The problems relate entirely to the integrity and competence of the entrepreneur. The entrepreneur may pay less attention to important information than he would if he bore all the risks himself. This can be dealt with, to some extent, by ensuring the entrepreneur remains significantly underinsured—in other words, that he holds a significant proportion of the equity himself. He needs to hold sufficient equity that loss of value will have a major adverse effect on his consumption plans. Material consumption is not everything to the entrepreneur, however, as noted earlier. An ethic of stewardship, and pride in his reputation, may be more important in helping the entrepreneur to keep other people's interests in mind.

Competence is the more difficult issue. Entrepreneurial competence is difficult to screen for, because it is often acquired through experience rather than formal education. It is revealed mainly by performance on the job. The entrepreneur's true competence will be slowly (and only partially) revealed as the coordination project proceeds. Escalating costs, or disappointing sales, may reflect misjudgement by the entrepreneur. But they could be explained by an adverse environment too. Diagnosing the cause of failure is itself an entrepreneurial task. Indeed, a difference of opinion is likely to emerge over the cause of failure, with the self-confident entrepreneur blaming the environment, while some of the equity holders blame the entrepreneur.

A successful equity holder requires knowledge of entrepreneurs, and their track records, to decide whether to back them or not. Equity holders also need to monitor the performance of the firms in which they invest, and interpret the causes of success and failure correctly. As they refine their own judgement in this way, they increase their investments in firms that they believe are run by competent entrepreneurs, and run down their investments in others.

The ability to hire and fire entrepreneurs is also important. A specialist equity holder can operate a market in entrepreneurs—or a market in management control, as it is sometimes called—'head-hunting' entrepreneurs from successful firms in order to 'turn around' failing ones. Indeed, specialized institutions such as investment banks are often formed for this sort of purpose. It is sometimes suggested that entrepreneurs who play an active role of this kind cross-subsidize the more passive entrepreneurs, and this is true—up to a point. There is plenty of scope, however, for these entrepreneurs to appropriate speculative profit from their superior judgement, by secretly buying up shares in the firms that they plan to turn around, and selling them off at a profit later. Although the appropriation may be incomplete, it is not obvious that it is any less complete than in other areas of entrepreneurial activity.

This situation is by no means unique to the firm, however. Most organizations have an élite of members—the stakeholders—who have contributed resources and in return demand a share of the control over the way they are used. They have the greatest authority because, generally speaking, they bear the brunt of the risk that a bad decision may be made. They therefore have the power to replace the head of the organization.

14. Conclusion

This chapter has embedded the theory of the firm within a holistic view of the economy, in which information flow is just as important as material flow. Co-ordination in a volatile economy depends on the continuing synthesis of new information. Processing this information is costly, and requires a division of labour. There is a vertical division of labour between observers and synthesizers, and a horizontal division of labour between different observers. The latter is particularly significant in dealing with regular changes in transitory factors, where an organization may hire full-time observers to submit routine reports. These observers also handle the implementation of the decisions that are made through a synthesis of their various reports, generating a pyramid of authority.

The pattern of variation in transitory factors depends in turn on persistent factors. It is difficult to set-up an organization to monitor persistent factors, because the relevant sources of information cannot be identified in advance. The synthesis of information about changes in persistent factors requires improvisation rather than routine: it requires the judgemental abilities of the entrepreneur.

It is difficult to be sure that the information used to identify persistent change is correct. Different entrepreneurs synthesize information from different sources, and even when they use the same sources they may interpret them differently. To encourage the most able entrepreneurs to specialize in monitoring persistent changes, and to give each individual as much scope as possible, the division of labour between synthesizers is structured in a highly flexible way. Flexibility is achieved through a market system, the institutions of which facilitate the trans-actions by which entrepreneurs gain access to the real resources they require. The formal specification of all the property rights that an entrepreneur may require is a formidable task. To economize on information costs, a comprehensive right of ownership, and an allied concept of rental, has therefore been developed to replace a wide spectrum of other more specific rights. Another institution is the use of money—a homogeneous stock that circulates in order to simplify trans-actions. The firm, too, falls into the same category; it is a specialized institution designed to act as a nexus of contracts, and as such is endowed with fiscal priv-ileges and unlimited life.

Embedded within this institutional framework, entrepreneurs implement their co-ordination projects by borrowing money and exchanging it for ownership or rental of productive resources, using their firm as a legal shell. In negotiating for command over resources, entrepreneurs are careful not to give away crucial infor-mation on which their synthesis is based. Entrepreneurs are organizers too. Because they cannot patent their own ideas, and cannot sell them as secrets either, they are obliged to internalize the market for their ideas. This involves them in the design of organizational structures—the most notable example being the or-ganization of intermediation effected by the market-making firm.

Successful entrepreneurs must be optimistic and self-confident in order to compete for resources with, and win them from rival entrepreneurs, and to live with the risk that their judgement may turn out to be wrong. To obtain the widest possible synthesis of the latest information they cultivate networks of social contacts who feed them the information they require. They are persuasive in raising finance, and astute in bargaining with customers and suppliers.

The high cost of information makes legal enforcement of business contracts problematic, and so trust engineered through moral values is very important in providing a climate of confidence within which risky co-ordination projects can take place. Traditional values such as honesty and hard work are particularly important for entrepreneurs in motivating their employees. While entrepreneurship thrives on plurality of opinion about co-ordination opportunities, it requires a degree of consensus on moral issues. The entrepreneurial theory of the firm suggests that a market economy driven by a combination of moral unanimity and pluralism of practical judgement is likely to prove the most successful.

References

BOISOT, M. H. 1995. *Information Space: A Framework for Learning in Organizations, Institutions and Culture*. London: Routledge.

BUCKLEY, PETER J., and MARK C. CASSON 1976. *The Future of the Multinational Enterprise*. London: Macmillan. (2nd edn., 1991.)

CANTILLON, RICHARD 1755, 1931. *Essai sur la Nature du Commerce en Generale*, ed. H. Higgs. London: Macmillan.

CASSON, MARK C. 1982. *The Entrepreneur: An Economic Theory*. Oxford: Martin Robertson (2nd edn., Cheltenham: Edward Elgar, 1999.)

—— 1985. 'Entrepreneurship and the dynamics of foreign direct investment', in P. J.Buckley and M. C. Casson, eds., *The Economic Theory of the Multinational Enterprise*. London: Macmillan, 172–91.

—— 1987. *The Firm and the Market*. Cambridge, MA: MIT Press.

—— 1991. *Economics of Business Culture: Game Theory, Transaction Costs and Economic Welfare*. Oxford: Oxford University Press.

—— 1995. *Studies in the Economics of Trust*. Cheltenham: Edward Elgar.

—— 1997. *Information and Organization: A New Perspective on the Theory of the Firm*. Oxford: Clarendon Press.

ELIASSON, GUNNAR, STEFAN FOLSTER, THOMAS LINDBERG, TOMAS POUSETTE, and EROL TAYMAZ 1990. *The Knowledge-Based Information Economy*. Stockholm: Almqvist and Wicksell.

FOSS, NICOLAI J. 1997. *Resources, Firms and Strategies: A Reader in the Resource-Based Theory of the Firm*. Oxford: Oxford University Press.

GRANOVETTER, MARK 1985. 'Economic action and social structure: The problem of embeddedness', *American Journal of Sociology* 91: 481–510.

HEDLUND, GUNNAR 1993. 'Assumptions of hierarchy and heterarchy: An application to the multinational corporation', in S. Ghoshal and E. Westney, eds., *Organization Theory and the Multinational Corporation*. London: Macmillan, 211–36.

KAY, NEIL M. 1993. 'Markets. False hierarchies, and the role of asset specificity', in C. Pitelis, ed., *Transaction Costs, Markets and Hierarchies*. Oxford: Blackwell, 242–61.

KLEIN, BURTON, R. G. CRAWFORD, and ARMEN A. ALCHIAN 1978. 'Vertical integration, appropriable rents and the competitive contracting process', *Journal of Law and Economics* 21: 297–326.

KNIGHT, FRANK H. 1921. *Risk, Uncertainty and Profit*. Boston, MA: Houghton Mifflin.

LANGLOIS, RICHARD N., and PAUL ROBERTSON 1995. *Firms, Markets and Economic Change*. London: Routledge.

LIPPMAN, S. A., and J. J. MCCALL, eds. 1979. *Studies in the Economics of Search*. Amsterdam: North-Holland.

MILGROM, PAUL R., and JOHN ROBERTS 1992. *Economics of Organization and Management*. Englewood Cliffs, NJ: Prentice Hall.

NELSON, RICHARD, and SIDNEY G. WINTER 1982. *An Evolutionary Theory of Economic Change*. Cambridge, MA: Harvard University Press.

NORTH, DOUGLASS C. 1981. *Structure and Change in Economic History.* New York: W. W. Norton.

PENROSE, EDITH T. 1959. *The Theory of the Growth of the Firm*. Oxford: Blackwell.

SAY, JEAN-BAPTISTE 1803, 1964. *A Treatise on Political Economy.* New York: Augustus M. Kelley.

SCHUMPETER, JOSEPH A. 1934. *The Theory of Economic Development,* trans. R. Opie. Cambridge, MA: Harvard University Press.

TEECE, DAVID J., RICHARD RUMELT, GIOVANNI DOSI and SIDNEY G. WINTER 1994. 'Understanding corporate coherence: Theory and evidence', *Journal of Economic Behaviour and Organization* 23: 1–30.

WILLIAMSON, OLIVER E. 1975. *Markets and Hierarchies: Analysis and Antitrust Implications*. New York: Free Press.

—— 1985. *The Economic Institutions of Capitalism.* New York: Free Press.

7

Organizing for Firm Growth: the Interaction between Resource-Accumulating and Organizing Processes

Sumantra Ghoshal, Martin Hahn, and Peter Moran

The interaction of institutional forms and entrepreneurial activity, the 'shaping' influence of the former and the 'bursting' influence of the latter, is . . . a major topic for further inquiry.   (Joseph Schumpeter 1947: 153.)

1. Introduction

With unfailing regularity, the growth of the firm expands the stock of resources that are within reach and thereby available for the firm to use. To the extent that these resources are used productively, the firm will continue to grow and will, therefore, accumulate even more resources and many more possibilities for further growth. But as every experienced manager knows, no firm is assured that its growth trajectory will continue indefinitely. Why does the growth of many, indeed most, firms eventually falter and often reverse itself, while other firms, including some that are already relatively large and complex, continue to grow?

In this chapter, we argue that the key to sustainable growth lies in the firm's organizing capability. Applying and extending an argument made by Moran and Ghoshal (1999) to describe the role of firms and markets in the process of economic development, we argue here that an organization which is not adequately enabling and motivating new possibilities will eventually witness its own decline—a destruction of its own economic structure that will have been induced from within. For any organization to remain viable, it needs to have an economic structure that encourages those institutional changes that would support what Schumpeter called the 'creative response'—that is, 'something that is outside of the range of existing practice' (1947: 153).

More specifically, firm growth is portrayed as the outcome of a symbiotic process of resource accumulation and administrative organization, a process

The authors are grateful to the Ashridge Strategic Management Centre for financial support for this work and to Michael Goold, Marcus Alexander, and Andrew Campbell for their helpful comments on earlier drafts of this chapter and in discussions on its subject-matter. The authors also wish to thank Volker Mahnke and Nicolai Foss for comments on earlier drafts.

unlike many symbiotic processes, that induces its own creating and destroying actions from within. We explore the process of creative destruction as it occurs *within* the firm and consider its implications for the long-term growth of the firm. It is this process, we argue, that determines not only the degree to which the firm's activities are expanded and the direction such expansion is likely to follow but also the likelihood that the firm will ultimately be able to sustain its growth or fall instead into decline.

In building our argument we need to consider how a growing firm affects and is affected by the development and use of resources. We draw on the insights of Penrose (1959), Schumpeter (1934), Langlois (1995), and others to piece together the argument that the process of firm growth and decline is similar to that of economic development (cf. Moran and Ghoshal 1999). Just as Schumpeter portrayed economic development as a process that is largely driven by 'the interaction of institutional forms and entrepreneurial activity' (1947: 153), we will illustrate how the same argument holds true for the process of firm growth. In other words, the growth of firms is driven by the interaction of the firm's processes of resource accumulation and organizing.

We begin by restating the essence of Penrose's theory and follow with an analysis of how the continuous accumulation of resources that accompanies firm growth induces the need for administrative reorganization. Reorganization is necessary to assimilate new resources with the old and also to facilitate the perception and exploitation of the wider set of productive possibilities that accrue to the growing firm. The tension-inducing symbiotic process of resource accumulation and administrative reorganization not only determines the success with which the firm's activities are expanded and the forces that constrain this expansion, it also provides an explanation of the historical evolution of corporate organizational forms and suggests a perspective on the roles and tasks of firm management. The chapter concludes with a brief discussion of some implications of the theory.

2. Growth as the Process of Accumulating Resources

Arguably the most significant breakthrough in the theory of the growth of the firm is Penrose's conceptualization of the nature of the firm itself—a collection of physical and human resources whose services are made more or less complementary, and thereby productive by (and specific to) the firm's 'coherent administrative organization' (Penrose 1995: xii). The unique collection of resources that make up any firm, particularly its 'existing human resources', provides 'both an inducement to expand and a limit to the rate of expansion' for the firm (ibid.). Although a system's productive possibilities always expand, in lock-step, with the number and variety of resources that are available, the continued growth of the system itself depends upon its productive opportunity, which does not necessarily expand with the growth or accumulation of resources.

As Penrose put it, 'a theory of the growth of firms is essentially an examination of the changing productive opportunity of firms' (1959: 31–2). Penrose
defined the firm's 'productive opportunity' as those possibilities for deploying
resources that its entrepreneurs and managers *can see* and which they are *willing*
and *able* to act on (1959: 32). Even though any growing firm accumulates an
ever-expanding set of productive possibilities that it can pursue (that is, from the
expanding set of resources that naturally accompanies any firm's growth), the
firm's productive opportunity will expand, and therefore the firm will grow, only
to the extent that these three conditions are met.

As we have argued elsewhere (see Moran and Ghoshal 1999), the extent to
which these conditions are met is largely influenced by three general forces that
collectively determine which resources are accessed and used and how they are
developed. The first of these forces results from the circumstances of time and
place, which define the constellation of resources as they happen to exist and the
services they are able to render at a given time. The mere presence or absence of
certain resources will render some services more or less available, productive, or
visible than others. The second force stems from the web of institutions in which
any set of resources is embedded (ibid.). We follow North (1994: 360) in defining 'institutions', as

the humanly devised constraints that structure political, economic and social interaction.
They consist of both informal constraints (sanctions, taboos, customs, traditions, and
codes of conduct), and formal rules (constitutions, laws, property rights). . . . Together
with the standard constraints of economics they define the choice set and therefore
determine transaction and production costs and hence the profitability and feasibility of
engaging in economic activity.

The firm's administrative organization (including its structure, policies, and
norms) is a very influential part of this institutional matrix that drives resource
deployment decisions (Moran and Ghoshal 1999). It is also the lever over which
management has the most immediate control.

The third force is the exertion of the individual's human will to defy, leverage,
or change these other two largely inertial forces, generally to accomplish something that otherwise could not get done. It is, we argue, an organization's unique
ability to influence and leverage 'the interaction of institutional forms and entrepreneurial activity, the "shaping" influence of the former and the "bursting"
influence of the latter' (Schumpeter 1947: 153), that gives firms the ability to
continue to create value and thereby remain viable over time.

To understand the dynamics of Penrosian growth requires an understanding
of how these forces of accumulation interact with the actions of the firm's entrepreneurs to expand and contract the firm's 'productive opportunity'. Consider
the model illustrated in Figure 7.1, as we explore the factors that determine how
the productive opportunity changes for a particular firm.

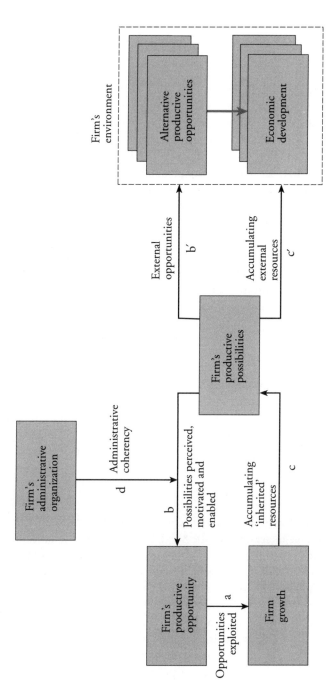

Figure 7.1. Penrosian growth: The process of accumulating and deploying resources

2.1. Productive Opportunity

Put simply, a firm grows or declines as its 'productive opportunity' expands or contracts (depicted in Figure 7.1 as relationship 'a'). The basic ingredients for the firm's productive opportunity are the resources whose services can be marshalled and co-ordinated for the benefit of the firm (that is, relationship 'b'). These resources include those 'inherited' by the firm (that is, relationship 'c'), as well as those that are available from the firm's external environment (that is, relationship 'c''). Collectively, the complete set of services that are possible from the many combinations and permutations that could be created by these resources constitute, for any firm, a unique set of productive possibilities. Although the access to external resources means that no firm's productive opportunity is confined to any particular set of resources, because of the firm-specific nature of the factors that shape its 'productive opportunity', no two firms enjoy the same set of opportunities.

The two factors emphasized by Penrose that most affect a firm's productive opportunity are the quality of its inherited resources (that is, relationship 'c') and the coherency of its administrative organization (that is, relationship 'd'). A 'bundle of possible services' accompanies each resource that a firm acquires or accumulates (Penrose 1959: 67). To the extent that some of these services are not needed or cannot be used to support current operations, they become available for adding to and shaping the set of possibilities for future growth. However, the firm's productive opportunity will be expanded by these newly added possibilities for growth (relationship 'b') only to the extent that they are perceived and motivated within the context of the firm's administrative organization (relationship 'd'). This is just another way of saying that each firm's productive opportunity is restricted to only those possibilities for productive resource deployment that its entrepreneurs and managers can *see* and are *willing* and *able* to act on (Penrose 1959: 32).

Both factors shape the firm's productive opportunity through their influence on all three determinants of the firm's productive opportunity—that is, what the firm's entrepreneurs and managers can see as opportunities and which of these they are willing and able to act on. But the first (along with the external institutional matrix in which the firm is embedded) more directly circumscribes the set of productive deployments that are possible for the firm at any given time. This is because the firm's inherited resources (including its stock of capabilities or routines, Nelson and Winter 1982) simultaneously enable and constrain (and, thereby, effectively specify) what the firm is *able* to do, at least for a time. Because most of the people who must see the firm's possibilities as opportunities they are willing to exploit are typically part of these 'inherited' resources, the firm's accumulated stock of resources also indirectly shapes what is seen as productive, or even possible.

The second factor emphasized by Penrose, the firm's administrative organization, plays the role of more or less accommodating the entrepreneurial judgement of members in the firm (that is, relationship 'd'). The coherency of the firm's administrative organization—that is, the degree to which the firm's resources are organized to produce services that are somehow complementary (or mutually enhancing)—reflects the ways in which the firm's administrative structure, values, rules, and incentives link these and other resources coherently with the abilities of, and in the minds of, the firm's employees.

Administrative coherency is essential for the productive deployment of the firm's resource base. The necessary 'administrative cohesion' that Penrose emphasized (1995: xviii) stems largely from the institutional context that is created by the existence of the firm itself. We will have more to say in the next section about the role that the firm's administrative organization plays in sustaining firm growth. For now, it is sufficient to note that just as the 'technical relatedness' of the firm's inherited resources defines a unique subset of possibilities that are or are likely to be seen as worth pursuing, the 'administrative coherency' of the firm's organization specifies another subset of these productive possibilities that are somehow made easier and more productive and more visible by the firm's administrative organization. The intersection of these two sets constitutes the firm's productive opportunity.

2.2. The Enabling and Constraining Environment

To the extent that the firm's productive opportunity involves resources that have alternative uses to others, the firm's environment exerts a disciplinary effect on the firm to use its resources productively. Competition for its resources and the services they can provide puts pressure on the firm to pursue only those opportunities that are at least as productive as those outside the firm—or to face, in time, a migration of its resources to those more productive external opportunities (that is, relationship 'b″'). Hence, this pressure of competition for the firm's accumulated resources influences the nature of the firm's 'productive opportunity' set and thereby the direction of a firm's growth—that is, towards activities that enhance the productivity of its scarce resources. The effect of the firm's environment on the size of the productive opportunity or the firm's potential growth rate is more complex.

Penrose (1959) suggested that the growth of the firm is most likely to be affected by the firm's external environment when the firm is still small and relatively more susceptible to market forces. Small firms are particularly likely to feel the sting from competing opportunities for their resources, as these alternative deployments restrict their access to resources (that is, relationship 'c″') and constrain not only the direction of their growth but also their ability to grow at all. But this effect should be attenuated, according to Penrose, as firms grow larger and accumulate a sufficient stock of their own resources to provide multiple avenues for growth. This accumulating stock of diverse resources that accompanies a firm's growth enables the firm to cope more easily with external forces that compete for its resources, by enhancing its opportunities to expand in a variety of new directions.

Because larger firms with access to more resources are generally free to expand in more directions, any resistance to growth they may encounter in one direction is less likely to limit their ability to grow in others. The more resources a firm controls, the more new possibilities it has for growing in new directions. Each increment of growth adds an *increasing* number of possibilities, for further growth to respond to external pressures, generally by avoiding those paths where competition is the fiercest. The growth of small firms is likely to be limited by the relatively small number of possibilities that stem from these firms' own limited resource bases. If, however, a small firm is somehow able to grow despite this constraint, it will soon amass a possibility set that contains a sufficient variety of possibilities so that there is always some productive opportunity to exploit—provided it has the appropriate administrative organization. Although this argument is consistent with that of Penrose (see also Montgomery and Hariharan 1991), it leaves unanswered, as did Penrose, the question of why so many successful firms stop growing and why some even begin a long spiral of decline.

The explanation, we suggest, lies in a shift in the relative importance of the two roles played by the firm's environment in affecting the firm's productive opportunity. As an important alternative source of resources (that is, relationship 'c''), the environment offers a veritable cornucopia of possibilities for productively combining and recombining these external resources with the accumulating stock of 'inherited' resources. The number and variety of resources available to the firm are a function of the size of both the firm and the stock of external resources to which it has access. As the stock of available resources grows in size and variety with the growth of the firm, the number of possibilities for growth expands (at a combinatorial rate; Weitzman 1996). But because external resources are generally also available to others, the environment is also a source of competing productive opportunities for these and other possibilities. Many of these possibilities are likely to be more productively exploited outside the focal firm (that is, relationship 'b''). Hence, a declining proportion of these possibilities are likely to end up as productive opportunities as the firm grows larger.

Because the firm's growth is accompanied by a concomitant growth in the firm's 'administrative responsibilities' (Penrose 1995: xvi), its growth must be accommodated by a process that successfully assimilates the old possibilities with the new. With further growth, the firm's accumulated stock of resources begins to tax the capacity of the firm's 'existing managerial resources' to 'maintain the coherency of the organization'. Hence, the firm's set of possibilities will expand more certainly and at a faster rate, with the firm's growth, than will the firm's productive opportunity. The size of the disparity, between its possibilities and those opportunities it exploits, that the firm can withstand will depend upon the strength of the alternative demands placed upon its resources by the firm's environment. Unless the firm is somehow able to adjust its 'coherent administrative organization' to accommodate its expanding possibilities, it cannot continue to grow, particularly in an environment with many opportunities. It may even face decline as other firms pursue its possibilities more productively and compete away the firm's resources and its productive opportunity.

We suggest, therefore, that as large firms continue to grow, the potential for sustainable growth lies less in the larger *number* of productive possibilities that past growth puts within the firm's reach and more in the extent to which these possibilities continue to be complementary—that is, jointly perceived, motivated, and enabled in the context of the firm's administrative organization. Thus, the pressure of competition for a firm's resources is likely to be felt *more* (not less) as the firm becomes larger. Even though the large firm has open to it a bigger set of avenues that it *might* pursue, most will lie outside the firm's 'productive opportunity' set, *given its current administrative organization*. That is, despite their relatively greater potential, it is increasingly more difficult for larger firms to change focus and direction because so much of the stock of their productive opportunity is specific to the path previously taken (see also Arthur 1989; Nelson 1991; Cohen and Levinthal 1990).

Hence, as a firm grows, a greater proportion of the possibilities within its reach will be likely to have more possibilities for complementarities within the context of alternative organizations that may exist or that may be possible outside the firm. Administrative reorganization is necessary to keep the firm's productive opportunity in balance with its possibilities or the firm will experience a migration of these possibilities to economic actors who reside outside the firm (that is, relationship 'b″').

This 'administrative reorganization', which Penrose deemed to be necessary for long-run growth, is neither automatic nor assured. As Penrose noted in the foreword to the third edition of her book, all the *successful* firms whose growth her theory was developed to explain 'seemed to undergo' such reorganization in both their 'managerial function' and their 'basic administrative structure' (1995: xvii). We submit that this accommodation process is the same change process, referred to as 'Schumpeterian integration' (Langlois 1995), that is used to describe the entrepreneurial process of 'carrying out new combinations' within new firms. As we argue below, this administrative reorganization is necessary, not only to enable an individual firm to grow over time, but also to retain its size in any dynamic environment, particularly one in which the forces of market discipline are particularly strong.

3. Organizing to Redefine what is Allocatively Efficient

Following from her definition of the firm as a 'coherent administrative organization' (1995: xii), Penrose opened up the 'black box' of the firm and argued why we should not be surprised to see even the largest firms continue to grow indefinitely. Although 'the necessity of using inputs from existing managerial resources to maintain the coherence of the organization' unavoidably limits a firm's *rate* of growth, it 'would not necessarily limit the ultimate size of a firm' (1995: xii).

Although Penrose took care to point out that firms may fail to grow for many reasons (1959: 7), her argument was explicitly aimed at explaining the growth of 'successful firms' (1959: 32–3). Penrose suggested, but did not develop the idea, that the key to sustainable growth lies in a firm's organizing capability. As she put it, in the foreword to the third edition of her book:

> [A] firm's rate of growth is limited by the growth of knowledge within it, but a firm's size by the extent to which administrative effectiveness can continue to reach its expanding boundaries. . . . With increasing size both the managerial function and the basic administrative structure of firms seemed to undergo an administrative reorganization to enable them to deal with the increasing growth.   (Penrose 1995: xvi–xvii.)

In other words, all the firms whose growth her theory was developed to explain 'seemed to undergo' a reorganization in both their 'managerial function' and their 'basic administrative structure' to maintain and accommodate the direction and magnitude of their growth within a coherent administrative organization (1995: xvii). We argue that the necessary accommodation requires the same change process referred to as 'Schumpeterian integration' (see, for example, Langlois 1995) and used to describe the entrepreneurial process of 'carrying out new combinations' within new firms. Administrative reorganization is necessary to enable an individual firm not only to grow over time but also to retain its size in any dynamic environment in which the forces of Schumpeterian integration also exist outside the focal firm.

No single institution, whether a firm or a market, can provide a context that sufficiently enables, motivates, and stimulates the perception of more than only a tiny fraction of the productive possibilities that are always within reach (see Moran and Ghoshal 1999). In other words, each institution favours a unique subset of economic activities over all other activities it might pursue under the influence of a different administrative organization. This institutional bias stems from the way the behavioural context of the firm's administrative organization affects both the objective and the subjective determination of the firm's productive opportunity (Penrose 1959: 41). For example, Eliasson (1990) attributes the fact that resources may not be deployed as needed to a lack of 'receiver competence' that may exist on the part of those who could gain from deploying their resources in a certain way but do not realize it. This may happen because they do not perceive the opportunity for gain, or because they believe they might not be able to appropriate enough of the gain. Consequently, many productive possibilities within the firm's reach are excluded from its productive opportunity set.

The forces that facilitate the perception of, the motivation to pursue, and the means to execute those resource deployments that collectively characterize a firm's productive opportunity can also impede the pursuit of many other alternative possibilities for deploying the same resources by making these alternatives more costly or less attractive. For example, the complementarities that make particular deployments collectively 'coherent' (see Teece, Rumelt, Dosi, and Winter 1994; Langlois 1995), and thereby more attractive in one use, inherently increase the opportunity cost of separating out the individual resource components for redeployment to most other uses. As a 'coherent administrative organization', a firm can only imperfectly adapt its institutional context and can never do so in ways that align its productive opportunity to more than only a fraction of all the possibilities within its reach. Hence, the very coherency of any institutional context must impede the pursuit of more possibilities than it enhances for deploying the same resources.

This institutional focus can be particularly troublesome for innovative alternative uses of resources that involve 'new combinations'. As Schumpeter (1934) argued, the 'new combinations' that generally precede subsequent leaps in economic progress are seldom if ever as productive initially as alternative deployments of the same resources that are also available at the time. Indeed, even if a particular 'new combination' is shown retrospectively to have triggered great progress (implying it to be among the best possible choices for resource deployment), it is seldom even among the most advantageous methods that were available at the time the combination was made (p. 83).

Whereas Penrose emphasized the value of an administrative organization's 'shaping influence', Schumpeter emphasized the value (indeed, the need) for the 'bursting influence' of entrepreneurial activity. Some change in the organization of economic activity is generally required to accommodate the entrepreneurial judgement that resides within the firm. This change can come in the form of an 'administrative reorganization' of an existing firm, as Penrose suggested had taken place in the successful growing firms that she studied, or as a new firm, as Schumpeter insisted is often necessary (see Figure 7.2). In either case, 'Schumpeterian integration' involves a substitution of the current organizational context (for example, firm or market) by a new one that involves some administrative reorganization.

By reorganizing certain resources within the context of a new institutional matrix (that is, Schumpeterian integration), the entrepreneur makes the services of certain resource deployments more complementary and/or more salient by enhancing the motivation and perception of these productive possibilities. This

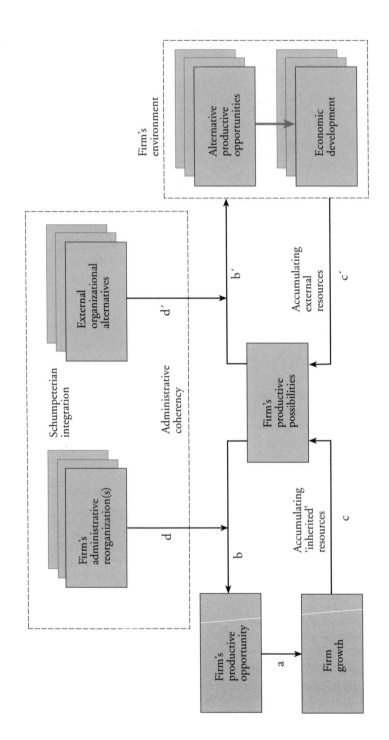

Figure 7.2. The process of firm growth: The integration of accumulating and organizing processes for productive resource use

then increases the likelihood of their being executed. Langlois (1995) argues that while Penrosian growth is essentially driven by the supply of resources and experiences that are within the firm's reach, Schumpeterian integration is driven more by 'the entrepreneur's demand for the capabilities necessary to bring about a *redesign of the chain of complementary activities*. As a consequence, Schumpeterian innovation normally involves integration into dissimilar activities that the entrepreneur would have preferred to leave to others' (p. 90; emphasis added).

The internalization of economic activity that Schumpeterian integration brings about arises not from the fact that the new organization is *better* than alternative institutions. Rather, it is simply because of the lack of a supporting (that is, an enabling, motivating, or perception-stimulating) context in either the market or another firm that would divert resources *away* from known 'best methods' towards the new combinations that may be more promising, but only appear so as perceived by the entrepreneur. As a consequence, activities that need to and which can complement the entrepreneur's competence are integrated within the boundaries of a new or existing firm. The firm provides, via its administrative organization, a coherent organizational context for co-ordinating these activities in ways that reinforce their complementarity (that is, relationship 'd'). It does this largely by influencing the perceptions and behaviour of its members in ways that are very different from those that may be induced, either by the nature of the resources themselves (that is, relationships 'c' and 'c''') or by any other context that may be 'within reach' (that is, relationship(s) 'd''').

We are now ready to explore why some firms can grow for long periods while others face decline. Although Penrose's theory explains why firms grow and the mechanisms through which growth is accomplished, continued growth over time requires Schumpeterian integration to fundamentally change the firm's administrative organization. Schumpeterian integration is needed to create a context that is hospitable for carrying out some new combinations. Further, as suggested by relationship 'd''' in Figure 7.2, the need for Schumpeterian integration becomes stronger with the number and variety of external organizational alternatives that are available to exploit the firm's productive possibilities. Hence, as economies develop and begin to exert significant market discipline, the need for (internal) Schumpeterian integration among growing firms only intensifies. Moreover, as we have shown above, the inability of a firm to undergo the needed administrative reorganization encourages the migration of the firm's entrepreneurial judgement outside the firm and, consequently, shifts the likely locus of the next round of Schumpeterian integration to occur outside the firm—by inducing the creation of new firms to accommodate the entrepreneurial judgement. The migration of other resources is likely to follow and to lead to stalled growth or even to decline.

4. The Symbiotic Process of Firm Growth

Because Penrosian growth and Schumpeterian integration are distinct processes, each affected by different drivers of growth, they tend to influence the direction of an individual firm's growth in different ways. While Penrosian growth is driven by *what the firm can do*—given its current institutional context— Schumpeterian integration is driven more by *what might be possible* in a different context. For example, Penrosian growth, on the one hand, seeks to extend the firm's existing organizational capabilities to exploit 'equilibrium' opportunities (that is, those that enhance the productivity of resources employed within the extended administrative framework). In the process, the firm becomes more efficient in allocating its resources to best known uses. This type of growth occurs generally through expansion into fields that are already in some way related to the existing firm-specific stock of knowledge.

Schumpeterian integration, on the other hand, focuses on 'disequilibrium' opportunities that demand a 'redesign of [those] complementary activities' (Langlois 1995: 90) that constitute the firm's organizational capability. Allocative efficiency is temporarily disturbed as the firm attempts to redefine what is efficient. Schumpeterian integration tends to induce growth more often by means of re-bundling activities and internalizing various stages of a product's or service's value chain. Whereas Penrosian growth exploits complementarities that are inherent in either the resources themselves or the administrative context in which they are embedded, Schumpeterian integration creates new complementarities that otherwise might not exist.

The interaction of these two forces can perhaps best be seen by tracing the emergence and growth of a hypothetical firm. In the first instance, the general inability of the current administrative framework to accommodate the entrepreneur's judgement to 'carry out new combinations' leads to the creation or expansion of a firm via Schumpeterian integration. This creation or expansion implies immediate demand for improved organizational capability to encompass the newly integrated activities with the old. For example, by integrating vertically related activities, a firm provides a new context for sharing knowledge among previously unrelated entities. This process directly contributes to the firm's growth by extending the complementarity of its activities. It also makes an indirect contribution to future growth by setting the stage for improved internal coordination and adaptation (that is, the enhancement of organizational capability) to enhance the firm's exploitation of this extension. As a result, the firm will be able to (indeed, must to some extent) take on new related resources or tasks in order to utilize this enhanced organizational capability efficiently (that is, undergo Penrosian growth).

Because each integration of activities leads in a similar fashion to growth of resources under the control of the firm and, consequently, an expanded set of productive opportunities within its reach, the firm creates a continuing cycle of inducements to initiate one form of growth or the other. First, it has to find more productive uses for its current resources (that is, Penrosian growth); then it must restructure its administrative organization in order to co-ordinate these or other uses more efficiently (that is, Schumpeterian integration); and finally new resources must be acquired or developed to exploit these new co-ordinative capabilities, only to start the cycle again. External competition for resources (as indicated by high levels of market discipline—relationship 'd″' in Figure 7.2) serves to reinforce these inducements and speed up the cycle. In a 'carrot and stick' fashion, the existence of many attractive alternatives for deploying resources encourages firms to *try* to grow faster, only to find it even more difficult to accommodate each new increment of growth to keep the market's forces (that is, the relevant environment) at bay.

There are various pieces of historical evidence to illustrate both the successes and failures of managing this dialectic process on firm growth. Consider, for instance, Langlois and Robertson's (1989) account of the acquisition of Fisher Body by General Motors (GM) in 1926, which made possible the necessary acquisition of related (but still non-complementary) knowledge that was needed by GM to exploit its vision of the closed-body vehicle. Integration is what made the activities associated with acquiring this knowledge complementary. Moreover, the integration also improved GM's internal production flow and thereby enabled workers to acquire skills about processes related to chassis assembly, which were applicable in neighbouring activities. These skills, and the associated learning and adaptation of GM's production line workers, increased GM's overall productivity, which in turn created incentives to increase scale to accommodate these newly acquired skills. This technological trajectory (Dosi 1988) that GM pursued contributed, for a while, to the firm's coherent context for motivating and enhancing the salience of many new resource deployment opportunities that were then within the firm's reach. In turn, GM's expanded 'productive opportunity' exposed a need for, and stimulated improvements in, the firm's organizational capability. The firm's ability to acquire specific knowledge, therefore, enabled it on the one hand to exploit economies of scope by moving into related markets, and on the other hand to expand geographically to exploit economies of scale (Chandler 1990).

Michael Best (1990) has described the institutionalization of Schumpeterian integration (which he refers to as 'Schumpeterian organizational innovation') within Japanese firms. He argues that 'the successful Japanese firm has combined Schumpeter and Penrose, and thereby altered the notion of entrepreneurship from "big ideas by individuals" to a social process of learning within which individual contributions can come from the bottom up, as well as from specialist staff' (Best 1990: 138).

5. Discussion

The insights of Penrose and Schumpeter give us the foundation for an integrative theory of dynamic firm growth. While Penrose's theory, on the one hand, offers a compelling explanation of why and how successful firms are able to grow, it does not offer any systematic explanation of why and how the growth of successful firms can stall. Schumpeter, on the other hand, explained—at least in his earlier work (1934)—why innovative new growth opportunities are more likely to be exploited by new firms, leading ultimately to a migration of resources away from existing firms. Thus, while his theory provides a powerful explanation for the decline of large established firms, it does not adequately explain why and how some of the largest firms in the world can continue to grow, often by continuing to proliferate innovative new products and services.

In this chapter, we have integrated the core ideas of both these pioneering authors to suggest a tension-inducing symbiotic process of firm growth and economic development. Growth begets growth, as Penrose suggested, because the expanding productive possibilities that inherently accompany resource accumulation generally lead to an expanded productive opportunity for the growing firm. But for growth to be sustainable, the firm's productive opportunity must be kept in balance by periodic administrative reorganization to motivate and accommodate the entrepreneurial judgement that is needed to exploit this expanding set of possibilities. Without such administrative reorganization to maintain coherence among a sufficient proportion of productive possibilities, the proportion of possibilities that remain dormant and unexploited by the firm will grow. In any vibrant economy (that is, one with many organizational alternatives or the possibility of such alternatives), such a growing imbalance of unexploited possibilities will lead ultimately to a migration of those resources and their deployment to those existing and potential alternatives outside the firm.

The story, at least for relatively large and complex companies, is of a continuous battle between the evolving organizational capability of the firm and the discipline of the firm's external markets. The more developed and sophisticated the markets, the greater the pressure on the firm and the greater the likelihood of a migration of resources and opportunities away from it. The more a firm is able to enhance its organizational capability (through a coherent administrative framework) to develop and accommodate a diversity of entrepreneurial judgements from its members, the more easily the firm will be able to continue to grow, in defiance of the market's discipline.

5.1. Diversification and Firm Performance

Several pieces of historical evidence exist that lend a degree of credibility to our story. The vast literature on the relationship between diversification and corporate performance provides one example. As has been widely documented (see the review in Markides 1995), empirical evidence on this topic—much of it based on studies conducted in the United States—has remained highly equivocal and inconsistent. Despite Rumelt's (1974) finding that the *way* in which a firm's businesses are related affects performance more than the degree of its diversification, a vast majority of these studies have attempted to relate some measure of the extent of product-market diversification with different aspects of firm performance, with no attention being paid to the issues of organizational capability. (Important exceptions include Jemison and Sitkin 1986; Grant 1988; Hill and Hoskisson 1987; Hill, Hitt, and Hoskisson 1992; Markides 1995.)

The theory we have presented suggests that the nature of the diversification–performance relationship will be strongly mediated by organizational capability, and the inconsistencies in past research findings may well be due to the omission of this contingency factor. Companies with superior ability to marshall the entrepreneurial abilities of their members without sacrificing administrative coherence can continue to perform well despite their larger size and greater degree of product-market diversity, when compared with companies that lack this capability.

Teece and colleagues' (Teece *et al.* 1994) finding of a high degree of coherence (measured in product market terms), across a broad range of corporations that vary markedly in the degree of their diversification (measured as the number of activities), lends support to the notion that coherence is important to firm growth. Moreover, the persistence of this finding across firms of varying diversity suggests that coherence stems less from product market or technical relatedness than from the firm's organizational or 'combinative' capabilities (see Kogut and Zander 1992)—a product of what Kogut and Zander (1992) have described as 'organizing principles' and Conner (1991) has referred to as 'linking mechanisms'. The ongoing superior performance of at least a few highly visible and highly diversified firms such as General Electric, 3M, and Motorola may well be due to their greater capacity to maintain coherence across a broader range of products and technologies. There is some evidence, even if not highly systematic, about the superior organizational ability of these companies and of the attention their managers pay to continuously protecting and enhancing that ability (for example, Tichy and Sherman 1993; Collins and Porras 1994).

Our framework also accounts for the inverted U-shape of the baseline relationship observed between diversification and performance in developed countries like the United States and the United Kingdom. Following directly from our earlier discussion on the role of the environment in firm growth, as a firm's stock of 'inherited' resources increases in size and diversity, its productive opportunity (and with it, performance) should grow—until the point is reached where it loses administrative coherence and, with it, some of its productive opportunity. Increasing diversity, beyond the firm's ability to maintain coherence, should have a negative impact on performance.

Our argument is also consistent with recent findings that this baseline relationship may not hold in developing economies such as South Korea, Indonesia, and India (Khanna and Palepu 1996). The relative scarcity of resources that generally prevails in developing nations may extend the particular challenge to growth faced by small firms to larger and more diverse firms as the munificence of their environment diminishes. Indeed, this 'small firm' effect may even be exacerbated, rather than attenuated by further growth. In the absence of an environment that is sufficiently endowed with resources and opportunities, firms may need to make up for a baseline level of coherence that is readily available in more advanced economies but not in developing ones. This is likely to have an adverse effect on performance until firms are large enough to benefit from their added investments in infrastructure and capabilities. Once they reach sufficient size, however, they are likely to have opportunities that do not exist elsewhere to any but the largest of firms. *Ceteris paribus* (and given a certain level of organizational capability), firms will be able to grow and diversify to a greater extent in economies characterized by relatively lower levels of market discipline than they can in economies where such discipline is much stronger.

5.2. The Evolution of Corporate Forms

At a broader historical level, the arguments we have presented here provide one explanation of the evolution of organizational forms in large corporations. The symbiotic process of growth we have described implies the periodic enhancement by the growing firm of its ability to facilitate the exercise of entrepreneurial judgement within its membership and the continuous preservation of its overall administrative coherence. The framework we have presented resonates with Thompson's (1967) dynamic open systems view of organization in which structure plays an instrumental role in accommodating the firm's co-ordination and control requirements. Complex organizations, according to Thompson, behave dynamically and adaptively by continually modifying and adjusting their structures as they seek 'determinateness' and 'certainty'. Thompson defined structure as the 'internal differentiation and patterning of relationships' and described it as a fundamental vehicle for organizations to create 'numerous spheres of bounded rationality [and] facilitate the coordinated action of those interdependent elements' (p. 54). As they grow, their need for both differentiation and integration increases—an argument that has been made and empirically supported by Lawrence and Lorsch (1967).

This is, indeed, the explanation provided by Chandler (1962) for the evolution and subsequent diffusion of the multidivisional organization. The functional organization, or F-form as Williamson (1975) labelled it, was instrumental in focusing firms on the development of specialized functions, particularly when no alternatives existed externally. This form, like any other, had an upper limit to what may be described as its 'carrying capacity of complexity'—that is, the extent to which it could accommodate the exercise of entrepreneurial judgement by its members, given the size and diversity of its accumulated stock of resources. Essentially, only the general manager in an F-form firm had the multifunctional perspective required to both perceive entrepreneurial opportunities and be able to act on such perceptions. However, as an F-form firm grew, the multifunctional possibilities created by the firm, and others like it, required a greater capacity for accommodating and exploiting the complexity they were generating. That is, they required an administrative organization that could continue to accommodate the growing diversity of people who could see what might be possible and would be willing and able to exploit their entrepreneurial judgement within the boundaries of the firm. Beyond a certain level of size and diversity—a level that was eventually exceeded by companies like General Motors and DuPont—companies operating under F-form structures found it increasingly more difficult to exploit the productive possibilities that were accumulating with their growing stocks of diverse resources. The innovation of the M-form by the managers of some of the largest companies in the early years of the twentieth century was the outcome of their efforts to relax this constraint. As Chandler has explained, the M-form created a new level of general managers, below the corporate chief executive, to whom strategic—that is, entrepreneurial—decisions could be delegated. What this decentralization accomplished was a significant broadening in the source of entrepreneurial judgement that could be accommodated within the company—an appreciable expansion in the organizations' carrying capacity of complexity. It is this expansion that ultimately allowed these pioneering companies to grow and diversify well beyond the limits imposed by the F-form.

Over the last seven decades, a vast majority of large companies around the world have made organizational changes similar to those documented by Chandler in his four famous cases (see Rumelt 1974; Dyas and Thanheiser 1976). This, indeed, is the general outcome that our story of firm growth would predict. What is at work here is the same continuing battle between firms and their managers, on the one hand, striving to preserve their ability to grow, and of market discipline, on the other hand, forcing them to expand their ability to accommodate a broader array of entrepreneurial judgement or else 'hand on' their productive possibilities and their associated resources and face a slackening of growth or even decline.

Several contemporary observers of large companies have suggested that another round of fairly fundamental organizational change is currently occurring among the largest companies (for example, Tushman and Anderson 1986; Handy 1990). In an article entitled 'Beyond the M-form', Bartlett and Ghoshal (1993) have described what they believe is an emergent new organizational form the defining characteristics of which are 'radical decentralization' and a focus on stimulating and supporting frontline entrepreneurship. In essence, the arguments of these authors can be interpreted as possible indicators of the next step in the evolution of corporate organizational forms: for the largest and most complex firms, the M-form may have reached the limits of its complexity-carrying capacity and the search is now on for another round of organizational innovation for expanding a firm's ability to accommodate more 'distributed' entrepreneurship, while still preserving administrative coherence.

While the evidence of such a change is still only anecdotal at best, the evolutionary process described by these authors is entirely consistent with the theoretical arguments we have presented in this chapter. That is, the largest firms—for which maintaining coherence in resource deployments is made more difficult by the breadth of deployment possibilities available—will be limited in their ability to grow further. This limit will be greater in advanced economies, where the pressure to deploy resources to their current best use is greater. Unless these companies are able to discover new organizational forms that will enable them to preserve coherence at historic levels, their growth will stall or even reverse itself.

5.3. The Role of Management

The arguments we have presented here also suggest a theory-grounded way to conceptualize the role of firm management. The recognition that the performance of organizations depends to a large extent on the ability of those who administer their operations does not require much insight into the real world of the successes or failures of established enterprises. Both Penrose and Schumpeter placed special importance on the entrepreneurial role of management in their theories. Indeed, Penrose defined the 'class of firms which are capable of growing' (1959: 33)—that is, the 'successful' firms whose growth her theory explains—as those 'possessing or able to attract competent management' (p. 33). Both Penrose and Schumpeter also took care to distinguish this entrepreneurial role of management from the more routine functions of administration that occupy a large part of the management literature (for example, see Penrose 1959: 31n.–32n.). Explicit in both Schumpeter's and Penrose's theories of growth is their notion of enterprise, as it is practised by entrepreneurs, which transcends the function of a 'mere manager' (Schumpeter 1934: 83), in that it is not restricted either to routine administrative tasks or to those few individuals who are in the position of 'manager'.

Schumpeter saw entrepreneurship (or innovation) as significantly different from invention: 'The inventor produces ideas, the entrepreneur "gets things done"' (1947: 152). The importance of this distinction between discovery of and exploitation of opportunity lies in the fact that many inventions never lead to the realization of the potential value that their discovery may have created.

While invention usually comprises the fruition of insight and capabilities that are resident in only a few minds, innovation more often requires the combination of insights and capabilities of many individuals.

Getting things done, especially new innovative things, often requires a substitution of one institutional context for another—that is, the internalization of some economic activity into a specific organization, often a new firm. Carrying out new combinations typically entails some reorganization of economic activities when the exigencies of established practice favour alternative deployments of the resources needed for the combinations (see Moran and Ghoshal, 1999). A new 'administrative organization' (Penrose 1959) is needed to meld the insights and capabilities of many into a workable whole, one that enhances the abilities of each individual to 'cope with the resistance and difficulties which action always meets with outside of the ruts of established practice' (Schumpeter 1947: 152). We have referred to this ability of accommodating the entrepreneurial judgement of many within a coherent administrative framework as organizational capability. Organizational capability facilitates the carrying out of new combinations by providing the means to cope with the resistance and difficulties typically imposed by established practice on attempts to exercise entrepreneurial judgement. In the views of Schumpeter and of Penrose, it is the development, protection, and continuous enhancement of organizational capability that defines the primary responsibility of management, at least for large firms where this capability—rather than the mere availability of accumulated resources— becomes the primary determinant of the extent to which the firm can exploit its productive opportunities.

Thus, by creating and shaping an institutional context that facilitates the accumulation of new resources and their accommodation with existing resources towards new productive opportunities, management determines the locus of Schumpeterian integration (see Figure 7.2). Without the ability to design an internal context that can accommodate new resource combinations, Schumpeterian integration is not possible. If it occurs at all, it will take place in new rather than existing firms, particularly as the discipline of the market's forces intensifies. Indeed, there is at least some evidence that the behavioural context provided by the firm is more strongly associated with a firm's performance as the firm's environment becomes increasingly more competitive (see Burt, Gabbay, Holt, and Moran 1994). Management's key role, then, is continuously to keep in balance the productive opportunities that are inherent in the firm's accumulating stock of resources, and the structure, processes, and context of the firm's organization, so as to allow the exploitation of these opportunities through the collective entrepreneurial judgement of its organizational members (see Ghoshal and Bartlett 1994). It is this accommodation, rather than the accumulating stock of resources, *per se*, that facilitates the use of those resources for an idiosyncratic set of activities—that is, what we describe as the firm's strategy.

References

ARTHUR, W. B. 1989. 'Competing technologies, increasing returns, and lock-in by historical events', *Economic Journal* 99: 116–31.

BARTLETT, C. A., and S. GHOSHAL 1993. 'Beyond the M-form: Toward a managerial theory of the firm', *Strategic Management Journal* 14 (Winter Special Issue): 23–46.

BEST, M. 1990. *The New Competition: Institutions of Industrial Restructuring*. Cambridge: Polity Press.

BURT, R. S., S. M. GABBAY, G. HOLT, and P. MORAN 1994. "Contingent organization as a network theory: The culture-performance contingency function', *Acta Sociologica* 37: 345–70.

CHANDLER, A. D. 1962. *Strategy and Structure: Chapters in the History of the American Industrial Enterprise*. Cambridge, MA: MIT Press.

CHANDLER, A. D., JR. 1990. *Scale and Scope: The Dynamics of Industrial Capitalism*. Cambridge, MA: Belknap/Harvard University Press.

COHEN, W. M., and D. A. LEVINTHAL 1990. 'Absorptive capacity: A new perspective on learning and innovation', *Administrative Science Quarterly* 35(1): 128–52.

COLLINS, J. C., and J. I. PORRAS 1994. *Built to Last: Successful Habits of Visionary Companies*. New York: Harper Business.

CONNER, K. R. 1991. 'A historical comparison of resource-based theory and five schools of thought within industrial organization economics: Do we have a new theory of the firm?', *Journal of Management* 17(1): 121–54.

DOSI, G. 1988. 'Sources, procedures and microeconomic effects of innovation', *Journal of Economic Literature* 26 (September): 1120–71.

DYAS, G. P., and H. T. THANHEISER 1976. *The Emerging European Enterprise, Strategy and Structure in French and German Industry*. London: Macmillan.

ELIASSON, G. 1990. 'The knowledge based information economy', in G. Eliasson, ed., *The Knowledge Based Information Economy*. Stockholm: IUI.

GHOSHAL, S., and C. A. BARTLETT 1994. 'Linking organizational context and managerial action: The dimensions of quality of management', *Strategic Management Journal* 15 (Summer Special Issue): 91–112.

GRANT, R. M. 1988. 'On "dominant logic," relatedness and the link between diversity and performance', *Strategic Management Journal* 12: 639–42.

HANDY, C. 1990. *The Age of Unreason*. Boston: Harvard Business School Press.

HILL, C. W. L., and R. E. HOSKISSON 1987. 'Strategy and structure in the multiproduct firm', *Academy of Management Review* 12: 331–41.

—— M. A. HITT, and R. E. HOSKISSON 1992. 'Cooperative versus competitive structures in related and unrelated diversified firms', *Organization Science* 3(4, November): 501–21.

JEMISON, D., and S. SITKIN 1986. 'Corporate acquisitions: A process perspective', *Academy of Management Review* 11(1): 145–264.

KHANNA, T., and K. PALEPU 1996. 'Corporate scope and (severe) market imperfections: An empirical analysis of diversified business groups in an emerging economy'. Mimeo, Harvard Business School.

KOGUT, B., and U. ZANDER 1992. 'Knowledge of the firm, combinative capabilities and the replication of technology', *Organization Science* 3 (August): 383–97.

LANGLOIS, R. N. 1995. 'Capabilities and coherence in firms and markets', in C. A. Montgomery, ed., *Resource-Based and Evolutionary Theories of the Firm: Towards a Synthesis*. Norwell, MA and Dordrecht: Kluwer Academic, 71–100.

—— and P. L. ROBERTSON 1989. 'Explaining vertical integration: Lessons from the American automobile industry', *Journal of Economic History* 49(2, June): 361–75.

LAWRENCE, P. R., and J. W. LORSCH 1967. *Organization and Environment: Managing Differentiation and Integration*. Boston: Harvard Business School Press.

MARKIDES, C. C. 1995. 'Diversification, restructuring and economic performance', *Strategic Management Journal* 16: 101–18.

MONTGOMERY, C. A., and S. HARIHARAN 1991. 'Diversified expansion in large established firms', *Journal of Economic Behavior and Organization* (January): 71–89.

MORAN, P., and S. GHOSHAL 1999. 'Markets, firms, and the process of economic development', *Academy of Management Review* 24(3): 390–412.

NELSON, R. R. 1991. 'Why do firms differ, and how does it matter?', *Strategic Management Journal* 12: 61–74.

—— and S. G. WINTER 1982. *An Evolutionary Theory of Economic Change*. Cambridge, MA: Harvard University Press.

NORTH, D. C. 1994. 'Economic performance through time', *American Economic Review* 84(3, June): 359–68.

PENROSE, E. T. 1959. *The Theory of the Growth of the Firm*. New York: Wiley.

—— 1995. *The Theory of the Growth of the Firm*, 3rd edn. Oxford: Oxford University Press.

RUMELT, R. P. 1974. *Strategy, Structure and Economic Performance*. Cambridge, MA: Harvard University Press.

SCHUMPETER, J. A. 1934. *The Theory of Economic Development*. Cambridge, MA: Harvard University Press.

—— 1947. 'The creative response in economic history', *Journal of Economic History* 7(2): 149–59.

TEECE, D. J., R. P. RUMELT, G. DOSI, and S. G. WINTER 1994. 'Understanding corporate coherence: Theory and evidence', *Journal of Economic Behavior and Organization* 23: 1–30.

THOMPSON, J. A. 1967. *Organizations in Action*. New York: McGraw-Hill.

TICHY, N., and S. SHERMAN 1993. *Control your Destiny or Someone Else Will: How Jack Welch is Making General Electric the World's Most Competitive Corporation*. New York: Doubleday.

TUSHMAN, M. L., and P. ANDERSON 1986. 'Technological discontinuities and organizational environments', *Administrative Science Quarterly* 31: 439–65.

WEITZMAN, M. L. 1996. 'Hybridizing growth theory', *American Economic Review* 86(2): 207–12.

WILLIAMSON, O. E. 1975. *Markets and Hierarchies: Analysis and Antitrust Implications*. New York: Free Press.

8

The Growth of Firms in Theory and in Practice

PAUL A. GEROSKI

1. Introduction

The modern theory of the firm has mainly been concerned with devising explanations of why firms exist. In fact, there is currently a broad consensus amongst economists that 'it remains one of the most profound challenges to identify the forces that determine whether transactions are conducted within the firm as opposed to through the market' (Moore 1992: 494). Interesting as this problem is, answering it does not actually take us very far in understanding what we observe about firms. It is, for example, hard to derive much of a theory of the growth of the firm from transaction-cost or governance-based theories of the firm. At best, one might argue that exogenous changes in transaction costs or governance technologies will induce changes in optimum firm size that, sooner or later, lead to changes in the size of firms. In fact, any of a number of potential determinants of optimum firm size can form the basis of a theory of corporate growth: when firms are away from their optimum, growth (or decline) occurs as competitive forces drive them towards equilibrium. However, in this view, growth is driven by exogenous events and it is a transitory phenomenon that occurs only until equilibrium is restored.

Older traditions of thinking have produced rather more satisfactory (or, at least, more interesting) models than this. There have, for example, been several attempts to develop stage theories of firm growth over the years (not all of which are based on simple biological analogies). These theories are often based on a conceptual framework which has more appreciative than predictive power, and they often seem to be a little over stylized or just too simple. Most of the interesting theorizing about the growth of the firm was either developed by Penrose (1959) or synthesized by her into her own work. She argued that the firm 'is basically a collection of resources' (p. 77), and then analysed the process of growth in terms of the speed with which firms could accumulate and assimilate such resources, and the opportunities for further growth which arise when a firm's internal resources are under-used. Following this tradition but shifting the focus slightly away from the resources themselves and towards the management of resources, many economic historians and management scholars have argued that:

the key concept . . . (which we need to use) . . . to explain . . . the beginnings and growth of modern industrial enterprises is that of organizational capabilities. These capabilities were created during the learning process involved in bringing a new or greatly improved technology on stream, in coming to know the requirements of markets for new or improved products, the availability and reliability of suppliers, the intricacies of recruiting and training managers and workers.   (Chandler 1992: 487.)

Different as they seem, all of these various ways of thinking about the growth of firms have at least one very important feature in common, namely that they are very hard to reconcile with much of what we have learned from econometric work on the growth performance of firms. This observation applies particularly to recent resource-based theories of the firm: the nature of competences and the process by which they are accumulated is hard to reconcile with the erratic growth performance that most firms display. This observation is the subject of the chapter, and documenting it forms its substance. The plan is as follows. In section 2, I will set out some of the basic 'facts' about the growth of firms which have been uncovered in recent econometric work. In section 3, I will confront these 'facts' with a set of predictions about corporate growth which have emerged from the two traditions of thinking about firms alluded to above. The main thrust of the argument is that most of these predictions are more or less inconsistent with the 'facts' on corporate growth. Section 4 contains some suggestions about the direction which future work on the theory of the firm might take.

2. The Growth of Firms in Practice

The most elementary 'fact' about corporate growth thrown up by econometric work on both large and small firms is that firm size follows a random walk. If we denote the size of firm i in period t by $S_i(t)$, then this observation can be written concisely as

$$\Delta \log S_i(t) \equiv \log S_i(t) - \log S_i(t-1) = \mu_i(t), \qquad (1)$$

where $\mu_i(t)$ is a normally distributed iid random variable with a mean of zero and a variance of δ^2.

It is worth being clear about just exactly what this 'fact' means. In the first place, equation (1) says that increases in firm size are driven by unexpected shocks. This is not quite the same as saying that growth is driven by 'mere chance' or 'good luck'. An unexpected shock may occur because we do not know what will happen, but it may also arise if we know what will happen to a particular firm but are not sure when it will happen. Put another way, equation (1) is a compact and succinct description of a process which may be very well understood, but hard to describe or predict with any precision. Moreover, unexpected means 'relative to some information set'; that is, what we expect depends on what we know. Hence, what may seem surprising to an econometrician may not, in fact, be very surprising to the managers of the firm to which it happens. In this case, equation (1) may turn out to be the best description of what happens to a firm that is available to outsiders.

Second and much more important, equation (1) says that unexpected shocks have permanent effects on the size of the firm: each idiosyncratic shock that affects the firm leaves a permanent mark. This means that corporate growth cannot be thought of as a process composed of a deterministic trend with some noise superimposed on it.[1] The trend itself is stochastic. Another way to make this point is to observe that equation (1) implies that

$$\log S_i(t) = S_0 + \Sigma\mu_i(s), \tag{2}$$

where the index s runs from 1 to t and S_0 is the initial value of $S(t)$, that is, the firm's start-up size. Thus, the size of a firm at any time is just the sum of the whole history of shocks, expected and unexpected, which it has received since it was founded in $t = 0$. To say that firm size follows a random walk, then, implies that corporate growth is a path-dependent process. The unpredictable nature of these shocks means that it is difficult, if not impossible, to predict what a firm's size will be at any time in the future, $t + \tau$.

Some will argue that equation (1) is an over-strong characterization of what we know about corporate growth, and there may be some truth in this. There is, in fact, a large empirical literature which has explored a variant of equation (1), namely

$$\Delta\log S_i(t) = \alpha + \beta\log S_i(t) + \mu_i(t), \tag{3}$$

where the observation that $\beta < 0$ is taken to indicate the existence of 'mean reversion'; that is, the proposition that larger firms grow relatively more slowly than smaller firms. A levelling out in growth rates between large and small firms in this manner bounds the overall rise in the variance of firm sizes. Further, if $\alpha > 0$ and is common to all firms, then firms whose size evolves over time according to equation (3) will all converge to the same, common long-run or steady-state size of $(-\alpha/\beta)$. The evidence on mean reversion and convergence is, however, quite mixed. Most estimates of β reported in the literature are quite small, and work using panel data almost invariably reveals that different firms display different estimated values of α. This means that firms (even those in the same industry) converge to different steady-state sizes; that is, that differences in firm size are permanent and not transitory. Further, direct (and arguably more powerful and persuasive) tests of convergence using long times series of data on different firms suggest that no stable or predictable differences in size or growth

---

[1] This is often described as the difference between a '*trend stationary*' and a '*difference stationary*' process in the macroeconomics literature; see Nelson and Plosser (1982). Most studies of GDP suggest that, like firm size, it is (more or less) difference stationary (that is, it follows a random walk).

exist in the short or the long run.[2] All of this means that the evidence against the proposition that firm sizes do not converge within or across industries is not very strong.[3] The simple fact is that firm size drifts unpredictably over time, and, as a consequence, predictions of $S_i(t + \tau)$ become increasingly uncertain as τ gets larger.

Two further implications of equation (1) are worth noting. The first is that since $\mu_i(t)$ is independently distributed across firms i, the growth rates of any two firms, i and j, chosen at random are likely to be uncorrelated. That is, corporate growth rates are likely to be idiosyncratic. This is a surprising observation, since common sense suggests that the growth rates of most firms should rise and fall with variations in the growth rate of the economy as a whole, or at least of the industry they inhabit. In fact, the evidence is that this tendency towards common growth rates across firms in the same industry (much less across the economy as a whole) is pretty weak. Including a macroeconomic growth variable in equations (1) or (3) typically generates a positive and significant coefficient that does not, however, add much explanatory power to a regression which (typically) already displays a tiny R^2. Further, studies of company performance in cyclical downturns usually show that most of the effects of recessions are concentrated in a few firms; many companies are not substantially affected and some actually prosper during cyclical downturns.[4] The upshot of all of this is that there is apparently very little in the current or recent past growth of rival company j that can be used to help predict the current or near future growth of firm i; corporate growth is history dependent and every firm seems to have its own particular history.

The second further implication of equation (1) is the absence of any dynamics associated with lagged dependent variables. A conventional dynamic econometric model of growth might take the form of

$$\Delta\log S_i(t) = \alpha + \theta(L) \, \Delta\log S_i(t{-}1) + \mu_i(t), \qquad (4)$$

where $\theta(L)$ is a polynomial in the lag operator L. Although it is occasionally possible to observe significant coefficients on $t{-}1$ and $t{-}2$ lags in the dependent variable, these terms rarely add much explanatory power to corporate growth

[2] For recent work, see Dunne and Hughes (1994); Evans (1987); Hall (1987); Hart and Oulton (1996); and others. Much of this literature is concerned with the evolution of industrial concentration, since Gibrat's law (which is what equation (1) is) predicts that the variance of firm sizes and, therefore, the concentration of economic activity in the hands of a few firms, will rise without bound.

[3] See Geroski, Walters, and Urga (1998). The major caveat to these conclusions is the literature on very small, new firms, which typically finds much larger and more precisely estimated effects associated with firm size (and age); see, for example, the references cited in note 2 above, and the papers in the 1995 *International Journal of Industrial Organization* special issue on 'The Post-Entry Performance of Firms'.

[4] See Davis, Haltiwanger, and Schuh (1996); Geroski and Gregg (1997); and others.

rate regressions.[5] Since the dynamics associated with the lagged dependent variable in equation (4) are typically interpreted in terms of adjustment costs, the fact that equation (4) reduces to equation (1) means that corporate growth rates are not smoothed. The implication is that firms do not appear to anticipate shocks and begin reacting before they occur; nor do they appear to be only partially adjusting to current shocks, postponing full adjustment to minimize adjustment costs.

Two further pieces of evidence complement the central 'fact' that firm size follows a random walk. The first is that adjustment costs seem to be fixed and not variable. The distinction may seem a little arcane, but it has a profound impact on the times series behaviour of output, investment, employment, and other choices made by firms. If adjustment costs are variable and increasing in the size of the desired adjustment, firms will have an incentive to spread out their adjustment to shocks, responding regularly but by a small amount. This type of behaviour will result in an equation like (4). If, on the other hand, adjustment costs are fixed, then firms have an incentive to 'save up' their desired changes until it is worth incurring the fixed costs to make them, and then they will make them all in one 'big bang'. This is sometimes called an (s,S) policy, and even if one knows the size of the adjustment that firms wish to make, the timing of when they choose to act is likely to be unpredictable. As a consequence, firm size will follow a path which looks more like equation (1) than equation (4). In fact, the evidence is that firms typically make large but infrequent and clearly discrete changes in their operations (for example in employment and investment), rather than continuous but small ones. This is perfectly consistent with equation (1), and is presumably why equation (4) gives a relatively poor fit on the data.[6]

The second added piece of evidence is that most firms are erratic and irregular innovators; that is, very few firms produce major innovations or patents on a regular basis (actually, very few firms ever innovate in this sense, but those that do are rarely persistent innovators). This evidence is difficult to interpret, since it depends on how frequently one observes firms and on what exactly one means by 'innovate'. On the one hand, most large firms regularly spend money on research and development, but, on the other, none has ever engineered a breakthrough as fundamental as splitting the atom. However, if we focus on activities

[5] For regression results which include one or more lags, see Geroski, Machin, and Walters (1997) and others. That $\theta(L) \approx 0$ is no surprise to those who believe that $\beta \approx 0$ in equation (3), since both simplifications yield the same outcome (namely, equation (1)); that is, both are tests of Gibrat's law.

[6] For some direct evidence based on establishment data taken from the Census, see Caballero, Engel, and Haltiwanger (1995, 1997); Geroski and Gregg (1997), and Davis, Haltiwanger, and Schuh (1996) notice much the same thing in their studies of how firms respond to recessionary pressures, observing that firms are much more likely to close whole plants than to make marginal adjustments in the size of their work-force. For a survey of work on labour adjustment costs, see also Hamermesh and Pfann (1994).

that lead to noticeable technical breakthroughs which are commercially success-ful (that is, 'major innovations') or patents, then the data suggest that very few firms manage to produce a regular sequence of innovative outputs. The typical pattern is that firms will innovate every once in a while, opening up what are sometimes very long periods of time between successive innovations.[7] Erratic innovative activity is likely to mean that the growth spurts experienced by firms will be unpredictable, and this is, of course, just what equation (1) describes.

3. Some Theories of Corporate Growth

Although they seem to be rather simple, it turns out that the 'facts' discussed in section 2 cast some doubt on the usefulness of a range of models of or hypothe-ses about corporate growth which have appeared in the literature. We begin by focusing on four rather different types of theories of growth: models of optimum firm size, stage theories of growth, models with Penrose effects, and models of organizational capabilities.[8]

3.1. Models of Optimum Firm Size

Most economists look for steady-state equilibrium configurations as a founda-tion upon which to do comparative static exercises, and much of the theory of the firm has been expressed in these terms. The oldest and best-known argument suggests that competition will drive firms to the bottom of their U-shaped aver-age cost curves. If firms have market power, then their optimum size may differ from this minimum cost position, and, if economies of scope exist, such differ-ences may be more noticeable (and, of course, firms will be diversified in this case). More recent arguments have suggested that the degree to which costs are (endogenously or exogenously) sunk and the intensity of competition may also be important determinants of firm size (and market structure). Further, many believe that internal organizational factors may be as important as market competition and technology in determining firm size. The ability of managers to control their firms may be limited by serial errors in communicating up and down a management hierarchy, or by other transaction costs. Although such problems can be mitigated by restructuring the organization in various ways, the bottom line is that sooner or later, firms are likely to become too large to

[7] See Geroski, van Reenen, and Walters (1997); Cefis (1996); Malerba and Orsenigo (1995); and others. Cefis observes much the same pattern of innovative activity over time as Geroski *et al.*, but interprets it slightly differently.

[8] For surveys of all or part of this literature, see You (1995); Sutton (1997); and others. There is also a literature which examines possible trade-offs between growth and profitability, focusing on the proposition that managerially controlled firms will grow 'too fast'. The 'facts' discussed in section 2 do not cast much light on this argument.

control.[9] Whatever the details, these models typically yield an outcome in which optimum firm size, S_i^*, depends on a number of exogenous variables.

The traditional way to get a model of growth out of this kind of argument is to use S^* as a benchmark, and then to interpret all observed changes in firm size either as white noise or as part of a transitional process of convergence to S^*. The most commonly used model of this type is a partial adjustment model of the form:

$$\Delta\log S_i(t) = \lambda\{\log S^* - \log S_i(t{-}1)\} + \mu_i(t). \tag{5}$$

λ is the interesting parameter in this model, as it governs the rate at which convergence occurs. If $\lambda = 0$, then convergence never occurs, while if $\lambda = 1$, then $\log S_i(t) = \log S^*$ always. Note that if S^* is constant over time, this model is equivalent to equation (3) when $\alpha \equiv \lambda\log S^*$ and $\lambda \equiv -\beta$.

Regarded as a model of the growth of the firm, equation (5) has the serious disadvantage of being inconsistent with the 'facts'. There are three problems. First, as we noted earlier, equation (3) and, therefore, equation (5) are at best only weakly consistent with the data: the values of λ which have been estimated using empirical models of this type imply that convergence is, at best, implausibly slow. Further, as we noted earlier, the very poor fit of these estimated models means that most of the variation in corporate growth rates is driven by $\mu_i(t)$. Secondly, and probably more seriously, most of the arguments used in these models generate predictions about the size or interindustry variation in S^* which are not firm specific. (For example, technology is typically assumed to be common to all firms in the industry, serial communication costs do not depend on who communicates but on the height of the hierarchy and the span of control, and so on.) This means that these models usually imply that all firms in the same industry will converge to the same size, S^*. This is clearly inconsistent with the data, which, as we saw earlier, suggest that there is, at best, only a very weak tendency for firms to converge towards a common size even in the same industry. Thirdly, and finally, the presumption that S^* is a fixed target towards which firms tend is impossible to reconcile with the 'fact' that firm size follows a random walk.

There are at least two ways to redesign this kind of model to make it consistent with equation (1). The basic trick is to let S^* drift unpredictably over time. Suppose, for example, that the exogenous variables which determine $\log S^*$ are

[9] See Scherer and Ross (1990) for a survey of many of the traditional arguments about optimum firm size; Sutton (1991) focuses on sunk costs and the intensity of competition. Williamson (1967) developed the model of hierarchy alluded to in the text; see also his 1970 book for early work on how restructuring may mitigate some of these problems. For a recent and fairly comprehensive textbook treatment of many of the issues originally raised by Williamson, see Milgrom and Roberts (1992). For recent related work on transactions and governance theories of the firm, see Hart (1995) and Williamson (1996).

altered by a large number of small, independent, firm-specific shocks which occur in each period. Then, if we suppose that $S_i(t) = S^*(t)$ (that is, that there are no transitional dynamics of the form of equation (5)), and collect these shocks together into one random variable $\mu_i(t)$, we arrive at equation (1). This is, of course, the standard explanation of what underlies Gibrat's law. A second version of this argument is the 'island markets' model.[10] The idea here is that each firm i is faced with a sequence of independent opportunities of varying sizes which arise exogenously over time. As each opportunity arises, there is a probability p that it will be taken up by a new entrant and a probability $(1 - p)$ that the firm will colonize it. If the size of the firm has an effect on the number of opportunities that it takes advantage of, then this argument produces a model like equation (3); if the size of the firm has no influence on the probability of colonizing a market in any period t, then this argument generates equation (1).

Thus, it is possible to reconcile the tradition of thinking in terms of optimum firm sizes with the 'facts' by letting S^* vary unpredictably, and by assuming that firms are always at (or only depart unpredictably from) their optimum sizes. The problem with these solutions is that they effectively make corporate growth an exogenously driven process, and this is not consistent with the many observations we have on how corporate decisions sometimes decisively alter the evolution of technology, the structure of transaction costs, or the development of demand.

3.2. Stage Theories of Growth

Although they are not much in fashion now, there have been a number of attempts over the years to identify life cycles of firms, model their evolution, or at least pick out identifiable stages through which they grow. For example, Greiner (1972) argued that firms evolve through five phases, each characterized by a period of relatively stable growth. These phases (which he identified with a label that indicates the nature of the management problem characteristic of each: 'creativity', 'direction', 'delegation', 'co-ordination', and 'collaboration') are separated by four crises (of 'leadership', 'autonomy', 'control', and 'red tape'). More recently, Garnsey (1998) has developed a model of corporate growth which traces out a set of phases which correspond to the development and deployment of new internal resources in young firms. Finally, in something of a different tradition, Mueller (1972) argued that what a firm does (that is, its propensity to maximize profits or sacrifice profits for growth) varies with age (and other factors, like investment opportunities). A strictly profit-maximizing firm is likely

---

[10] See Sutton (1997, 1998), who attributes it to Simon. Sutton is arguably not interested in the growth of firms, but, rather, in developing a lower bound on industry concentration, and this makes one reluctant to see it as a serious attempt to construct a model of corporate growth.

to enjoy only a finite burst of growth associated with each innovation. However, if the innovation fuels enough growth to weaken the power of shareholders, then managers will gradually acquire some room to exercise discretion. Since they are liable to be more interested in the size or growth of the firm than in its profits, they will take advantage of this discretion to reinvest too much of the proceeds from the innovation into this or other investment opportunities. As a consequence, 'too much' growth is likely to be associated with each innovation, and it is likely to go on for 'too long'.

These arguments have more than a little superficial plausibility. Stage theories of growth have some basis in fact (entrepreneurial firms eventually outgrow their founders and become bureaucratic institutions, all firms mature, and many decline and disappear, and so on), and they are often a useful aid to conceptualization. However, even if all firms progress through all five of Greiner's phases, they are likely to do so at very different rates and will probably enjoy different growth rates in each phase. Similarly, although it is not hard to believe that the goals of firms change systematically over time, it is hard to know exactly how one might see this in the data on annual growth rates which form the basis of the 'facts' discussed in section 2. The basic problem with these arguments is that they are built up around the view that there are secular (or long-run), deterministic trends in the pattern of growth of firms. The 'fact' is that growth rates display stochastic trends, meaning that firm size evolves in an erratic and unpredictable manner over time. Further, since the data on corporate growth rates display very little in the way of transitional dynamics, it is hard to draw a meaningful distinction between short- and long-run effects of exogenous factors on firm size. The current-period shocks which propel a random walk are permanent, and, as a consequence, their effect in the long run is almost the same as it is in the short run.

3.3. Models with Penrose Effects

The classic study of the growth of firms by Penrose contains two quite different types of argument. One is a 'resources push' theory of (endogenously driven) growth, which I will deal with when we look at models with organizational capabilities. The other argument in her book is the famous 'managerial limits to growth' hypothesis, and that is our concern here.

This argument starts with the premise that management is a team effort in which individuals deploy specialized, functional skills as well as highly team-specific skills that enable them to collectively co-ordinate their many activities in a coherent manner. The knowledge which underlies these specific skills is likely to be tacit, and can only be learned experientially or by direct instruction from existing managers. Hence, as the firm expands, it needs to recruit new managers and it must divert at least some existing managers from their current operational responsibilities to help manage the process of expanding the management team. Since diverting existing managerial resources to training new managers carries an opportunity cost, the faster is the planned rate of growth of the firm, the higher are these costs of growth likely to be (that is, adjustment costs are variable and not fixed). Under these circumstances, firms are likely to smooth out their responses to current growth opportunities, sacrificing current profits but saving some of the costs of growth which they might otherwise incur to gain those profits.

Penrose argued that firms had no determinant long-run or optimum size, but only a constraint on current-period growth rates. This yields a model like equation (4): the $\theta(L)$ are determined by the size of adjustment costs (and the rate at which they increase increases with increases in the rate of growth), while the lack of an optimum size means that α is effectively zero (that is, in the long run, firm size is unpredictable). It should be clear by now that this argument is not consistent with the 'facts'. As we noted earlier, equation (4) frequently reduces to equation (1) in practice, and when it does not, estimates of $\theta(L)$ suggest that lags higher than order 1 are almost always insignificant. This means that most adjustment costs associated with growth are incurred within a year, which is rather implausible (since we know that it can take years to mould a successful management team). Further, estimates of $\theta(1)$ are typically very small (that is, adjustment costs are not very large), and the collective contribution of all lagged dependent variables to the overall explanation of the regressions is usually extremely modest (which is to say that managerial limits to growth do not appear to explain much of what we observe). More decisively, most of the direct evidence on adjustment costs that we have suggests that they are fixed and not variable. However hard one tries, it is difficult to reconstruct Penrose's managerial limits to growth argument in a way that makes the costs of expanding management teams independent of the number of new managers to be recruited into the team.

It is possible to rescue at least some of this argument. A somewhat more modern and more formal version of it would start from the realization that a firm faced with variable adjustment costs of whatever type will have an incentive to begin adjusting to shocks which it expects to occur in the near future. This means that its optimum size will depend, *inter alia*, on cost and demand conditions which are expected to prevail in the near future. In a standard, optimizing model, these are captured by current-period expectations of future margins. Since, at the optimum, firm size depends on current expectations of future margins, growth will depend on current-period changes in those expectations. It turns out that this very simple model of growth is consistent with equation (1) under certain not entirely uninteresting circumstances. In particular, if firms form rational expectations about future conditions, then changes in these expectations are unpredictable. Rational expectations about a future period $t + \tau$ held at time t basically are those which use all the information available to decision makers at time t. This, in turn, implies that current changes in expectations will be unpredictable (or their expected value will be zero). Since, in this simple model, growth is driven by current changes in expectations, this means that growth rates are also unpredictable.[11]

That a rational, profit-maximizing firm might display unpredictable growth rates as a matter of course makes (1) considerably easier to accept (or, at least it makes equation (1) seem like less of an affront to orthodox neoclassical theory). However, expectations matter only when current actions have undoable future consequences (adjustment costs are only one example of this kind of phenomenon), and this means that current actions depend on past actions. This is a feature of equation (4) but not of equation (1). The history dependence displayed in equation (1) arises from the fact that each burst of growth has a permanent effect on the size of the firm. The history dependence displayed in equation (4) is one in which the realized outcomes of current decisions depend on the realized outcomes of recent past decisions, and, as we have seen, it is inconsistent with the 'facts'. These are quite different types of 'history dependence' (being permanent and transitory respectively), and the 'facts' sit more easily with the former than with the latter.

3.4. Models of Organizational Capabilities

Penrose thought of firms as bundles of resources bound together by a set of administrative skills or capabilities which are used to deploy them as effectively as possible. Others have followed in this spirit. Nelson, for example, has argued that 'successful firms can be understood in terms of a hierarchy of practised organizational routines, which define lower order organizational skills and how these are co-ordinated, and higher order decision procedures for choosing what is to be done at lower levels' (1991: 67–8). These routines are, of course, part of a firm's resource base, and they define what the organization is capable of doing (or what its competences are). These capabilities are almost always thought of as bundles of skills, and, indeed, they are one of the more important repositories of tacit knowledge inside firms. The fact that knowledge is the foundation of organizational capabilities or competences means (at least) two things: first, these competences are not assets (and do not, therefore, appear on balance sheets, and

---

[11] For a formal exposition of the Penrose model in terms of variable adjustment costs, see Slater (1980) and, for an ambitious effort to extend and develop Penrose's work, see Ghoshal, Hahn, and Moran (1997). The argument, which argues that growth is driven by changes in current-period expectations about the future, and shows that current-period growth rates must be unpredictable if expectations are rational, is set out in Geroski, Machin, and Walters (1997). It claims some empirical support from correlations between firm growth and change in stock market value (which act as proxy for changes in current expectations about future profits).

cannot be bought and sold), and, secondly, they can only be learned or maintained through use (hence, people typically talk of 'practised' routines). Each firm is likely to be born with some particular skill or knowledge base, and then to develop, idiosyncratically over time as it uses what it has inherited and what it has learned to develop, new skills and an augmented knowledge base. This means that each firm's development is likely to be path dependent. Further, if, as Penrose argued, internal resources are discrete, then firms may have stocks of underutilized resources which 'push' it on to further expansion.[12]

The basic premise of this work is that competitive advantage is based on the possession of a few key resources and routines, organizational capabilities, or core competences and, despite the proliferation of labels, there is some measure of agreement on what this means. A 'core competence' (to choose the label used in most popular discussions) is something which: creates value for consumers, is unique (or at least better than that possessed by rivals), is durable, generates returns that are appropriable, and is (or should be) inimitable. There are many possible sources of inimitability: the resource may be physically scarce, its accumulation may be path dependent, and there may be causal ambiguity about just how it works or what its driving feature is. If competitive advantage is based on the possession of core competences defined in this way, then firms are likely to be heterogeneous (because competences are unique) and to realize different levels of performance (depending on the value created for consumers by using the competence and the degree of appropriability of the resulting gains) over long periods of time (because the resources which sustain competences are durable, and the competences themselves are difficult to imitate).[13] These arguments are roughly consistent with what we know about accounting profitability: firm profitability is idiosyncratic (meaning that aggregate or industry-level determinants are weak relative to idiosyncratic, firm-specific determinants of profitability) and profit differences between firms persist for long periods of time.[14] It does not, however, seem to be quite so consistent with what we observe about company growth.

To see this last argument, consider the following simple model. Suppose that firm i has a competence which enables it to generate more revenue growth than

---

[12] See Wernerfelt (1984); Dierickx and Cool (1989); Rumelt (1987); and others; Peteraf (1993) surveys some of this literature while Hamel and Pralahad (1994) and Collis and Montgomery (1995) are more popular discussions. Foss (1997), Chandler, Hagström, and Solvell (1998) and Dosi, Teece, and Chytry (1998) are good collections of papers in this area. Helfat (1997) and Teece, Pisano, and Shuen (1997) discuss the related notion of 'dynamic capabilities'.

[13] The notion of core competences has also been extensively applied to the question of choosing the right diversification strategies for firms, the idea being that diversification should be based on a clear understanding of what any particular firm is capable of doing or designed around the acquisition of particular skills or routines. Indeed, 'mergers and acquisitions are an opportunity to trade otherwise non-marketable resources' (Wernerfelt 1984: 175); see also Montgomery and Wernerfelt (1988) and, more generally, Markides (1995).

[14] See, for example, the survey in Geroski (1998); Rumelt (1991) is frequently cited in the management literature in this context.

rivals. Let $\theta_i(t)$ be an index of firm i's competence, measured in units so that i grows at rate:

$$\Delta \log S_i(t) = g(t) + \theta_i(t), \tag{6}$$

when it has a competence level of $\theta_i(t)$. Firms with no particular competence ($\theta = 0$) grow at rate $g(t)$, while those that are incompetent ($\theta < 0$) grow even more slowly. Everything that we know about competences suggests that they evolve over time in a systematic way, with each increment in ability that is realized depending on the previous ability of the firm. An easy way in which to model this is to suppose that

$$\theta_i(t) = \rho_1 \theta_i(t-1) + \rho_2 \theta_i(t-2) + \varepsilon_i(t), \tag{7}$$

where $\varepsilon_i(t)$ is an unpredictable change in competence. If $\rho_1 + \rho_2 > 1$, then the growth of firm i's competence is explosive, increasing at ever increasing rates (there must obviously be a limit to this); if $\rho_1 + \rho_2 < 1$, then equation (7) describes a process in which competence levels gradually revert to some long-run mean level. A little manipulation of equations (6) and (7) reveals that

$$\Delta \log S_i(t) = \rho_1 \Delta \log S_i(t-1) + \rho_2 \Delta \log S_i(t-2) + v(t) + \varepsilon_i(t), \tag{8}$$

where $v(t) \equiv g(t) - \rho_1 g(t-1) + \rho_2 g(t-2)$. If $E\{\varepsilon_i(t)\} \equiv \alpha + \mu_i(t)$, then equation (8) effectively reduces to equation (4) with the addition of a common time trend, $v(t)$. However, as we have seen, equation (4) is not a satisfactory description of corporate growth rates, and this means that the argument that corporate growth is driven by competences is not consistent with the 'facts'.

The basic problem should be clear: most of the literature on competences has sprung up to explain persistent differences in accounting profitability between firms, but firms do not display persistent differences in their growth performance. Whatever it is that fuels corporate growth seems to be much more transitory than whatever it is that fuels changes in corporate profitability. Notice that equation (8) reduces to equation (1) if $\alpha = \rho_1 = \rho_2 = 0$; that is, if there is no trend change in $\theta_i(t)$ and if changes in a firm's competences over time are random (that is, if $\theta_i(t)$ follows a random walk). While this simplification makes the model consistent with the 'facts', it is now basically inconsistent with everything we know and believe about how competences evolve over time. To put the matter another way, if the accumulation of competences is really what powers growth, then the kinds of competences that we need to identify are those which either have very transitory lives, or have only very temporary effects on growth.

4. Where do we Go from Here?

There is much to be said for the modern, Coasian theory of the firm, but one thing that it simply does not do is address the growth, development, and diversification of firms which we observe going on around us day in and day out. Economists have developed many arguments and theories over the years which do try to explain what we observe, but, as we have seen, many of them are not easily reconciled with the 'facts'. The most promising recent development is probably the literature on organizational capabilities or core competences. It has the major virtue of accounting for the ubiquitous heterogeneities between firms that we observe, and it offers a plausible, history-dependent story of organizational growth and development. The problem is that the literature on competences has been much influenced by empirical studies of accounting profitability, which show persistent and stable differences in performance between firms. However, this is not a feature of many other measures of corporate performance. Corporate growth rates, for example, differ between firms in temporary and unpredictable ways, and it is hard to reconcile the inimitability and durability of organizational capabilities with these data. The consequence of all of this is that theorizing about competences is being driven by a correspondence with the 'facts' which is, at best, partial.

The way forward seems to be reasonably clear: work on the theory of the firm needs to be redirected towards models which help to account for the uneven, erratic performance of firms over time. It is, of course, possible to argue that exogenous factors are entirely responsible for the unpredictable nature of corporate growth rates. But, this is hard to believe: many firms try to alter their environment in various ways and, further, many competitive shocks are endogenous. It is also hard to accept that growth is largely driven by exogenous shocks because many firms do not react quickly or well to market shocks, and others try to resist innovation. This inertia makes the timing of corporate activity difficult to predict, and, hence, it makes corporate behaviour seem erratic. Since this is what we observe, it seems possible that models which focus more on *when* firms act than on *what* they do may be a useful step forward.

There is, in fact, a model of aggregate economic growth which has a number of properties that are roughly consistent with the data we discussed earlier, and it turns out to be relatively easy to translate that model into a theory of the firm.[15] I will conclude this chapter by sketching out this model very briefly, and showing why it seems to fit the 'facts'.

Suppose that a firm generates revenue, y, in each period by spending an amount of money, x, on labour inputs, the services of physical capital, advertising, and so on. In particular, let

$$\pi = y(x) - x = Ax^{\alpha} - x, \tag{9}$$

where $0 < \alpha < 1$. The optimum choice of x satisfies: $\alpha y = x$, so

---

[15] See Aghion and Howitt (1992) and, more generally on models of endogenous growth, their 1998 textbook.

$$\pi = (1 - \alpha)y. \tag{10}$$

Innovations occur in response to expenditures on x, and we date each innovation by the time it arrives, τ. For simplicity, assume that each innovation has the same effect on the firm's performance, namely that it raises A by a factor γ; that is,

$$A_\tau = A_0 \gamma^\tau. \tag{11}$$

Note that τ does not record calendar time: τ increases every time an innovation occurs, not every year. The implication of equation (11) is that

$$y_\tau = \gamma y_{\tau-1}. \tag{12}$$

The core of this model is in the choice of how much research a firm does. For simplicity, reinterpret that x_τ is the amount of money the firm chooses to spend on research after the arrival of an innovation in period τ, and we assume that the more money it spends the sooner will be the arrival date of the next innovation in period $\tau + 1$. To be more precise, suppose that the rate of innovation conditional on x_τ is a Poisson process, so that the length of time between the τth and the $(\tau + 1)^{st}$ innovation is exponentially distributed with parameter $\phi(x_\tau)$, where we take it that $\phi' > 0$ and $\phi'' < 0$. Since an innovation in τ yields profits for a period of time which is a random variable, its expected value is $\xi_{\tau-1} = \pi_\tau\{r + \phi(x_\tau)\}^{-1}$, where r is the discount rate. The expected value of doing research is then

$$\xi_\tau = \gamma\phi(x_{\tau+1})\pi_{\tau+1}\{r + \phi(x_{+1})\}^{-1} - x_{\tau+1}. \tag{13}$$

A profit-maximizing firm will choose a sequence of values of x_τ which satisfy

$$\gamma\phi'(x_\tau)\pi_\tau - r - \phi(x_\tau) = 0. \tag{14}$$

There are two results that emerge from all of this. Equation (14) shows the first. It basically says that x_τ and $x_{\tau+1}$ will be negatively correlated over time; that is, if $x_{\tau+1}$ is expected to be large, then x_τ will be small. The basic idea is that if a firm knows that $x_{\tau+1}$ is going to be large, then it also knows that the innovation which x_τ will (sooner or later) generate will be short lived (because the large spending in period $\tau + 1$ will quickly generate an innovation to displace it. The innovation in τ will not, therefore, be particularly valuable, and the firm will not be willing to spend much to get it. Hence, the firm will not choose a large value of x_τ.[16] The common sense of this proposition is that firms are unlikely to sustain a regular sequence of innovations. Instead, an innovator is going to have an incentive to delay the introduction of subsequent innovations as long as possible in order to preserve returns from the first. The result will be an erratic pattern of innovative activity.

[16] This is the well-known 'displacement effect', which describes a situation where firms will be reluctant to introduce a second innovation which displaces returns from an earlier innovation (or to cannibalize the returns from existing products). See Tirole (1988: chap. 10) for a discussion.

This is a conclusion that is consistent with much of what we observe in markets, and the pattern of behaviour it describes is not model specific. Successful innovators are often reluctant to introduce subsequent innovations which either are competence destroying or cannibalize some of the rents that flow in from the original innovation. The consequence is that they are not quite willing or able to follow up an initial innovation with subsequent innovations unless, by chance, they are forced to (or unless these subsequent innovations are competence enhancing or do not cannibalize existing rent streams). Further, this pattern of apparently erratic behaviour is likely to be a property of models in which firms face fixed adjustment costs, and do not respond to performance deteriorations until some threshold of poor performance has been reached. Many firms do not immediately respond to cost and demand shocks. Instead, they tolerate a little deterioration in their performance until they are sure that the shocks are permanent and important. They may also need to take some time to work out just exactly how to deal with the shocks that they have experienced. The consequence is that adjustment to shocks will occur only when 'enough' pressure has built up (this is basically an (s,S) strategy of response). If shocks are Poisson distributed, then the time between responses will be exponentially distributed. Further, if the firm expects to make a major initiative to improve its performance in period $\tau+1$, then it is unlikely to make much of an investment in period τ. This is, of course, just the kind of behaviour that equation (14) describes.

The second interesting result follows from this, since an erratic pattern of innovation ought to induce an erratic pattern of growth. Equation (12) can be written in calendar time (t, not τ time) as:

$$\log y_t = \log y_{t-1} + \varepsilon_t, \tag{15}$$

where $\varepsilon_t \equiv N(t-1,t)\log \gamma$, and $N(t-1,t)$ is the number of innovations that arrive between period $t-1$ and period t. Our earlier assumptions imply that this is a Poisson random variable whose expected value is ϕ. Hence, if we define $e_t \equiv \varepsilon_t - \phi$, then

$$\log y_t = \theta + \log y_{t-1} + e_t \tag{16}$$

where $\theta \equiv \phi\log \gamma$. Note that e_t is a normally distributed random variable with zero mean and variance $\phi(\log \gamma)^2$; that is, equation (16) looks like a classical regression model. Basically, it says that firm size follows a random walk with drift. Again, the intuition is straightforward: the natural cycle of activity from the point of view of the firm's actions is the 'calendar' based on innovative activity (and tracked by τ), but we, as econometricians, observe the firm only at arbitrarily fixed yearly intervals. Since our observations are not synchronized with the actions of the firm, it is hardly surprising that we are inclined to find its activities erratic and unpredictable.

This conclusion springs from an observation that is sufficiently deep to be worth stressing. As econometricians, we observe firms on a regular but arbitrary basis. Financial data appear annually (say in April or October), and that is when we observe the firm and collect data on its size (and other things). However, the important events which affect the firm's performance happen at all kinds of times, and none of these is necessarily tied in with the firm's normal financial reporting cycle. Further, many of the choices (investments in research and development, competitive initiatives, and so on) that firms make do not have natural gestation periods of twelve months; nor are their consequences delivered in neat twelve-month intervals conveniently dated to coincide with the release of an annual report. As a consequence, when we view firms through the lens of a twelve-month financial reporting cycle, we are bound to be somewhat out of phase with the natural but irregular rhythms of its day-to-day competitive life. In the circumstances, it is not hard to believe that accounting for variations in its performance will be difficult, and that is basically what equation (16) says. Notice that the sole exception to this is accounting profits, since this is the one measurable aspect of corporate performance that is perfectly synchronized with its annual reporting cycle.

The bottom line is that this sketch of a model of corporate growth displays two properties which are consistent with the facts outlined in section 2 above: it generates a pattern of innovative activity over time (firms in this model are rarely rapid or persistent innovators), and the resulting evolution of firm size follows a random walk over time. This is not, of course, the only model which displays (or can be made to display) these properties. But, it is characteristic of what I think may be the defining feature of models of the firm which try to come to terms with the 'facts', namely that it is *when* things happens that matters and not (so much) *what* it is that happens.

References

AGHION, P., and P. HOWITT 1992. 'A model of growth through creative destruction', *Econometrica* 60: 232–351.

—— 1998. *Endogenous Growth Theory*. Cambridge, MA: MIT Press.

CABALLERO, R., E. ENGEL and J. HALTIWANGER 1995. 'Plant level adjustment and aggregate investment dynamics', *Brookings Papers on Economic Activity* 2: 1–39.

—— 1997. 'Aggregate employment dynamics: Building from microeconomic evidence', *American Economic Review* 87: 115–37.

CEFIS, E. 1996. 'Is there any persistence in innovative activities?' Mimeo, Florence: European University Institute.

CHANDLER, A. 1992. 'What is a firm? A historical perspective', *European Economic Review* 36: 483–92.

—— P. HAGSTRÖM, and Ö. SOLVELL, eds. 1998. *The Dynamic Firm*. Oxford: Oxford University Press.

COLLIS, D., and C. MONTGOMERY 1995. 'Competing on Resources: Strategy in the 1990's', *Harvard Business Review* (July–August): 118–28.

DAVIS, S., J. HALTIWANGER, and S. SCHUH 1996. *Job Creation and Destruction*. Cambridge, MA: MIT Press.

DIERICKX, I., and K. COOL 1989. 'Asset Stock Accumulation and Sustainability of Competitive Advantage', *Management Science* 35: 1504–14.

DOSI, G., D. TEECE, and J. CHYTRY, eds. 1998. *Technology, Organization and Competitiveness*. Oxford: Oxford University Press.

DUNNE, P., and A. HUGHES 1994. 'Age, Size, Growth and Survival: UK Companies in the 1980's', *Journal of Industrial Economics* 42: 115–40.

EVANS, D. 1987. 'Tests of Alternative Theories of Firm Growth', *Journal of Political Economy* 95: 657–74.

FOSS, N. 1997. *Resources, Firms and Strategies*. Oxford: Oxford University Press.

GARNSEY, E. 1998. 'A Theory of the Early Growth of the Firm', *Industrial and Corporate Change* 7: 523–56.

GEROSKI, P. 1998. 'An applied econometrician's view of large company performance', *Review of Industrial Organization* 13: 271–93.

—— and P. GREGG 1997. *Coping with Recession*. Cambridge: Cambridge University Press.

—— J. VAN REENEN, and C. WALTERS 1997. 'How persistently do firms innovate?', *Research Policy* 26: 33–48.

—— S. MACHIN, and C. WALTERS 1997. 'Corporate growth and profitability', *Journal of Industrial Economics* 45: 171–89.

—— C. WALTERS, and G. URGA 1998. 'Are Differences in Comparing Size Transitory or Permanent?', Mimeo, London: London Business School.

GHOSHAL, S., M. HAHN, and P. MORAN 1997. 'An integrative theory of firm growth'. Mimeo, London: London Business School.

GREINER, L. 1972. 'Evolution and revolution as organizations grow', *Harvard Business Review* (July–August): 37–46.

HALL, B. 1987. 'The relationship between firm size and firm growth in the US manufacturing sector', *Journal of Industrial Economics* 35: 583–606.

HAMEL, G., and C. K. PRALAHAD 1994. *Competing for the Future*. Boston, MA: Harvard Business School Press.

HAMERMESH, D., and G. PFANN 1994. 'Adjustment costs in factor demand', *Journal of Economic Literature* 34: 1264–92.

HART, O. 1995. *Firms, Contracts and Financial Structure*. Oxford: Oxford University Press.

HART, P., and N. OULTON 1996. 'Growth and size of firms', *Economic Journal* 106: 1242–52.

HELFAT, C. 1997. 'Know-how and asset complementarity and dynamic capability accumulation: The case of R&D', *Strategic Management Journal* 18: 339–60.

MALERBA, F., and L. ORSENIGO 1995. 'Schumpeterian patterns of innovation', *Cambridge Journal of Economics* 19: 47–65.

MARKIDES, C. 1995. *Diversification, Refocusing and Economic Performance*. Cambridge, MA: MIT Press.

MILGROM, P., and J. ROBERTS 1992. *Economics, Organization and Management.* Englewood Cliffs, NJ: Prentice Hall.

MONTGOMERY, C., and B. WERNERFELT 1988. 'Diversification, Ricardian rents and Tobin's-q', *Rand Journal of Economics* 19: 623–32.

MOORE, J. 1992. 'The firm as a collection of assets', *European Economic Review* 36: 493–508.

MUELLER, D. 1972. 'A life cycle theory of the firm', *Journal of Industrial Economics* 20: 199–219.

NELSON, C. and C. PLOSSER 1982. 'Trends and random walks in macro-economic times series', *Journal of Monetary Economics* 10: 139–69.

NELSON, R. 1991. 'Why do firms differ and how does it matter?', *Strategic Management Journal* 12: 61–74.

PENROSE, E. 1959. *The Theory of the Growth of the Firm.* Oxford: Basil Blackwell.

PETERAF, M. 1993. 'The cornerstones of competitive advantage: A resource-based view', *Strategic Management Journal* 14: 179–91.

RUMELT, R. 1987. 'Theory, strategy and entrepreneurship', in D. Teece, ed., *The Competitive Challenge: Strategies for Industrial Innovation and Renewal.* Cambridge, MA: Ballinger.

—— 1991. 'How much does industry matter?', *Strategic Management Journal* 12: 167–85.

SCHERER, M., and T. ROSS 1990. *Industrial Market Structure and Economic Performance,* 3rd edn. Boston: Houghton Mifflin.

SLATER, M. 1980. 'The Managerial limitation to the growth of firms', *Economic Journal* 90: 520–8.

SUTTON, J. 1991. *Sunk Costs and Market Structure.* Cambridge, MA: MIT Press.

—— 1997. 'Gibrat's legacy', *Journal of Economic Literature* 35: 40–59.

—— 1998. *Technology and Market Structure.* Cambridge, MA: MIT Press.

TEECE, D., G. PISANO, and A. SHUEN 1997. 'Dynamic capabilities and strategic management', *Strategic Management Journal* 18: 509–33.

TIROLE, J. 1988. *The Theory of Industrial Organization.* Cambridge, MA: MIT Press.

WERNERFELT, B. 1984. 'A resource-based view of the firm', *Strategic Management Journal* 5: 171–80.

WILLIAMSON, O. 1967. 'Hierarchical control and optimum firm size', *Journal of Political Economy* 75: 123–38.

—— 1970. *Corporate Control and Business Behavior.* Englewood Cliffs, NJ: Prentice Hall.

—— 1996. *The Mechanisms of Governance.* Oxford: Oxford University Press.

YOU, JONG-IP 1995. 'Small firms in economic theory', *Cambridge Journal of Economics* 19: 441–62.

9

The Growth of Firms

NEIL KAY

1. Introduction

One major issue emerging from the conference around which this collection of papers is based is the prospect of progressing with work into the existence, boundaries, and internal organization of the firm by drawing together insights from the capabilities and post-Coasian literatures. If possible, this could provide an invaluable corrective to the natural tendency to Balkanization that has developed in the study of the economics of organization. For the purposes of this chapter we shall focus on the possibility of complementarity between approaches that look at costs of co-ordinating economic organization, such as transaction cost economics (Williamson 1975, 1985) and those that build on foundations for resource-based economics built by Penrose (1959). A good collection and overview of relevant approaches in this latter camp is provided by Foss, ed. (1997).

This chapter offers some rude thoughts (by which I mean, of course, rough or preliminary thoughts) on these issues, as well as on the possibilities of finding common ground between the major streams of analysis. The position taken in this chapter is that it is indeed possible to find complementarities between the major approaches but that there are dangers on the way. The chapter is divided into two main parts, the first concerned with possible complications that may be encountered in such a programme, and the second with how an integrated agenda in this area might be sketched (and appropriately, the sketch is a rude or rough one). It is also suggested that the process of *decision making* is an element that tends to be missing or underplayed in these approaches, and that this area may be central to helping us understand the economics of organization.

2. Some Rude Thoughts on the Economics of Organization

One common barrier to communication and understanding using the English language is that some words may constitute non-specific assets in that they may have a number of different applications and interpretations. We talk on the one hand of the 'theory of value' in economics where 'value' means price, and on the other of the need to use 'value judgements' where 'value' clearly does not mean price. In consumer theory, 'utility' refers to satisfaction, in regulatory theory it is a particular type of firm. And when I talk of 'rude thoughts', 'rude' can mean rough or unrefined, or it can mean impolite or discourteous. The uses to which words can be put are many and varied and indeed even the word 'use' can mean different things. This brings us to our first comment on the possibility of integrating resource-based and transaction cost economics.

2.1. 'Specialized Uses' Means very Different Things in Resource-Based and Transaction Cost Economics

Penrose did consider at length the value-enhancing consequences of 'the specialized use of resources' (Penrose 1959: 71). Williamson defines asset specificity as 'a specialized investment that cannot be redeployed in alternative uses or by alternative users except at a loss of productive value' (Williamson 1996: 377) and at first sight it does seem that asset specificity means very much the same thing as Penrose's 'specialized resources'. However, there are in fact significant differences between the two approaches. The problem is that both 'specialization' and 'use' mean very different things in Penrose's and Williamson's view of the firm. When Penrose talked of 'specialized uses' she was referring to the type and range of things a resource could do, or what Richardson (1972) calls *activities*. When Williamson talks of 'specialized uses' for an asset, he is referring to final applications, product or services, that is, *end-outcomes*.

An example may help clarify this point. Suppose we have a graphics designer whose productive value entirely lies in her mastery of a single computer graphics programme. This is clearly a highly specialized set of skills and uses in the Penrose/Richardson sense. However, this graphics designer can design brochures, advertising copy, book covers, record labels, maps, and cartoons, *inter alia*. At the moment she is contemplating job offers from a cartographer, an advertising agency, and three publishers. Given the range of potential end-uses and potential employers for this individual, clearly she must rate very low in terms of asset specificity. Thus, she has highly 'specialized uses' in a resource-based perspective, but not in a transaction cost one.

These different interpretations leads to fundamentally different perspectives in resource-based and transaction cost economics. In transaction cost economics, 'specialized uses' of assets represent a barrier to diversification; if assets cannot be applied to other products or services, there are no potential economies of scope from related diversification. But in resource-based economics, resource specialization can be the *basis* for diversification, as Penrose herself noted; 'a firm's opportunities are necessarily widened when it develops *a specialized knowledge* of a technology which is *not* in itself *very specific* to any particular kind of product, for example, knowledge of different types of engineering or industrial chemistry' (1959: 115, emphasis added). This illustrates how resource specialization in the Penrose sense is entirely consistent with the absence of asset specificity in the transaction cost sense. The different interpretations of resource specialization in the respective approaches also helps explain why the paradigm case associated with resource specialization in transaction cost economics is vertical integration, while in resource-based economics it is diversification.

2.2. There Is more to the Boundaries of the Firm than Asset Specificity

In practice, asset specificity appears to be neither necessary nor sufficient for internalization of assets within the firm. In turn, this limits its ability to provide a satisfactory explanation of the boundaries of the firm.

Transaction cost economics has treated the make-or-buy decision in vertical integration as its paradigm case (Williamson 1996: 41–2). It predicts that transactions that are characterized by asset specificity (and its associated transactional hazards) will be more likely to be internalized within firms, while transactions characterized by the absence of asset specificity will be more likely to be carried out through market contracting, *ceteris paribus*. There has been a considerable amount of empirical work in this field, and as Shelanski and Klein (1995) report, most of this has tended to support this prediction. However, most of these studies have focused on the make-or-buy decision in the production department, which is only one area of resource allocation within the modern multifunctional and multidivisional firm. Unfortunately asset specificity explanations for the boundaries of the firm do not perform so convincingly outside the production department (Kay 1997, forthcoming).

First, related diversification by firms tends to be built around assets that are by definition not specialized to one particular use. Secondly, many firms tend to internalize research and development activities and to steer clear of licensing technology because of appropriability problems; if such problems exist it is because assets in the form of intellectual property may *not* be specialized by use or to user. Consequently, it is difficult to deal with horizontal moves in the form of diversification and multinational enterprise in transaction cost economics. The framework's dependence on asset specificity means it is difficult for it to widen its focus away from vertical relations.

It is possible to develop explanations for these phenomena (Kay 1997: 33–57), but the explanations tend not to build on asset specificity.[1] Once we step outside the confines of this particular problem in vertical integration, asset specificity ceases to provide such an obvious explanation for the setting of the boundaries of the firm.

---

[1] There are approaches that look at transactional issues relevant to related diversification, but these approaches are based on the recognition that assets may not be specialized to a particular application (Teece 1997 and Kay 1982) and so are difficult to reconcile with transaction cost economics emphasis on asset specificity.

2.3. Resource-Based Approaches Find Vertical Integration Difficult to Explain

Just as transaction cost economics finds it difficult to deal with diversification, so resource-based approaches find it difficult to deal with vertical integration. There can be considerable differences in technological and marketing characteristics associated with different stages in the vertical chain of production. The operational and marketing problems associated with drilling for oil bears little resemblance to those encountered in running a refinery, and both sets of problems are again quite distinct from the day-to-day issues encountered by a service station manager. The competences and capabilities required to make and sell aluminium ingots are quite different from those required to make and sell aluminium pots and pans. Yet these very different activities may be internalized within the firm through vertical integration despite the very dissimilar nature of the activities involved in the respective cases.

One of the least satisfactory parts of Penrose's seminal work is the part where she looks at vertical integration (1959: 145–9). Although she prefaces her account by suggesting that much of the earlier discussion of diversification is equally applicable to vertical integration, in reality the reasons she identifies for vertical integration (while credible in themselves) tend to have no obvious or necessary connection with sharing competences between applications. For example, she identifies two categories of reasons for backward integration; first, the desire to maintain control over quality, quantity, and delivery of supplies; and secondly, the desire for security and avoidance of fluctuations in the face of risk and uncertainty (pp. 146–7)—objectives which may be pursued though vertical integration irrespective of similarity or dissimilarity in the resource characteristics across stages. She does also state that integration may allow 'efficient management' to be shared across stages where it is a scarce resource, but this seems a rather weak reason since it does not explain why such management is not diverted into related fields where there may be more obvious scope for sharing competences and capabilities. Penrose's resource-based approach is simply not designed to deal with the problem of vertical integration and it is interesting to note that when she turned her attention to the archetypal vertically integrated industry (petroleum), she made no systematic attempt to show how her resource-based approach could be applied in this context (Penrose 1968, 1971). So why can it be so difficult to apply resource-based explanations to vertical integration? There is one crucial difference between horizontal and vertical relations as far as the firm is concerned; horizontal relations are optional but vertical relations are compulsory. While a firm can choose to specialize or not, it has no choice but to be part of at least one vertical chain of production if it wishes to stay in business, though within this remit firms may choose different ways to create or participate in a vertical chain, for example, single or multiple sourcing, domestic or international distribution. In addition, as transaction cost economics has shown, there are alternative means through which firms can obtain access to components and reach final consumers, such as spot markets, long-term contracts, and vertical integration.

The compulsory nature of vertical relations may help explain why the resource-based approach is so difficult to apply to the case of vertical integration. If the management of a firm is looking at horizontal opportunities and finds that they would fail to make sufficient use of the firm's capabilities, it can simply forget about them. However, vertical relations cannot be ignored in this way. If a petroleum firm finds that service station retailing makes little or no use of its existing capabilities, it cannot simply walk away from this element in the vertical chain and say it does not matter. Instead it may be forced to turn its attention to the best way of dealing with these elements in the chain. If vertical integration offers control advantages of the type discussed by Penrose, then it may be pursued, regardless of any lack of similarity in the capabilities required at different stages in the chain.

2.4. 'Uniqueness' Has Become a much Abused Concept in this Area

Both resource-based economics and transaction cost economics have shown interest in 'unique' resources and assets and their role in adding value for the firm. One problem with this approach in transaction cost economics is that it has become a fairly common practice to analyse an asset in terms of degrees of uniqueness: for example different studies have considered whether an asset is 'relatively unique' or 'highly unique', or 'how unique' an asset is. Another study discussed a firm investing in firm-specific assets to 'enhance its uniqueness'. It has to be said that these are meaningless concepts since unique, like 'simultaneous' and 'perfect' denotes an absolute state that is not subject to qualification. Something either is or is not unique, and it is no more appropriate to imply degrees of uniqueness than it is to talk of degrees of perfection. If it was possible to identify a continuous variable to which 'degrees of uniqueness' could correspond, then this point might be dismissed as a mere quibble. However, it has to be said that it is not clear what this variable would be, or how it would be defined.

At the same time, the resource-based perspective in strategy research has been concerned with the issue of unique assets or resources, though more from the perspective of such assets as rent generators (see, for example, a number of the readings in Part 3 of Foss, ed. (1997)). From this perspective, unique assets are generally regarded as potential sources of competitive advantage that may allow the firm to outperform its rivals.

Possible difficulties are created by the emphasis in this approach on individual assets and resources. There are at least two problems with this perspective; first, uniqueness is not generally contingent on unique components, and secondly, uniqueness at any level is not a guarantor of success. My telephone number is 'unique' and indeed I subscribe to the telephone company on the implicit understanding that my number is not possessed by anybody else in the world. However, it is composed of the same ten Arabic numerals used by the rest of the global telecommunications system. James Joyce's *Ulysses* and Stramash University's *Parking Regulations* are both unique works, but both are also composed of the same 26 letters and sundry punctuation marks that makes up much of the rest of the world's literature.[2] What makes *Ulysses* and my telephone number unique has nothing to do with the individual components making up these entities, and everything to do with the way that these components are combined. In turn, distinctiveness or uniqueness is not in itself sufficient to guarantee that something has merit or value. Both *Ulysses* and Stramash University's *Parking Regulations* may be unique publications, but it is only the former that is likely to have a real claim to literary merit (and a competitive advantage in the global literary market).

Once one begins looking for it, 'uniqueness' actually turns out to be a very ordinary quality that is more the norm than the exception in many contexts. However, there are warnings here for any analyses of competitive advantage in terms of distinctive, unique, or inimitable assets. These run the danger of being reductionist exercises in which the truly distinctive aspects of the firm are simply not visible in any audit of individual resources or assets. Attempts to pin down 'distinctiveness' that ignores how assets and resources are combined can all too easily lead to a situation where what is being looked for is filtered out, like grains of sand dribbling through the fingers.[3]

The problem with the term 'uniqueness' when used at any level of analysis is that it carries the weight of implying something about both the *value* and the *incidence* of the phenomenon in question. This is not a problem that tends to be encountered in evolutionary theories where questions of the value of character-istics are contingent on environment,[4] and questions of incidence are dealt with in more neutral terms such as 'variation' and 'diversity'. In these approaches, path dependency and variation is in the natural order of things, not something that is exceptional or unusual; 'diversity of firms is just what one would expect under evolutionary theory' (Nelson 1991: 69).

---

[2] As Shackle (1979: 21) points out, 'the letters of an alphabet are constant, essentially invariant against changes of context and circumstance, yet they are capable of embodiments in language-constructs of strictly *endless* variety and novelty' (emphasis in original).

[3] This has implications for the recent emphasis on outsourcing in strategic management. If what are perceived to be non-critical activities are contracted out, then competitive advantage may be affected if that competitive advantage lies in combinations or bundles of activities, rather than any individual activities.

[4] Foss (1997: 11) notes that the nature of the environment (including other firms as elements) is critical if notions of firm heterogeneity are to have any meaning and he also notes, encouragingly, that there are signs that such issues are entering into resource-based approaches.

This suggests that caution may be warranted in terms of searching for distinctive characteristics at individual level as potential sources of competitive advantage. In the resource-based approach this may be expressed in terms of resources being unique, rare, heterogeneous, distinctive, superior, inimitable, immobile, specialized, firm-specific, non-tradeable, idiosyncratic. What this may obscure is that these resources may only begin to generate competitive advantage when they become organized. It may not be individual assets that turn out to be the important level of analysis in practice, but rather how they combine and complement each other.[5] Langlois (1997: 287) makes a similar point when he comments that the firm's capabilities may in part be due to how it organizes human and machine-based routines.

One of the lessons coming out of the Santa Fe Institute in New Mexico is that many systems behave in a non-linear fashion, with eventual outcomes being profoundly affected by marginal differences in initial or subsequent conditions.[6] If we were to take two identical firms, set them down in virtually identical environments, and come back some time later, we should not be surprised to find we have two firms that now bear little resemblance to each other. The biologist Stephen J. Gould argues that behaviour of this type is the 'essence of history': 'Each step proceeds for cause, but no finale can be specified at the start, and none would ever occur a second time in the same way, because any pathway proceeds through thousands of improbable stages. Alter any early event, ever so slightly and without apparent importance at the time, and evolution cascades into a radically different channel' (Gould 1989: 51). These arguments would not seem too strange to organization theorists capturing organizational processes in garbage can models of organizational choice (Cohen, March, and Olsen 1972; March and Olsen 1986).

Firms do not survive because they are different, they are different because they survive. Analysis of firms has to start from this premise if it is to have any hope of making sense of the competitive process in practice.

2.5. Capabilities are not Necessarily Firm Specific

One aspect of the resource-based approach is that it tends to see capabilities and competences as firm specific. However, the graphics designer example above suggests that capabilities may be more portable than might be thought at first sight, and here the transaction cost perspective may be useful.

It is certainly the case that some capabilities may be firm specific, but it is not clear a priori whether these cases are general, frequent, or unusual. If capabilities are *always* firm specific and have no or little value in other uses, then it leads to

---

[5] Richardson's (1972) notion of complementarity may be of relevance here.
[6] See Arthur (1994) for a number of studies of such processes.

the strong conclusion that there would be no external market for the resources which embody them. I am not sure this would always be a convincing position. If the coaching team responsible for Brazil's national soccer side were to offer itself for employment on the open market, it is highly likely there would be some expressions of interest, just as it is likely that there would be interest in the skills and expertise of individual members of that team. Nor does embodiment in teams necessarily encourage unified governance within the firm or long-term contracts; session musicians may contribute to orchestral teams and club-based players to international soccer teams. In both such cases the individual members of the respective teams may be contracted and paid for on a performance basis.

In general, capabilities do not have to be contained within the firm, as Coase himself argued: 'the fact that certain people have better judgement or better knowledge does not mean that they can only get an income from it by them-selves actively taking part in production. They can sell advice or knowledge. Every business buys the services of a host of advisers. We can imagine a system where all advice or knowledge was bought as required' (1937: 400–1). Coase's observations are still pertinent today. The first few pages of my *Yellow Pages* tell me I can go into the market-place and obtain the wisdom and expertise of Accountants, Actuaries, Advertising Agencies, Advice Agencies (of various kinds), Appliance Testers, Architects, and even Astrologers. The 'As' even flag competences that help to make markets work, such as Arbitrators, Assessors, and Auctioneers.

The issue here is that there are outside sources for external knowledge and expertise of various kinds that can help firms, and indeed Langlois (1997) has already explored how 'external capabilities' may be available to the firm from outside sources. John Kay (1996: 45–6) also describes how shared knowledge and established routines may be exploited by whole networks, as in the case of Silicon Valley (Kay 1996: 99–101). The important points are that capabilities may not be firm specific and that sources external to the firm may contribute to an individual firm's capabilities.

3. A Rude Agenda for Looking at Organizations

The various issues discussed in the last section all have implications for the devel-opment of integrative efforts in these areas. In this section we concentrate on the issue of how these integrative efforts might be framed. We shall approach this issue from the perspective of transaction cost economics and set out a transac-tion cost question. Suppose a manufacturer has acquired one of its foreign suppliers. *Question:* Why did it do that? In general the transaction cost literature treats this as a single question with a single answer. *Answer:* Asset specificity may create transactional hazards and so the firm may decide to replace market with hierarchy.

However, we saw earlier the problem of words with more than one meaning. The same problem can exist with whole questions. The standard transaction cost question *'Why did it do that?'* may be interpretable as three separate questions, one relating to the method or *mode* by which the transaction is carried out, one to where the transaction is carried out or the *domain* within which (or over which) it takes place, and one relating to the *strategic direction* associated with the transaction. The transaction explanation above takes the strategic direction for granted and fuses the domain and mode explanations together; if you explain domain you explain mode (if you know *where* the relationship is located, you typically know *how* it will be governed).

However, if there are three different questions here, it would be reasonable to expect three different sets of possible answers to these questions. If we are interested in *mode* then we might expect answers to the question of how the firm is going to co-ordinate the allocation of resources; for example, will it simply send instructions to the unit taken over, set-up a transfer pricing system, or what? If we are interested in *domain*, we might expect answers to why the firm is bringing certain resources within the firm as opposed to obtaining these services from outside the firm. Alternatively, if we are interested in *strategic direction* then we might expect answers to the question of why the firm is pursuing this particular direction rather than alternative directions. For example, why is the firm pursuing foreign rather than domestic supplies, backward relations rather than forward or horizontal?

It may be conceded that there is a distinction between the question of strategic direction and the other two questions, but the distinction between domain and mode may be less obvious. When Coase (1937: 388) said, 'within a firm in place of the complicated market structure with exchange transactions is substituted the entrepreneur-co-ordinator who directs production', he was stating a one-to-one correspondence between domain and mode; exchange transactions *across* firms and hierarchy *inside* the firm. However, this one-to-one correspondence between domain and mode has already been blurred by Williamson (1975), who carried out much of his transaction cost analysis in terms of internal capital, labour, and intermediate product markets. It is not difficult to find markets *inside* the firm once you start looking for them. Is it also possible to identify hierarchy *across* firms in much the same way that exchange transactions can link these firms?

To answer this question, we need first to be clear about what is meant by a firm. Cowling and Sugden define the firm as 'the means of co-ordinating production from one centre of strategic decision-making' (1993: 68). Alternatively, Grossman and Hart 'define a firm to consist of these assets that it owns or over which it has control; we do not distinguish between ownership and control and virtually define ownership as the power to exercise control' (1986: 693–4). Figure 9.1 shows two cases of hierarchy: the M-form and the joint

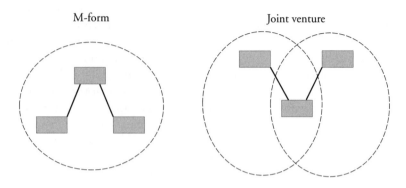

Figure 9.1. Hierarchy within and between firms

venture. The boundaries of firms in the respective cases are represented by the dotted circles. In the case of our M-form, the corporation owns and controls two divisions and the boundaries of the firm clearly include the headquarters and the two divisions. This is consistent with both Cowling and Sugden's control definition and Grossman and Hart's ownership definition of the firm. However, we shall use Cowling and Sugden's definition as more appropriate for our purposes.

The case of a joint venture inverts normally hierarchical relationships as Figure 9.1 illustrates. Instead of having headquarters as the master of two servants, as in the case of our M-form, we now have the joint venture subsidiary as the servant of two masters. The two parent firms co-own and co-administer the subsidiary, as Figure 9.1 illustrates. There is now a dual line of authority and control as indicated by the V-shaped hierarchy in Figure 9.1. Since the subsidiary is co-owned, the boundaries of the two parent firms overlap according to Grossman and Hart's ownership definition of the firm. The boundaries of the firms also overlap if they are analysed in control terms as in Cowling and Sugden's definition, since the subsidiary is ultimately co-administered from two separate centres of strategic decision making. Thus, whether we use ownership or control definitions of the firm, the boundaries of the two firms in Figure 9.1 overlap around the joint venture, and the joint venture itself appears as a case of a hierarchy which may cross or transcend firms.

If joint ventures were infrequent it might be possible to treat this case as simply a curiosity. However, some firms now have the bulk of their business tied up in joint ventures and it is no longer possible to dismiss this form of organization as being of minor importance. Thus, not only can markets be internal or external to firms, so also can hierarchies. This suggests that it may be possible to develop taxonomies based around direction, domain, and mode dimensions, as in Figure 9.2.

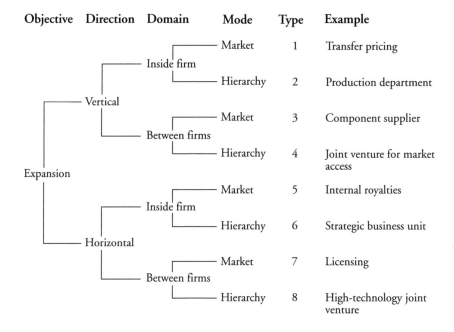

Objective	Direction	Domain	Mode	Type	Example
		Inside firm	Market	1	Transfer pricing
			Hierarchy	2	Production department
	Vertical	Between firms	Market	3	Component supplier
			Hierarchy	4	Joint venture for market access
Expansion		Inside firm	Market	5	Internal royalties
			Hierarchy	6	Strategic business unit
	Horizontal	Between firms	Market	7	Licensing
			Hierarchy	8	High-technology joint venture

Figure 9.2. A taxonomy of directions, domains, and modes

As Figure 9.2 shows, there are eight possible variants of direction, domain, and mode characteristics. The first four types are examples of vertical relations. Types 1 and 2 in Figure 9.2 indicate that vertical integration may be organized internally *within* the firm using either exchange relations or the exercise of authority. For example, components may be directed by transfer prices (Type 1) or a production manager's instructions (Type 2). As we have noted, both markets and hierarchies may exist *between* firms, with external supplies from a components supplier being an example of Type 3, and market access joint ventures[7] being an example of Type 4.

The second group of four types represent horizontal relations. Within the firm, resources such as technology may be shared using internal markets (Type 5) or hierarchy (Type 6). For example, while it is usual to think of royalty payments as taking place between firms, Dunning (1993: 288) notes that about 80 per cent of the cross-border receipts and payments of royalties and fees of the

[7] See Buckley and Casson (1996) for discussion of both backward and forward integration using joint ventures.

USA and Germany represent intra-firm (and Type 5) transactions. An example of a Type 6 case is where management administers the exploitation of economies of scope within a strategic business unit, for example by arranging the sharing of technology or distribution channels. Finally, horizontal relations may be organized between firms using market (Type 7) or hierarchical (Type 8) means. For example, a firm can share its technology with another firm through licensing (Type 7) or jointly administer its use with the other firm in a joint venture (Type 8).

Different approaches have tended to emphasize different types. Coase (1937) was really concerned with Types 2 and 3, while Williamson (1975) extended analysis of unified governance to include Type 1. Penrose's resource-based approach has always been most comfortable in the company of Type 6 situations.

There are some points that serve to complicate the picture painted in Figure 9.2. First, the hierarchy/market dichotomy is an idealized one. In practice, relations may combine elements of both. For example, joint ventures typically involve contractual as well as hierarchical relations between the parties, while internal markets and transfer prices may be influenced or constrained by administrative decisions. Secondly, the relations between a unit and the rest of the firm may be complex and vary according to circumstances and the nature of decisions; for example a unit may compete with the rest of the firm in a relatively free internal labour market, have its transfer prices regulated by group headquarters, and find itself subject to the undiluted authority of corporate headquarters as far as decisions relating to its expansion, divestment, or termination are concerned. Thirdly, the authority (or hierarchy) versus market (or exchange) distinction may conceal other modes of co-ordination.[8] Individuals and groups do not simply instruct, agree exchanges, or receive instructions. They also consult, co-operate, liaise, ask for help, and advise, amongst other things; indeed, as Chisholm (1989) shows, such informal co-ordination mechanisms should be regarded as both complements and substitutes for hierarchical and contractual methods of co-ordination. Co-ordination is a more subtle and complex process than is generally acknowledged in economic analysis.

However, our simple taxonomy in Figure 9.2 should serve its purpose if it helps to show that direction, domain, and mode are separate but complementary questions. For example, management would do well to reconsider horizontal moves if there is no cost-effective combination of domain and mode that would allow such moves to proceed profitably. None the less, while the questions of direction, domain, and mode may be interdependent, they are still distinctive and influenced by different considerations. Most crucially, it is important to avoid the danger of interpreting the question, 'why did it do that?', in an inappropriate or incomplete way. For example, it was noted in Kay (1997: 58–61)

---

[8] For example, see Mintzberg (1979) for a review of many of these techniques.

that the transaction cost explanation of the conglomerate as an internal capital market may help to explain why this *mode* of organization was preferred to the external capital market, but not why the conglomerate *direction* was chosen. More specialized strategies could also achieve the efficiency gains associated with an internal capital market and add specialization gains and economies sacrificed by the conglomerate strategy. Similarly, transaction cost explanations of multi-national enterprise tend to focus on the relative costs of governance associated with this solution analysed as a *mode*, but this does not explain why firms may wish to expand in an international *direction* when domestic expansion usually offers more opportunities for exploitation of economies of scope associated with managerial capabilities.[9]

In the next three subsections we shall look at issues relating to the framing of mode, domain, and direction agendas respectively.

3.1. Mode of Co-ordination

What influences *how* activities are co-ordinated? Why employ organization or hierarchy in some contexts, market contracts in others? In Kay (1997: 51–5) it is suggested that the nature and the timing of *decisions* are important influences in this context. For example, if all the relevant technical specifications have been established for a technology on the basis of past decisions, a licensing contract may be the preferred means to transfer technology to a third party. If major technical decisions remain to be made in the future, then setting up a hierarchy in the form of a joint venture to deal with future uncertainties may be deemed to be a more appropriate form of organization.

However, economics has traditionally tended to take a fairly limited view of what constitutes decision making in the past. Neoclassical theory and managerial theory were preoccupied with decision makers maximizing some objective function, while at the same time behavioural theorists developed analysis based around the notion of satisficing decision makers. Indeed, a consensus picture of *Homo economicus* began to emerge. This was an individual wandering through time and space, perhaps maximizing here if information was sufficient, possibly satisficing there if information was inadequate or too costly to obtain. Nelson and Winter (1982) probably represents the best developed view of this individual from a decision-making perspective.

Homo economicus is, and always was, an impatient decision maker. He is

---

[9] In Kay (1997: 177) it was also pointed out that many studies of collaborative and merger activity interpreted the 'Why did it do that?' question in terms of strategic direction. Unfortunately, this leads to checklists of reasons for joint venture, licensing, strategic alliances, and mergers all looking very similar. This is not surprising since these modes are indeed alternative ways of doing the same thing. What the studies need to do to explain the incidence of a particular mode is explain not *where* they are going, but *why* a particular mode was chosen instead of its alternatives.

presented with information and immediately makes a decision, whether satisficing or optimizing depending on the circumstances and/or the assumptions of his
modeller. Even when more than one decision maker is recognized, as in game
theory, it is usual to assume that decision making is done by individual decision
makers and takes place instantaneously, such as in Cournot and Bertrand competition. If sequential decision making is recognized, the decisions are still generally assumed to come in discrete packets. Economics is really about acts of choice
and selection, not processes of decision.

However, anyone tracing the history of the theory of the firm over recent
years might reasonably begin to wonder where all the decisions have gone.
There is not much evidence of individuals actually making decisions (whether
of a maximizing or a satisficing kind) in resource-based economics or transaction cost economics. In the former, there are competences and capabilities, but
decision making is less visible. In the latter, there is attitude (primarily opportunism), but no clear indications as to how parties with such attitude make
decisions.

This neglect is all the more noteworthy when the processes of strategic decision making in the firm are actually studied. Such decisions bear little resemblance to the picture of decision making associated with economic models.
These decisions do not just allocate resources, they are major consumers of
resources. Hickson *et al.* (1986) studied 150 strategic decisions made by large
organizations and found that these decisions typically took several months or
years, usually involved numerous internal and external units, and were likely to
link with numerous other major and minor decisions.

A strategic choice (build a new warehouse?) can be expressed in a few words
or a discounted cash flow calculation, but it can take a book such as Loasby
(1973) to analyse the decision to build that warehouse. Hamlet may have had a
couple of strategic choices (Kill the King? . . . Kill himself?) that could have been
distilled down to Act 1, Scene 1, Line 1, but such a consummation would almost
certainly have prompted theatre patrons to demand their money back. It is the
process of making decisions that creates the play, much as it appears the process
of making decisions creates organizations.

Earlier we used a working definition of a firm as a bundle of resources
controlled from a single centre of strategic decision making. Our discussion
here suggests that decision processes are more than simply acts of choice or
selection, but this is not sufficient to demonstrate that these provide the key to
understanding the reasons for the existence of organizations. However, we do
feel justified in suggesting that it would be reasonable to suppose that clues as
to why these centres of strategic decision making exist are to be found in the
kinds of strategic decisions that these centres make—decisions of the kind that
Hickson and colleagues investigated. When Monteverde and Teece (1982)
asked the management of Ford and General Motors which components were

produced in-house and which were produced by outside suppliers,[10] their results might tell us something about how their respective production departments worked, but this is not the same thing as telling us why organizations such as Ford and General Motors existed. The answers to this question are likely to be found in the capabilities of Ford and General Motors in strategic decision making, not because the making of steering gear and crankshafts is a specialized activity compared with the production of paint and antifreeze. Indeed, if the senior management of Ford or GM were to spend meetings debating whether to make or buy a certain type of oil or a particular kind of seat trim, shareholders would be well advised to reconsider their investment or to sack the CEO. Make-or-buy decisions are normally made at lower levels.[11] There are more important things for these organizations to worry about.

This all suggests that transaction costs and capabilities are only part of the story. There is no point in saying that transaction costs result in markets being substituted by hierarchies if we do not have a sense of how these hierarchies actually work in practice. There is no point in saying that capabilities are important unless we go one step further and study what they actually do. Hierarchy and capabilities are both tools, but tools are only useful if they actually do something. What the modern business firm actually does is to operate as 'an organization for making and implementing decisions within a market economy' (March 1988: 101). It is the nature of practice of these decisions which is likely to mark the difference between hierarchy and the market-place.

3.2. Domain

What considerations influence the domain over which activities are conducted? This is the stamping-ground of transaction cost economics and, as we have seen, studies here have concentrated on the paradigm case of vertical integration—especially in the form of the make-or-buy decision. However, as we have also seen, Penrose also offered explanations as to why firms may vertically integrate, though her explanations for vertical integration turn out to be more convincing when they are seen in terms of the need for managerial *control* over resources rather than in resource-based terms. She argued that

where efficient management is a scarce resource, there will be a strong tendency to (vertically) integrate in order to reduce the managerial difficulties not only of controlling and

---

[10] Monteverde and Teece did not claim more for their study than that it told us something about vertical integration. It is the wider claims of transaction cost theorists to be able to explain the existence of the firms (based on empirical evidence such as Monteverde and Teece) which are regarded as questionable here.

[11] At the same time a distinction can be made between particular make-or-buy decisions and the strategies such as outsourcing which may be formulated at the highest level and provide an umbrella or context for specific make-or-buy decisions at lower levels.

planning existing operations but also, and sometimes especially, of planning future investment . . . much (vertical) integration is directly traceable to the technical efficiency of conducting a sequence of operations in close proximity, and to the maintenance of a smooth flow of supplies and more stable markets (1959: 148–9).

It should be noted that while these arguments are not inconsistent with asset specificity explanations of vertical integration, they do not require the existence of this condition. The key words in Penrose's explanation of vertical integration are 'control' and 'planning'. For example, vertical integration may help to reduce uncertainty by controlling and smoothing the throughput of standardized inter-mediate inputs at various stages in the oil industry.[12] As we noted earlier, it is difficult to explain the phenomenon of vertical integration in such cases in terms of the particular control problems associated with asset specificity.

Similar points can be made about long-term contracts, which are regarded in transaction cost economics as potential substitutes for vertical integration in cases where the latter is prohibited or impeded (Williamson 1985: 106). In early 1998 two of the most publicized long-term contracts in the UK were those for the coaches of the Scottish and English national soccer teams, with both national associations pressing their respective coaches to sign new contracts[13] that would extend beyond the summer of 2000. It is difficult to see how asset specificity could explain such contracts since they are stimulated by both coaches being potentially highly mobile and marketable (non-specific) assets that could be difficult to replace. Instead, the long-term nature of these contracts lies in the wishes of the management of the respective national teams to maintain control over the continuity and quality of coaching services supplied to them: tying them down to prevent them walking out of the door. Long-term contracts are similarly found in many cases of sports stars and performing artists, again to prevent valuable and mobile assets cutting and running (Kay 1997: 49–50).

Maintaining control over the use of the assets is also a fundamental issue in the widespread internalization of research and development activity within the firm. It is precisely because R&D may *not* be a specific asset that management may decide to internalize it—rivals may be interested in appropriating the hard work commissioned by the firm in this context, so wise firms may decide to control and conceal their innovative efforts in-house (Kay 1997: 45–8).

One point that can be said immediately about these control-based arguments for internalization of activity within the firm is that they are potentially less straightforward than asset specificity considerations: in-house control for stabil-ity, continuity, and/or appropriability may be a more varied set of reasons and

---

[12] Penrose cites the oil industry as an example of vertical integration in this context (1959: 147 and 149, footnotes).

[13] *Scotsman* (Sport section), 18 January 1998, p. 27 and *Observer* (Sport Section), 18 January 1998, p. 5.

more difficult to operationalize than explanations based around asset specificity. However, while a simple explanation should always be preferred to a complex one, *ceteris paribus*, in this context it does seem that the asset specificity explanations may have been stretched too far. Management may want to bring resources under its direct control for a variety of reasons, and asset specificity may not be one of them.

It is not suggested here that control-based reasons are necessarily sufficient for a general explanation as to why management may wish to bring activities within the scope of the firm.[14] Our main purpose here has been to argue that mode and domain are separate but complementary questions, and that recognition of this is essential if questions relating to the economics of organization are to be properly formulated.

3.3. Strategic Direction

What determines the strategic *directions* that the firm may pursue? Bearing in mind that we are only dealing in rude thoughts at the moment, the rude answer is, whatever senior management decides to do. We do have the caveat from our earlier discussion that vertical relations are compulsory but horizontal directions are optional; this means that whatever business a firm is in, it must at least be aware of needs to make, maintain, improve, and/or alter vertical relations wherever appropriate. It has to have a route or routes to final customers, and it has to have access to supplies. These relations may be internal to the domain of the firm or mediated in conjunction with other firms, and there are a variety of modes through which they may be expressed, as we have seen.

However, the directions in which the firm goes ultimately depend on what Cowling and Sugden's single 'centre of decision making' wants to do and the freedom with which it is allowed to pursue its wishes. If senior management wishes to pursue growth of the firm, there are usually clear limits for doing so up and down the vertical chain; beginning with raw material and ending with the final consumer. These limits may be exacerbated to the extent that it is inefficient or otherwise impractical to bring many vertical transactions within the domain of the firm. Vertical expansion has roofs and floors, which is why it is difficult to conceive of a transaction cost theory of the growth of the firm. Thus, the firm that wishes to expand will be forced to look at possible horizontal paths, sooner or later. Once horizontal perspectives are recognized, opportunities for expansion are opened up and may proceed indefinitely along a variety of routes. These routes may or may not make extensive use of the existing capabilities of the firm.

[14] For simplicity and to aid comparison with transaction cost economics, we have concentrated here on the case of domain in the context of vertical relations. In the case of *horizontal* relations, horizontal integration may be preferred because it is simpler and cheaper than a system of market contracts. See Kay (1997: 66–9) for further discussion.

Why would a firm choose to explore technological linkages rather then marketing linkages, go international rather than concentrate on expanding within its home country? Questions such as these will depend on the objectives of the firm, the linkages open to the firm, the constraints imposed by policy makers, and the effectiveness of alternative modes and domains through which a particular strategic direction could be organized. Each strategy will typically have an opportunity cost in terms of alternative strategies that could be pursued with the managerial and financial resources available to the firm at any one time. Thus the question can still be framed as an economic one, and indeed unless it is, the logic of strategic direction may be obscured in particular cases. Clearly these are issues beyond the scope of this chapter, but Kay (1997) does provide a framework for analysing questions of strategic direction along these lines.

4. Conclusions

Two main sets of conclusions are drawn here. First, a number of issues must receive attention if we are to move forward in looking at issues of capabilities and co-ordination in the economics of organization. Some of these have been raised in this chapter.

Secondly, it has been suggested that there are three main questions that are important in this area, and that analysis has not always been effective in the past in differentiating these questions. The three questions relate to the mode of co-ordination of resources, the domain over which resources are controlled, and the strategic direction of the firm. These are complementary but distinct issues, and each may be affected by different considerations. It has been emphasized that it is especially important to distinguish between mode and domain if we are to make progress in this area. This would facilitate recognition of the central role of decision making in influencing choice of mode of co-ordination and would create the possibility of integrating this issue with the rest of the research agenda discussed here.

Our last rude thought is that 'decision' can mean different things, much like other words we have looked at, and these meanings can influence and sometimes distort analysis. It can mean instantaneous selection or choice, or a process that can take months or years. It shares this duality of meaning in economics with 'innovation', which can mean the act of introducing a new product or the search process leading up to and including the act of new product introduction. Duality of meaning is not a problem as long as those who study the final act are not misled into thinking that this always represents a sufficient description of the phenomenon they are studying. However, it is felt here that the decision process lies at the heart of the reasons for the existence of organization and that these issues must be incorporated in to the agenda of the economics of organization if it is to move forward.

References

ARTHUR, W. B. 1994. *Increasing Returns and Path Dependence in the Economy.* Ann Arbor, MI: University of Michigan Press.

BUCKLEY, P. J., and M. CASSON 1996. 'Joint ventures', in P. J. Buckley and J. Michie, eds., *Firms, Organizations and Contracts: A Reader in Industrial Organization.* Oxford: Oxford University Press, 410–28.

CHISHOLM, D. 1989. *Co-ordination without Hierarchy.* Berkeley: California University Press.

COASE, R. H. 1937. 'The nature of the firm', *Economica* 4: 386–405.

COHEN, M. D., J. G. MARCH, and J. P. OLSEN 1972. 'A garbage can model of organizational choice', *Administrative Science Quarterly* 17: 1–25.

COWLING, K., and R. SUGDEN 1993. 'Control, markets and firms', in C. Pitelis, ed., *Transaction Costs, Markets and Hierarchies.* Oxford: Blackwell, 66–76.

DUNNING, J. H. 1993. *Multinational Enterprises and the Global Economy.* Wokingham: Addison-Wesley.

FOSS, N. J. 1997. 'Resources and strategies: a brief overview of themes and contributions', in N. J. Foss, ed.: 3–18.

—— ed. 1997. *Resources, Firms and Strategies.* Oxford: Oxford University Press.

GOULD, S. J. 1989. *Wonderful Life: The Burgess Shale and the Nature of History.* New York: J. J. Norton.

GROSSMAN, S. J., and O. D. HART 1986. 'The costs and benefits of ownership: a theory of vertical and lateral integration', *Journal of Political Economy* 94: 691–719.

HICKSON, D. J., R. J. BUTLER, D. CRAY, G. R. MALLORY, and D. C. WILSON 1986. *Top Decisions: Strategic Decision-making in Organizations.* San Francisco: Jossey-Bass.

KAY, J. 1996. *The Business of Economics.* Oxford: Oxford University Press.

KAY, N. M. 1982. *The Evolving Firm: Strategy and Structure in Industrial Organization.* London: Macmillan.

—— 1997. *Pattern in Corporate Evolution.* Oxford: Oxford University Press.

—— forthcoming. 'Loasby and decisions: a non-Coasian perspective on the nature of the firm', in S. Dow and P. Earl, eds., *Contingency, Complexity and the Theory of the Firm: Essays in Honour of Brian Loasby.* London: Edward Elgar.

LANGLOIS, R. N. 1997. 'Transaction cost economics in real time', in N. J. Foss, ed.: 286–305.

LOASBY, B. J. 1973. *The Swindon Project.* London: Pitman.

MARCH, J. G. 1988. *Decisions and Organizations.* Oxford: Basil Blackwell.

—— and J. P. OLSEN 1986. 'Garbage can models of decision making in organizations', in J. G. March and R. Weissinger-Baylon, eds., *Ambiguity and Command: Organizational Perspectives on Military Decision Making.* Cambridge, MA: Ballinger, 11–35.

MINTZBERG, H. 1979. *The Structuring of Organizations.* Englewood Cliffs, NJ: Prentice Hall.

MONTEVERDE, K., and D. J. TEECE 1982. 'Supplier switching costs and vertical integration in the automobile industry', *Bell Journal of Economics* 13: 206–13.

NELSON, R. R. 1991. 'Why do firms differ, and how does it matter?' *Strategic Management Journal* 12: 61–74.

NELSON, R. R., and S. G. WINTER 1982. *An Evolutionary Theory of Economic Change.* Cambridge, MA: Harvard University Press.

PENROSE, E. T. 1959. *The Theory of the Growth of the Firm.* Oxford: Blackwell.

——— 1968. *The Large International Firm in Developing Countries: The International Petroleum Industry.* London: Allen & Unwin.

——— 1971. *The Growth of Firms, Middle East Oil and Other Essays.* London: Frank Cass.

RICHARDSON, G. B. 1972. 'The organization of industry', *Economic Journal* 82: 883–96.

SHACKLE, G. L. S. 1979. *Imagination and the Nature of Choice.* Edinburgh: Edinburgh University Press.

SHELANSKI, H. A., and P. G. KLEIN 1995. 'Empirical research in transaction cost economics: a review and assessment', *Journal of Law, Economics and Organization* 11: 335–61.

TEECE, D. J. 1997. 'Economies of scope and the scope of the enterprise', in N. J. Foss, ed.: 103–6.

WILLIAMSON, O. E. 1975. *Markets and Hierarchies: Analysis and Antitrust Implications.* New York: Free Press.

——— 1985. *The Economic Institutions of Capitalism.* New York: Free Press.

——— 1996. *The Mechanisms of Governance.* New York: Oxford University Press.

Part C

The Dynamics of Governance

10

Organizing for Innovation: Co-ordinating Distributed Innovation Capabilities

Rod Coombs and J. Stan Metcalfe

1. Introduction

The central theme of this chapter is the need to combine a capabilities perspective on the innovating firm with the increasingly complex division of labour in the generation of science and technology. It is increasingly the case that technological innovations cannot be accomplished by individual firms acting independently. It is more and more common for firms to act in collaboration with other firms, whether suppliers, customers, or competitors, and with other non-commercial knowledge-generating organizations. The nature of these collaborative linkages varies from formal contractual links to informal networks of knowledge exchange, with all sorts of intermediate varieties.

In explaining how and why firms differ in their market performance, the capabilities view of the firm has placed its primary emphasis on the internal accumulation of the knowledge and skills which underpin its productive activity. While this certainly is an important part of the explanation of the differential innovative trajectories of firms, it is deficient in two important respects. First, it fails to pick up on one of the principal features of the modern innovation process, namely, its collective, combinatorial character. Secondly, it fails to recognize that a distinguishing feature of the competitive performance of firms is their differential ability to manage the external collaborative relationships required by modern innovation conditions.

These developments have several strong implications for the capabilities view of the firm, for the nature of corporate governance, and for systemic perspectives on the innovation process. They also allow us to develop the theory of the firm beyond the idea that the firm is its production function. Input–output relationships are of course central to an understanding of economic performance but they are not to be taken for granted. What they are and how they develop over time depends on a wider set of instituted relationships in which the firm is embedded. Consequently, the boundary of the firm is never entirely clear. The creation of new capabilities is increasingly taking place through the combination of the capabilities of several firms and research organizations and this raises fundamental questions about the co-ordination of capability formation. The governance of extra-firm relationships adds new layers of complexity to intra-firm governance and indeed to our understanding of the boundaries of the firm itself. The 'distributed innovation process', which rests upon the newly created 'cross-firm capabilities', also raises the need for substantial elaboration and development of received models of innovation and technology management. This distributed innovation perspective casts new light on the innovation systems literature and shows that a systemic perspective on the innovation process is a special case of a more general phenomenon of institutional embed-dedness.

The ensuing discussion will bring us to a paradox, which can be expressed as follows. We will argue in section 2 that innovation processes are increasingly distributed across firm boundaries, and that they are implemented through structures which co-ordinate the contributions of the various participating firms. Then in section 3 we will review the treatment of the innovation process within the capabilities theory of the firm, and conclude that, up to now at least, capabilities and their exploitation have been presented as matters for individual firms acting alone. There is clearly a mismatch between this single firm perspective on capabilities, and the multiple organization perspective on innovation. We therefore need to consider how the capabilities perspective can be extended to embrace a multi-firm perspective on innovation.

In order to make progress in understanding these issues it is necessary to shift from a framework which sees legally distinct firms as the only unit of analysis, and towards a framework in which firms are still important, but capabilities themselves become an important unit of analysis which is not coterminous with the firm. In such a framework, incentives, opportunities, entrepreneurial behaviour, and indeed the long-term defence of the interests of legally distinct firms, can be reconstructed as the search for and imple-mentation of new combinations of capabilities. Furthermore, the new combi-nations, and the cross-firm structures in which they are managed, may then become the site for the creation and accumulation of genuinely new capabil-ities (and technologies) which did not exist prior to the creation of the cross-firm structure.[1] This is the basis for the notion of a 'distributed innovation process' which forms part of the argument of this chapter. In section 3, we examine how far the current literature on the capabilities model of the firm enables us to accommodate this notion of a distributed innovation process. In section 4, we propose extensions to the capabilities model in order to achieve this aim.

---

[1] Chesnais (1996) provides a very persuasive and detailed analysis of the resource-creating role of inter-firm agreements and their potential as stimulants to growth.

2. The Distributed Nature of Innovation Capabilities

During the last two decades or so, the nature of the innovations produced in advanced economies has been changing, along with changes in the nature of the innovation processes which give rise to those innovations. We begin by identifying three of these changes in innovations and their creation processes as 'stylized facts', which then deserve further exploration.

The first stylized fact is that innovations (and indeed products, services, and processes more generally) tend to embody or draw on a wider and wider range of constituent technologies and knowledge bases. We call this the *technological diversity* thesis.

The second stylized fact is that the products and processes created through innovation are placed into a context of use which is becoming increasingly *systemic*. We refer to this as the *systemic complexity* thesis.

The third stylized fact relates to the nature of the evolving relationship between scientific and technological disciplines. We call this the *connectedness* thesis.

The significance of these three trends is that the individual innovating firm now faces a *tougher and tougher* challenge to its range of technological knowledge and its broader capabilities. As the number of technologies in a product increases, and the context of use becomes more systemic and complex, the ability of a firm to meet these requirements from its own resources must reduce, other things being equal. However, before we consider these implications for the innovating firm, and its responses, we first need to elaborate and exemplify the three broad trends which have been introduced above.

2.1. Technological Diversity

The first piece of evidence for the technological diversity thesis comes from analysis of trends in the technology portfolios of large companies. Recent work by Granstrand *et al.* (1997) using US patent data has shown that during the 1970s and 1980s large corporations increased the absolute number of distinct technological fields in which they maintained a capability. What is particularly interesting is that this increase in technological diversity was greater than the increase in product diversity of these companies, and occurred even in cases where product diversity had *decreased* at the corporate level. Using complementary case study data Granstrand and his co-authors argue that this broadening of the technology base of a company is mirrored at the product level. This evidence suggests that the innovation process to produce new or modified products is increasingly required to mobilize a wider array of technological capabilities than hitherto. Quite simply, companies have to 'know more' even if they wish to maintain a relatively stable position in a given product market.

This increasing technological diversity of products means that the research and development (R&D) budgets of firms experience strong upward pressure. New technologies have to be acquired, and they also have to be integrated with the existing technologies in the companies. This in turn places greater demands on the organizational capabilities of the firm as it struggles to deploy this wider portfolio of technologies.

The second piece of evidence for the technology diversity thesis arises from the now widely accepted notion that we are witnessing the diffusion of a number of important *generic technologies* across nearly all industrial sectors. The most developed version of this argument is the 'techno-economic paradigms' thesis associated with the work of Perez (1983). However, it is not necessary to agree with all aspects of these arguments to see the truth in the proposition that the generic technology of information technology has had powerful impacts on all industrial sectors; new materials technologies have had impacts on several sectors; and bio-technology is impacting on a smaller number of sectors but in a very thoroughgoing way. All three of these generic technologies provide firms with opportunities not just to substitute new technology for old, but to *combine* new technologies with existing technologies in order to upgrade the functionality of products. Indeed Kodama's (1991) concept of technology fusion was coined out of the need to give a name (mechatronics) to the powerful combination of mechanical and electronics technologies which emerged in engineering and consumer products in the 1980s.

The third phenomenon we cite as contributing to the technological diversity trend is the intensification of supply chain linkages. The classical example here is the vehicles sector. As the sector has matured, an increasing proportion of the modern car has come to consist of components and sub-assemblies manufactured by the first-tier suppliers to the big vehicle assemblers. The first-tier suppliers in turn purchase components from their suppliers and so on. Much of the design sovereignty, however, still lies with the assemblers, although they are increasingly reliant on the expertise of the first-tier suppliers in technologies such as, for example, engine management chips and software. Thus a company such as General Motors, with the highest private R&D spend in the world, has to do enough electronics R&D to be an intelligent specifier and customer for the IT embedded in its cars. But it does not want to incur the full R&D costs associated with actually developing all of that IT. For this it relies on first-tier suppliers such as Lucas-Varity. These suppliers, in their turn, have to do enough R&D on vehicles, vehicle systems, and their behaviour to enable them to collaborate with GM, but not enough to actually build vehicles. Thus each player in a tightly structured supply chain for a complex end-product has to have R&D capability that extends well upstream and downstream of their own product position in that chain. It is plain enough that this pressure will contribute to the increase of technological diversity at firm level.

To summarize so far: we have seen that patent data paint a picture of company technological diversity increasing over time, and we have argued that the desire to exploit generic technologies, and to organize innovation processes across supply chains, have both contributed to this trend. We now turn to the second stylized fact: the increasing systemic complexity thesis.

2.2. Systemic Complexity

The argument here is that innovations increasingly face a complex systemic environment, and that they have to reflect this in their design by ensuring compatibility with this environment. This requirement presents in two forms, which we can label the weak and the strong forms of the systemic compatibility requirement.

In the weak case, the innovating firm finds itself developing a new product which has not only to provide novel functionality, but also to inter-operate with various established technical systems in the customer's environment. These established systems may be based on technologies of which the supplier firm knows little. An example will illustrate the point.

The gases company BOC has a division which manufactures anaesthetic gases for use in hospital operating rooms. The gases are chemically novel, and patent protected, but cannot be delivered with conventional anaesthetic equipment. Consequently the company entered into the design and manufacture of specialized equipment to deliver its own gases. Many aspects of this equipment design problem were familiar to BOC, since it frequently finds itself involved in precisely this situation with customers from a wide variety of industries. Indeed this provision of a combined 'gases and equipment solution' is a central feature of its innovation and business strategy. In this case, however, the anaesthesia equipment has the added requirement that it has to interface with the hospital information systems. US hospitals in particular have complex information systems which record the details of medical procedures administered to patients and integrate them into patient databases which serve both for clinical records and for cost control. Because of the need to meet this system integration requirement, BOC formed a strategic alliance with Hewlett Packard to enable them to access the relevant electronic and information technologies. This means that their equipment can be marketed as having the necessary features of systems compatibility with the hospital environment. The point here is twofold. First, BOC had to face the need to mobilize technologies beyond their existing internal portfolio. This creates a pressure similar to the technological diversity thesis described in the previous section. Secondly, in this case they chose not to develop the technology internally, nor to simply specify it to a supplier, but to engage in a joint development effort through a strategic alliance. This underlines the fact that there can be a variety of responses to the need to mobilize technology unfamiliar to the firm. We return to this point in section 4 of the chapter.

We turn now to the stronger form of the systems compatibility requirement on innovation. In this case it is not a process of placing an innovation within an existing system, but of having to innovate a *new system* in order to achieve the primary innovation aim. Again we will use an example to explain the point.

In the early 1980s Marks and Spencer were dissatisfied with the quality and customer appeal of the 'ready meals' available to them to sell in their retail food activity.[2] They began to explore the possibility that both fresh meat and fish, and also 'recipe meals' incorporating meat, fish, cheese, etc., could be prepared in a form which only required heating. However, they did not want to deep-freeze these meals, since there are limitations on the recipes that are suitable for freezing, and there are additional costs both to the retailer and to the customer. The concepts they developed were 'chill-fresh' (for uncooked products), and 'cook chill' (for products which are cooked but require reheating).

In order for these products to be realized, a new 'system' was required, in which products are prepared, shipped, and displayed with the temperature being maintained within the range 0 to +2 degrees centigrade at all times, in order to control bacteriological and other hazards. Three major new technologies (or more precisely, clusters of technology) were required for this to be achieved. These are first, *the chilling technologies and temperature control procedures*; second, the *controlled atmosphere packing* which, together with the chilling, prolongs the shelf life of the fresh product; and third, the *transport and logistics systems* to bring together the inputs and deliver the outputs while never varying more than one degree C within the 0 to +2 range.

Marks and Spencer initiated and then actively co-ordinated the efforts of food processing equipment manufacturers, which made the chillers; and gases companies and packaging companies, which developed controlled atmosphere packaging. They then formed a joint venture company with one of the gases companies in order to develop and implement the transport of the chilled products between production sites, distribution centres, and retail sites. The resulting system is known in the industry as the 'chill-chain' and has now diffused widely amongst food product producers and food retailers in the UK. The retailers continue to play a prominent part in improving this system despite themselves having a technology base which only covers a modest part of the whole system.

In this example then, the retailers' desire for a new *end-product* was fulfilled by the creation of a series of new intermediate products, welded together into a system, involving a variety of players from other sectors.

---

[2] At that time such meals were often in a form that required reconstitution with water and the addition of other ingredients, and had poor reputations for quality.

2.3. The Connected Nature of Modern Science and Technology

Turning to the third of our stylized facts, we begin by advancing a rather bold hypothesis concerning the nature of modern science and technology. Since the late nineteenth century and the emergence of modern physics and chemistry, and even more during this century with the emergence of molecular biology, there has tended to be an increase in the interconnectedness and 'completeness' of scientific understanding. Examples are numerous: quantum mechanics explains not only subatomic issues important to physics, but also the principles of chemical bonding which underpin modern chemistry. Biochemistry shows how the form and function of living organisms are modulated by chemical bonds. Mathematics provides a set of tools and a language across all the physical and biological sciences.

This accelerating process of 'closure' in understanding nature has contradictory effects on its economic exploitation by firms. On the one hand, discrete technological artefacts are increasingly dependent on wider and wider swathes of this set of connected scientific disciplines and sub-disciplines. In that sense it can be said that the *complementarity* of different elements of technology is always increasing. On the other hand however, the specialization of these various technical and scientific fields multiplies; the volumes of knowledge in each field become greater and greater, and the modes of enquiry and distinctive skills of each discipline become more specialized. Thus despite being complementary, different parts of the technological universe become more and more *dissimilar* in terms of the skills required to conduct and manage them. This increases the absolute incentive for the firm to internalize interesting technologies, but reduces the relative probability of doing it successfully. Consequently the external acquisition of the capabilities associated with that technology becomes an attractive alternative. It is this process we have been discussing in the earlier part of this section.

2.4. Co-ordinating 'Distributed' Innovation Capabilities

From the discussion of the three stylized facts above, we have seen that the technologies and the other capabilities[3] required for certain innovations are now less frequently located within single firms and increasingly distributed across a range of firms and other knowledge-generating institutions. Such innovations therefore require the co-ordination of these existing capabilities (wherever they may be) and, possibly, the generation of new combinatorial capabilities. They therefore

---

[3] The sense in which we are using the term 'capabilities' will be clarified in section 3. For the time being we simply use it to denote accumulated skills and organizational routines with which firms can carry out certain complex tasks with reliability and with some degree of distinctiveness from other firms.

require specific forms of governance structures which run in parallel with the existing governance structures. Put simply, the issue is this. We cannot explain how these innovations come about if we construe all economic activity as happening either inside single firms, or through arm's-length market transactions between firms. Cross-firm structures are being used in which firms voluntarily subordinate part of their autonomy in exchange for access to capabilities which they do not possess. They are doing this instead of relying on the market to purchase the services of those capabilities; and instead of fully internalizing those capabilities through mergers or through internal capability development.

3. Capabilities

3.1. Capabilities and the Development of the Firm

Our purpose in this section is not to review the considerable and rapidly growing literature on the capabilities-based view of the firm, for that has been achieved more efficiently elsewhere (Foss and Knudsen 1996; Montgomery 1995). Rather, our purpose is to draw upon some of the central threads of a capabilities perspective as background to our treatment in section 4 of distributed innovation processes. Our general conclusion will be that it is necessary to see the formation and articulation of capabilities as dependent as much on external relations as they are on the internal workings of the firm. Indeed we shall argue that the latter have been given excessive emphasis in the capabilities literature. The idiosyncrasies of individual firms is one matter, their process of generation is quite another, and a quite proper focus on idiosyncrasies should not lead to an excessively internalist perspective on capability generation. This leads us to view the generation of capabilities as dependent on the division of labour in the generation and exploitation of knowledge and on the particular methods for co-ordinating the division of labour.[4]

As with many other contributions to this literature our starting-point is Edith Penrose's (1959) view of the firm as an administrative unit which generates bundles of productive services from bundles of physical and human productive factors. This perspective presupposes organization, and purpose, and the existence of a theory of the particular business to provide the framework which justifies and evaluates the operation of that business.[5] Each of these elements plays a

[4] In the final stages of revising this chapter a referee drew our attention to the complementary paper by Dyer and Singh (1998). They too argue that the ability to generate competitive positions depends upon what they call relational factors, that is to say, the wider network of relationships in which the firm is embedded. As they rightly emphasize, the capability to identify, form, and manage such productive complementarities is not evenly distributed across firms nor is it developed without appropriate investments.

[5] Penrose refers in this context to the image of the business opportunity; others have proposed similar framing concepts, for example the dominant logic, proposed by Bettis and Prahalad (1995).

role in the capabilities perspective, as we shall explore below. Our second point of departure is provided by Richardson (1972), who presents firms as sets of activities which for their operation require knowledge, expertise, and skills in their performance. In other words, capabilities are the ability to carry out specific actions. It is immediately clear that the nature of capabilities may be approached in different ways. Richardson begins by distinguishing broad activities, such as production, marketing, and research and development, and progressively refines and subdivides these so that they relate increasingly to the execution of specific, narrow tasks. Alternatively, one can think of capabilities at different levels from top strategic management, Eliasson's top competent team (1988), down through various levels of operation to the 'shop-floor'. The point is that capabilities are bundles of behaviours, they are multidimensional, and they differ according to the function and level at which they are identified. For example, in her influential book *Wellsprings of Knowledge*, Leonard-Barton (1995) distinguishes core capabilities from supplemental and enabling capabilities in relation to their link to competitive advantage and goes on to distinguish physical systems, skills, managerial systems, and cultural values as elements which shape capabilities. Small wonder that their precise measurement at this general level proves to be so elusive.

It is more important, we believe, to recognize and exploit the micro detail of capabilities, particularly the technological capabilities which are our principal concern. They are domain specific, linked to well-defined transformation processes, and accumulated and articulated in the specific contexts that arise in the operation of these processes by firms.

Before we go further it is necessary to understand that a central purpose of a capabilities view of the firm is to explain why firms differ, not why they are similar. It is the idiosyncratic individuality of the firm, in terms of its characteristics at a particular time and its pattern of development over time, that becomes the defining issue. It is not surprising therefore that evolutionary scholars have been able to link a broad capabilities perspective to questions of competition and industrial change (Nelson and Winter 1984). As Foss (1996) has so clearly explained, the emphasis shifts to individual firm diversity in the context of populations of competing firms and to an abandonment of essentialist modes of explanation. One might add also that it leads to a recognition of competition as a dynamic process dependent for its rate and direction on *differences* in firm behaviour, and hence upon differences in the rate at which those firm behaviours develop over time.

We now explore the nature of capabilities more carefully, and begin with a distinction between resources, routines, organization, and intent. Some of the major contributions to the literature have espoused a resource-based view of the firm to explain firm heterogeneity and emphasize the importance of a lack of inter-firm resource mobility (Barney 1991; Amit and Shoemaker 1993). We can explain this more clearly by distinguishing productive factors, employees, capital and intermediate goods, and organizational structures from the *factor services or resources* which are derived in Penrose fashion from the factors. Now the point is that the resources are not entirely intrinsic properties of the factors; what each productive resource flow is depends upon the other resource flows with which it is combined, on the context in which that combination takes place, and on the purpose underlying the activity in question. The same skilled employee may be very productive in one function, and quite unproductive in another; in one firm she may work successfully, in another company not. Consequently, while the productive factors are highly tradeable, the collective bundle of interdependent, complementary services is not; it is a unity, which if it is to be traded at all in the market for corporate control must be traded as a single entity. Here it is important to recognize that the firm, *tout court*, is not always the appropriate unitary entity that can be traded. The more significant concept is the business unit, that particular organization charged with articulating a particular set of transformation processes addressing a specified product market. This is why we observe far more trading in business units in the market for corporate control than we do trading in entire companies.[6] An active market in corporate control is an extremely important complement to the process of capability formation. Indeed it is vital if the right incentive structure is to be created for the often highly uncertain process of capability formation. The bundle of resources in this Penrosian approach creates competitive advantage only to the extent that it is associated with products or production methods superior to at least one rival; to the extent that it is not widely imitated; and to the extent that other firms are not able to create effective, alternative, substitute routes to competitive advantage. Two further aspects now fall into place.

First, it is clear that the collective capability represented by the bundle of resources is dependent on the way in which the firm organizes its many activities. The organization is an operator for translating the individual resources into a collective bundle, the capability. One need not stress here how important this dimension can be, or that it has formal and informal components in terms of the social capital of patterns of trust, reputation, and authority which are continuously created within the firm (Eriksen and Mikkelsen 1996). Secondly, the focus on services and activities leads naturally to the question of what is done by whom and how, that is to say the question of routines (Nelson and Winter 1984). Routines are stabilized patterns of behaviour but of widely differing degrees of specificity. Some routines are precise templates for action, specifying to the 'nth' degree what must be done in each set of conceivable circumstances. Others, typically those associated with higher management, may offer far greater degrees of

---

[6] Of course, in the case of small companies, firm and business unit are coterminous; but not in general.

interpretative flexibility; some indeed may be routines for defining new routines, or for improving existing ones.

This assembly of concepts promises a rich theory of the internal workings of the firm and a basis for linking this with competitive advantage. Bundles of productive factors are deployed to yield productive services through the execution of activity routines in organization contexts. Fundamental to all of this is the idea that it is knowledge which is the common denominator, which ties the capability into a co-ordinated unity, so that the capabilities perspective could just as easily be seen as overlapping with a knowledge-based view of the firm (Itami 1987). However, before taking this further we need to recognize the final element in the capabilities perspective, that of intent and purpose, for it is intent combined with capabilities which gives rise to productive opportunities (Loasby 1994, 1999). Now intent implies a 'theory' of the business, what shall be done and how, a framework which allows the various resource services to be combined to a purpose. Such a framework, a paradigm, an image, or a dominant logic (Bettis and Prahalad 1995), identifies productive opportunities, guides action and decision, provides tests of performance, and acts as a filter in relation to the accumulation of new internal or external knowledge. In determining which questions are asked it necessarily determines which questions are off the agenda. Here we find one of the strong themes in the capabilities literature, that firms are subject to inertia: not only physical and organizational capital but human intellectual capital is sunk as they develop their distinctive patterns of activity. This theory of business specialization recognizes constraints as well as opportunities: as with all knowledge, competence in particular activities brings with it a trained *incapacity* to think beyond the region of specialist expertise. Thus a capabilities perspectives not only speaks to why firms are different; it also speaks to why they develop in different ways and how that development is often channelled in specific directions and is unresponsive to even major shifts in the competitive environment. All this, it will be immediately recognized, is a natural consequence of specialization and the division of labour. The acquisition of expertise in one domain forecloses its acquisition in some other domains; this is part of the reason why such investments are risky and subject to unplanned obsolescence.

With these preliminary remarks in mind we may now turn to what is for us the central feature of the capabilities view, namely its link with the creation of valuable knowledge, knowledge which is the basis of competitive advantage. For firms are frameworks in which knowledge is generated as well as used and there is not the slightest reason to expect that the process of knowledge generation ever approaches a state of rest. As Richardson (1972) emphasized, this brings knowledge, experience, and skills to the foreground. We shall interpret these distinctions as follows. By knowledge we mean codifiable understanding which may be shared by virtue of its transmissability in hard copy form. By skills we mean all those tacit components of understanding, which may not be replicated in hard copy form but depend for their transmission upon mutual observation and social interaction. Finally, expertise is constituted by the combinations of knowledge and skills *appropriate* to the task in hand. Thus expertise may be related to the carrying through of production transformations, the identification of markets for outputs and inputs, and, crucially, that integrative expertise through which the multiple capabilities of the firm are combined and directed at its objectives. Knowledge necessarily rests in the minds of individuals (either directly or indirectly), is shared in groups or teams (organization again), and may be expressed in some symbolic form even if only incompletely. Thus to understand the knowledge of the firm one must, in principle, know how that firm is organized and how its patterns and language of communication are articulated. Now this is exactly Penrose's point: capabilities depend upon team activity in which the knowledge and skills of the individuals are transformed into the integrated knowledge of the organization. Thus the organization, in all its aspects, becomes an operator for creating the collective from the individual. Since these phenomena are often less than transparent to the external observer and certainly complex, in that they may lack apparent order, this has given rise to the idea of causal ambiguity. In short the link between capabilities and competitive performance is not readily decipherable, even perhaps by the management of the firm, to which its operations are partly a 'black box' (Rumelt 1984). Of course, this raises particular difficulties when a firm comes to choose which other imperfectly understood organizations to engage with in co-operative arrangements to generate new capabilities (Metcalfe and James 1998).

It is here that the Richardson and Penrose themes come together and complement our earlier discussion. For the processes by which experience is gained inevitably generate *imbalances* in the capabilities of the firm, imbalances which disrupt or fall short of the requirements of close complementarity of capabilities for the operation of the firm. Expertise is acquired which no longer fits with the existing capabilities and if this slack is to be exploited this can only be done by attending to the gaps which prevent its classification as a capability. By contrast, the imbalance can take the form not of an underutilized capability, but of a 'missing' capability, needed for the optimal exploitation of other capabilities which are present.[7] If we add to this the above-mentioned connectedness in the development of modern science and technology (section 2.3) we can see how the firm finds itself continually faced with emergent opportunities to bring together complementary but discriminate bodies of expertise, to create capabilities where imbalances existed previously. The crucial point, though, is that it is not axiomatic that internal generation and exploitation of the capabilities is always

---

[7] Indeed, given the fact that the exploitation might take place within the existing firm or outside it, the 'surplus' problem and the 'missing' problem can be two sides of the same coin.

the most rational option. Thus the options of internal and external acquisition become different but complementary routes to the same end, namely to exploit imbalances in knowledge, skill, and expertise. The issue is one of careful judgement, of the appropriate choice of external and internal methods of accumulation, and of the effective integration of the two methods.

Once more Richardson provides us with the important insight. There is an entire spectrum of methods for external acquisition which lie between the limiting case of spot market transactions and direct administrative control, a spectrum summarized by the phrase co-operative arrangements: agreements between firms which guarantee their conduct for the duration of the agreement. Here lies a rich vein of possibilities. On the one hand it points to the idea of the embeddedness of co-operative arrangements in a network of social relationships (Granovetter 1985; Gulati 1999), in which matters of trust, reputation, authority, and competence are constructed in the process of forming and working together in co-operative arrangements, and are essential to the effective operation of such arrangements. On the other hand it points to the idea of the distributed and decentralized accumulation of competences in the economy, that is, to the division of labour in the accumulation of expertise and the co-ordination of that accumulation in systems of interacting organizations, as, for example, in the innovations system perspective (Nelson 1991; Carlsson 1995; Edquist 1997). To summarize: the process of capability formation is driven by factors external and internal to the firm. The activities of all expertise-generating organizations create for each of them *underutilized expertise* and thus the opportunities to engage in co-operative arrangements to exploit that expertise and to develop any further expertise necessary to the fulfilment of the objectives of the co-operative agreement. The question which arises now is that of the choice of co-operative arrangement for the elimination of imbalances in capability. The range of co-operative arrangements will be sketched later in the chapter. As we shall see, the choice between them is in part a matter of comparative efficiency, and in part a matter of the expertise to be acquired, and depends in part on the manner in which it is intended that the capability gained is to be exploited.

3.2. Capabilities and the Accumulation of Knowledge

The argument we examine here is in two parts. First, the question of how the firm acquires capabilities is closely related to the question of how it acquires knowledge and skill. Secondly, the choice of co-operative arrangements is influenced considerably by the nature of the knowledge to be acquired or transacted. Here the capabilities perspective has taken a predominantly internalist view, in part based on the observation that markets for knowledge are often imperfect and in many cases conspicuous by their absence. This essentially Arrovian market failure perspective (Arrow 1962) errs significantly in failing to recognize a full spectrum of possibilities between the limits of internal direction and external spot market transactions for the acquisition of knowledge (Howells 1999). The difficulties here are considerable and depend in part on a confusion between information and knowledge. Public information cannot be equated to public knowledge; indeed the restlessness of firms to which Penrose draws attention (1959: 78) depends on the fact that the same information flow will generate different accretions of knowledge in different firms. Moreover, knowledge is not in general in the atmosphere, despite its non-rival nature. It has to be searched for and acquired through positive steps: steps that presuppose investment (Langlois and Robertson 1999). To be able to communicate internally, members of the firm must make joint investments in the knowledge needed to understand one another and this point applies *a fortiori* to the acquisition of external knowledge (Rosenberg 1990). Knowledge may not be consumed in the traditional sense but, equally, it does not flow freely as if it were a drop of water on a frictionless plane. As Cohen and Levinthal (1989, 1990) have made clear this requires a firm to develop an appropriate absorptive capacity in order that it may read its external technological environment and that it can draw upon that external knowledge as and when appropriate. A model of information as publicly available to all-comers at a minimal transmission cost is very wide of the mark.

Now, of course, one cannot have half a piece of workable knowledge: it is all or nothing. While the firm at any one time may have many items of new knowledge in process as it were, it can only make use of its completed and interrelated bits of understanding, its practically applicable knowledge. It needs both a workable design architecture and all of the components required to translate that architecture into practice, as Henderson and Clark (1990) have emphasized. This takes us immediately to the indivisibility of the investments in capability generation, which has three powerful consequences. First, the accumulated capabilities of the firm give rise to increasing returns in their application and thus create incentives to find a wider scale of application. The return to capabilities formation increases with the scale of the firm's activities and it does not matter in this regard whether the capability has been acquired singly or co-operatively. Secondly, as Penrose emphasized, once knowledge has been acquired, the resources absorbed in its creation become free for the further generation of new capabilities within the domain of the firm's theory of business. Thus capabilities become self-generating if only the firm is willing to see and exploit the possibility. Thirdly, a point which is much underemphasized, namely the fact that much knowledge arises not as a result of planned search but as a consequence of the current activities of the firm: capabilities are a joint product with activity, perhaps the most significant way to consider learning by doing, and, as we shall see below, learning by interacting. Such processes are inherently path-dependent and serve to reinforce the idiosyncratic nature of the firm. It is this autocatalytic aspect of knowledge accumulation that is central to understanding capabilities as cumulative, path-dependent characteristics of each individual enterprise. Of course, autocatalytic systems are self-organizing systems *par excellence*.

Some final observations must be made before we turn more specifically to the choosing of co-operative arrangements. First, capabilities clearly connect with the importance given to intangible assets in some treatments of the firm (Itami 1987). Secondly, capabilities help one understand that the debate about markets versus hierarchies can mislead. Markets and firms are not substitutes; they are necessary complements: neither can do what the other does. The prerogative of the firm is to decide what is to be produced and how, a matter of transformation not exchange (McNulty 1984; Egidi 1996). By contrast, the market's role is to make public knowledge of the rival offers of *all* competing firms. From a capabilities viewpoint one cannot be made sense of without the other. Finally, capabilities take us to the question of design of the firm, how it comes to have the properties it has and how design is an ongoing process (Bausor 1994). This matters greatly since the design of a firm's external relationships is, we have argued, as significant for the generation of innovative capabilities as are its internal relationships.

4. Towards an Extension of the Capabilities Model

A useful first step in this process is to list and classify the different organizational structures that firms can use to co-ordinate their respective contributions to a multi-firm innovation process. Once this has been achieved, it will be possible to consider the different possibilities of these organizational structures for the combination, creation, and exploitation of capabilities. It will also be possible to consider the various factors which influence the choices made by firms between these alternative modes.

4.1. Organizational Forms of the Distributed Innovation Process: A Preliminary Classification

The general form of the problem we are dealing with here is as follows. If a firm wishes to engage in an innovation which requires knowledge or capabilities it does not currently possess, it needs to make a choice between developing that resource internally or acquiring all or part of it from outside the firm. Only exceptionally will it be possible for a genuine arm's-length market transaction to provide for that need. It is much more likely that the sourcing mechanism will involve some sort of hybrid governance structure which combines elements of joint working and contractual relations in various ways. These various organizational forms are presented below in five broad groups.[8] Before we present them

---

[8] There are other typologies available, such as the excellent one in Chesnais (1988). The simple grouping provided here is not meant to be complete or exhaustive; it is intended to serve as a basis for considering issues of choice between major alternative modes of collaboration.

we must make an important proviso. The various options in the five groups should not be seen as stable, optimal solutions to clear, given contingencies. Rather, they will frequently be found in dynamically changing sequences. As technical and commercial uncertainties unfold in the innovation process, the appropriate mode of inter-firm co-operation may change. We return to this point later. Notice also that we wish to distinguish our five groups from the more informal kinds of interaction and exchange of knowledge which take place on a day-to-day basis between and within communities of practitioners in any modern economy (Freeman 1991; von Hippel 1988). They are an important background to the external accumulation of capabilities but not, we believe, its decisive form in relation to the strategic development of competitive advantage.

4.1.1. Group 1: Predominantly market-mediated relationships   Examples of this form are the use of consultancy services; the hiring of key individuals or teams from other firms; the purchase of licences; the use of contract R&D services; and the special case of purchasing firms solely in order to acquire their specific technologies. The common feature of these situations is that the external technology or capability is transferred to the acquiring firm with the payment of a fee of some kind. However, these transactions are clearly not made in spot markets. There are considerable subsequent uncertainties, search costs, and transaction costs involved; as well as considerable effort expended in managing the actual transfer process and in successfully integrating the acquired knowledge with the firm's pre-existing knowledge. Recent calculations suggest that some 15 per cent of UK R&D is outsourced and that this figure is growing (Howells 1999). To the extent that this figure excludes the outsourcing of other forms of expertise, for example market research, it is no doubt a significant understatement of the role of market transactions in the accumulation of capabilities.

4.1.2. Group 2: Multi-firm collaborations to produce generic knowledge   Firms can collaborate in various ways to produce new knowledge which is sufficiently generic to be used by all the participants. Industrial research associations are the oldest institutional form for doing this. More recently, technology-focused research 'clubs' have been set-up around research groups in universities or other research organizations. In some cases separate companies have been set up as research-only ventures, with share capital and staff coming from a number of contributing companies. Finally, bilateral R&D collaborative agreements between firms are an increasingly frequently used device (Hagedoorn 1992). In addition to being less market mediated than the arrangements listed in group 1, these arrangements share the distinction that they focus more on the production of new knowledge than on the transfer of existing knowledge.

4.1.3. Group 3: Application-oriented collaborations   These arrangements are similar to those in group 2 except that they embrace a longer stretch of the 'innovation pipeline'. Rather than producing only 'pre-competitive' technology they progress the work closer to the marketable product, with the important proviso that the firms may then choose to separate and produce and sell the products independently. The significance of this type of arrangement for capability theory is that it may involve the combination of firm capabilities in marketing and production as well as those centred on the R&D function.

4.1.4. Group 4: Joint venture companies   Joint ventures in which products are developed, manufactured, and sold are clearly larger-scale commitments to combine existing capabilities from participating firms and to develop new capabilities across the board. They combine elements of the arrangements in groups 1, 2, and 3 above with other features which give a greater institutional and legal stability to the activity. It is worth remembering, though, that even in the case of joint ventures, there can be a later stage in which the newly created capabilities are absorbed back into one of the participating firms.[9]

4.1.5. Group 5: Strategic alliances   Strategic alliances are difficult to define in terms as clear as those used for the four groups discussed above. In some respects they could be seen as portfolios of arrangements drawn from those in groups 1 to 4, but with the added indefinable ingredient of some public manifestation of 'trust' between the partners. They will often be driven not only by innovation and capability issues, but by larger issues of industrial and market restructuring. However, they will often have powerful consequences for the exchange and creation of capabilities and knowledge.

As we have already noted, these five sets of arrangements can be seen in the short term as alternatives for the solution of the problem which a company faces if it does not have the complete set of capabilities required for an innovation. The actual choice between the alternatives depends on a variety of factors, in which the scale of the innovation relative to the size of the participating firms will play a particularly important role. In the longer term, however, they can be seen as stages (though not necessarily in a predetermined order) through which inter-firm co-operations can evolve. To give an obvious example, technology-centred collaboration can evolve into joint product development, and from there to a formal joint venture. The degrees of technical risk, financial risk, and exposure of existing proprietary technology are quite different as one passes through these stages.

---

[9] This happened when the joint venture in ceramics formed by Johnson Matthey and Cookson plc was dissolved and Cookson sold out their share to Johnson Matthey.

To summarize: these various organizational forms for capability transfer, capability combination, and joint capability creation emphasize that there is an important intermediate territory, between market transactions on the one hand and fully internalized capability development on the other. The forms of cooperation described above create options for firms to experiment with their capability portfolio in a manner which allows some degree of risk management. This type of behaviour is clearly of great importance for the conduct of specific innovations, but also of great strategic importance for the direction of evolution of the distinctiveness of the firms themselves. Since firm distinctiveness is at the heart of the capability model, this is significant.

4.2. Issues Affecting the External Acquisition of Technology, Knowledge, and Capabilities

Having reviewed the alternative organizational manifestations of external capability acquisition we now turn to the question of what drives the actions and choices of firms in this broad intermediate territory between market transactions and autarkic technology development.

We have suggested that the processes of knowledge, skill, and expertise accumulation internal to and external to the firm play a central role in generating opportunities for the distributed accumulation of capabilities. Now an equally important factor is that of the comparative cost of self versus joint accumulation. Indeed, in discussion of collaborative arrangements cost sharing appears as a principal motive for co-operative arrangements.

Now this requires careful treatment, for cost sharing in the development of jointly shared capabilities carries with it a threat of profit dissipation, since one's partner can later turn into a rival. If costs are shared and profits dissipated pro rata there will be no economic gain from collaboration (Metcalfe 1992). However, since collaborations do occur, what is it that shifts the balance in their favour?

One approach is to co-operate with non-rivals. Universities and other non-commercial generators of knowledge fit this category admirably, but this does not account for the majority of arrangements which are inter-firm and often with close competitors. The answer is perhaps to be found in the fact that profit dissipation is more than offset by profit enhancement: the jointly developed capability shows a greater return because it creates capabilities which could not be generated economically by a firm acting in isolation (Dyer and Singh 1998). Taken jointly, the co-operating firms create a 'group advantage' relative to their rivals which makes an external arrangement profitable even when it is jointly exploited. This possibility is further enhanced by the practical details in relation to the domain specificity of capability exploitation. The new knowledge may be exploited by the partners in different markets (a frequent specification of licence agreements) or may be exploited in different ways because the partners possess different complementary capabilities when it comes to exploitation.

All this amounts to a general argument in favour of co-operative arrangements but it does not help explain the particular merits of the different forms of co-operation outlined in section 4.1. We now turn finally to this point. To do this we consider the following list of attributes which present as important issues bearing on the relevance of the alternative forms of co-operation to a given situation:

- *Creation versus exploitation of new capabilities.* 'Market-mediated' and 'precompetitive research' forms of collaboration are clearly focused on capability creation rather than exploitation. Collaborative product development arrangements and joint ventures are obviously geared to both the creation and the exploitation of capabilities.
- *Relative size and power of the collaborators.* At first sight it might appear that collaborators of 'equal power' might choose joint ventures or precompetitive research arrangements, whereas in conditions of power disparity the stronger partner would enforce a market-mediated relationship or a joint product development arrangement. In practice, however, this issue interacts with the issue of the relative importance of the capability contribution each partner makes to the venture in question. In some cases the 'smaller or less powerful' partner may be able to negotiate a joint venture rather than a subordinate contractual position, if that partner's capability contribution is proportionately more important.
- *Availability of exploitation routes.* In cases where new capabilities are to be not only created but quickly exploited, the availability of the complementary capabilities for exploitation (for example manufacturing and distribution channels) becomes an important issue. If partners are equally well endowed with these complementary assets, they will not bear upon choice of collaborative arrangements. Where one partner has distinctive strengths in this area, it may shift the choice, away from the joint venture for example, and towards a restricted product development co-operation. Thus trade-offs between technology contributions from one partner and market access contribution from another partner can become very finely balanced.
- *Levels of uncertainty and risk.* The different co-operative arrangement options clearly confer different possibilities for dealing with technical uncertainties in the capability creation process, and for dealing with commercial risk in the exploitation process. Different combinations of internalized, contractual, and equity-based devices can be deployed in the various cases.

Thus we see that the choice between co-operative forms is not an exact calculus, but a delicate balance of the contingencies of power asymmetries, availability of complementary capabilities, and risk-shifting and risk-sharing devices. The choice is all the more complex given that these contingencies are all likely to be subject to the peculiarities of 'embeddedness' in the sense mentioned in section 3, and to the related issue of the effects of different national systems of innovation. In practical terms, for example, different legal systems and business cultures will have a significant influence on the relative feasibility of different collaborative governance arrangements. Inevitably, the choice of collaborative structure is bound to be a trial and error process, a process in which experience is accumulated, a process in which the generation of capabilities becomes inseparable from the conduct of wider market relationships.

Two final points are worth noting about these alternative arrangements and the choices between them. First, the decisions to enter into these arrangements can be seen as formally similar, in terms of a capability model, to the other major business decisions made by the firms in question. That is, they involve mobilizing the distinctive 'theory of the business' already present in the firm; they involve assessing the capabilities of the firm and the uses to which they can be put; and they involve devoting resources to the creation of new capabilities and new modes of exploitation. Furthermore, and this is particularly important, they contribute to the development of the idiosyncrasies and distinctive differences of each participating firm, as in other such decisions. However, they also contribute to some new processes which could in principle reduce some differences between firms with respect to some capabilities, while at the same time creating new capabilities that create new sources of difference with respect to other firms outside the collaborating group. The only difference between this set of decisions, and those already described in the capability model, is the vitally important one that the content and context of the decisions concerns relationships between firms which are neither fully market based nor fully administratively determined.

The second noteworthy point is one mentioned earlier, but worth repeating here. This is that the decisions are not necessarily one-off choices which are then fixed for some time. They represent an array of possibilities which can provide a flexible territory for adaptation of inter-firm co-operation structures, in order to reflect the changes that occur in technical and business uncertainty, as a direct result of the creation of the new capabilities themselves.

In conclusion, then, we have argued the following. The capabilities model of the firm has been developed in a way that has made it very attractive to scholars of innovation. Its emphasis on how firms differ, and on the economic consequences of such differences, has led to major fruitful interactions with the innovation literature, the evolutionary economics literature, and the understanding of the embeddedness of firms in varying national and regional institutional structures. However, the model as it stands is unable to encompass the observation that the process of innovation is becoming more distributed across firm boundaries. In order to rectify this problem we have explored an approach in which capabilities are combined, created, and exploited in Richardson's territory of co-operation between firms which is neither market nor integrated single firm in character. This has the immediate benefit of resolving some of the tension and mismatch between theory and observation. It also has the more radical long-term implication for our research agenda that capabilities themselves deserve a status as a unit of analysis of near similar stature to that of the firm; rather than being assumed to be always subordinate in stature to the firm. A rich research agenda emerges when we view the economic system as being populated by a wide variety of diverse, locally embedded, and evolving capabilities, the ownership, creation and mobilization of which, within and between firms, is continually in flux. It then becomes possible to view entrepreneurial decisions about a firm's development and collaborative relationships as being conceived and implemented in terms of these capability combinations.

References

AMIT, R., and P. J. H. SHOEMAKER 1993. 'Strategic assets and organizational rent', *Strategic Management Journal* 14: 33–46.

ARROW, K. 1962. 'Economic welfare and the allocation of resources to invention', in R. Nelson ed., *The Rate and Direction of Inventive Activity*. New York: National Bureau of Economic Research.

BARNEY, J. 1991. 'Firm resources and sustained competitive advantage', *Journal of Management* 17: 99–120.

BAUSOR, R. 1994. 'Entrepreneurial imagination, information and the evolution of the firm', in R. W. England, ed., *Evolutionary Concepts in Contemporary Economics*. Ann Arbor, MI: University of Michigan Press.

BETTIS, R. A., and C. K. PRAHALAD 1995. 'The dominant logic: Retrospective and extension', *Strategic Management Journal* 16: 5–14.

CARLSSON, B., ed. 1995. *Technological Systems and Economic Performance*. Dordrecht: Kluwer Academic.

CHESNAIS, F. 1988. 'Technical co-operation agreements between independent firms', *STI Review* 4, Paris: OECD.

—— 1996. 'Technological agreements, networks and economic theory', in R. Coombs, A. Richards, P. Saviotti, and V. Walsh, eds., *Technological Collaboration*. Cheltenham: Edward Elgar.

COHEN, W. M., and D.A. LEVINTHAL 1989. 'Innovation and learning: The two faces of R&D', *Economic Journal* 99: 569–96.

—— 1990. 'Absorptive capacity: A new perspective on learning and innovation', *Administrative Science Quarterly* 35: 128–52.

DYER, J. H., and H. SINGH 1998. 'The relational view: Co-operative strategy and sources of interorganizational competitive advantage', *Academy of Management Review* 23: 660–79.

EDQUIST, C. 1997. *Systems of Innovation: Technologies, Institutions and Organizations*. London: Pinter.

EGIDI, M. 1996. 'Virtuousness and adverse selection in economic organizations', Mimeo. Laxenberg: IIASA.

ELIASSON, G. 1988. 'The firm as a competent team', Mimeo. Stockholm: II ESR.

ERIKSEN, B., and J. MIKKELSEN 1996. 'Competitive advantage and the concept of core competence', in N. J. Foss and C. Knudson, eds.: 54–75.

FOSS, N. J. 1996. 'Whither the competence perspective', in N. J. Foss and C. Knudsen, eds.: 1–12.

—— and C. KNUDSEN 1996. *Towards a Competence Theory of the Firm*. London: Routledge.

FREEMAN, C. 1991. 'Networks of innovators: A synthesis of research issues', *Research Policy* 20: 499–514.

GRANOVETTER, M. 1985. 'Economic action and social structure: The problem of embeddedness', *American Journal of Sociology* 91: 481–510.

GRANSTRAND, O., P. PATEL, and K. PAVITT 1997. 'Multi-technology corporations: Why they have "distributed" rather than "distinctive core" competences', *California Management Review* 39: 8–25.

GULATI, R. 1999. 'Network location and learning: The influence of network resources and firm capabilities in alliance formation', *Strategic Management Journal* 20: 397–420.

HAGEDOORN, J. 1992. 'Trends and patterns in strategic technology partnering since the early seventies', *Review of Industrial Organization* 11: 601–16.

HENDERSON, R., and K. CLARK 1990. 'Architectural innovation', *Administrative Science Quarterly* 35: 87–109.

HIPPEL, E. VON 1988. *The Sources of Innovation*. Oxford: Oxford University Press.

HOWELLS, J. 1999. 'Research and technology outsourcing and systems of innovation', in J. S. Metcalfe and I. Miles, eds., *Innovation Systems in the Service Economy*. Dordrecht: Kluwer.

KODAMA, F. 1991. *Emerging Patterns of Innovation: Sources of Japan's Technological Edge*. Boston: Harvard Business School Press.

ITAMI, H. 1987. *Mobilising Invisible Assets*. Cambridge, MA: Harvard University Press.

LANGLOIS, R. N., and P. L. ROBERTSON 1999. 'Stop crying over spilt knowledge: A critical look at the theory of spill-overs and technical change', Mimeo. University of Connecticut and University of Wollongong.

LEONARD-BARTON, D. 1995. *The Well-Springs of Knowledge*. Cambridge, MA: Harvard University Press.

LOASBY, B. 1994. 'The organization of knowledge and the organization of industry', Mimeo: University of Stirling.

—— *Knowledge, Institutions and Evolution in Economics*. London: Routledge.

McNULTY, P. 1984. 'On the nature and theory of economic organization: The role of the firm reconsidered', *History of Political Economy* 16: 223–53.

METCALFE, J. S. 1992. 'Competition and collaboration in the innovation process', in M. Bowen and M. Ricketts, eds., *Stimulating Innovation in Industry*. London: Kogan Page.

—— and A. JAMES 1998. 'Knowledge and capabilities: A new view of the firm', Mimeo. University of Manchester, CRIC.

MONTGOMERY, C. 1995. *Resource-Based and Evolutionary Theories of the Firm.* Dordrecht: Kluwer Academic.

NELSON, R. 1991. 'Why do firms differ, and how does it matter?', *Strategic Management Journal* 12: 61–74.

—— and S. WINTER 1984. *An Evolutionary Theory of Economic Change.* Cambridge, MA: Harvard University Press.

PENROSE, E. 1959. *The Theory of the Growth of the Firm.* Oxford: Basil Blackwell.

PEREZ, C. 1983. 'Structural change and the assimilation of new technologies in the economic and social system', *Futures* 15: 357–75.

RICHARDSON, G. B. 1972. 'The organization of industry', *Economic Journal* 82: 883–96.

ROSENBERG, R. 1990. 'Why firms do basic research (with their own money)', *Research Policy* 19: 165–174.

RUMELT, R. 1984. 'Towards a strategic theory of the firm', in R. Lamb, ed., *Competitive Strategic Management.* Englewood Cliffs, NJ: Prentice Hall.

11

The Role of Prior Commitment in Governance Choice

NICHOLAS ARGYRES AND JULIA PORTER LIEBESKIND

1. Introduction

The trade-off between commitment and flexibility is a major theme in the economics literature on business strategy. Much of this work has focused on the strategic benefits to the firm from credibly committing to a course of action. Industrial organization theories have shown that committing to a future level of production can deter the entry of competitors (Spence 1977, 1979), especially when that commitment can be made credible (Dixit 1980). Entry can also be deterred when sellers make contractual commitments with buyers (Aghion and Bolton 1987). Profits can also be increased by committing to product quality through sunk cost investments in brand equity (Klein and Leffler 1981; Shapiro 1983). The economics of organization literature also emphasizes the benefits of commitment. For example, Williamson (1983) showed how the ability to credibly commit not to harm the interests of the contractual partner can increase a party's gains from trade by increasing the level of specific investment in a transaction. In Milgrom and Roberts (1988), superiors can control costly influence activities by committing to limit communication with subordinates.

The economic benefits of commitment are thus increasingly well understood in the economics of organization and business strategy literatures. The other side of the trade-off, however, is arguably less well developed. The costs and risks of commitment in terms of lost flexibility have been analysed at an abstract level (Dixit and Pindyck 1994), and many writers on strategy have advocated flexibility in broad terms. However, the specific mechanisms through which commitments can act as strategic constraints remain poorly understood. Ghemawat has begun to address some of these mechanisms in his analyses of strategic situations where commitments acted as binding constraints when environmental conditions develop in unanticipated ways (Ghemawat 1991, 1993; Ghemawat and del Sol 1998).

Whereas Ghemawat addresses the general benefits and costs of commitments in terms of their implications for strategic investments, our interest is more specifically with situations in which prior contractual commitments constrain the firm's future choices about the way it governs its activities. These are situations that involve what we call *governance inseparability* (Argyres and Liebeskind

1999*a*, 1999*b*). We argue that in many cases a firm's governance choices reflect not only the characteristics of the particular transaction being governed, but also previous governance choices. Previous choices can make it difficult for a firm to change the way it governs a transaction, imposing a *governance switching constraint* on its choice of governance mode. Previous governance choices can also make it difficult for a firm to tailor governance arrangements to the special requirements of various transactions, imposing a *governance differentiation constraint*. We begin this chapter by discussing the sources of governance inseparability in terms of these two types of constraint. We then briefly discuss how governance inseparability is related to transaction cost theory (Williamson 1975, 1985; Klein, Crawford, and Alchian 1978) and to a real options approach to governance. Finally, we discuss some implications of governance inseparability for industry evolution and make some concluding remarks.

2. Governance Inseparability

2.1. Constraints on Governance Switching

A firm faces a governance switching constraint when it is constrained from entering into a governance arrangement of Type Y in future periods for a particular transaction, if it already has a governance arrangement of Type X in place with another party for that transaction.[1] This constraint on altering governance structures for the same type of transaction may prevent firms from taking advantage of new economic opportunities such as entering new markets, undertaking or outsourcing stages of production, or adopting new technologies.

A straightforward example of this type of constraint on governance modes is offered by franchising arrangements. Outstanding contractual commitments in the form of franchise agreements and exclusive dealerships pose significant barriers to further agreements, and also limit moves toward forward integration by the franchisor. For example, Coca-Cola entered into a number of exclusive franchising agreement with independent bottling companies in the USA. These agreements prevent Coca-Cola from forward integrating, because they do not allow any company other than the franchisee to bottle Coca-Cola products within a given territory. By granting such local monopolies, Coca-Cola was able both to induce investment in use-specific bottling equipment, and to motivate aggressive marketing by franchisees. However, when Coca-Cola decided to forward integrate in the 1980s in order to rationalize bottling capacity in the face of increasing price competition, the contractual commitments that the company had in place meant that it could forward integrate only by buying out its bottling franchisees in the open market for corporate control. To do so, it had to pay a

---

[1] This section borrows from Argyres and Liebeskind (1999*a*).

considerable price premium relative to the costs of forward integrating through internal expansion. Moreover, in some cases Coca-Cola has been unable to buy out its franchisees. In others, it has elected not to do so, because the costs of acquisition were too high relative to the benefits of internalization and subsequent rationalization.

Governance-switching constraints may also be engendered by unforeseen changes in bargaining power. For example, a seller S and a buyer B may enter into an efficiently structured long-term contract to support investment in transaction-specific assets by both parties (see, for example, Joskow 1988). Because there is some uncertainty about prices and/or demand in the future, they agree upon a long-term contract that allows some scope for renegotiation of prices and/or quantities. At the time of contracting, these undefined or 'residual' rights are not considered a problem by either party, since they are both making specific investments to bond the contract (Williamson 1983). However, as time passes, B's market share increases and S now has fewer alternative buyers to B, so that B can more credibly threaten S with withdrawing its business if S does not behave in certain ways. At the time of contract renegotiation, B may use this increased bargaining power to constrain S's governance options. For instance, B may prevent S from internalizing any activities that are similar to B's business, forcing S to continue to sell across markets rather than vertically integrate. Alternatively, B may impose more terms and conditions on S concerning the way that it produces its output, so that S is obligated to reward its workers in particular ways. (For example, B may lower its prices paid to S so that S must pay its workers less, or move to longer shifts, or introduce piece-work pay rates.) Thus, the change in B's bargaining power relative to S over time has imposed a degree of governance inseparability on S that was not anticipated, and therefore could not be prevented, in its original contract with B.

One common example of the operation of bargaining power to create governance-switching constraints is when unionized labour uses its bargaining power to restrict a firm from shifting production from hierarchy to market by outsourcing. In recent years a number of US companies have attempted to outsource production or service activities but have been opposed by their own workers. Examples include Deere, Ameritech, McDonnell Douglas, Boeing, United Parcel Service, Chrysler, and General Motors.[2] In several of these instances—most prominently in the case of General Motors—workers managed to prevent outsourcing moves that otherwise would have taken place.[3]

Changes in bargaining power have also led to governance-switching

[2] See, respectively, *Des Moines Register*, 19 February 1996; *Crain's Chicago Business*, 24 January 1994; *Los Angeles Times*, 6 June 1996; *New York Times*, 22 March 1996; *Wall Street Journal*, 5 August 1995.
[3] For details of the General Motors strike, see McGahan (1998) and Argyres and Liebeskind (1999*a*).

constraints in franchising. During the 1990s, franchisees in a large number of US chains became more organized, increasing their membership of national franchisee groups and forming new chain-specific franchisee groups.[4] One chain-specific group, the Meineke Mufflers Dealers Association, won a major lawsuit against the franchisor—a victory that was made by the financial clout of a national association, the American Association of Franchise Dealers (AAFD) (Harris 1997). This increased bargaining power enjoyed by franchisees is allowing them to impose new constraints on the contracts that franchisors can write. Even when this increased power is partly anticipated, and contractual safeguards protecting the franchisor's specific investments are included in franchise agreements, legal decisions favouring franchisees have invalidated the safeguards. In one case, Naugles, Inc., a fast-food franchisor, issued franchise contracts which specifically ruled out territorial exclusivity for its franchisees, allowing Naugles to sell new franchises close to existing ones as population densities increased (Harris 1997). Naugles' franchisees originally agreed to this contract provision. However, when Naugles attempted to open a new franchise close to an existing one, its franchisees collectively sued. A California federal court essentially ignored the fact that Naugles' franchise contract did not stipulate territorial protection, and found in favour of the franchisees. Victories such as these increase the bargaining power of franchisees in future contracts, and aggravate governance inseparability.

2.2. Constraints on Governance Differentiation

Governance inseparability may also disallow governance differentiation for different transactions. That is, a firm may be obliged to enter into a governance arrangement of Type X with one party for one type of transaction, because it already has a governance arrangement of Type X in place for another type of transaction with a different party.

This type of inseparability commonly arises when firms want to differentiate their internal organizational arrangements, such as transfer pricing rules. Transaction cost theory would predict that internal transactions featuring asset specificity would use cost-based transfer prices that are set by corporate management, while generic transactions would use market-based transfer prices. Hence, firms encompassing both types of transactions could be expected to combine both types of transfer pricing rules in a highly tailored way. However, such tailored transfer pricing schemes are difficult to find in practice.[5]

---

[4] According to Harris (1997), the American Franchisee Association grew from roughly 4,000 members to about 7,500 during the years 1993–7, and the AAFD grew from 20 members in 1992 to about 6,000 in 1998. Chain-specific franchisee groups have also become more widespread.

[5] In a study of transfer pricing in 13 chemical and electronics firms, Eccles (1985) found that

Why are transfer pricing rules so often standardized, rather than tailored to the characteristics of the transaction to which they are applied? One answer to this question may involve understanding the firm's incentive system and decision-making structure as constituting a set of implicit contractual commitments between the top management of a firm and its divisional managers (Argyres 1995, 1996). For instance, top management may commit to non-intervention in divisional affairs, decentralized decision making, and tight links between divisional performance and rewards for division managers. This kind of organization is often consistent with market-based transfer pricing, but not with cost-based rules. Similarly, a more centralized structure supported by weaker links between divisional performance and rewards would be more consistent with cost-based, rather than market-based, transfer prices. By committing to either of these system–structure combinations, firms may sacrifice efficiency for certain individual transactions in order to elicit desired managerial behaviour over a *cluster* of the firm's internal transactions. Thus, more than reflecting economizing on transaction costs on a transaction-by-transaction basis, the selection of transfer pricing rules may reflect concerns about upholding prior implicit commitments to managers—commitments which cut across individual internal transactions.

This argument should be distinguished from Williamson's (1985) argument that the limits to internal differentiation result from limits to selective intervention. Williamson's argument can be explained in the context of internal corporate venturing, in which firms start new venture units to develop and commercialize new products. Frequently, new venture units are deliberately placed outside the authority of existing divisions so that they can operate more autonomously and circumvent the governance arrangements that apply to established divisions. However, efforts to start and/or sustain new venture units have failed at many large firms (Hlavacek 1974; Fast 1978; Sykes 1986; Burgelman and Sayles 1986). Williamson (1985) explains this failure as resulting from the inability of firms to make credible commitments to the 'market-like' governance arrangements often needed to support new ventures. It is argued that ventures which are internal to a firm cannot operate under market-like, 'high-powered incentives', because corporate management may be tempted to abrogate those incentives if at some point it becomes in their interest to do so. Hence, internal ventures often fail, or are never initiated.

Governance inseparability considerations provide a different explanation of this phenomenon: contractual commitments to established divisions can make specialized governance arrangements difficult to sustain because these latter

each firm tended to use only one method of establishing transfer prices for all interdivisional exchanges, based either on 'full costs' or on market prices. More recently, Poppo (1995) found that, among the Fortune 500 companies responding to her survey, 63 per cent reported using a single transfer pricing method only, 27 per cent reported using two methods, while only 5 per cent reported using three methods.

arrangements may violate established commitments to established divisions. For instance, paying high-powered incentives to managers in new venture divisions before they reap profits may undermine less high-powered, profit-based reward schemes elsewhere in the firm. Such specialized arrangements will therefore be opposed, or even sabotaged, by managers elsewhere in the firm. Fast (1978), for example, documented instances of retaliation and interdivisional conflict over new ventures in several case studies. These arguments do not deny that credible commitments by the firm to its venture divisions are problematic for internal venturing. Rather, they provide one reason why the inability of top management to make credible commitments should be so problematical in this particular instance.

Extrapolating from this example, considerations of governance inseparability suggest that a given firm may be able to govern efficiently only a subset of those transactions that overall are more efficiently governed by a hierarchy as opposed to a market. That is, governance inseparability can help to explain why all transactions are not governed by one large firm (Teece 1992). Commitments that are made to internal parties related to the governance of transactions that are internalized early on in a firm's life will constrain that firm's ability efficiently to internalize transactions later on that require differentiated governance arrangements. Hence, each firm will evolve over time into a bundle of specialized internal governance arrangements and the transactions that are most efficiently governed by these arrangements.

As in the case of governance switching, bargaining power may also constrain a firm's ability to differentiate its internal governance arrangements. One example of this phenomenon is offered by the trucking industry. The demand for long-haul trucking stagnated during the 1980s, but the demand for short-haul trucking grew rapidly. Accordingly, the three major US long-haul trucking firms (Yellow Corp., Consolidated, and Roadway) have attempted to enter new short-haul markets. But these companies have been unable to differentiate their organizational arrangements to suit this new market. Yellow Corp., for example, tried to establish a new subsidiary to conduct its short-haul business, and to negotiate a new, more flexible union contract for this firm. However, the union refused to negotiate with Yellow.[6] Thus, bargaining power that resulted in governance inseparability served to limit Yellow's overall scope.[7]

A parallel set of circumstances has arisen in the US airline industry. Some large airlines maintain separate subsidiary firms to handle shorter routes. The pilots working for these subsidiaries earn much lower salaries, allowing (for

[6] See *Kansas City Business Journal*, 26 November 1993.

[7] While the Teamsters were successful in this instance, their bargaining power has been weaker on other occasions. For example, Consolidated and Roadway have been able to circumvent union agreements by purchasing small, non-union trucking concerns, allowing them to gain a competitive advantage over Yellow.

example) American Airlines' American Eagle subsidary to compete with smaller, non-unionized airlines such as Southwest. In the late 1990s, however, American sought to increase the proportion of flights handled by American Eagle by adding short-haul jets to its previously entirely turboprop fleets. The pilots of American Airlines, arguing that they alone should be allowed to fly the short-haul jets, threatened a strike, rather than allow internal differentiation of jet pilots' pay. Some other airlines have avoided this problem by conducting their short-haul businesses through partially owned subsidiaries (for example Delta); through long-term contracts or strategic alliances with short-haul carriers (such as Continental); or through employee ownership, which aligns the incentives of all the parties involved (for example United).

It is important to note that in each of these examples, *parties are able to obtain bargaining power because initial contractual commitments are in place*, and these commitments make it costly for a firm to seek alternatives to dealing with the parties who have the bargaining power. This implies that contractual commitments not only expose a firm directly to a risk of increased governance inseparability; they also expose a firm to an indirect risk by exposing it to a second risk, that of changes in bargaining power over time. Thus, the two key variables that determine governance inseparability in our arguments—contractual commitments and bargaining power—can interact in their effects on governance choices. First, the presence of contractual commitments increases the effects of relative bargaining power on governance choices, especially for firms with low bargaining power. Secondly, and conversely, the greater a firm's relative bargaining power, the greater its ability to negotiate so as to curb contractual restrictions on its future activity.

3. Governance Inseparability and Transaction Cost Theory

Transaction cost theory makes predictions about governance choice at the level of the transaction (Williamson 1985). The most prominent hypothesis is that transactions featuring high levels of asset specificity will tend to be internalized within the firm, whereas generic transactions tend to be governed by the market (Williamson 1975, 1985; Klein, Crawford, and Alchian 1978). This focus on the transaction as the unit of analysis can obscure interdependencies between transactions. Thus, Williamson (1985: 393) noted that transaction cost economics

normally examines each trading nexus separately. Albeit useful for displaying core features of each contract, interdependencies among a series of related contracts may be missed or undervalued as a consequence. Greater attention to the multilateral ramifications of contract is sometimes needed.

One of the main theoretical ramifications of governance inseparability is that governance choices that would be efficient for a transaction considered in isolation may become infeasible or inefficient if the impacts of related transactions are taken into account. For instance, in the automobiles, trucking, and airlines examples above, the firms in question were attempting to respond to increased competition or changes in the composition of demand. In each case, the responses involved seeking organizational changes that would enhance the efficiency with which a particular set of transactions were carried out. However, in each case, prior commitments to labour unions, combined with difficult-to-foresee increases in unions's bargaining power with respect to those commitments, prevented the firm from implementing the efficiency-enhancing adjustment in governance it was seeking. This would imply, as a general matter, that some transactions which transaction cost theory would predict would be conducted through the market, might in fact be internalized when prior commitments are binding and/or bargaining power changes are difficult to foresee. And, conversely, transactions that transaction cost theory would predict would be conducted internally, might be carried out through long-term contracts or the spot market if prior commitments to specific parties are in force. Hence, when considerations of governance inseparability are important, they can change the predictions about governance choices offered by transaction cost theory.[8]

The examples in section 2 illustrate that governance inseparability becomes particularly important when changes in the firm's economic environment are difficult to foresee. For instance, if a firm could anticipate changes in the bargaining power of a contractual partner, it could take actions to mitigate associated hazards. Indeed, this is the essence of established transaction cost theory; firms are assumed to anticipate future contractual hazards and to construct contractual safeguards in response. If such safeguards are not sufficient, vertical integration is assumed to be available as a last resort (Williamson 1985). Governance inseparability, on the other hand, arises when the relevant hazards cannot be anticipated.

Governance inseparability also arises when changes in scope technologies cannot be anticipated. For instance, if a firm anticipated that an activity might need to be moved from the market or a long-term contract to its own hierarchy in the future, it might make provision for this move in its early contracts. For instance, Coca-Cola might have provided a limited franchise period to bottlers if it could have anticipated the need to forward integrate in the future.

In other instances, there are no feasible safeguards against the hazards that can engender governance inseparability. This is particularly the case with hazards that arise in relation to employees. Even if it is possible to foresee increases in employee bargaining power, vertical integration cannot be used as a safeguard,

---

[8] There a number of circumstances under which one might expect governance inseparability considerations to be especially important: when unions are active and enjoy support from the state; when social or consumer groups are well organized; and when firms have greater commitments to their local communities (older firms are often implicated here).

because a firm cannot establish full control rights over employees; the law accords far more extensive ownership rights to other kinds of tangible and intangible asset. Except where slavery is legal, employees will always comprise third parties that can engender the hazard of increased bargaining power. Note that part-time employment cannot protect against this threat. Similar considerations apply to a firm's customers.

When future hazards are difficult to anticipate, firms face *governance inseparability risks*: these are the risks associated with being locked into a governance structure that is inefficient for a new or changed transaction. Given these risks, firms may prefer to avoid contractual commitments in order to remain flexible. Thus, increases in environmental uncertainty may lead firms to eschew vertical integration in favour of market-based governance, or perhaps strategic alliances (Argyres and Liebeskind 1999*a*). This prediction reverses that made by Williamson (1975), who argued that greater uncertainty, because it increases the difficulty of using contracts for exchange, increases the likelihood of vertical integration.

4. Governance Inseparability and Real Options

The positive association between environmental uncertainty and the use of market-based or alliance-based forms of governance that is suggested by governance inseparability considerations is consistent with a 'real options' approach to governance choice (Kogut 1991; Folta 1998; Barney and Lee 1998; Sanchez 1998).[9] This approach emphasizes that some governance choices, besides influencing the level of transaction costs associated with a given transaction, can also generate real option value. In particular, these choices can affect the future opportunity set faced by the firm with respect to future governance choices. Kogut (1991) argued that joint ventures can serve this purpose. By entering into a joint venture with a particular partner, a firm may gain information about the value of the partner's assets which can be useful in subsequent investment decisions, including the decision about whether to acquire the partner or not. Entering into a joint venture thus offers the option of waiting to invest further, through acquisition for example. In this way, it is argued, joint ventures can offer the benefit of greater flexibility than is possible with full integration because they allow investments to be made sequentially, rather than as one-time, irreversible commitments. In support of this view, Folta (1998) finds evidence that greater technological uncertainty increases the likelihood that a joint venture will be chosen in preference to an acquisition in a large sample of bio-technology alliances and acquisitions.

---

[9] A real option is defined as a right to make a future investment in operating capital. A financial option, by contrast, refers to a similar right to invest in financial capital (Myers 1977).

One difficulty with this real options argument, however, is that it is not fully comparative, in the sense that it does not explicitly compare the option value of a joint venture with the option value of an acquisition. Instead, it is assumed that only the joint venture can provide option value.[10] If information about a target firm is unavailable to non-owners, however, acquiring that firm immediately also furnishes an option value to an acquirer. Just as in a joint venture, the acquiring firm can gain information: indeed, more information. Consider, for instance, the case where the target firm is conducting research and development (R&D), as would be the case in the bio-technology industry as studied by Folta (1998). Acquisition may allow a potential acquirer to obtain more information about the value of the target's R&D projects. If this information is favourable, the acquirer will continue to invest in the projects. If the information is unfavourable, the acquirer may disinvest in the projects, and may even choose to divest the acquired firm. Divestiture may be accomplished by partial or complete sale of the firm. Of course, acquisition involves greater risk than a joint venture, but it also offers greater returns if the target's projects pay-off. It would seem, however, that without a symmetric treatment of the option value of the two modes, the real options theory reduces to the simple argument that joint ventures are formed to spread investment risk.

Despite this criticism, we agree that the acquisition and joint venture modes of organization are indeed asymmetric in their option values. However, the nature of this asymmetry has not been spelled out carefully. Specifically, governance inseparability considerations are necessary to complete the theory. Investment in an acquisition may be less reversible than investment in a joint venture because acquisition may involve making implicit and explicit contractual commitments to employees and managers in the target firm. These commitments can then make it difficult or costly for the acquiring firm to later divest the target. For instance, an acquisition may be understood as an implicit or explicit commitment to invest over a relatively long period. Hence, attempts to disinvest, or to divest partly or entirely, may be seen as violations of this commitment. Employees may then attempt to enforce the original commitment by, for example, collective action, perhaps organized by unions. Managers may engage in influence activities (Milgrom and Roberts 1988; Schaefer 1998) in order to affect the decision-making calculus for the divestiture, or take actions that reduce the value of the firm to make its sale less attractive (such as through accounting

---

[10] The following quotation illustrates this implicit assumption: 'The question of why do the parties not agree to an immediate acquisition underscores the critical roles of learning and pre-emption. Through the joint venture, the divesting party is contracted to pass on complex know-how on the running of the business, as well as to slow an erosion in customer confidence. Since this know-how may be essentially organizational . . . a joint venture serves as a vehicle of managerial and technological learning' (Kogut 1991: 26). Whether and how acquisition (that is, integration) can accomplish these same purposes is left untreated.

contrivances that are difficult to detect). Thus, what may give a joint venture greater option value than an acquisition is the relative absence of irreversible contractual commitments that are concomitant with full ownership of another firm. In a joint venture, divestiture is expected and is usually accommodated in the founding contracts. Hence, governance inseparability arguments are necessary to complete the real options theory of governance.

5. Implications for Industry Evolution: The Example of Bio-Technology

Established transaction cost theory is mostly concerned with predicting how individual transactions will be governed.[11] Hence, it is not particularly useful for generating predictions about the proportion of transactions governed by markets or hierarchies at the industry level. For instance, transaction cost theory might predict that industries featuring high capital:labour ratios would be more concentrated, since capital:labour ratios might be correlated with both firm size and physical asset specificity. But such a prediction would also be consistent with explanations based on economies of scale in production. To generate precise industry-level predictions from transaction cost economics, one would have to measure the level of asset specificity in each of the crucial stages of production within the industry. This task would be especially difficult if, as is usually the case, the firms within the industry used somewhat different production technologies. Governance inseparability considerations, on the other hand, by focusing on prior commitments as constraints on future activity and drawing attention to the intertemporal linkages between transactions, can generate predictions about industry-level phenomena. For example, these considerations can help predict the identity of entrants into new and established industries. They can also offer explanations for the size distribution of firms within an industry and for the evolution of the industry. We consider these two aspects in turn below.

5.1. Governance Inseparability and the Identity of Industry Entrants

The question of what firms enter a new industry is an important one in industrial economics. Issues of entry can be understood to embrace two broad-reaching questions. The first is the question of what firms 'enter' when a new economic opportunity arises. Will this new opportunity be exploited by existing firms, or will it generate a population of new firms and, hence, a new industry? The second is the question of patterns of entry into established industries. Competition is of course attenuated, for example, if entry is constrained by barriers to entry created by incumbent firms (see, for example, Sutton 1990).

---

[11] This section draws from Argyres and Liebeskind (1999*b*).

However, if certain types of firms—those with 'deep pockets' for example, or those with certain types of production technologies—are prevented from entering a given industry, competition within that industry may be attenuated in particular ways. Governance inseparability considerations may affect the character of entrants in established industries.

Consider, for example, the development of the bio-technology industry. At the time of writing, this industry consists of over a thousand small, recently founded 'new bio-technology firms' (NBFs) (Pollack 1998). These NBFs continue to proliferate, contrary to predictions that these firms would be displaced by incumbent pharmaceutical, chemical, and agribusiness firms that serve the same markets.

Bio-technology as a technology is applicable to the 'upstream' activities of R&D and manufacturing. The downstream activities needed to market and distribute bio-technology products are essentially identical to those required for established pharmaceutical, chemical, and agribusiness products. The expectation would therefore be that incumbent firms, benefiting as they do from economies of scale and experience in these downstream activities, would eventually integrate backwards into bio-technology. Indeed, this has happened in a few cases, albeit with a considerable lag. However, it is now over twenty-five years since the first NBF was founded, and bio-technology—far from becoming merely a new research and production technology being carried out by established firms within a variety of different industries—is instead the core technology of a new 'bio-technology industry' (Kenney 1986).

In our view, the evolution of this new industry can be explained at least in part by constraints—engendered by considerations of governance inseparability—on the ability of established firms to backward integrate into bio-technology. Specifically, our argument is that, at the inception of this new technology, large incumbent firms were unable to credibly commit to offering and sustaining the kinds of high-powered incentives that small firms could offer to attract, retain, and motivate bio-technology researchers.

An NBF is founded in order to commercialize scientific discoveries made by research scientists. Many of these scientists work originally in universities (Kenney 1986). In order to induce them to work for a commercial firm, high-powered incentives are required. These are of two types. First, scientists in NBFs typically own a substantial portion of the firm's equity, in the form of direct share ownership and share options (Liebeskind 1999). These ownership stakes provide high-powered incentives for a scientist to vest her human capital in the firm. For example, option structures with long vesting horizons serve as 'golden handcuffs' that can help tie a scientist to a specific firm for a period of time sufficient to allow basic research ideas to be transformed into intellectual property in the form of patents and other codified, and hence legally protectable, knowledge (Liebeskind 1997, 1999). Secondly, the capital raised by an NBF increases and supports the value of scientists' ownership stakes, since large amounts of capital are required to bring bio-technology products to market.

Established firms cannot credibly commit to providing either type of incentive, as we have discussed earlier. Yet, without such incentives in place, a firm cannot conduct a bio-technology business. Hence, established firms have been constrained from directly entering the bio-technology industry. Furthermore, because complete acquisition of a new bio-technology firm by an incumbent would attenuate the high-powered incentives in place in the smaller firm, large established firms have also been unable to buy out NBFs. They have only been able to enter through partial holdings and by forging strategic alliances with the smaller firms.

A parallel phenomenon in the bio-technology industry is the infrequency of forward integration moves by NBFs. This is surprising in light of the publicly announced intentions of many of their chief executives to lead them toward becoming fully integrated pharmaceutical or chemical firms. We argue that this surprising scarcity of forward-integrated bio-technology firms can also be explained by considerations of governance inseparability.

First of all, forward integration presents a problem because it would undermine the contracts that an NBF has in place with its scientists. Prominent scientists in NBFs, especially those who join the firm at its founding, are typically members of the board of directors. This combination of share ownership and board representation can be considered to be a 'constitutional' commitment—affecting in the most basic way how an NBF is organized and controlled. If an NBF expands its equity base in order to raise new capital, these constitutional commitments may be abrogated and their incentive effects thereby attenuated. For example, diluting the equity base may engender 'free rider' effects (Grossman and Hart 1986; Zenger 1994), or promote the formation of block shareholdings whose voting power may be used to oppose scientists' long-run economic interests (see, for example, Hellman 1998). Obviously, some levels of new equity will be compatible with incentives, if they provide for wealth gains sufficient to offset the wealth effects of dilution of control. None the less, as an NBF expands, individual scientists' incentives may be weakened. Hence, by remaining small in size, an NBF may be better able to sustain an incentive structure that secures the interests of its critical employees.

A second problem that may stem from forward integration by an NBF is the difficulty of differentiating incentive schemes for managers and employees in different vertically related activities. Although scientists require high-powered, wealth-sharing contracts, workers in downstream activities such as manufacturing, marketing, and distribution are performing more generic work, and do not require such high-powered contracts. Yet, given the incentives in place within an NBF, other employees may insist on similar rewards for reasons of envy, etc. Because equity ownership gains by one party are losses for the other, any addition to the equity base of a firm that is not offset by a parallel contribution of capital (intellectual or financial) will reduce the wealth of outstanding equity holders. Hence, adding downstream workers in an NBF may dilute the wealth of existing owners, both internal and external.

Finally, an NBF's degree of forward integration—as well as its overall growth rate and its direction of horizontal expansion—may be stemmed by its outstanding R&D alliances. Typically, NBFs raise capital from venture capitalists and other equity investors. However, capital markets are cyclical, and delays in funding may result in a firm losing a critical patent race. Therefore, NBFs also typically obtain funding by entering into R&D contracts with large established firms, especially early on in their development (Pisano 1989; Kogut, Shan, and Walker 1992). In such contracts, an NBF typically receives research funding for developing a specific product from an estabished firm, in exchange for supplying know-how in the form of exclusive licences to market and distribute the resulting product.

While these contracts may enhance the survival of a young NBF, they may also constrain its future growth, if the scope of intellectual property rights they define is too broad. For example, some contracts call for the NBF to carry out research to discover a new drug useful to combat a particular disease. This research may yield a number of valuable ideas, some of which may turn out to have applications to other disease classes. Unanticipated discoveries are of course very common in basic research. It is therefore impossible to write a 'complete contract' that clearly specifies the allocation of ownership rights *ex ante* (Grossman and Hart 1986). As a result, firms must rely on incomplete contracts that specify quite general 'rights to control' the intellectual property produced by the NBF. Obviously, it is in the interests of the NBF to keep rights narrow, and in the interest of an incumbent firm to make them as broad as possible. Two factors may favour the interests of the established firm in these circumstances. First, the NBF may be quite desperate for capital to fund its research. Secondly, the large firm may have much 'deeper pockets' than the small firm to finance litigation to assert its ownership over intellectual property rights (Lanjouw and Lerner 1996). For both of these reasons, an NBF may relinquish more intellectual property to an established firm in an R&D contract, than would a firm that is less capital constrained. This conjecture is supported by Lerner and Merges (1998), who find that small firms that are capital constrained cede more control rights in contracts with large firms than do small firms that are more financially secure.

These early contractual provisions may constrain the direction and rate of firm growth in later periods. For instance, a capital-constrained NBF will face diminished incentives to invest in new research projects that are closely related to its outstanding contract research, since the results of these projects are more likely to be claimed by the established firm as its property. And even if the established firm promises not to make such claims, in order to see further research carried out, it cannot credibly commit not to enforce its contracted rights.[12] Hence, a capital-constrained NBF is at a competitive disadvantage, relative to rival NBFs that can exploit economies of scope in an unencumbered fashion. These constraints on growth will also tend to limit an NBF's vertical scope: without new projects an NBF cannot develop enough output volume to cover the high fixed costs of downstream activities. Thus, we can conjecture that NBFs founded when capital markets were relatively illiquid are less likely to expand their product lines and forward integrate in later periods than firms that were originally founded under more favourable capital market conditions.

To summarize: we explain the persistent fragmentation of the biotechnology industry as being based on two sets of governance-inseparability arguments. First, large established firms have not absorbed more NBFs because they have been unable to replicate the high-powered incentive systems that an NBF can offer to its critical scientists. This is because large firms face governance-differentiation constraints enforced by managers of their established divisions. Secondly, because many NBF firms were capital constrained early in their lives, they entered into R&D contracts with large established firms that also constrained their ability to add product lines and integrate forward. Taken together, these factors have served to promote the founding and survival of NBFs while constraining their growth and forward integration, contributing to the leftward skew in the size distribution of firms in the bio-technology industry.

6. Concluding Remarks

This chapter has discussed some important ways in which prior contractual commitments can act as binding constraints on firms' ability to change their organizational arrangements in response to changes in their scale or scope, or in response to changes in their competitive environment. Most accounts of the strategic role of commitments in the industrial organization and economics of organizations literatures emphasize the various benefits that can accrue from them; but such commitments are more properly seen as double-edged swords. Thus, we have argued that contractual commitments originally made to support

---

[12] One solution to this type of constraint, proposed by Williamson (1983), is for the large firm to post a bond by making an equity investment in the NBF. Pisano (1989) finds that research alliances between large firms and NBFs are frequently accompanied by equity investments. However, equity investments are not neutral: they increase the likelihood that the investing firm will strategically interfere in the affairs of the biotechnology firm (Hellman 1998). Hence, such investments may exacerbate rather than moderate the relative bargaining power of the large firm. Moreover, these equity investments tend to be small in size, because NBFs have small market capitalizations. As an illustration of this fact, in 1997, according to *Fortune*, the market value of Merck exceeded the total market value of the entire population of US NBFs. It would therefore be difficult for a large pharmaceutical firm to post a credible bond.

transaction-specific investments by contractual partners, or to provide them with efficient performance incentives, can prevent efficient adaptation in later periods, when the governance needs of the transaction have changed. In addition, contractual commitments made to one party for one transaction may constrain the way other transactions with other parties can be governed. Moreover, there appears to be evidence that governance-inseparability conditions of this sort have been present in a wide range of industries, including automobiles, bio-technology, airlines, trucking, fast food, beverages, and others. These conditions, we argue, play an important role in explaining why the predictions of transaction costs are sometimes not borne out. In addition, we have argued that considerations of governance inseparability may be important in affecting the relative options values of various governance modes. They may also affect industry evolution by affecting both the nature of entering firms, and the competition between entrants and incumbents.

Understanding both the benefits and costs of contractual commitments is clearly crucial for understanding firms' strategic choices. We hope that future research will help achieve a more balanced understanding of the consequences of commitment.

References

AGHION, P., and P. BOLTON 1987. 'Contracts as a barrier to entry', *American Economic Review* 77: 388–401.

ARGYRES, N. S. 1995. 'Technology strategy, governance structure and interdivisional coordination', *Journal of Economic Behavior and Organization* 28: 337–58.

—— 1996. 'Capabilities, technological diversification and divisionalization', *Strategic Management Journal* 17: 395–410.

—— and J. P. Liebeskind 1999a. 'Contractual commitments, bargaining power and governance inseparability: Incorporating history into transaction cost theory', *Academy of Management Review* 24: 49–63.

—— —— 1999b. 'Governance inseparability, competition and industry evolution', unpublished paper, Marshall School of Business, University of Southern California.

BARNEY, J., and W. LEE 1998. 'Governance under uncertainty: Transaction costs, real options, and property rights', paper delivered to the 1998 DRUID conference.

BURGELMAN, R. A., and L. R. SAYLES 1986. *Inside Corporate Innovation: Strategy, Structure, and Managerial Skills.* New York: The Free Press.

CHANDLER, A. 1990. *Scale and Scope.* Cambridge, MA: The Belknap Press of Harvard University Press.

DIXIT, A. 1980. 'The role of investment in entry deterrence', *Economic Journal* 90: 95–106.

—— and R. PINDYCK 1994. *Investment under Uncertainty.* Princeton, NJ: Princeton University Press.

ECCLES, R. 1985. *The Transfer Pricing Problem: A Theory for Practice.* Lexington, MA: Lexington Books.

FAST, N. 1978. *The Rise and Fall of Corporate New Venture Divisions*. Ann Arbor, MI: University of Michigan Press.

FOLTA, T. 1998. 'Governance and uncertainty: The trade-off between administrative control and commitment', *Strategic Management Journal* 19: 1007–28.

GHEMAWAT, P. 1991. *Commitment: The Dynamic of Strategy*. New York: The Free Press.

—— 1993. 'Commitment to a process innovation: Nucor, USX, and thin-slab casting', *Journal of Economics and Management Strategy* 2: 135–61.

—— and P. DEL SOL 1998. 'Commitment versus flexibility?', *California Management Review* 40: 26–42.

GROSSMAN, S., and O. HART 1986. 'The costs and benefits of ownership: A theory of vertical and lateral integration', *Journal of Political Economy* 94: 691–719.

HARRIS, N. 1997. 'Franchisees get feisty', *BusinessWeek*, 14 February.

HELLMAN, T. 1998. 'A theory of venture capital investing', unpublished paper, Stanford Business School.

HLAVACEK, J. D. 1974. 'Toward more successful venture management', *Journal of Marketing* 38: 56–60.

JOSKOW, P. 1988. 'Asset specificity and the structure of vertical relationships: Empirical evidence', *Journal of Law, Economics and Organization* 4: 98–115.

KENNEY, M. 1986. *Bio-technology: The University-Industrial Complex*. New Haven, CT: Yale University Press.

KLEIN, B., and K. LEFFLER 1981. 'The role of market forces in assuring contractual performance', *Journal of Political Economy* 89: 615–41.

—— R. CRAWFORD, and A. ALCHIAN 1978. 'Vertical integration, appropriable rents and the competitive contracting process', *Journal of Law and Economics* 21: 297–326.

KOGUT, B. 1991. 'Joint ventures and the option to expand and acquire', *Management Science* 37: 19–33.

—— SHAN, W., and G. WALKER 1992. 'The make or cooperate decision in the context of an industry network', in N. Nohria and R. Eccles, eds., *Networks and Organizations*. Cambridge, MA: Harvard Business School Press.

LANJOUW, J., and J. LERNER 1996. 'Preliminary injunctive relief: Theory and evidence from patent litigation',unpublished paper, Harvard Business School.

LERNER, J., and R. MERGES 1998. 'The control of strategic alliances: An empirical analysis of the biotechnology industry', *Journal of Industrial Economics* 46: 125–55.

LIEBESKIND, J. 1997. 'Keeping organizational secrets: Institutional protective mechanisms and their costs', *Industrial and Corporate Change* 6: 623–64.

—— 1999. 'Ownership, incentives and control in human-capital intensive firms: evidence from the biotechnology industry', in M. Blair and T. Kochan, eds., *The Corporation and Human Capital*. Washington, DC: Brookings Institution Press.

MCGAHAN, A. 1998. 'Saturn Corporation in 1998', Harvard Business School Case No. 9-799-021.

MILGROM, P., and J. ROBERTS 1988. 'An economic approach to influence activities', *American Journal of Sociology* (supplement) 94: S154–S179.

MYERS, S. C. 1977. 'Determinants of corporate borrowing', *Journal of Financial Economics* 5: 147–75.

PISANO, G. 1989. 'Using equity participation to support exchange: Evidence from the biotechnology industry', *Journal of Law, Economics and Organization* 5: 109–26.

POLLACK, A. 1998. 'Weed-out time in biotechnology', *New York Times*, 16 December.

POPPO, L. 1995. 'Influence activities and strategic co-ordination: Two distinctions of internal and external markets', *Management Science* 41: 1845–60.

SANCHEZ, R. 1998. 'Uncertainty, flexibility and economic organization: foundations for an option theory of the firm', paper delivered to the 1998 DRUID conference.

SCHAEFER, S. 1998. 'Influence costs, structural inertia, and organizational change', *Journal of Economics and Management Strategy* 7: 237–63.

SHAPIRO, C. 1983. 'Premiums for high quality products as returns to reputations', *Quarterly Journal of Economics* 98: 659–79.

SPENCE, M. 1977. 'Entry, investment and oligopolistic pricing', *Bell Journal of Economics* 8: 534–44.

—— 1979. 'Investment, strategy and growth in a new market', *Bell Journal of Economics* 10: 1–19.

SUTTON, J. 1990. *Sunk Costs and Market Structure: Price Competition, Advertising, and the Evolution of Concentration.* Cambridge, MA: MIT Press.

SYKES, H. 1986. 'The anatomy of a corporate venturing program: Factors influencing success', *Journal of Business Venturing* 1: 275–93.

TEECE, D. 1992. 'Competition, cooperation, and innovation: Organizational arrangements for regimes of rapid technological progress', *Journal of Economic Behavior and Organization* 18: 1–25.

WILLIAMSON, O. E. 1975. *Markets and Hierarchies: Analysis and Antitrust Implications.* New York: Free Press.

—— 1983. 'Credible commitments: Using hostages to support exchange', *American Economic Review* 73: 519–40.

—— 1985. *The Economic Institutions of Capitalism.* New York: Free Press.

ZENGER, T. 1994. 'Explaining organizational diseconomies of scale in R&D: Agency problems and the allocation of engineering talent, ideas and effort by firm size', *Management Science* 40: 708–30.

12

Knowledge Maturity of Products, Modularity, and the Vertical Boundaries of the Firm

ERIC PFAFFMANN

1. Introduction

This chapter introduces a knowledge-based theory of vertical firm boundaries, in which 'products' make up the unit of analysis. Such an analytical framework enables examination of the processes of creating and co-ordinating productive knowledge and tasks, and exploration of the relationship between knowledge and vertical firm boundaries. From the outset, the approach to determining vertical firm boundaries is dynamic, since knowledge, tasks, and products change over time (Langlois and Robertson 1995). The theory builds on the assumptions that: (1) economic actors (individuals or organizational units) are partially ignorant (Loasby 1976) and possess only incomplete knowledge; and (2) problems of economic co-ordination arise as a consequence of change (Hayek 1945). The approach of this theory differs in some respects from that pursued in transaction cost economics (Williamson 1985, 1998). In the latter, the unit of analysis is transactions (not products). Furthermore, when tackling the question of whether and when to vertically integrate, transaction cost economics places the main emphasis on the alignment of incentives. The efficiency criterion is to minimize transaction costs. In the transaction cost approach, a causal link is established between the potential for opportunistic behaviour and the amount of the transaction costs. This chapter does not address incentive problems. Rather, it takes the position that efficiency considerations are based on the consequences of incomplete knowledge and partial ignorance. The efficiency criterion is to minimize *knowledge costs*. Hence, the chapter deals with the issue of vertical integration from a knowledge-based perspective, but does not elaborate on how to mitigate hazards of contracting. Nevertheless, the extension of the knowledge-based perspective to address co-ordination problems due to both incomplete knowledge and opportunistic behaviour (Scheuble 1998; Foss 1999) is a promising avenue.

In this chapter, 'firms' are viewed as a part of a value chain. Firms develop and manufacture components of knowledge-intensive consumer and investment goods such as automobiles, high-speed trains, or computers. At the end of this value chain is the final manufacturer, who integrates components to assemble the final good. In section 2, I shall introduce the determinants of vertical firm boundaries. I am especially concerned with the definition of the minimum scope of vertical firm activities (or tasks).[1] It will be argued that a firm should vertically integrate those activities that are both *similar* and *closely complementary* (Richardson 1972). While this argument is not new, this chapter provides a novel rationale by explicitly including a knowledge level. The introduction of a knowledge level permits the integration of the concept of *knowledge maturity*. Knowledge maturity refers to the idea that the use of a product requires different knowledge from that required for the production of this product. A product is sufficiently knowledge mature if knowledge for its application can be separated from knowledge of how to produce it. When this condition is met, a product can be transferred across firm boundaries without the necessity to teach the user how to produce the product himself (Demsetz 1988). Before a sufficient degree of knowledge maturity is achieved, productive tasks are closely complementary and should be carried out only within an organizational entity.

In section 3, I will apply the concept of modular product architectures and different degrees of task interdependence to analyse the transfer and downstream use of products. I argue that modular product architectures consist of a hierarchy of sufficiently knowledge-mature products or product components. Integrating knowledge-mature products into a larger product architecture makes it possible to access and *use* specialized competences of supplier firms without learning the underlying productive knowledge itself. The term *competence* refers to the ability to co-ordinate the deployment of scarce firm resources in the course of productive activities (Sanchez, Heene, and Thomas 1996; Sanchez and Heene 1997). In section 4, I shall examine the kind of competences an integrating (downstream) firm should possess to ensure the beneficial use and to co-ordinate the development of the product architecture. I shall derive a typology of products and associated buyer–supplier interactions based on different levels of competences. In section 5, I conclude by juxtaposing the conventional view of 'ownership integration' with that of 'co-ordination integration' (Langlois and Robertson 1995) presented in this chapter.

2. A Knowledge-Based Explanation of Vertical Integration

This section develops an exclusively knowledge-based perspective of vertical integration.[2] It shows that it is efficient to vertically integrate similar and closely complementary activities. Products that are based on the execution of similar

---

[1] In the following discussion, 'activities' and 'tasks' are used synonymously.

[2] The structure and arguments of this section have benefited from co-operation with Sven Scheuble, which resulted in a joint paper (Pfaffmann and Scheuble 1998).

and closely complementary tasks are knowledge *im*mature. I start the analysis by distinguishing between three different levels of economic organization, outlining what knowledge is needed for and what kinds of vertical interaction take place within productive processes. Furthermore, I specify two kinds of productive knowledge that are required for the production and use of a product, and introduce (dis-)similar and (non-)complementary tasks and the connection to the knowledge base. Finally, I illuminate the relationship between productive tasks, on the basis of specialized repertoires of knowledge, knowledge-mature products, and the minimal degree of vertical integration.

2.1. Levels of Economic Organization

If we take a knowledge perspective, we can distinguish three different levels of economic organization: (1) a knowledge level, (2) a process level, and (3) an output level (see Figure 12.1). The *knowledge level* contains specialized repertoires of knowledge that are neither directly visible nor clearly separable from each other. Specialized repertoires of knowledge are fundamental for the implementation of any productive activity. Activities can be directly viewed, separated from each other, and assessed, as can the results of these activities. On the *process*

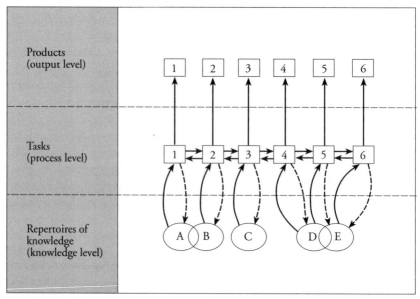

Key:
——— Implementation
– – – Learning by doing

Figure 12.1. Organization of vertical activities

level, activities are implemented that lead to results at the *output level.* The results of productive activities are products, which comprise all kinds of goods and services. The introduction of three levels of economic organization allows us to analyse the *interactions* between output level, process level, and knowledge level as well as to examine the degree of task similarity and complementarity that arises in the course of productive processes. I start with the knowledge level and distinguish the areas for which knowledge is put to use.

Knowledge is not pre-given, but has to be learned by each individual actor. Learning processes need time, and the results of learning processes as well as the utility derived from these results cannot be completely determined *ex ante.* Thus, dynamic learning processes are inherently uncertain, are time consuming, and incur costs. Therefore, the characteristics of learning processes are very similar to capital investments. *Knowledge costs* that arise during learning processes are sunk costs. This holds for individuals and for teams, such as organizational units. The amount of knowledge that has to be learned and the corresponding knowledge costs depend on the stock of knowledge that already exists in the heads of the individual actors.

2.2. *Substantive and Functional Knowledge*

Basically, one can differentiate between two kinds of knowledge: (1) substantive knowledge, and (2) functional knowledge.[3] *Substantive* knowledge is the knowledge of *how* a product is developed and produced. This knowledge is held by an individual or a team of individuals. *Functional* product knowledge is knowledge of *what.* It contains information about the functions, applications, and correct uses of a product. Functional knowledge is predominantly theoretical knowledge, which, can be found for instance, in a user's manual. A characteristic of specialization and distribution of labour is that the user of a product requires only functional product knowledge while the producer needs substantive knowledge (Pfaffmann and Scheuble 1998). Substantive knowledge is embedded in the product itself and does not need to be explicitly transferred between producer and user. For instance, if one wishes to use a personal computer, one should know *what* one can do with it rather than *how* it was produced or what kind of physical components the PC contains or *why* it works. The same holds for the use of a car. One may know how to drive, and, when driving, one should

---

[3] This distinction is based on Gilbert Ryle's classification of 'know how' to do something and 'know that'. See Ryle (1949). See Loasby (1998) for a discussion of knowing how and knowing that in the context of the organization of competences. Ron Sanchez suggests a distinction between knowing how, knowing why, and knowing what. Knowing *how* relates to descriptions of states and knowing *why* descriptions of processes in system theory. Knowing *what,* however, refers to the perceptions of economic actors in relation to potential product applications and new product and process developments (see Sanchez 1997). Clearly, knowing how and knowing why are the elements of substantive knowledge while knowing what concerns functional knowledge.

UWE LIBRARY SERVICES

know where to find the brakes before one has to use them. For the user of the car, the knowledge of why the brakes brake is irrelevant.

The distinction between substantive and functional knowledge derives its economic importance from differential *transfer* properties of substantive and functional knowledge. Specifically, the more difficult it is to transfer productive knowledge between economic actors, the higher are the knowledge costs that must be invested to transfer the knowledge. In principle, the size of knowledge costs depends on the *competence gap* between the sender and receiver (Heiner 1983; Foss 1993). If this gap is large, it can be an awkward process and take a long time for the receiver to learn what the sender teaches. But existing competence gaps also depend on the *consistency* of the knowledge. Knowledge, as is widely recognized among non-orthodox scholars, can be tacit (Polanyi 1966), that is, difficult to codify, and hence, to articulate. Productive knowledge may be complex, not visible, and very difficult to teach (Winter 1988). It may be presumed that, as the amount of tacit knowledge increases, the greater and more persistent do the competence gaps become.

To a large extent, substantive knowledge of how to carry out productive tasks is rooted in skills and experiences of individuals which they have accumulated in the course of their (working) lives. In this context, substantive knowledge cannot be entirely codified, is complex, and is fundamentally implicit (Polanyi 1966). Thus, the transfer of substantive knowledge can raise prohibitively high knowledge costs. On the other hand, functional knowledge as theoretical knowledge is easier to codify, less complex, and, hence, easier to transfer. While functional knowledge is also based on implicit knowledge, the amount of 'easy-to-transfer' *explicit* knowledge elements is much larger than in the case of substantive knowledge (Pfaffmann and Scheuble 1998). Therefore, when functional knowledge is transferred, knowledge costs are lower.

2.3. Similarity and Complementarity of Tasks

On the basis of the differentiation of substantive and functional knowledge, it is now possible to analyse the interactions of process and knowledge levels as well as task interdependencies that occur within productive processes. In order to explain the organization of vertical activities from a knowledge perspective, it is essential to examine the similarity and complementarity of tasks. The degree of similarity and complementarity of tasks provides a rationale for the co-ordination of activities.

Tasks are similar if they are based on the same substantive repertoires of knowledge (Pfaffmann and Scheuble 1998). Tasks are dissimilar if they do not have in common some substantive knowledge. Hence, it is the repertoires of substantive knowledge that make tasks similar or dissimilar. This is illustrated in Figure 12.1 on the basis of tasks 1–6 and repertoires of knowledge A–E. Tasks 1 and 2 are similar, because they require the *intersected* repertoires of knowledge of A and B for their implementation (Argyres 1996). In other words, tasks 1 and 2 are similar because they need some identical knowledge elements to be carried out (intersection A ∩ B). The same holds for tasks 4 to 6 with the intersection of D and E. Compared with the other five tasks, task 3 is dissimilar because there are no intersections between other specialized repertoires of knowledge and repertoire C. Accordingly, the task groups comprising 1 and 2, and 4 to 6, are dissimilar. However, tasks are not simply similar *or* dissimilar. Rather, they are put in order along a continuum ranging from complete heterogeneity to entire homogeneity. The more similar tasks are, the larger the intersection of the under-lying substantive repertoires of knowledge become (Pfaffmann and Scheuble 1998).

As well as examining the relationship between tasks and repertoires of substantive knowledge, it is necessary to look at how tasks are related to each other. Tasks that jointly contribute to the creation of products at the output level are complementary tasks (Richardson 1972; Milgrom and Roberts 1992). Similarly, tasks 1–6 can be interpreted as different phases of a productive process, which points to task complementarity in time. Furthermore, complementary tasks have to be co-ordinated in time and space with respect to their quantity and quality. Thus, although tasks are not all similar, they may nevertheless be complementary (Richardson 1972). For instance, in the development and production process of automobiles, the development of components such as drive shafts, car bodies, or gears must be co-ordinated in order to achieve compatibility and smooth functioning of the finished vehicle.

The complementarity of tasks translates into the necessity to co-ordinate the activities of individuals who are engaged in development and production processes. Co-ordination requires the interaction of individuals, and this in turn calls for *communication*. In general, communication is based on codes that are accumulated by the co-operating actors during their joint productive activities (Arrow 1974; Crémer 1990). Thus, the co-ordination of complementary tasks demands as a first prerequisite the continuous interaction of individuals. Furthermore, the continuity of co-operation encourages the creation and use of the interdependent division of knowledge and the division of labour (Loasby 1994). At the same time, individuals not only learn to master specific tasks, but also accumulate shared repertoires of knowledge. Thus, continuous interaction is a salient feature of the co-ordination of complementary activities (Pfaffmann and Scheuble 1998).

More specifically, during the time of their continuous interaction, individuals develop what Brian Loasby calls a 'frame of reference' (Loasby 1996). This frame of reference consists of organizational facts and codes, the meaning of which is shared collectively by all individuals who belong to the organization (Dosi and Marengo 1995):

By speaking, acting, writing, playing, producing and using tools and marks, individuals continuously participate in the creation of social knowledge of a firm. This knowledge allows people to observe and make a shared sense of organizational events as well as to act in a co-ordinated manner.   (Krogh and Roos 1995: 64.)

Since this knowledge is shared by all interacting individuals, it can be considered as the *social* knowledge of productive processes. Social knowledge is vital for reasonable communication, and thus, a second prerequisite for qualitative and quantitative co-ordination. Shared social knowledge can also be interpreted as *intersections* of individual repertoires of knowledge. But shared social knowledge comprising the repertoires of knowledge of individuals does not refer to substantive intersections of knowledge. Rather, shared social knowledge refers to the *functional* knowledge of individual actors (Pfaffmann and Scheuble 1998). In Figure 12.1, the intersections of the repertoires A and B, and D and E, consist not only of common substantive knowledge but also of shared elements of functional knowledge.

The intersections of repertoires of functional knowledge emerge during the co-ordination of complementary tasks. For analytical reasons, one may draw the distinction that an organizational frame of reference of shared knowledge consists of organization-specific knowledge containing facts and codes, and of organization-specific knowledge containing norms and values. The former could be called *organizational knowledge*, and the latter organizational *identity*. The term 'identity' denominates a self-description of the organization (Krogh, Roos, and Slocum 1994; Kogut and Zander 1996). The identity of the organization conveys criteria that determine what kind of information individuals absorb from their environment, and what kind of information they ignore at the same time. Furthermore, learning and co-ordinating activities are guided by the organizational identity, which provides rules and routines of why, how, and when tasks should be carried out (March and Simon 1958; Nelson and Winter 1982).

The existence of an organizational knowledge and identity is essential for the co-ordination of complementary tasks. The co-evolution of organizational knowledge and specialized repertoires attenuates the trade-off between the extent of substantive repertoires of knowledge and shared functional knowledge in a population of specialists (Crémer 1990). This trade-off limits the division of knowledge and the division of labour which can efficiently be achieved, because, at its extreme, specialists who do not share a common code of symbols are not able to communicate the value of their services to other specialists and, thus, cannot trade their services. In sum, a shared frame of reference allows individuals to communicate, and to be *directed* by those who know (other things) better, and, hence, convert their specialized substantive knowledge into utility for others (Demsetz 1988). Thus, co-ordination serves as a substitute for the transfer of substantive knowledge. In fact, it is the continuity of co-operation that drives specialization among individuals and substitutes for the transfer of knowledge from one individual to another (Demsetz 1988; Conner and Prahalad 1996).[4]

As with the similarity of tasks, tasks are not simply complementary or non-complementary. The complementarity of tasks ranges in a continuum from complete independence to close complementarity (Pfaffmann and Scheuble 1998). An increasing degree of task complementarity implies an increasing demand for co-ordination and communication. Accordingly, the importance of shared functional knowledge grows along the continuum, since both the complexity and frequency of communication expand. The higher the degree of task complementarity, the more extensive and differentiated are the shared or-ganizational knowledge and identity required for the interaction of individuals. Hence, the efficient implementation of tasks within productive processes is based on the match between the degree of complementarity and the extent of shared functional knowledge (Pfaffmann and Scheuble 1998).

2.4. Knowledge Maturity of Products and Vertical Integration

On the basis of the analysis of the knowledge and process levels, one can now proceed to include the output level and to examine the link to vertical integra-tion.[5] This permits us to define the activities that a firm should implement in-house, and to determine the efficient *minimal* degree of vertical integration. In particular, we discuss the connection between task similarity and complemen-tarity, and the distribution of decision rights with respect to the implementation of tasks.

The concept of *knowledge maturity* makes suggestions about the distribution of decision rights (Dietl 1995). The basic idea of the concept is that the results of productive activities ensuing from the underlying repertoires of substantive knowledge must be made available for potential users without the need for users to acquire the particular substantive knowledge themselves. In other words, the fundamental condition to economize on costs of knowledge and to realize productivity gains through specialization is that the user of a product does not need to have the underlying substantive knowledge. That is, that the product can be transferred from the producer to the user without explicitly transferring the substantive production knowledge. Products that meet this condition can be said to be knowledge mature. The implication for vertical integration is that tasks carried out in a productive process should be kept under *joint decision*

---

[4] 'Those who are to produce on the basis of this knowledge, but are not to be possessed of it themselves, must have their activities *directed* by those who possess (more of) the knowledge. Direction substitutes for education (that is, for the transfer of the knowledge itself).' (Demsetz 1988: 159.)

[5] The following analysis is presented in greater detail in Pfaffmann and Scheuble (1998: 17–21).

authority as subsequent value chain stages require the substantive knowledge of former stages (Dietl 1995).

However, the concept of knowledge maturity advanced by Dietl (1995) considers repertoires of substantive knowledge only and neglects functional knowledge required for the use of a product. It is not possible, on the basis of substantive knowledge alone, to *denominate* knowledge-immature products. This deficiency can be overcome by amending the concept and taking repertoires of functional product knowledge into consideration.[6]

As mentioned above, the origin of productive knowledge is a dynamic learning process comparable to an investment in capital goods. Consider the similarity of tasks and the underlying repertoires of substantive knowledge. It has been argued that similar tasks are characterized by the intersections in the repertoires of substantive knowledge. The investment nature of the accumulation of productive knowledge is entailed in the intersections of repertoires of substantive knowledge. Thus, economies of scope that accrue from the use of repertoires of intersected substantive knowledge can be achieved by the execution of similar tasks. This is an argument in favour of *specialization* on similar tasks. Otherwise, the very same repertoires of substantive knowledge would have to be built by several actors.

However, on the basis of repertoires of intersected substantive knowledge, it is possible to draw conclusions about the distribution of *tasks*, but nothing can be said about the distribution of *decision rights*, and accordingly, the design of the relationships among specialized actors. The relationship design refers to the social element in the distribution of labour and the complementarity of tasks. Therefore, one has to consider the complementarity of tasks and the underlying repertoires of shared functional knowledge. As outlined above, the co-ordination of complementary tasks demands the interaction of individual actors and presumes the accumulation of a shared frame of reference which consists of intersections of functional knowledge. In line with the evolution of similar tasks and the economics of substantive knowledge the evolution of a common frame of reference also influences the costs of productive activities. The more differentiated and intense the co-operation of two actors, the larger is the base of shared knowledge and the easier and less expensive is the interaction of the individuals involved. The extent to which a frame of reference has to be built depends on the intensity of mutual interaction. This cost advantage is lost if individuals frequently change their co-operating partners and impede the evolution of a shared frame of reference. This means that the frame of reference among interacting individuals is specific and exists solely in a particular relationship config-

---

[6] Furthermore, integrating functional knowledge enables recommendations of a more refined nature for different governance forms (vertical integration, co-operation, market transactions) to be given. For details, see Pfaffmann and Scheuble (1998).

uration. The size of the attainable cost advantage depends on two factors. First, it depends on the degree of complementarity, and, secondly, it is influenced by the duration of the co-operation. Thus, the higher the degree of task complementarity, the higher is the intensity of interaction and the more important is the shared frame of reference of co-operating partners.

While the similarity of tasks provides arguments in favour of specialization, the complementarity of tasks contains a reasoning for the relationship design of specialized actors. If the realization of a product is accompanied by both similar and closely complementary tasks, these tasks should be co-ordinated in-house (under joint decision authority). A distribution of these tasks to several independent actors would be inefficient because this kind of division of labour would demand a multiplication of the same repertoires of substantive knowledge. In addition, closely complementary tasks call for a large amount of intersected functional knowledge. Thus, the vertical integration of closely complementary and similar tasks is efficient because cost advantages can be realized for both kinds of intersection.

Since intersections of repertoires of both substantive and functional knowledge are necessary for realizing the product, this product can be termed *knowledge immature*. In contrast, a product is *sufficiently knowledge mature* if the underlying tasks are complementary but dissimilar.[7] In the case of sufficient knowledge maturity, only intersections of functional knowledge are required. Again, the extent of these intersections depends on the degree of task complementarities. The minimal boundaries of the firm should comprise all productive activities that contribute to the realization of a knowledge-immature product, while sufficiently knowledge-mature products can be realized by inter-firm co-operation. The in-house co-ordination of knowledge-immature products and the inter-firm co-ordination of sufficiently knowledge-mature products minimize the total knowledge costs required to realize a complex product along a value chain.

Knowledge-immature products include, for example, the development of designs for new car bodies or the development of a new pharmaceutical substance for the treatment of infectious diseases. Sufficiently knowledge-mature products include finished components such as a chassis, a clutch or a drive shaft that may, when completed, be used in the assembly process of a car. The development and production of these components can be carried out by separate organizational entities which co-ordinate their activities quantitatively and qualitatively. From this perspective, it becomes clear that sufficient knowledge-mature products are needed for vertical interaction across firm boundaries to be carried out efficiently. Specifically, once sufficient knowledge maturity is

---

[7] See Pfaffmann and Scheuble (1998) for a differentiation of degrees of knowledge maturity based on the existence of substantive and/or functional intersections of knowledge.

achieved, it becomes possible to *access* and *use* specialized competences of supplier firms without having to acquire the underlying substantive knowledge itself. This implies that *decisions to buy* (in relation to product components) which precede vertical inter-firm interaction are feasible only for product components that are sufficiently knowledge mature. Thus, the purchase of components from upstream suppliers constitutes a substitute for the transfer of substantive knowledge.[8]

The arguments developed in this section do not make any reference to the relationship between the architecture of a product and the vertical organization of its realization. However, the arguments indicate that an 'upstream' market for supplier products exists only if downstream users can integrate a product into their (supposedly more complex) products, or use it for their specific purposes, if there is no need to possess large amounts of substantive product knowledge. Thus, sufficient knowledge maturity is the fundamental condition a product must meet in order to be saleable, and, in turn, purchasable for downstream producers or consumers.

3. Product Architecture and the Organization of Task Complementarities along the Value Chain

As has been outlined so far, the interaction between different organizational entities commences beyond the separated transfer of functional and substantive product knowledge. But, if all the firms engaged in the development of a complex (final) good like aircraft, automobiles, computers, power stations, etc., produce knowledge-mature products, why is there any need at all for them to interact and co-operate to a degree that is distinct from neoclassical market relations? The fundamental answer to this question can be found in the distribution of distinct competences along the value chain: because no firm possesses all the substantive knowledge that is necessary to develop and produce a complex final product, each firm is a specialist for a certain element or aspect of this product, and delivers components which may be specific to the development and production process of the final product. In this section, I shall illuminate the relationship between the decomposition of a complex (final) product into its constituent parts and the intensity of buyer–supplier interaction resulting from the distribu-

---

[8] It is also evident that co-operation between independent firms for research and development activities is fundamentally different from vertical inter-firm co-operation along a value chain. Very often, co-operation for R&D is institutionalized as strategic alliances or joint ventures. Their target is, for instance, to jointly develop a (still) knowledge-immature product, such as a drug. Therefore, they build repertoires of substantive and functional knowledge repertoires by pooling their resources under a joint (project) decision authority. In the arguments developed above, this marks vertical integration although the co-operation for R&D may be restricted to certain activities and to a particular time.

tion of tasks among them. I start by introducing the product as a system of inter-related product architectures.

3.1. A Product as a System of Nested Architectures

In general, a product can be viewed as a complex system which consists of 'a set of components that together provide utility to users. System performance is dependent not only upon constituent components, but also on the extent to which they are compatible with each other' (Garud and Kumaraswamy 1993: 353). This implies that constituent elements of a system relate to each other in a specific way, which can be called the *architecture* of a product. More precisely, a product architecture is a 'scheme by which the function of the product is allocated to physical components' (Ulrich 1995: 420). The architecture defines the layout of functional elements, the relation between functional elements of the product and the physical components—parts, components, modules, or subsystems—which implement these functions, and the specification of the interfaces among interacting physical components (Ulrich 1995).

Two fundamental kinds of product architecture can be distinguished (Ulrich 1995; Ulrich and Eppinger 1995; Goepfert 1998). A *modular* architecture is one where the functional elements and the physical components are *relatively independent* of each other. In relation to the functional independence of a component, one physical component carries out exactly one functional element. Functional independence is at its maximum if each functional element is implemented by exactly one physical component. In contrast, functional dependence between components emerges if more than one component implements one functional element. The independence of physical components refers to the interfaces of physical product components. Components are the more independent the more easily they can be *separated* from each other, or in other words, the less they are *coupled* (Goepfert 1998). Within an *integral* product architecture, many functions are implemented by one physical component, and interfaces between physical components are not well defined or coupled.

The notion of a modular product architecture infers the existence of a *hierarchy* within an architecture (Simon 1962, 1996). Indeed, a modular product architecture permits the definition of 'nested' subsystems, where each subsystem consists of a distinct subsystem architecture, which again can be modular or integral. 'Nesting refers to the idea that components within a larger system are self-contained, such as the audio system within a vehicle. . . . Simply, products which at one level can be viewed as complex architected systems act as components in systems at a higher level' (Gulati and Eppinger 1996: 5–6). The modularity of the product architecture permits a flexible combination and integration of components at different nested levels which interact by way of clearly specified interfaces, and in its entirety results in the complex final product.

3.2. Product Architectures and Degrees of Task Complementarity in Product Development Processes

The definition of a modular architecture has a direct impact on the organization of activities and competences within and across firms. Because the modular architecture specifies the interfaces between the physical elements of interacting components, teams that are assigned as task owners in the development of distinct components can organize their activities nearly independently from each other, and co-ordinate their activities by agreeing on interface specifications. A modular architecture permits a concurrent development of product constituents by processes that can be carried out by de-coupled organizational structures (Sanchez and Mahoney 1996). Thus, the design of the product architecture translates into the design of the organization, and also contains implications for vertical integration. In the remaining part of this section, I will discuss this relationship in more detail.

In section 2, it was shown that tasks which should be co-ordinated within the firm are closely complementary and similar. As outlined above, the complementarity of tasks ranges from complete independence to close complementarity. The following analysis focuses on different stages of a productive process or a value chain. In the context of detailed product development processes, it may add to the understanding to apply a typology of different degrees of task interdependence, developed by Thompson (1967). Thompson (1967) studied work flows and distinguished between pooled, sequential, and reciprocal tasks. As with different degrees of complementarity, Thompson's typology (1967) is based on locational separability and complementarity in time. Tasks which are *pooled* can be completed independently, but depend on each other in an economic sense.[9] *Sequential* tasks have to be resolved step by step according to a predefined sequence. *Reciprocal* interdependence means that the solution of one task needs the simultaneous resolution of the other tasks as its input. In addition, going beyond the notion of reciprocal tasks, van de Ven, Delbecq, and Koenig (1976) suggest the notion of *team-based* task interdependences. Team-based task interdependences are those that exist in a situation in which individuals have to carry out their tasks jointly and simultaneously.[10] Reciprocal and team-based tasks correspond with *closely* complementary tasks, and pooled as well as sequential tasks with a lower degree of complementarity. While pooled and sequential tasks

---

[9] 'Yet they may be interdependent in the sense that unless each performs adequately, the total organization is jeopardized; failure of any one can threaten the whole and thus the other parts' (Thompson 1967: 54).

[10] 'In team work flow, there is no measurable temporal lapse in the flow of work between unit members, as there is in the sequential and reciprocal cases; the work is acted upon jointly and simultaneously by unit personnel at the same point in time' (van de Ven, Delbecq, and Koenig 1976: 325).

can be assigned to several teams, reciprocal and team-based tasks cannot. As I argued above, the implementation of reciprocal and team-based tasks requires frequent interactions and intense communication between the individuals involved.

The degree of task complementarity in development and production processes basically depends on the design of the product architecture. An integral architecture implies the existence of reciprocal and team-based task interdependences. The interdependences result from non-specification of clear interfaces between physical components, and from the complex (non one-to-one) mapping of functions to physical components. If the arrangement of functions to components as well as the interaction between components is fuzzy, *task boundaries* cannot be exactly defined, nor can the input:output relations of team members be clearly determined. Hence, if a sufficient degree of modularity between the components of the final product cannot be derived, it is impossible in a timely fashion and/or locally to de-couple multipersonal development processes. Again, these processes can be managed only by explicit co-ordination using frequent interaction and direct communication. A modular architecture, on the other hand, goes hand in hand with pooled and sequential task interdependences. The relative independence of functional elements and physical components, and clearly specified interfaces of interacting components, mean that development tasks can be defined, structured, and separated from each other. Reciprocal and team-based interdependences can be kept *inside* the development processes of components. Thus, a modular product architecture allows the 'embedded co-ordination' of development tasks, in the sense that specifications of functions and interfaces clearly define the output of each system element (Sanchez and Mahoney 1996). The relationship between increasing architectural integrality and increasing degrees of task complementarity is illustrated in Figure 12.2.

The development of an appropriate modular architecture is carried out in the early phases of a product development process and is a core problem in the development of a new product. Hence, the development of appropriate product architectures may be considered as an indication of *sufficient knowledge maturity*. In the case of knowledge immaturity, later stages of the development process will require the substantive knowledge of former process stages. Furthermore, if a firm does not succeed in developing a sufficiently modular architecture, it will have to vertically integrate all complementary tasks and cannot use the 'upstream' competences of specialized supplier firms to provide certain functions and (related) components, since it cannot define and communicate reliable specifications to supplier firms, nor does it know how to *integrate* supplier components. In addition, because of inadequate modularity, the firm may not even be aware which functions could improve the performance of the product or upgrade its utility for customers and, thus, it may not know that there is a market for

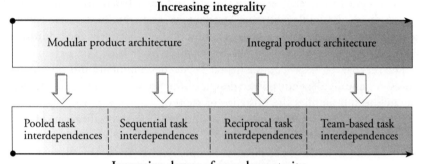

Figure 12.2. Continuum of increasing architectural integrity and complementarity of tasks

these components to which the firm could have access. The same holds for the 'downstream' market for a firm's product: if a firm cannot adjust its product to the specifications of customers (particularly in the case of a final consumer), the product will be of little utility for prospective buyers.

Principally, the architecture of a complex product consists of a spectrum of modular and integral nested (component) architectures. However, one may simply distinguish between (1) a completely modular architecture (and, hence, an organization that has to co-ordinate pooled and sequential task interdependences), and (2) a completely integral architecture accompanied by an organization which has to manage reciprocal and team-based task interdependences. While pure modularity and integrality are not of empirical importance,[11] several implications can be derived from the relationship between product and organization architectures. First, modularity in product design reduces the complexity of the product and the development process as a whole. A modular design represents a successful decomposition of complex tasks into less complex tasks which can be assigned to specialist actors who co-ordinate their activities nearly autonomously of each other. Secondly, product or problem decomposition corresponds to a similar organizational structure (Henderson and Clark 1990). Thus, modularity drives the division of labour and knowledge, but a flawed architecture is fraught with danger since it may create insurmountable impediments for the organization when structures become routinized. In addition, if a product architecture turns out to be incorrect and incomplete, the modular organizational design will also be

---

[11] A complete modular architecture is neither technically feasible nor economically advantageous. The modularity and the integrality of architectures have direct impact on the efficiency characteristics of a product. An integral architecture, for example, is beneficial if the performance of the product rests on size, design, or mass. This is the case because an integral architecture permits 'function sharing', that is, where many functions are implemented by one physical component. For details, see Ulrich (1995) and Goepfert (1998).

incorrect and incomplete. Accordingly, adjustments to the product architecture in the later stages of the development process directly affect the organizational (inter-firm) design (Pfaffmann and Bensaou 1998). Thirdly, a product with a higher degree of modularity contains more interfaces than a less modular product, and thus provides more options for learning and more flexibility for integrating new or improved functions and related physical components. Fourthly, while co-ordination across component development and production is encapsulated in specifications and can be left to specialists, modularity requires sophisticated knowledge of *how* components interact in a specific product design.[12] But substantive knowledge of a complex product may be dispersed within a population of specialists, and applications of components may be novel and/or specific to a certain system architecture. Interactions between components in a nested system hierarchy may therefore reveal unforeseen technical difficulties and externalities, and consequently give rise to enhanced *uncertainty*.[13]

In sum, the product architecture determines the task boundaries and the interdependences between tasks. Within a modular architecture, task boundaries are precisely defined and can be allocated among a population of internal or external teams. These teams can act almost autonomously and co-ordinate their activities by means of their output, which is captured as a set of specifications. An integral architecture has the opposite consequences: no precise task boundaries can be defined, and neither a clear decomposition of independent tasks nor the assignment of (nearly) autonomous teams is feasible. The design of the product architecture has profound implications for the opportunity to use upstream supplier competences during the development and production of a complex product. The architecture works as a *plan* with which suppliers and buyers co-ordinate their activities during the product development process. From the value chain perspective, the architecture decomposes the complex product and ascribes tasks to specialized firms, and thus, assigns firms their own specific roles and affiliated responsibilities as suppliers and buyers.

4. The Inter-Firm Transfer of Products: Buyer–Supplier Interaction and Competence in the Product Development Process

In this section, I shall analyse the interaction of buyers and suppliers on a value chain in greater detail. In particular, I develop a typology of transferred products

---

[12] The information needed for co-ordinating product development processes within a modular organization must include: (1) an adequate technical description of the components to be created; (2) clear assignments of specific development tasks to participating organizations; and (3) a schedule for carrying out and completing development and delivery tasks. See Sanchez and Mahoney (1996).

[13] Sometimes these problems can prove to be disastrous. Take for example the failure of the Mercedes-Benz class A car in the now famous 'moose test'.

from the perspective of buyers and investigate the linkage between the intensity of buyer-supplier interaction and the type of products buyers and suppliers transfer. Furthermore, I focus on the distribution of competences with regard to the realization of specific components by suppliers and the integration into a larger system implemented by buyers. In general, the division of labour among firms along a value chain is not pre-given but designed by the firms which develop the architecture of this product. If there is only one such firm, as is the case in the automobile or aviation industry, this firm exerts significant control over the companies which participate in the development and production of the final product. If this is the case, a kind of inter-firm hierarchy is put in place and each participant's position is determined by its contribution to the final product, that is, by the component it delivers.

4.1. A Typology of Transferred Products and the Intensity of Buyer–Supplier Interaction

During the concept development of a new product, the product architecture is typically designed by the firm which delivers the final good. This firm may derive a modular architecture which allows the purchase of components from specialized suppliers. A component supplier designs the architecture for their product, given the constraints of the integrator's specifications, and may outsource the development and production of some sub-components to other upstream specialists. Again, sufficient modularity is the key requirement for the decomposition process and the division of labour.

Products which are transferred along the value chain between buyers (meaning integrators or users) and suppliers (that is, producers) can be classified according to the amount of substantive product knowledge and the amount of functional product knowledge a *user firm* possesses. One can distinguish between three principal product classes: (a) 'white box' products, (b) 'black box' products, and (c) 'grey box' products. Since the product classes are based on the existing stock of knowledge of the user firm, they do not make any reference to (absolute) physical properties of the products classified. Therefore, a product can be a 'black box' product for firm X and at the same time a 'white box' product for firm Z. We now look in more detail at these product classes.

1. *'White box' products.* If a user firm is able to achieve the development of a product itself, it will have accumulated the corresponding competences in the past, and may now apply this *substantive product knowledge* to make the product in-house. On the other hand, for reasons of efficiency, the firm may decide to outsource the development and production to a supplier firm. However, in a decision to buy, the firm retains detailed substantive knowledge. If the integrating firm possesses a large amount of

functional product knowledge, it knows reasonably well what kinds of interaction problems and behaviours are likely to occur, as a result of its record
of multiple applications and its past experience. Therefore, the integrating
firm holds an almost complete knowledge of this product, which makes it
transparent. This product may therefore be called a 'white box' product.

2. *'Black box' products.* If a user firm is not able to achieve the detailed development of an upstream product on the basis of substantive knowledge in-
house (although this product exists and the user firm is acquainted with its
existence), the firm must rely on the competences of specialized suppliers
to develop it. In this instance, the integrating firm does not possess
substantive product knowledge but has sufficient comprehension of the
product's functions to appreciate them. Moreover, if the upstream product
is of relatively large physical complexity and/or is highly innovative, the
integrating firm may not have adequate *functional knowledge* to assess the
interactions and behaviour of this product within the larger system. This
product may therefore be classified as a 'black box' product.

3. *'Grey box' products.* Obviously, black box and white box products are op-
posites. There is no doubt that a more refined differentiation could be
derived along the 'substantive knowledge' and 'functional knowledge'
dimensions of the integrated product. However, the characterization of
grey box products may suffice. A firm may possess some substantive
knowledge of the development of an upstream product because it possesses
competences in the development of similar products or it has developed
the upstream product in the past. If this is the case, the user firm has some
fragmented *substantive knowledge* of the details of the procedure for developing an upstream product, and could, in principle, develop the product
in-house. However, it may rely on the competences of the suppliers,
because it may not consider the development of a specific upstream
component as a core activity and/or it may prefer to use competitive offers
by supplier firms. Although the amount of substantive product knowledge
in-house is incomplete, the integrating firm may have good comprehension of the functions of the upstream product. The integrating firm may
possess some *functional product knowledge* and experience from former
applications, and thus, may be able reliably to assess the behaviour of the
product within the larger system. The transfer properties of this product
are between the black box and the white box, and it may therefore be
denominated a 'grey box' product.

On the basis of the former typology, we can now relate the intensity of
buyer–supplier interaction to the product classes discussed above.

1. *Intensity of interaction concerning the integration of 'black box' products.* As
the preceding discussion elucidates, it is misleading to conclude that the

integration of black box products suggests that buyer–supplier interaction is redundant after component specifications have been fixed. Rather, the opposite is true. Since knowledge maturity is incomplete, suppliers may not know the effect of their components on the interplay of the larger system, and, for several reasons, buyers may not even be certain that they have worked out the 'right' specifications. Buyers develop architectures which, at the very beginning, may be of only a preliminary nature, as are specifications derived on the basis of these architectures. In addition, specifications may turn out to be restrictive, in the sense that they interfere too much with supplier domains of competence, and as a result, produce obstacles to their work. However, the concept development phase, which marks the start of buyer–supplier interaction, may include the necessity for some experiments and provides many opportunities for mutual inter-firm learning. This translates into the requirement for close interaction, which can be institutionalized by regular meetings of multifunctional teams (Schrader and Goepfert 1997). During this stage of development, buyers and suppliers may also co-locate important team members to support information flows that can be 'sticky' (Hippel 1994), that is, consist of messages which it is difficult to use to bridge different frames of reference and large competence gaps.

2. *Intensity of interaction concerning the integration of 'white box' products.* Since buyers and suppliers have accumulated both extensive substantive and extensive functional knowledge, specifications should be set appropriately, task boundaries for interacting parties should be clearly defined, and interaction should be confined to the purchasing and sales departments. There is no need for suppliers to participate in buyers' development processes. As a result, the intensity of buyer–supplier interaction can be quite low.

3. *Intensity of interaction concerning the integration of 'grey box' products.* The defining characteristics of grey box products favour more extensive buyer–supplier interaction than do those of white box products. Suppliers must be involved in the development process of the final product, because early specifications may not be optimal, and unforeseen problems may occur. However, the amount of substantive and functional knowledge held by the integrating firm is higher than for white box products and the corresponding integration may be fixed in the early stages of the development process. It follows that occasional meetings should be sufficient to facilitate information transfer and problem resolution.

4.2. *The Competences of the Firm as an Integrator of Transferred Products*

In analysing buyer–supplier interaction, I assigned different roles to buyers and suppliers. Buyers were associated with the design of the product architecture and the integration of components, and suppliers with the detailed development of the respective components. I now examine the principal competences which underlie this division of labour between buyers and suppliers.

Designing a product architecture is an iterative process in which the decomposability of the product concept has to be assessed, specifications defined, and negotiations with suppliers initiated. These activities are part of each new product development, regardless of whether outside suppliers are brought in, or internal departments are assigned. The underlying competences may be called *architectural competence*.[14] Architectural competence refers to the co-ordination and integration of dissimilar repertoires of substantive knowledge and tasks which are fundamental parts of every productive activity. However, in the terminology proposed here, architectural competence refers to the integration of heterogeneous components of which the integrator does not necessarily hold significant repertoires of substantive knowledge. Apart from the capability to design an appropriate modular system architecture and to set specifications which best fit the requirements of suppliers and buyers, architectural competence also embraces capabilities which are indispensable for understanding and evaluating the *functions* of external upstream products as well as the appraisals of potential interdependences among heterogeneous components within a nested system hierarchy.

Conversely, the development and production of components requires in-depth substantive product knowledge which also comprises new developments in related domains of technological knowledge. Following Henderson and Cockburn (1994), the required competence may be called *component competence*.

The consequences of lacking architectural and component competences are obvious. The supplier does not know how to produce a high quality product, nor does the buying firm know how to integrate a component. In the following discussion, I concentrate on the architectural and component competences of buyer firms, and assume that suppliers possess the relevant component competence. The use of dichotomous degrees of architectural and component competences (high or low) makes it possible to integrate the product typology derived above and the precariousness of buyer–supplier interaction.

1. If both architectural and component competence is high, the integrator draws from a great amount of substantive and functional product knowledge, although this might not meet the standards of specialized supplier companies. Consequently, from the perspective of the integrating firm,

---

[14] Rebecca Henderson and Kim Clark introduced the notion of 'architectural knowledge', which is supposed to be embedded in the firm's communication channels, information filters, and problem solving strategies (see Henderson and Clark 1990). Other authors recognize the importance of architectural knowledge, and add that it is stored in the firm's managerial systems (Leonard-Barton 1992), or norms and values (Henderson and Cockburn 1994; Henderson 1994).

upstream components are white box products, and integration should not cause many obstacles.

2. If the integrator's component competence is low but architectural competence is high, black and grey box products are sourced and integration may cause problems. As suggested above, to deal with integration and application problems, buyers and suppliers should set up and maintain sufficient intensity of interaction.

3. Where low architectural and high component competence are combined, the integrator is a good component producer but does not know how to develop sufficient system modularity, or how to integrate components into the larger system. This may be the case if the firm is about to accumulate architectural competences by forward integrating into new downstream domains in the value chain.

4. Where low architectural and component competences are combined, buyers obtain black box products, the functions of which they do not know, nor do they have the means to integrate these components, because they do not possess functional knowledge and have not developed an appropriate architecture. In this situation, inter-firm learning does not seem to be promising, as the competence gap with respect to component knowledge is too large, and architectural knowledge may only be acquired from direct competitors.

5. Conclusions

In this chapter, I have attempted to outline a knowledge-based theory of vertical integration in which 'products' are the unit of analysis. I differentiated between three levels in the organization of vertical activities in order to analyse the interaction between knowledge, tasks, and products. I then distinguished between two kinds of productive knowledge as well as between similar and complementary tasks. I showed that the similarity of tasks rests upon the intersections of repertoires of substantive knowledge, while the complementarity of tasks is based on intersections of repertoires of functional knowledge. Furthermore, I provided a rationale for the minimal degree of vertical integration, arguing that knowledge costs can be saved if productive activities that are either (highly) similar and (closely) complementary are integrated. If tasks are both similar and closely complementary, the resulting product is termed knowledge immature.

This approach is based on subjectivist grounds, that is, on the necessity of a frame of reference in which individuals co-ordinate and learn the activities they pursue, and on the existence of competence gaps between individuals and firms. A competence gap is a result of specialization and psychological requirements as well as limits to learning. Competence gaps are responsible for the trade-off between shared knowledge and substantive knowledge within a population of specialists. This, in turn, impedes communication and co-ordination among interacting individuals. Thus, a firm is an institution that facilitates co-ordination among its members by providing social knowledge in the form of a shared identity and organizational knowledge.

However, this research implies that vertical integration is a matter of 'co-ordination integration' and not exclusively 'ownership integration'. This insight has been made explicit by Richard Langlois and Paul Robertson. In their analysis of vertical integration, they use the dimensions 'ownership integration' *and* 'co-ordination integration' (Langlois and Robertson 1995; Robertson and Langlois 1995). In the conventional view, vertical integration is considered as the degree of ownership integration (Teece 1986; Gerybadze 1995). Ownership is treated as being almost synonymous with *control* since owners hold (residual) rights of control (Grossman and Hart 1986) and thus can exert control over people who carry out integrated activities. This line of argument sees control as ensuring the enforcement of owners' interests and as preventing others from cheating. This is considered to be particularly important in the context of change (Langlois 1989). However, the perspective of vertical integration proposed in this chapter is one of integration of co-ordination.

Again, ownership includes the right to exert control over the co-ordination of complementary activities. It is worth examining the activities that must be carried out in order to exert control. First, information about relevant activities has to be obtained. Secondly, understanding of these activities is required. Thirdly, on the basis of identified activities and adequate comprehension, *ex ante* targets have to be set, which individuals must use to guide their behaviour. Fourthly, the behaviour of individuals and the *ex post* results of this behaviour must be 'screened' and evaluated. Fifthly, potential deviations from *ex ante* targets and *ex post* results have to be analysed, conclusions drawn, and decisions agreed upon. Finally, the decisions must be implemented.

Now, compare these control activities with the activities a firm carries out in order to integrate and use the embedded competences of others. First, the firm needs information on the functions of products. Secondly, it must understand and assess the use of these functions. Thirdly, appropriate specifications have to be set, and interactions evaluated. Fourthly, the firm has to check whether specifications are met. Fifthly, deviations must be analysed, conclusions drawn, and decisions made. Finally, the decisions must be implemented. However, the salient feature of ownership rights seems to be that their execution requires architectural competence. It is only at the final step in the decision process that ownership rights facilitate control of activities. Thus, I argue that, to a large extent, ownership substitutes for architectural competence, that is, for gaining access and integrating the embedded competences of others.

While internal firm organization builds a frame of reference that fits the requirement of learning particular competences, and, in addition, offers a solution for co-ordinating closely complementary tasks by delivering organizational knowledge that facilitates communication, this, of course, has its limits. This is where product modularity enables vertical co-operation which extends the division of knowledge and the division of labour beyond the point where this division could effectively be co-ordinated in-house. This is not to say that vertically co-operating firms do not need any shared knowledge for their joint activities. However, the amount and richness of interorganizationally shared knowledge can diminish concomitantly with a reduced degree of integration of co-ordination; in other words, it can fluctuate with the degree of task interdependence. To a certain extent, shared organizational knowledge of vertically co-operating firms is then encapsulated in specifications by which the development and transfer of products are co-ordinated concurrently. Obviously, the de-coupling of component development has strong implications for the organization of development processes (Sanchez 1996), and for inter-firm learning. Modularity allows concurrent product development of many firms which can be used to upgrade final goods or to develop completely new products.

References

ARGYRES, N. 1996. 'Evidence on the role of firm capabilities in vertical integration decisions', *Strategic Management Journal* 17: 129–50.

ARROW, K. J. 1974. *The Limits of Organization*. New York: Northern & Company.

CONNER, K. R., and C. K. PRAHALAD 1996. 'A resource-based theory of the firm: Knowledge versus opportunism', *Organization Science* 7(5): 477–501.

CRÉMER, J. 1990. 'Common knowledge and the co-ordination of economic activities', in Aoki, M., B. Gustafsson, and O. E. Williamson, eds., *The Firm as a Nexus of Treaties*. London and Delhi: Sage, 53–76.

DEMSETZ, H. 1988. 'The theory of the firm revisited', in H. Demsetz, *Ownership, Control, and the Firm: The Organization of Economic Activity*. Oxford and New York: Blackwell, 144–65.

DIETL, H. 1995. 'Institutionelle Koordination spezialisierungsbedingter wirtschaftlicher Abhängigkeiten', *Zeitschrift für Betriebswirtschaft* 65(6): 569–85.

DOSI, G., and L. MARENGO 1995. 'Some elements of an evolutionary theory of organizational competences', in R. W. England, ed., *Evolutionary Concepts in Contemporary Economics*. Ann Arbor MI: University of Michigan Press, 157–78.

FOSS, N. J. 1993. 'Theories of the firm: Contractual and competence perspectives', *Journal of Evolutionary Economics* 3(2): 127–44.

—— 1999. 'Research in the strategic theory of the firm: "Isolationism" and "Integrationism" ', *Journal of Management Studies*, forthcoming.

GARUD, R., and A. KUMARASWAMY 1993. 'Changing competitive dynamics in network industries: An exploration of Sun Microsystems' Open Systems Strategy', *Strategic Management Journal* 14: 351–69.

GERYBADZE, A. 1995. *Strategic Alliances and Process Redesign: Effective Management and Restructuring of Cooperative Projects and Networks*. Berlin, New York: de Gruyter.

GOEPFERT, JAN 1998, *Modularisierung in der Produktentwicklung: Ein Ansatz zur gemeinsamen Gestaltung von Technik und Organization.*

GROSSMAN, S., and O. HART 1986.'The costs and benefits of ownership: A theory of vertical and lateral integration', *Journal of Political Economy* 94: 691–719.

GULATI, R., and S. D. EPPINGER 1996. 'The coupling of product architecture and organizational structure decisions', Working Paper No. 3906, Sloan School of Management, Cambridge, MA.

HAYEK, F. VON 1945. 'The use of knowledge in society', *American Economic Review* 35(4): 519–30.

HEINER, R. A. 1983. 'The origin of predictable behavior', *American Economic Review* 73(4): 560–95.

HENDERSON, R. 1994. 'The evolution of integrative capability: Innovation in cardiovascular drug discovery', *Industrial and Corporate Change* 3(3): 607–30.

—— and K. B. CLARK 1990. 'Architectural innovation: The reconfiguration of existing product technologies and the failure of established firms', *Administrative Science Quarterly* 35: 9–30.

—— and I. COCKBURN 1994. 'Measuring competence? Exploring firm effects in pharmaceutical research', *Strategic Management Journal* 15: 63–84.

HIPPEL, E. VON 1994. ' "Sticky information" and the locus of problem solving: Implications for innovation', *Management Science* 40(4): 429–39.

KOGUT, B., and U. ZANDER 1996. 'What do firms do? Co-ordination, identity, and learning', *Organization Science* 7(5): 502–18.

KROGH, G. VON, and J. ROOS 1995. 'A perspective on knowledge, competence and strategy', *Personnel Review* 24(3): 56–76.

—— —— and K. SLOCUM 1994. 'An essay on corporate epistemology', *Strategic Management Journal* 15: 53–71.

LANGLOIS, R. N. 1989. 'Economic change and the boundaries of the firm', *Journal of Institutional and Theoretical Economics* 144(4): 635–57.

—— and P. L. ROBERTSON 1995. *Firms, Markets and Economic Change.* London and New York: Routledge.

LEONARD-BARTON, D. 1992. 'Core capabilities and core rigidities: A paradox in managing new product development', *Strategic Management Journal* 13: 111–25.

LOASBY, B. J. 1976. *Choice, Complexity and Ignorance.* Cambridge: Cambridge University Press.

—— 1994. 'Organizational capabilities and inter-firm relations', *Metroeconomica* 45(3): 248–65.

—— 1996. 'The organization of industry', in N. J. FOSS, and C. Knudson, eds., *Towards a Competence Theory of the Firm.* London: Routledge, 38–53.

—— 1998. 'The organization of capabilities', *Journal of Economic Behavior & Organization* 35(2): 139–60.

MARCH, J. G., and H. A. SIMON 1958. *Organizations.* New York: Wiley.

MILGROM, P., and J. ROBERTS 1992 *Economics, Organization and Management.* Englewood Cliffs, NJ: Prentice Hall.

NELSON, R. R., and S .G. WINTER 1982. *An Evolutionary Theory of Economic Change.* Cambridge, MA: Belknap Press.

PFAFFMANN, E., and B. M. BENSAOU 1998. 'Mercedes-Benz and "Swatch": Inventing the smart and the networked organization', INSEAD Case Study No. 07/98-4765. Fontainebleau: INSEAD.

—— and S. SCHEUBLE 1998. 'Eine wissensbasierte Erklärung der vertikalen Grenzen einheitlicher Entscheidungshoheit', Discussion paper, Hohenheim University, Ludwig Maximilians University, Munich.

POLANYI, M. 1966. *The Tacit Dimension*. London: Routledge & Kegan Paul.

RICHARDSON, G. B. 1972. 'The organization of industry', *Economic Journal* 82(2): 883–96.

ROBERTSON, P. L., and R. N. LANGLOIS 1995. 'Innovation, networks, and vertical integration', *Research Policy* 24: 543–62.

RYLE, G. 1949. *The Concept of Mind*. London: Macmillan.

SANCHEZ, R. 1996. 'Strategic product creation: Managing new interactions of technology, markets, and organizations', *European Management Journal* 14(2): 121–38.

—— 1997. 'Managing articulated knowledge in competence-based competition', in R. Sanchez and A. Heene, eds., *Strategic Learning and Knowledge Management*. Chichester: Wiley, 163–87.

—— and A. HEENE 1997. 'Competence-based strategic management: Concepts, and issues for theory, research, and practice', in A. Heene and R. Sanchez, eds., *Competence-based Strategic Management*. Chichester: Wiley, 3–42.

—— and J. T. MAHONEY 1996. 'Modularity, flexibility, and knowledge management in product and organization design', *Strategic Management Journal* 17 (Winter Special Issue): 63–76.

—— A. HEENE, and H. THOMAS 1996. 'Introduction: Towards the theory and practice of competence-based competition', in R. Sanchez, A. Heene, and H. Thomas, eds., *Dynamics of Competence-based Competition*. Oxford: Pergamon Press, 1–35.

SCHEUBLE, SVEN 1998. *Wissen und Wissenssurrogate: Eine Theorie der Unternehmung*. Wiesbaden: Gabler.

SCHRADER, S., and J. GOEPFERT 1997. 'Task partitioning among manufacturers and suppliers', in H. G. Gemünden, T. Ritter, and A. Walter, eds., *Relationships and Networks in International Markets*. Oxford: Pergamon Press, 248–68.

SIMON, H. A. 1962. 'The architecture of complexity', *Proceedings of the American Philosophical Society* 106(6): 467–82.

—— 1996. *The Sciences of the Artificial*, 3rd edn. Cambridge, MA, and London: MIT Press.

TEECE, D. J. 1986. 'Profiting from technological innovation: Implications for integration, collaboration, licensing and public policy', *Research Policy*, 15: 285–305.

THOMPSON, J. D. 1967. *Organizations in Action: Social Science Bases of Administrative Theory* . New York: McGraw-Hill.

ULRICH, K. 1995. ' The role of product architecture in the manufacturing firm', *Research Policy* 24: 419–40.

—— and S. D. EPPINGER 1995. *Product Design and Development*. New York: McGraw-Hill.

VEN, A. VAN DE, A. L. DELBECQ, and R. KOENIG, JR. 1976. 'Determinants of coordination modes within organizations', *American Sociological Review* 41: 332–8.

WILLIAMSON, O. E. 1985. *The Economic Institutions of Capitalism: Firms, Markets, Relational Contracting.* New York: Free Press.

—— 1998. 'Transaction cost economics: How it works; Where it is headed', *De Economist* 146(1): 23–58.

WINTER, S. G. 1988. 'On Coase, competence, and the corporation', *Journal of Law, Economics, and Organization* 4(1): 163–80.

13

Inter-Firm Collaboration: Contractual and Capabilities-Based Perspectives

ANOOP MADHOK

1. Introduction

The recognition of collaboration as an indispensable tool in the successful conduct of business today is manifested in the phenomenal increase in the number of collaborative ventures between firms in recent years, both domestic and international. Paradoxically, however, the level of dissatisfaction with their outcome, in the light of their intended purpose, tends to be high (Parkhe 1993*a*; Dodgson 1993; Pearce 1997). The unprecedented popularity of yet simultaneous dissatisfaction with collaborations seems incongruent. However, it also poses an interesting intellectual puzzle with respect to the formation and management of collaborations, one which opens up a potentially fruitful area of research with important implications for theory and practice. It raises three related questions: Why do firms collaborate? Why do collaborations evidence so much difficulty in attaining their intended purpose? And what can firms do to reduce such dissatisfaction?

The goal of this chapter is to extend the current state of understanding of the above questions, mainly the latter two. The first question has to do with organizational form while the second and third have to do with the process of managing inter-firm collaborations.[1] Osborn and Hagedoorn (1997) have contended that the study of collaborations is both in need of and ripe for more integrative theoretical development of a kind which combines multifaceted approaches to the phenomenon in a more complex and sophisticated manner. Responding to this call, this chapter builds upon and combines two currently prominent theoretical approaches in order to address these questions—one more contractually focused and primarily concerned with the difficulties and costs of transacting and the other oriented more towards the organizational capabilities of firms.[2]

---

[1] In this chapter, although I address both form and process, my primary interest lies in the latter, with the discussion of the former serving primarily to provide the platform upon which I build the subsequent arguments.

[2] Capabilities are more dynamic and refer to the ability to manage the more static resources. Moreover, capabilities and their underlying routines can be considered as forms of knowledge about

Transaction cost (CT) theory (Williamson 1975, 1985) places prime importance on the contractability of the transaction. It is principally concerned with the potential for opportunistic behaviour in economic interactions and with the design of contractual mechanisms to safeguard against such behaviour. In a nutshell, the theory posits that, in the light of the opportunistic tendency of economic actors, firms seek the most efficient means by which to organize an activity, such efficiency being defined in terms of economizing on TC. This is occasioned through the fit between transaction and governance characteristics, such fit being the driving force underlying the choice of organizational form— be it a pure market, a hierarchy, or a collaborative hybrid. Here, the governance characteristics of the hybrid form are of a level which is intermediate between markets and hierarchies (Williamson 1991*a*).

Organizational capabilities theory places greater emphasis on the bounded rationality of firms and envisions the firm as a repository of knowledge and capabilities—both generic and idiosyncratic—which provides the prime source of its competitive advantage but also behaves as a constraint. The primary concern here is the pursuit of competitive advantage through the efficient and effective development and deployment of a firm's capabilities (Winter 1988; Madhok 1996; Langlois and Robertson 1995; Teece, Pisano, and Shuen 1997) as it goes about conducting its economic activities. From this approach, the reason for collaborations between firms is to combine synergistically two sets of complementary but dissimilar resources and capabilities in a manner which will generate greater returns than will either a market transaction or complete internalization (Madhok and Tallman 1998; Loasby 1994; Richardson 1972).[3]

The two theories were originally developed to address different questions: governance and competitive advantage respectively. Accordingly, the TC perspective addresses the firm primarily in terms of its governance and exchange attributes rather than its productive attributes, whereas the primary interest of the capabilities perspective is in the productive attributes of firms (Winter 1988), and the associated competitive advantage, rather than the governance attributes. Yet, if we bear in mind that the essence of firm strategy is the search for economic rents (Rumelt 1984; Teece 1990; Lado, Boyd, and Hanlon 1997), there is an

---

how to carry out productive tasks (Langlois and Robertson 1995; Kogut and Zander 1992). Although one can get into detailed semantics about the difference between capabilities, competences, knowledge, know-how, and the like, for the purposes of this chapter, and for convenience, I do not distinguish between these various terms but use them interchangeably to denote, along with resources, the collective technological, organizational, and ultimately commercial capacity of the firm. That is, for convenience, the capabilities-based view is used as an 'umbrella' term to include all the above.

[3] There might be reasons for collaborations other than TC- or capability-related ones, for example, strategic rivalry ones such as pre-emptively blocking a competitor's move. These are acknowledged but are not the focus of this chapter.

element of convergence across the two theories in the broader sense, in that both production and governance relations are central to the earning of rents.

In spite of the differing orientations, the domain of the two theories has begun to overlap in recent years. Capability-based arguments have been applied to the issue of firm boundaries (Kogut and Zander 1992; Madhok 1996, 1997; Langlois and Robertson 1995; Conner 1991), traditionally the concern of TC theory. Similarly, TC theory argues that efficient governance results in competitive advantage, and that TC economics deals with many of the key issues pertinent to the behaviour and organization of firms, with which business strategy is concerned or should be concerned (Williamson 1991*b*). With respect to collaborations, both TC (Williamson 1991*a*; Balakrishnan and Koza 1993; Hennart 1998) and capabilities-based (Eisenhardt and Schoonhoven 1996; Hamel, Doz, and Prahalad 1989) arguments have been utilized as a basis for furthering understanding of inter-firm collaboration.

Although the two theories respectively offer useful insights, their differences in basic orientation as well as in primary emphases—costs and benefits respectively— have resulted in their evolving in parallel and somewhat independent of one another. (Teece's work (for example 1982, 1986) is a notable exception.) It is important to address this lacuna since production and exchange are both essential and frequently interdependent counterparts in the conduct of economic activity. A more integrative and comprehensive approach towards the topic, one which stresses the interrelatedness of these two perspectives with respect to governance and competitive advantage, would not only address this lacuna but also contribute towards further insight into increasingly important economic phenomena such as inter-firm collaborations. This is the task that the chapter seeks to accomplish.

Researchers tracking the trend have observed that the overwhelming majority of collaborations being formed today occur in rapidly changing industries and involve complex linkages in technology, research and development, and other knowledge-intensive activities (Hagedoorn 1993) that tend to be characterized by reciprocal knowledge flows of a tacit nature (Mowery, Oxley, and Silverman 1997). This chapter is accordingly concerned with primarily those inter-firm collaborative relationships (IFRs) which are characterized by potential synergies of a more substantive kind, arising from 'the combining of complementary, but scarce, resources or capabilities (typically through multiple functional interfaces), which results in the joint creation of unique new products, services or technologies' (Dyer and Singh 1998: 662). Such IFRs often involve relationship-specific investments as well as substantial sharing of knowledge and enable firms to accomplish activities which they could not perform otherwise, at least not as cost effectively.[4]

---

[4] More than the actual legal form, the key issue in these collaborations is the strategic intent to combine the relevant organizational resources and capabilities of two (or more) partners in the search for a sustainable competitive advantage.

Synergy tends to remain a somewhat underspecified concept in the literature, which largely takes a more static and snapshot approach towards synergy, that is, that aspect of synergy which is visible *ex ante* on the surface due to seeming complementarities. This, however, ignores that such synergy, while potentially available, may be unattainable without concomitant and relationship-specific organizational complementarities.[5] Besides enabling realization of the more visible synergies, a more dynamic and evolutionary argument would suggest that organizational synergy—the ability to relate to one another (culture, systems, personnel, mindset, etc.)—over the course of the relationship could also enable firms jointly to uncover opportunities which it might not have been possible to anticipate *ex ante* from a static and structural assessment alone.

Drawing upon the discussion of synergy above, I take the position here that even though TC may be a consideration, the essential reason, one which can be taken as an underlying assumption (Powell 1990), why two firms enter into a relationship is that they anticipate the generation of idiosyncratic (that is collaboration-specific) rents through synergistic and interdependent complementarities (Dietrich 1994; Zajac and Olsen 1993; Jarillo 1988). Yet there is a crucial distinction between the latent synergistic potential and the actual realization of such potential, which then places a premium on a firm's 'collaborating technology'.

In making my arguments, I utilize a novel conceptual tool as an indicator of a firm's 'collaborating technology', namely the Type I/Type II TC ratio, and apply it to further our insight into the management of collaborations. Type I TC entails the search, selection, evaluation, bargaining, and enforcement costs traditionally associated with TC theory, assuming potential opportunism. Type II TC refers broadly to the costs dedicated towards persuading, training, teaching, and learning, and generally 'educating' one another. While Type I TC is primarily oriented towards protection against opportunistic behaviour, the Type II TC, which is more concerned with firm capabilities, is of a more dynamic nature and is more explicitly oriented towards the active and actual creation and realization of entrepreneurial rents through inter-firm collaborative relationships.[6] I expand

---

[5] The two dimensions can be viewed as the 'hard' and 'soft' dimensions of synergy, each of which is necessary but not sufficient.

[6] Milgrom and Roberts (1992) also distinguish between two types of costs: motivation based and co-ordination based. While the former stem from the potential for opportunism, the latter stem from the costs of information transmission, namely, acquisition, assimilation, and dissemination, associated with the process of search, selection, and negotiation. The Type II cost in this chapter differs in that, as will become apparent, it is associated more with the entrepreneurial management of relationships in line with the active creation of value. Also, while my approach towards Type II TC is closer to that of Langlois (1992), the treatment is distinctly different in two ways. First, Langlois's argument is more unilateral in its orientation in that, as a result of differences in firm capabilities, an innovating firm that possesses some unique know-how faces difficulties and costs in earning rents by transacting through inter-firm organization. Instead, I much more visibly emphasize joint creation of value, and the quality of the relationship that underlies this. Secondly, as will

upon and demonstrate the significance of this second kind of TC in some detail.[7]

2. The Firm as a Manager: Contractual and Capability-Based Considerations

From the standpoint of this chapter, firms do not compete on the basis of costs alone but rather on the basis of overall value (Madhok 1996, 1997; Zajac and Olson 1993; Dyer 1997). Value is envisioned as the net rent-earning capacity of an asset or resource, tangible or intangible. Rather than seek efficiency through economizing on (transaction) costs, the value perspective approaches boundary-related phenomena in terms of cost effectiveness with respect to rent-earning capacity over the longer term (Madhok and Tallman 1998). This is comprised of both a static and a dynamic dimension.

Value can conceptually be unpacked and disaggregated into two aspects: that which can be anticipated and that which cannot. In the former case, the desired outcome can be considered as a given and the predominant concern is the most economical means of attaining this outcome. In the latter case, value cannot be fully contemplated in advance since it is partially occasioned through the dynamic process of interaction among economic actors. As a result, the benefits are variable, are only partially specifiable up front, and are partially generated through the behaviour and conduct of the parties concerned. Essentially, the future is continually being created on the basis of current and real-time actions, and partner resources and capabilities tend to co-evolve over time. This argument has important implications and emphasizes the need for entrepreneurship, especially in more fluid and tacit situations.

The distinction between the two aspects of value is underlined in Dyer and Singh's (1998) distinction between efficient and effective governance. While efficient governance may yield relational rents through lower TC, effective governance, and the associated mechanisms, allow additional collaboration-specific rents through value-creating initiatives that enable a greater realization of synergies than may be possible otherwise (see also Madhok and Tallman 1998). Effective governance impacts on critical issues such as the nature and extent of specialized investments, knowledge sharing, etc. Such initiatives, whether in technology to support the transaction or in specialized routines that

be evident from the arguments in the subsequent sections, I am more specifically interested in the allocation of expenditures between the two types and the implications thereof.

[7] I focus mostly on non-opportunism-based Type II TC and the implications thereof in the subsequent analysis. The reason for this is twofold: the arguments underlying the opportunism-based TC are well known and the arguments underlying Type II TC, and the relations between the two types, is where the significance of this chapter lies. The position I take on opportunism is that the assumption of potential opportunism is necessary but certainly not sufficient for the fuller attainment of value.

facilitate co-ordination and knowledge transfer, behave as efficiency-enhancing investments that translate into both greater revenue (for example through greater quality, speed of development, etc.) and lower costs (for example through superior production technology, communication economies, etc). (Nickerson 1998). In fact, such initiatives can become unique and inimitable assets which then form the basis of sustainable competitive advantage (ibid.). Yet it is difficult, if not impossible, to contract for such value-creation initiatives, such as sharing fine-grained tacit knowledge, exchanging resources that are difficult to price, or offering innovations or responsiveness not explicitly called for in the contract (Dyer and Singh 1998).

To anticipate some of the key arguments in the rest of the chapter, the actual value attained through an IFR depends not just on what resources are combined, but on how this combination is accomplished. This difference has to do with the explicit recognition that the relationship is in and of itself a potential value-bearing asset and, accordingly, that expenditures specific to the relationship not only are costs but also act as investments in future value (Madhok and Tallman 1998). The shift in orientation towards transaction-specific expenditures from costs to investment in future value is critical to value creation and realization. The Type II TC is central to this process. Inadequate appreciation of Type II costs would detract from the value potentially available through IFRs, yet attention to this value requires a fundamental attitudinal shift toward collaborations, one which significantly influences how firms approach and structure their interaction with other firms. This does not mean to suggest that opportunism and opportunism-based TCs are not important but, rather, that the *level* and *composition* of the two types of costs, as they apply to a particular situation, are critical factors.

But first let us briefly examine the two theories' preference for IFRs from a value perspective. As mentioned, from the organizational capabilities view, IFRs are considered attractive when they support the firm's search for sustainable rents through the efficient and effective development and deployment of capabilities in situations where competitive advantage requires the synergistic combination of resources which a firm is unable to develop in-house in a timely and cost-effective manner or to purchase through a market transaction (Madhok and Tallman 1998; Loasby 1994). The constraint on internal development lies in the path-dependent nature of knowledge. On the other hand, the constraint on arm's-length market exchange lies in the inherent incapacity of the price mechanism to support the nature and extent of the interaction that undergirds the fuller realization of substantive synergies (Loasby 1994; Richardson 1972; Powell 1990).

The general argument of the TC perspective above is not necessarily incompatible with the capability argument above. For example, TC theory also reasons that markets are better at exchanging more general and substitutable resources. The focus, however, is different: the pursuit of efficient governance by aligning governance and transaction characteristics in a TC minimizing manner, under the assumption of potential opportunism. Particularly central to TC economics is the notion of the transaction specificity of assets (Williamson 1985, 1991*a*; Klein, Crawford, and Alchian 1978). Basically, transaction-specific investment transforms an *ex ante* market scenario of competitive bidding into an *ex post* 'unmarket-like', small numbers bargaining situation since, once the investment is made, a firm is locked into the transaction due to switching costs and therefore rendered vulnerable to opportunistic rent-extracting behaviour. As the level of such investment increases, it escalates the risks associated with transacting through the mechanism of the market and results in a preference for hierarchical governance. Here, IFRs (or organizational hybrids in TC parlance) occupy the middle ground and tend to be preferred when the transaction is characterized by an intermediate level of asset specificity. This is so since the characteristics of the hybrid governance structure, such as intermediate levels of adaptability to changing circumstances, of incentive intensity in terms of the linkage between effort and outcome, and of administrative control between markets and hierarchies, tend to be more optimally in alignment with the transaction characteristics (Williamson 1991*a*).

Note that from both the theories, if a firm resorts to an IFR, it is because this form is deemed more attractive than the alternatives for organizing the particular activity, in line with the respective concerns of the two theories. Yet the focal concerns are fundamentally different. In contrast to economizing on TC, the superiority of IFRs from the capability perspective lies in the ability to generate greater rents than other organizational forms as a result of synergies.

With respect to the two aspects of value distinguished earlier, it becomes fairly apparent that TC economics is primarily concerned with the more static aspect of value, with the primary consideration in the choice of an organizational form being the comparative differential in TC (Jones and Hill 1988; Madhok 1996). In effect, the theory (implicitly) assumes that the desired outcome is a given. Since there are various impediments to attaining this outcome, which increase the costs and difficulties associated with effecting the transaction, the net benefit of organizing it through various governance forms must reflect these costs in the overall cost-benefit calculus. Yet, the benefit, and the primary source of value, is expressed implicitly in the form of lower (transaction) costs and the appropriate governance structure is the one which has the greatest cost efficiency in attaining this outcome.

To further elaborate on this point, while on the one hand Williamson (1985: 61) states that the choice of governance structure (in a comparative static analysis) depends on a comparison of the sum of production and transaction costs across organizational forms, and recognizes that trade-offs are possible, yet in substance, to correct for prior neglect, the exposition of the argument concentrates almost exclusively on TC at the expense of underemphasizing production costs (Williamson 1985, 1988a).[8] Accordingly, inputs, outputs, technology, and prices are held constant (Nickerson 1998; Foss 1994) and the choice effectively rests on a TC assessment (Williamson 1985: 71),[9] where TCs vary, being lowest when the level of asset specificity of the investment is matched to the degree of internalization (Williamson 1991a).

Such a treatment, however, results in the rent potential, rooted in the manner in which resources are created and utilized, being implicitly (and unrealistically) held constant across organizational forms (Dietrich 1994; Conner 1991), and leaves little room for entrepreneurial rent creation (Foss 1994). This more dynamic aspect of value is an important thrust of the capabilities perspective. The heretofore neglected but intrinsic interdependence between the two theories in the pursuit of rents by firms promises to yield greater insight into the rent-generation and realization process. This is the focus of the next section.

3. Managing Inter-Firm Collaboration: The Interdependence of the Two Perspectives

As I explain in this section, the realization of synergistic benefits through the combination of complementary resources and capabilities is not independent of the TCs incurred in doing so. Similarly, the TCs incurred in the exchange of resources are not independent of the nature of the resources to be transacted (see also Madhok and Tallman 1998). This raises the question of what really is required in order to realize the synergistic potential. Type II TCs play an important role in this context. Dahlman (1979) argues that all TCs are ultimately information costs associated with lack of information and bounded rationality. On a somewhat related note, Demsetz (1988) contends that information costs are an intrinsic component of TCs but in a more fundamental way than theories such as TC contemplate. I embellish this argument and demonstrate how the creation and realization of value through IFRs necessarily involve TCs of both types.

3.1. Type I TC

In the search for value through IFRs, partner compatibility, in terms of both compatibility of vision, direction, and general outlook as well as more specific resources and competences, is especially important (Geringer 1988; Dodgson 1993) since it affects both the synergistic rent potential and the ability to realize

---

[8] To be more accurate, differences in production costs are allowed in Williamson's (1985, 1996) approach. These are, however, primarily in the form of economies of scale that distinguish suppliers from in-house production. Technology is still held constant.

[9] Accordingly, as Ring (1997) points out, most of those who work in the TC framework in the management field have tended to focus narrowly on TC.

such rents. The partner-selection process necessarily entails the incurrence of TCs, such as search, selection, evaluation, negotiation, and enforcement costs, in order to safeguard against opportunism (Williamson 1985). Two issues, both directly related to TC theory, are important for anticipated rents to be more fully realized: adverse selection and moral hazard. Both of these have to do with information asymmetries due to bounded rationality and can have detrimental consequences with respect to the choice of partner. Adverse selection is concerned with the ability of the partner to provide the complementary resources and capabilities, and with reducing the probability of misrepresentation of such capabilities. On the other hand, moral hazard is concerned with the willingness and commitment of a partner to provide the requisite resources and capabilities, and with reducing the probability of opportunistic behaviour, once the investment is in place, in pursuit of a greater share of the income stream. Both the adverse selection and moral hazard problems therefore increase TCs.

Vulnerability to opportunistic behaviour increases in situations where a partner's behaviour is not readily transparent. Ironically, while tacit resources and capabilities are often valuable and frequently underlie IFR formation, they are also more difficult and costly to identify and evaluate *ex ante* and ultimately transact (Chi 1994; Dyer and Singh 1998). By their very nature (being intangible, complex, embedded), they intensify the extent of information asymmetries between partners as well as the extent of ambiguity in specification, measurement, and evaluation of input, output, or contribution. This aggravates the adverse selection and moral hazard concerns by creating more scope for opportunistic behaviour and, consequently, increases the difficulties and costs of transacting. These concerns are further exacerbated by the fact that, in order to realize the underlying purpose of transferring, absorbing, and, more generally, effectively combining complementary capabilities at the heart of the IFR, the firm also exposes such organizational resources and capabilities to the partner firm (Hamel 1991).

Note, however, and this is a crucial point, that even when there is no opportunistic intent, firms still face difficulties in combining their resources successfully. One needs to differentiate between resource complementarity, which leads firms to co-operate for economic purposes, and the organizational and process dimension which creates strains and makes IFRs difficult to maintain and to manage (Tallman and Shenkar 1994; Parkhe 1991). In this regard, a number of authors (Dodgson 1994; Ring and van de Ven 1994) have emphasized the inordinate amount of time and effort that it takes and the long-term perspective required to build a compatible framework and create the 'intimate connection' (Loasby 1994) necessary to realize the true value of the relationship. Cultivating such relations increases the relationship management costs.

3.2. Type II TC

It is important to keep in mind the important distinction between avoiding a negative and creating a positive (Conner 1991; Madhok 1995). The TC argument above (Type I TC) was oriented towards protecting against opportunism, which could potentially occur as a result of information asymmetries due to bounded rationality. In contrast to safeguarding behaviour, however, an alternative course of behaviour is to reduce the extent of asymmetry through sharing information, thus occasioning a greater cognitive alignment. However, this also entails TC, albeit of a different kind (Type II TC), one which is associated more closely with the active creation and realization of value.

The gist of the argument, basically rooted in the capabilities-based view of the firm, is that the set of resources and capabilities in a firm's possession arises cumulatively from its past experiences. The bounded rationality of firms, along with the subjective and path-dependent nature of knowledge and capability accumulation, results in the perception, attention, processing, and action-selection processes of firms being filtered, shaped, and generally biased and even constrained by their particular histories. The net outcome is that firms perceive, interpret, evaluate, and act on different things and even on the same things differently. This can lead to genuine differences between firms, even if there is an intention to co-operate (Beije 1996; Dietrich 1996; Conner and Prahalad 1996). In other words, there are 'natural' frictions between economic actors which are rooted in bounded rationality and information asymmetries as a result of idiosyncratic differences in their knowledge base.

Dietrich (1996) argues for the need to separate issues related to opportunism from those related to conflicting cognitions and cognitive distance arising from bounded rationality. This issue deserves more careful consideration since it has important implications. While complementarities may have been the motive behind the IFR, fuller creation and attainment of value requires firms to reduce cognitive distance between them and to mutually align themselves in order to appreciate each other's needs and capabilities and to adapt their own needs and capabilities accordingly (Beije 1996; Nooteboom 1996). Thus, the alignment here, rather than being one between transaction and governance characteristics, is more one of cognition between the transacting parties. Creating such a mutual alignment requires a substantial level of communication and information flows of a richer and more textured nature, richer than would be attainable through more formal and arm's-length contractual exchange, which in turn facilitates mutual knowledge transfer, absorption, and synthesis through the presence of a variety of mechanisms. Examples in firms would be joint cross-functional teams at each other's sites, frequent joint meetings, closer and more sustained interaction among boundary personnel at various levels, harmonizing of management systems for particular purposes, and the like. Clark and Fujimoto (1991) show, for example, how greater information sharing and interaction among design engineers from buying and supplying firms allowed them to read and interpret blueprints more accurately, reduce errors, rapidly disseminate and absorb new, particularly tacit, knowledge, improve quality, and hasten new product development.

True value creation and realization, therefore, emerge through the process of interaction and consequent learning and adapting between firms. The potential for value arises from the unique and diverse but complementary knowledge that firms bring to the particular activity, while overlapping or common knowledge enables disparate bodies of knowledge to combine more easily by increasing each other's competence or ability to interpret and make sense of information in a similar manner. On the one hand, then, greater cognitive distance increases the 'natural' friction in interaction and the difficulty and cost of interacting in a value-creating manner, even more so in the case of fast-changing environments where there is a scope for greater cognitive divergence as events unfold. On the other hand, greater cognitive convergence brings the communication between sender and receiver more into alignment and thereby provides a common platform for engaging in such interaction for the joint creation of value (Beije 1996; Nooteboom 1996). There is a necessary and delicate balance between the two.

In essence then, realization of underlying value within an IFR requires that the transacting partners proactively and entrepreneurially engage in the relationship and make relationally oriented investments, as I illustrate below. However, the bridging of cognitive differences involves additional TC of a different kind, one that is more dynamic in nature (Langlois 1992) and involves transaction-specific investments in the form of expenditures—not just monies but also time, effort, and sheer managerial energy—dedicated towards persuading, training, teaching, and learning, and generally 'educating' each other in order to (a) bring about greater inter-firm alignment and (b) jointly embark on actions conducive to entrepreneurial discovery.

3.3. 'Collaborating Technology': The Type I:Type II TC Ratio

To paraphrase the argument above, the potential for synergistic complementarities which motivates firms to collaborate simultaneously requires them to incur greater expenditures in cultivating the relationship in order to realize the very potential. Interestingly, dissimilar but complementary skills provide scope for greater synergistic value, yet the resultant greater cognitive distance would call for higher Type II expenditures to realize it. At the same time though, greater cognitive asymmetries due to the dissimilarities also occasion the need for higher Type I TC in order to safeguard against exploitation of such asymmetry by the partner. In both cases, the situation is exacerbated when tacit resources are involved, since the embeddedness both increases the complexity of combining them, in order to realize the underlying synergies, and increases the transactional difficulties.

From a stricter interpretation of TC theory, not only would the rent-seeking firm strive for the most efficient form in terms of TC but would, furthermore, try to attain the minimum TC feasible within this form. Yet, to the extent that the operational specification is TC economizing and not TC minimizing, the difference between the minimal level of TC between IFRs and the next lowest organizational form represents the amount of latitude that the firm has in making transaction-specific expenditures, over and above strict TC minimizing ones, while still remaining the TC economizing form of organizing.

But why should a firm undertake such costs under the assumption that the other may be an opportunistic actor? This is a legitimate question. On the one hand, the resolution of differences between firms can be attempted through further strictures on firms' behaviour and actions through contractual safeguards (Type I TC). On the other hand, another avenue for resolving differences is through Type II TC which, the reader will recall, is oriented towards 'education' in the form of cognitive alignment in the pursuit of value. Clearly, with an expectation of opportunism, firms would be reluctant to make unilateral and voluntary commitments outside the terms of the contract, and would tend to perceive a greater need to take costly and elaborate safeguards (Parkhe 1993a; Ring and van de Ven 1992; Lado, Boyd, and Hanlon 1997). This reduces the level of value created and realized through the relationship (Hill 1990; Pearce 1997; Dyer 1997).

Broadly speaking, a firm would be willing to incur additional transaction-specific expenditures only if doing so enabled it to realize greater synergies than it could have attained in the absence of such expenditures, and of a magnitude large enough to offset the increase in expenditures. That is, it would do so when the additional benefits justify the additional costs, thus increasing the net value realized. In other words, such transaction-specific expenditures are of a value-creating nature and can be considered an investment in the relationship which potentially yields subsequent returns. Without such relationally oriented investments, the dynamic aspect of value will be sacrificed. However, to capture this, firms need to incur costs. A careful balance must be struck between the two. The pay-off is in future benefits, which could be in terms of both forbearance of opportunistic behaviour and greater and more willing contributions towards the relationship. In fact, a firm may even choose to incur such specific expenditures to the point where IFRs are no longer the TC minimizing form, so long as there are sufficient returns from doing so.

The key argument here is that full exploitation of the underlying value of collaborative relationships requires a different mindset, oriented towards value maximization rather than cost minimization, which entails treating the relationship intrinsically as a potential asset and, accordingly, making transaction-specific investments in the relationship itself. To the extent that the value is attached uniquely to a particular relationship and unavailable outside it, whether in another organizational form or in another inter-firm collaboration, the relationship can also be considered a specialized asset. The rents earned by firms through the IFR are related directly to the quality of the relationship, the development of which can therefore be considered as an investment in future value (Madhok and Tallman 1998). In this regard, while on the one hand 'transaction costs become a sunk cost of relationship development inhibiting mobility' (Dietrich 1994: 10; Pearce 1997), on the other, such expenditures behave as relational (and asset-specific) investments and positive relational signals which enable the co-ordination of commitments in the process of creating and realizing the associated value. Such signals are important when we remember that the efficient and effective flows of richer and more complex information across firms' boundaries are difficult to attain without more flexible and committed interaction.

The need for both Type I and Type II TC is especially high in the initial stages of a relationship. Higher Type I expenditures during the initial stages of the relationship increase TC up front but, by reducing the adverse selection and moral hazard problems, may lower it over the longer term since less monitoring and enforcement would be required (Jarillo 1988; Ring and van de Ven 1994; Dyer 1997; Parkhe 1993a). Moreover, with respect to Type II TC, a pattern of mutually oriented interaction from the outset has the potential both to generate greater confidence and to enable the formation of norms which facilitate co-ordination and reduce the probability and scope of conflict later (Madhok 1995; Ring and van de Ven 1994). As a result of Type II expenditures, the governance of the relationship begins to shift in emphasis from a formal and contractual nature to a more informal and mutually oriented one (Parkhe 1993a; Ring and van de Ven 1994; Pearce 1997; Dyer 1997).

Basically, the above suggests that the relationship within which the transaction is embedded must be actively managed in order to benefit from it. The ensuing paragraphs examine this argument more carefully through an illustrative example.

What will happen if a co-operating firm is confronted with a situation where a partner, in whose competences it may have a critical (even if limited) interest, misuses an asset or fails to meet contractual specifications, that is, the partner engages in seemingly opportunistic behaviour? To protect against this eventuality, firms would need to incur Type I costs, say through the deployment of on-site personnel for monitoring purposes, in order to safeguard against the abuse of an asset through opportunism. Note, however, that non-performance in the form of behaviour by a partner who diverges from his commitments may not in fact be due to any opportunistic intent but could be due simply to honest misunderstanding, misinterpretation of environmental signals, or inadequate capabilities on his part. The distinction is important since, in such a case, what appeared to be an action of 'defection', being actually unintentional, was really not so. Given that mutual synergies still exist, that is, that there are potential joint gains from co-operation, such a situation may require expenditures of a Type II kind to correct it, in the form of teaching, training, etc. A simplistic and vengeful 'eye for an eye and a tooth for a tooth' response may potentially be shortsighted in the context of long-term value. In fact, where there are significant size asymmetries, such a response could have the effect of a 'knockout punch' on the partner or, at least, even without size asymmetries, on the relationship (Dixit and Nalebuff 1991).[10]

Instead, in order to generate and realize value, the firm may need to monitor closely how the asset or technology is being developed and employed, since this enables the firm to supervise, teach, and guide its application and use and, in general, to facilitate or even ensure that the relevant activities have been understood and are being performed in the requisite manner in line with the buyer's particular needs.

This argument becomes even more significant when the two parties are engaged in the pursuit of a mutually beneficial joint discovery, which by its nature cannot be fully anticipated in advance. For one thing, a Type II orientation enables the focal firm itself to learn and better understand what is hindering the appropriate utilization and application of the technology or asset as anticipated. Moreover, in addition to understanding the supplier's competences and needs, the firm may find that there was some 'noise' in the communication process and that it was unable adequately to communicate its own needs and competences to the supplier. The importance of the user in the innovation process has been emphasized by von Hippel (1988).

In other words monitoring, as well as being a policing device, can also play an educational role, in terms of providing an occasion for mutual teaching/learning. Such teaching/learning not only facilitates value creation through greater cognitive alignment but, at the same time, by lowering information asymmetries through greater sharing of information, reduces the potential for opportunism (Ring and van de Ven 1992; Dyer 1997). Therefore, there are both efficiency and effectiveness implications.

The difficulty of assessing a partner's performance and reacting appropriately can also be examined in a different light. For an opportunism-protecting regime to work effectively, it is necessary for firms to have unhindered ability to observe the partner's behaviour. If instead, as Kreps (1990) points out, one only observes

---

[10] Of course, this does not mean to suggest that repeated behaviour of this type should be tolerated. If non-performance continued to occur, for reasons to do with capabilities, it suggests a wrong choice of partner due to adverse selection (rather than moral hazard).

the outcome, which is found to be wanting, and the outcome is the result of a probabilistic rather than a deterministic (production) function, then one has to decide whether to impute deliberate defection or chance (or both) as the reason for the poor result. As can be imagined, with complex and multidimensional products/services, and especially those that involve innovative (knowledge-creating) aspects, such as product development, the outcome is always probabilistic to some extent and thus 'judgement' comes into the evaluation of the product/service delivered and the subsequent reaction.

In line with the above, monitoring, therefore, plays a dual function in guarding against dissipation of the rent stream, both through checking opportunistic behaviour and through facilitating the creation and realization of value. Now, if a firm places a team on-site primarily for purposes associated with value creation, then monitoring costs associated with Type I TC are basically incremental (Alston and Gillespie 1989). This does not negate the opportunism-protecting monitoring element but suggests that the balance, in terms of resource allocation—financial, temporal, managerial—between the two, will tilt towards actions more consonant with Type II TC. Similarly, where the monitoring is of a Type I nature, the costs associated with Type II TC are only incremental. In effect, the Type I:Type II TC ratio is an indicator of the quality of the relationship. While Type I TC may dominate in the earlier stages of the relationship (Parkhe 1993*a*, Ring and van de Ven 1994), the composite has the potential to shift towards Type II as the relationship progresses. Differently put, if the relationship evolves positively over time through a process of successful interaction, which draws the two actors closer together, then at some stage the relationship has the potential to undergo a 'fundamental transformation', in which the balance shifts from checking opportunism to creating value.

Process is important to Williamson also. He states (1988*b*: 71) that, 'Although TC economics is underdeveloped in process aspects, process arguments nevertheless play a prominent role', and then goes on to discuss the 'Fundamental Transformation' as the central processing element, where a 'locking in' to a small numbers bargaining situation may evolve through the gradual process of increasing the specificity of relations and assets between the two parties. Being concerned with protecting against the potential for opportunistic behaviour, the fundamental transformation proposed by Williamson clearly has more of a Type I nature. The fundamental transformation I propose (we can term it Type II fundamental transformation), in terms of managing the relationship in a manner that engineers a shift in the TC from a Type I to a Type II disposition, is of a clearly different nature since it is more oriented towards the active creation of value. It also develops in an important way the underdeveloped process aspect that Williamson notes.

The nature of the Type I:Type II balance puts into context Ghoshal and

Moran's (1996) argument that economic actors are, at their core, characterized by the potential for both self-interested and mutually oriented behaviour and are not predisposed towards one or the other, opportunism or co-operation. Rather, it is managerial action and the context surrounding such action that results in one or the other becoming operationally dominant. In other words, rather than being an assumption, as it is in TC theory, opportunism is a variable that can be managed. In this context, a number of authors have pointed out the trade-off involved when committing to a specialized investment, with productivity gains from specialization on the one hand and reduced flexibility due to switching costs on the other (Richardson 1972; Parkhe 1993a). What is being suggested here is that to realize value from these 'harder' flexibility-reducing commitments (examples of which include specialized designs or machinery), a firm may need to incur 'softer' transaction-specific commitments, the two going hand in hand in the pursuit of value. In fact, the latter also mitigate the potentially adverse impact associated with reduced flexibility, a point supported by Dyer's (1997) study of IFRs in the automotive industry.

4. Discussion and Implications

I have assumed in this chapter that a synergistic potential through resource combination underlies IFRs. Were this not so, then perhaps Type I TC to safeguard against opportunism would suffice to attain the intended outcome, and a value orientation would result in unnecessary expenditures of money, time, and energy without proportionate returns. However, given such potential, my argument is that firms which go beyond safeguarding against opportunism, and approach the relationship with an entrepreneurial bent and in a more proactive and positive manner, have a greater potential to generate and realize value more fully through synergistic relations. The de-emphasis on opportunism and cost minimization and the shift in frame from cost to value, and accordingly towards transaction-specific expenditures as investments in future value, have important implications for research, theory, and practice with respect to the management of IFRs and, for that matter, firm boundaries and economic organization and governance in general.

While I may have emphasized value creation and realization and de-emphasized opportunism, I am not suggesting that one should not pay heed to opportunism-related concerns, say in the form of unintended leakage of knowledge, or factor these concerns into the calculus through investment in protection mechanisms. Clearly, that is not the case and, of course, a firm needs to have recourse to safeguards. In fact, safeguards may enable a firm to undertake value-creating initiatives. The more important point is that Type I TC may not be sufficient in and of itself to realize more fully the potential synergies that IFRs occasion, and overemphasis on this point alone may be short-sighted in terms of value, a result which manifests itself through disappointment with the outcome of the collaboration.

From TC theory's predominant emphasis on rent distribution and (mis)appropriation by economic actors, each actor effectively assumes that the other would in all likelihood behave opportunistically and appropriate the knowledge of the other, and related rents, given the opportunity to do so. Accordingly, interaction becomes characterized by a more guarded and zero-sum nature, with each party intent on taking measures to safeguard against such an occurrence. Under such a scenario, there will tend to be relatively limited valuable flows of information, and consequent learning, which then hinder the pursuit of value. However, although the risk of leakage is ever present, there is a need to distinguish between the 'natural' knowledge flows, which are intrinsic elements of the conduct of normal commercial activity, and active opportunism in the form of deliberate and self-serving (mis)appropriation. From a value perspective, inward and outward information flows are a necessary, healthy, and integral part of the process of capability development and exploitation, benefiting the parties involved, and should be treated as such rather than as a leakage (Saxenian 1994).

In the light of the potential value of collaborations, opportunism-related concerns may therefore need to be traded off against the benefits (Mody 1993). In fact, given the effect of reputation (Hill 1990) and the difficulty in appropriating others' tacit knowledge due to bounded rationality (Langlois 1995), the trade-off may not be as ominous as it appears on the surface.

4.1. Implications for Theory Regarding Management of Firm Boundaries

Broadly speaking, from the standpoint of this chapter, a more apt representation of the behaviour of the modern firm would be as a manager of value. The strategy and organization of the firm, as represented, has more to do with how its resource/capability base can best be developed and co-ordinated, both internally and externally, so as to create and realize value. Such a perspective is particularly important in the current business context, which is characterized by a high incidence of inter-firm engagements, since it provides greater scope to the firm for more entrepreneurial behaviour than merely designing better contractual safeguards against opportunism. A shift from cost to value is a potentially pivotal one, where the fundamental question shifts from how exchange relationships can be structured to economize on TC to how they can be structured to maximize transaction value (Zajac and Olsen 1993; Dyer 1997). Accordingly, this chapter proposes a shift in relative focus from the form of governance, with its emphasis on the governance structure and formal safeguards against opportunism, to embrace also the process of governance, which has direct implications for the value creation and realization associated with exchange. The nature of governance plays a key role in the creation of relationship-specific rents by influencing not only TC (of a Type I nature) but also the willingness of partners to engage in value-creating initiatives (Dyer and Singh 1998: 669).

A true understanding of the relationship between economic organization and performance requires a closer appreciation of the value-creating aspects of different organizational modes (Lazonick 1991). In essence, in the context of IFRs, instead of the object of a transaction being viewed as something static and atemporal, in that it does not change during transfer, it is actually part of an active social and temporal process wherein it can be transformed in the course of inter-action. This argument supports Loasby's contention that 'What is at stake in most of these relationships is more than economizing of the transaction costs . . . such intimate connections are forms of organization which aid the growth of knowledge' (1994: 261). In a similar vein, Dietrich (1994: 4–5) emphasizes that:

In a dynamic setting, governance structures may gain their rationale from benefit advantages, the attendant costs may or may not change . . . Benefits of this sort are based on the use to which resources are put and introduce an important dynamic element into the analysis of the firm.

The focus of TC theory on the containment of costs under the assumption of opportunism, on contractual safeguards, and on the static exchange of a good or service possessing 'given utility-value characteristics' (Lundvall 1993: 52), along with its implicit assumption of the relationship being an exogenous rather than an intrinsic and 'soft' factor of production with an endogenous impact on the production function, hinders a fuller appreciation of the dynamic nature of value creation and realization associated with the exchange process. Treating knowledge as inanimate tends to disregard the dynamic aspect of the knowledge transfer process, which can transform knowledge and enhance its value through novel combinations. This then enables entrepreneurial engagement and joint discovery.

The argument I have made in this chapter departs from the primary thrust of TC economics in an important way. What it is really pointing at is an alternative, more evolutionary foundation of the nature of governance—both the choice and the manner—where efficient and effective governance is discovered through social learning processes and where various governance mechanisms and partner resources and capabilities co-evolve over time. The argument also suggests that, for more fully realizing the potential of a governance structure, in this case IFRs, it is necessary for the relevant agents in a relationship to perform 'dynamic programming'.

On the other hand, extant capabilities-based theory has yet to fully appreciate the various costs that must necessarily be incurred in effectively bringing together synergistic firm-specific resources and capabilities through IFRs. The theory does not fully or clearly recognize Type I TC, in particular, or the nature and extent of Type II TC associated with realizing the synergistic benefits.

To sum up, the perspective of value calls for a more proactive, mutually oriented, and flexible approach towards collaborations, one that is more able to view transaction-specific expenditures more entrepreneurially as not just costs but potential investments in future value. Although in a somewhat different way, the arguments provide further insight into Winter's (1988) comment that TC economics provides too central an emphasis on the structuring of deals to the neglect of the economics of production itself, not just cost but more importantly the processes underlying them. Consequently, as a result of its predisposition that just 'tinkering around' with the governance and the incentive structure suffi- ciently provides the basis for the solution to co-ordination problems commonly present in IFRs, the theory tends to neglect many of the operational issues and difficulties that characterize IFRs in managing the value creation and realization process (Borys and Jemison 1989). Such a predisposition disregards the full set of tools that management possess to add value to a transaction. As Dodgson (1995) states:

> The cooperative rather than the universally competitive model of inter-firm relationships . . . has implications for those theories that reduce all firm transactions to cost and price considerations without regard to the mutually valuable synergies achievable through the sharing of competencies and knowledge (1995: 291).

Achieving such synergies, however, requires an entrepreneurial orientation and greater attention to 'collaborating technology', as illustrated earlier.

Attention to value also invites, even demands, greater attention to issues such as innovation and learning, phenomena which are increasingly important to competitive advantage in the modern economy but which have admittedly not been of central importance to TC theory (Williamson, Chapter 2, this volume). Explicit attention to the simultaneous presence of commonality (both in compe- tence and objectives) and diversity (unique capabilities) provides an opportunity to learn and create value, if the opportunity is tapped productively. In their insightful paper, Moran and Ghoshal (1996) show that the theory misses this very point, which then 'tends to eliminate the opportunity for discovery and learning among transaction partners' (p. 65) and add that 'it is not the elimina- tion of hazards but the ability to learn and use the learning of others that is the prerequisite for "healthy progress" ' (p. 66). Exploiting such an opportunity may require a greater mutual orientation in that attaining the exchange potential requires a 'social context necessary to build the trust and commitment that are needed for maintaining co-operation' (Ghoshal and Moran 1996: 42). Since knowledge sharing entails costs, such a social context provides the incentive that enables partners to engage in rent-creating activities through specialized invest- ments and knowledge sharing (Dyer and Singh 1998). In this regard, Ghoshal and Moran claim that, in an evolving theory of the firm, learning and trust may well take the place that opportunism and the narrow concept of efficiency occupy in the theory of the firm today.

Foss, Knudsen, and Montgomery (1995: 14) have argued that 'there has been very little systematic work on the precise relations between the resource and evolutionary approaches on one hand and transaction costs on the other', and urged the need for work in this direction. Along similar lines, Knudsen (1995: 214) asserts:

One of the most significant attempts of integration within [the] modern theory of the firm involves exploring the possibility of bridging the perception of the firm as a 'productive unit' within evolutionary and resource-based theory and the perception of the firm as an 'exchange structure' within transaction cost theory.

This is precisely what I have attempted to accomplish in this chapter, in the context of IFRs. From the perspective of value, the relational capital which enables the realization of such synergies is just as important as the structural capital in the form of synergistic complementarities. Earlier I mentioned that the relationship itself behaves as an endogenous factor of production, albeit a 'soft' one. Putting it differently, the joint production function is partially created by the transacting partners. Where the firm's and the market's capabilities are limited, and the joint production function is potentially superior to the hierarchical one, (over)expending resources on in-house production or contractual safeguards in order to protect against opportunism (that is, Type I TC), instead of investing in the relational capital (Type II TC), can be value inefficient and can amount to a misallocation of resources. This, of course, requires a recognition that production and exchange relations are intertwined and cannot be easily separated from one another.

4.2. The Type I:Type II TC Ratio: Implications for Research and Practice

The relations between the two types of TC and value raise some interesting research questions. Broadly speaking, inter-firm collaboration is clearly a mixed-motive game where the relationship is characterized by a spirit of collaboration (for creation of the pie) and competition (for distribution of the pie). Clearly, co-operation and conflict go hand in hand, with there being a level of dialectical tension between the two. In this regard, interaction has both conflict-generating and relationship-bonding properties. Some conflict is probably healthy since it tests the commitment of the partners. Successful resolution of differences not only further strengthens the relationship but, if done properly, brings diverse capabilities together constructively and thus facilitates the pursuit of value. It is therefore important to know when to collaborate and when to compete. How is such tension balanced? How are the necessary trade-offs made? When and under what situations? Moreover, given the considerable costs of relationship development, under what circumstances would such expenditures be justified? Greater research is needed in this regard. Longitudinal case studies would be especially useful in providing further insights.

One can also ask whether TC theory, at its current state of development, operates at too aggregated a level. Perhaps a further and more fine-grained disaggregation of TC would offer a more informed understanding of important issues and decisions pertaining to governance. In this regard, I submit that the Type I:Type II TC ratio could potentially turn out to be an important concept, one which provides the core of an interesting and important set of ideas which are currently not being pushed far enough, and the further development and investigation of which could potentially yield very fruitful results for theory, research, and practice. Moreover, besides being an important conceptual notion, the Type I:Type II TC ratio also potentially offers a relatively concrete research and measurement tool for carrying out more informed enquiry into relevant topics.

Let me elaborate on this issue in the remainder of this section. For one, these two kinds of cost and the ratio between them could be related to key questions of why firms experience high dissatisfaction with collaborations or how firms might manage alliances for a more positive outcome.[11] As an illustration, consider the following. A distinction can be made between alliances in which partners contribute similar kinds of assets to the IFR (for instance, in alliances between direct competitors) and alliances in which partners contribute different sets of assets (for instance, between firms from different industries or knowledge bases). It is unlikely that successful alliances of both kinds would (or should) have similar Type I:Type II TC ratios, especially at similar points of time. While this chapter suggests that increasing the ratio of Type II TC relative to Type I TC is desirable, the argument clearly needs to be contingent. When collaborating with a direct competitor, a firm may be better served by a higher ratio of monitoring costs to educating costs (high Type I:Type II TC), as differences in knowledge bases are likely to be smaller and the risk of opportunistic behaviour, especially if within the same segment of the value chain, is likely to be greater. Similarly, when collaborating with a firm from a different knowledge or industry base, one might prefer a lower Type I:Type II TC ratio, as opportunistic behaviour is likely to be less of a problem than cognitive differences. Perhaps one of the reasons for high levels of dissatisfaction with their IFRs may stem from managers picking inappropriate ratios between the two kinds of cost. This is an interesting and important research issue.

Secondly, deeper thought about the contrasting thrusts stemming from the

---

[11] One argument that is commonly used to explain collaboration failures is that firms make commitments too hastily, without adequate screening, and end up repenting later because of a poor choice of partner, which then hinders the realization of desired outcomes. The arguments below go beyond this simple argument.

logic of the two approaches could generate important additional insights. For instance, drawing upon the focus on transaction value rather than transaction costs, one could suggest, as this chapter has done, that firms are sometimes better off *increasing* transaction costs than necessarily trying to reduce them. Extending the suggested notion of opportunism as a variable and combining it with this argument, one could argue that in fact the level of transaction costs for a given transaction is itself a decision variable. Conceptually, there is no reason to believe that, even for a given IFR, the TC minimizing level of costs is the one that will also maximize value from that relationship. Given that the ultimate interest of the firm is in maximizing value rather than minimizing costs, managers are probably better off treating both the *level* of transaction costs and their *composition* as strategic variables. Providing some kind of framework that can help and guide managers or researchers think through what level and composition of TC I and TC II would be appropriate for a given kind of IFR would indeed be a significant contribution.

Thirdly, one could use conventional TC analysis to enrich understanding of decisions based on a value criterion. For example, the decision to form an IFR may be decided on value terms yet its actual form—joint venture, joint development arrangement, etc.—and some of the more microlevel governance arrangements could be informed by TC economics (Kogut 1988). Again, the considerations of Type I and Type II transaction costs could be relevant, since different forms of IFRs may be more or less appropriate for implementing different levels and compositions of TC I and TC II.

Fourthly, the chapter raised the possibility of a dynamic analysis of transaction costs through the evolution of an IFR. This needs to be extended in a more significant way. For instance, one could argue that, even though a particular ratio of Type I:Type II TC may be appropriate for the initial stages of an IFR, as the IFR develops a firm may prefer to re-examine continually its level and composition of transaction costs. Extending the illustration above, one could argue that when direct competitors collaborate there may initially be a need for high TC I relative to TC II. Yet, both partners should realize that high levels of TC I represent relatively less productive use of resources. Perhaps over time they could develop mechanisms that would help them bring about 'the Type II fundamental transformation'. Greater research into these mechanisms, and their nature and evolution over the life cycle of the relationship, would be informative. Combining this notion with the point in the previous paragraph that different forms of IFRs may be more or less appropriate for implementing different levels and compositions of TC I and TC II, another possible path for dynamic analysis would be to consider the evolution of the IFR as it adopts different forms over its life cycle.

Fifthly, in the same vein, there is no reason to believe that the 'fundamental transformation' should always entail an increase of TC II relative to TC I.

Although the argument as developed in this chapter is suggestive in this direction, this need not be true across different kinds of alliances, and across time within a given alliance, as is richly illustrated in the case research by Doz (1996) and Arino and de la Torre (1998). One can envisage situations in which the appropriate 'transformation' would be to increase Type I TC relative to Type II. For instance, if a partner is initially from a different industry and knowledge base but shows indications of becoming a direct competitor, the appropriate corporate response might be to increase 'monitoring' relative to 'educating'.

5. Concluding Remarks

Increasingly, economic organization and the management of firm boundaries has to do with the management of value. In light of the anticipated level of synergy which characterizes the formation of IFRs, the extent of disappointment with their outcome is ironic and suggests that, even though such synergies may potentially be present, firms face substantial difficulties in attaining them, resulting in a high rate of dissatisfaction. Basing itself on TC and capabilities/competence-based theory, this chapter explains why this might be so. In making its argument, the chapter contributes towards a fuller appreciation of the process of creating and realizing such value through IFRs.

The effective realization of the synergistic potential in IFRs is often a lengthy and laborious process, especially so in the transacting of tacit resources/capabilities, with the benefits being more variable and uncertain, and highly dependent on the nature and pattern of transaction-specific expenditures in the earlier stages. Yet it could well be a worthwhile endeavour, one with potentially high pay-offs, for firms to pay greater attention to cultivating their 'collaborating technology'. A longer-term value orientation points towards a reassessment of co-operation as a strategic tool, where greater sophistication in relationship management skills and routines would leverage both firms' investment in IFRs as well as other pertinent resources and capabilities resident in the firm. If used effectively, the approach towards relationships from a management of value perspective can enable firms to attain a competitive advantage over those that remain stuck in the TC minimizing mould (Barney and Hansen, 1994; Lado, Boyd, and Hanlon 1997).

Williamson (Chapter 2, this volume) unequivocally acknowledges that the capabilities/competence-based perspective raises some good issues that TC theory would do well to appreciate, especially the importance of learning and the evolutionary potential of inter-firm interaction over the longer term. However, as he correctly contends, the more contractual TC theory also raises important issues to which capabilities/competence-based arguments must be more responsive. Resolving these tensions and challenges would increase the rigour of both theories and be beneficial for the development of the field.

In the light of the arguments made in this chapter, I submit that the management of value perspective is particularly appropriate to the organization and management of economic activity today and needs to receive greater prominence when issues pertinent to firm strategy, the theory of the firm, and, more generally, of economic organization and governance. Ilinitch, D'Aveni, and Lewin claim that, in today's 'hypercompetitive' environment, scholars and managers face a paradox, namely that 'strategies and organizational forms that were effective at a past competitive juncture ... are entirely inadequate for the future' (1996: 218). I would suggest the reverse as a paradox: strategies and organizational forms, in this case IFRs, that were not so effective at a past competitive juncture, may be increasingly effective for the future, the caveat of course being that they are organized and managed appropriately. The above authors added that 'today's problems require frame-breaking approaches to research' (ibid.). The purported shift in orientation proposed in this chapter, away from opportunism and from cost to value, is a potentially pivotal and frame-breaking one, in both a structural and an attitudinal sense, with critical implications for the manner in which inter-firm co-operative relationships are managed. Theorists need to adopt value as their criterion in the formation and governance of IFRs, and for that matter economic organization in general, in that it incorporates both efficiency (both static and dynamic) and effectiveness considerations. While I do not disagree about the potential for opportunism, I do believe that the extent of emphasis on it by TC theory is unwarranted and there needs to be a more realistic balance in the pursuit of value. I hope the ideas put forward in this chapter provoke further work in this regard.

References

ALSTON, L. J., and W. GILLESPIE 1989. 'Resource coordination and transaction costs', *Journal of Economic Behavior and Organization* 11: 191–212.

ARINO, A., and J. DE LA TORRE 1998. 'Action and reaction: Toward an evolutionary model of collaborative ventures', *Organization Science* 9: 306–25.

BALAKRISHNAN, S., and M. P. KOZA 1993. 'Information asymmetry, adverse selection and joint ventures: Theory and evidence', *Journal of Economic Behavior and Organization* 20(1): 99–117.

BARNEY, J. B., and M. H. HANSEN 1994. 'Trustworthiness as a source of competitive advantage', *Strategic Management Journal* 15 (Special Winter Issue): 175–90.

BEIJE, P. R. 1996. 'Transaction costs and technological learning', in J. Groenewegen, ed., *Transaction Cost Economics and Beyond*. Boston: Kluwer, 309–26.

BORYS, B., and D. B. JEMISON 1989. 'Hybrid arrangements as strategic alliances: Theoretical issues in organizational combinations', *Academy of Management Review* 14: 234–49.

CHI, T. 1994. 'Trading in strategic resources: Necessary conditions, transaction cost problems, and choice of exchange structure', *Strategic Management Journal* 15(4): 271–90.

CLARK, K. B., and T. FUJIMOTO 1991. *Product Development Performance*. Boston, MA: Harvard Business School Press.

CONNER, K. R. 1991. 'A historical comparison of resource-based theory and five schools of thought within industrial organization economics: Do we have a new theory of the firm?', *Journal of Management* 17: 121–54.

—— and C. K. PRAHALAD 1996. 'A Resource-based theory of the firm: Knowledge versus opportunism', *Organization Science* 7(5): 477–501.

DAHLMAN, C. 1979. 'The Problem of Externality', *Journal of Law and Economics* 21: 141–62.

DEMSETZ, H. 1988. 'The theory of the firm revisited', *Journal of Law, Economics and Organization* 4(1): 141–61.

DIETRICH, M. 1994. *Transaction Cost Economics and Beyond: Towards a New Economics of the Firm*. London: Routledge.

—— 1996. 'Opportunism, learning and organizational evolution', in J. Groenewegen, ed., *Transaction Cost Economics and Beyond*. Boston: Kluwer, 225–48.

DIXIT, A. K., and B. J. NALEBUFF 1991. *Thinking Strategically*. New York: W. W. Norton.

DODGSON, M. 1993. *Technological Collaboration in Industry*. London: Routledge.

—— 1994. 'Technology and collaboration', In M. Dodgson and R. Rothwell, eds., *The Handbook of Industrial Innovation*. Brookfield, VT: Edward Elgar.

—— 1995. 'Technological collaboration and innovation', In M. Dodgson and R. Rothwell, eds., *The Handbook of Industrial Innovation*. Brookfield, VT: Edward Elgar, 285–92.

DOZ, Y. L. 1996. 'The evolution of cooperation in strategic alliances: Initial conditions or learning processes', *Strategic Management Journal* 17 (Summer Special Issue): 55–84.

DYER, J. H. 1997. 'Effective interfirm collaboration: How transactors minimize transaction costs and maximize transaction value', *Strategic Management Journal* 18: 535–56.

—— and H. SINGH 1998. 'The relational view: Cooperative strategy and sources of interorganizational competitive advantage', *Academy of Management Review* 23: 660–79.

EISENHARDT, K. M., and C. B. SCHOONHOVEN 1996. 'Resource-based view of strategic alliance formation: Strategic and social effects in entrepreneurial firms', *Organization Science* 7(2): 136–50.

FOSS, N. J. 1994. 'The two Coasian traditions', *Review of Political Economy* 6(1): 37–61.

—— C. KNUDSEN, and C. A. MONTGOMERY 1995. 'An exploration of common ground: Integrating evolutionary and strategic theories of the firm', in C. A. Montgomery, ed., *Resource-Based and Evolutionary Theories of the Firm: Towards a Synthesis*. Boston: Kluwer, 1–18.

GERINGER, J. M. 1988. *Joint Venture Partner Selection*. Westport, CT: Quorum Books.

GHOSHAL, S., and P. MORAN 1996. 'Bad for practice: A critique of transaction cost theory', *Academy of Management Review* 21(1): 13–47.

HAGEDOORN, J. 1993. 'Understanding the rationale of strategic technology partnering: Interorganizational modes of cooperation and sectoral differences', *Strategic Management Journal* 14: 371–86.

HAMEL, G. 1991. 'Competition for competence and inter-partner learning within international strategic alliances', *Strategic Management Journal* 12 (Summer Issue): 83–103.

—— Y. L. DOZ, and C. K. PRAHALAD 1989. 'Collaborate with your competitors—and win', *Harvard Business Review* 67(1): 133–9.

HENNART, J. F. 1998. 'A transaction costs theory of equity joint ventures', *Strategic Management Journal* 9: 361–74.

HILL, C. W. L. 1990. 'Cooperation, opportunism, and the invisible hand: Implications for transaction cost theory', *Academy of Management Review* 15(3): 500–13.

HIPPEL, E. VON 1988. *The Sources of Innovation*. New York: Oxford University Press.

IINITCH, A. Y., R. A. D'AVENI, and A. Y. LEWIN 1996. 'New organizational forms and strategies for managing in hypercompetitive environments', *Organization Science* 7(3): 211–220.

JARILLO, J. C. 1988. 'On strategic networks', *Strategic Management Journal* 9: 31–41.

JONES, G. J., and C. W. L. HILL 1988. 'A transaction cost analysis of strategy-structure choice', *Strategic Management Journal* 9: 159–72.

KLEIN, B., R. G. CRAWFORD, and A. A. ALCHIAN 1978. 'Vertical integration, appropriable rents, and the competitive contracting process', *Journal of Law and Economics* 21(2): 297–325.

KNUDSEN, C. 1995. 'Theories of the firm, strategic management and leadership', in C. MONTGOMERY, ed., *Resource-Based and Evolutionary Theories of the Firm: Towards a Synthesis*. Boston: Kluwer, 179–217.

KOGUT, B. 1988. 'Joint ventures: Theoretical and empirical perspectives', *Strategic Management Journal* 9: 319–32.

—— and U. ZANDER 1992. 'Knowledge of the firm, combinative capabilities, and the replication of technology', *Organizational Science* 3(3): 383–97.

KREPS, D. 1990. 'Corporate culture and economic theory', in J. Alt and K. Shepsle, eds., *Perspectives on Positive Political Economy*. New York: Cambridge University Press, 90–143.

LADO, A. A., N. G. BOYD, and S. C. HANLON 1997. 'Competition, cooperation, and the search for economic rents: A syncretic model', *Academy of Management Review* 22(1): 110–41.

LANGLOIS, R. N. 1992. 'Transaction Cost Economics in Real Time', *Industrial and Corporate Change* 1: 99–127.

—— 1995. 'Capabilities and coherence in firms and market', in C. Montgomery, ed., *Resource-Based and Evolutionary Theories of the Firm: Towards a Synthesis*. Boston: Kluwer, 71–100.

—— and P. L. ROBERTSON 1995. *Firms, Markets and Economic Change*. London: Routledge.

LAZONICK, W. 1991. *Business Organization and the Myth of the Market Economy*. Cambridge: Cambridge University Press.

LOASBY, B. 1994. 'Organizational capabilities and interfirm relations', *Metroeconomica* 45: 248–65.

LUNDVALL, B. 1993. 'Explaining interfirm cooperation and innovation: Limits of the transaction cost approach', in G. Grabher, ed., *The Embedded Firm*. London: Routledge, 52–64.

MADHOK, A. 1995. 'Revisiting multinational firms' tolerance for joint ventures: A trust-based approach', *Journal of International Business Studies* 26: 117–37.

—— 1996. 'The organization of economic activity: Transaction costs, firm capabilities and the nature of governance', *Organization Science* 7(5): 577–90.

—— 1997. 'Cost, value and foreign market entry mode: The transaction and the firm', *Strategic Management Journal* 18: 39–61.

—— and S. B. TALLMAN 1998. 'Resources, transactions and rents: Managing value through interfirm collaborative relationships', *Organization Science* 9: 326–39.

MILGROM P., and J. ROBERTS 1992. *Economics, Organization and Management*. Englewood Cliffs, NJ: Prentice Hall.

MODY, A. 1993. 'Learning through alliances', *Journal of Economic Behavior and Organization* 20: 151–70.

MORAN, P., and S. GHOSHAL 1996. 'Theories of economic organization. The case for realism and balance', *Academy of Management Review* 21(1): 58–72.

MOWERY, D. C., J. OXLEY, and B. SILVERMAN 1997. 'Strategic alliances and interfirm knowledge transfer', *Strategic Management Journal* 17 (Winter Special Issue): 77–92.

NICKERSON, J. 1998. 'Toward an economizing theory of strategy'. Paper presented at the DRUID conference on Competences, Governance and Entrepreneurship. Denmark, 9–11 June.

NOOTEBOOM, B. 1996. 'Towards a learning based model of transactions', in J. Groenewegen, ed., *Transaction Cost Economics and Beyond*. Boston: Kluwer, 327–50.

OSBORN, R. N., and J. HAGEDOORN. 1997. 'The institutionalization and evolutionary dynamics of interorganizational alliances and networks', *Academy of Management Journal* 40: 261–78.

PARKHE, A. 1991. 'Interfirm diversity, organizational learning and longevity in global strategic alliances', *Journal of International Business Studies* 22(4): 579–602.

—— 1993a. ' "Messy" research, methodological predispositions and theory development in international joint ventures', *Academy of Management Review* 18(2): 227–68.

—— 1993b. 'Strategic alliance structuring: A game theoretic and transaction cost examination of interfirm cooperation', *Academy of Management Journal* 36(4): 794–829.

PEARCE, R. J. 1997. 'Toward understanding joint venture performance and survival: A bargaining and influence approach to transaction cost theory', *Academy of Management Review* 22(1): 203–25.

POWELL, W. W. 1990. 'Neither market nor hierarchy: Network forms of organization', *Research in Organizational Behavior* 12: 295–336.

RICHARDSON, G. B. 1972. 'The organization of industry', *The Economic Journal* 82: 883–96.

RING, P. S. 1997. 'Costs of network organization', in Anna Grandori, ed., *The Game of Networks*. London: Routledge.

—— and A. H. VAN DE VEN 1992. 'Structuring cooperative relationships between organizations', *Strategic Management Journal* 13: 483–98.

—— —— 1994. 'Developmental processes of cooperative interorganizational relationships', *Academy of Management Review* 19(1): 90–118.

RUMELT R. P. 1984. 'Toward a strategic theory of the firm', in R. B. Lamb, ed., *Competitive Strategic Management*. Englewood Cliffs, NJ: Prentice Hall, 566–70.

SAXENIAN, A. 1994. *Regional Advantage.* Cambridge, MA: Harvard University Press.

TALLMAN, S. B., and O. SHENKAR 1994. 'A managerial decision model of international cooperative venture formation', *Journal of International Business Studies* 25(1): 91–114.

TEECE, D. J. 1982. 'Towards an economic theory of the multiproduct firm', *Journal of Economic Behavior and Organization* 3(1): 39–63.

—— 1986. 'Profiting from technological innovation: Implications for integration, collaboration, licensing and public policy', *Research Policy* 15: 285–305.

—— 1990. 'Contribution and impediments of economic analysis to the study of strategic management', in J. W. Frederickson, ed., *Persectives on Strategic Planning.* New York: Harper, 39–80.

—— G. PISANO, and A. SHUEN 1997. 'Dynamic capabilities and strategic management', *Strategic Management Journal* 18: 509–34.

WILLIAMSON, O. E. 1975. *Markets and Hierarchies.* New York: Free Press.

—— 1985. *The Economic Institutions of Capitalism.* New York: Free Press.

—— 1988a. 'Technology and transaction cost economics', *Journal of Economic Behavior and Organization* 10: 355–63.

—— 1988b. 'The logic of economic organization', *Journal of Law, Economics and Organization* 4: 65–93.

—— 1991a. 'Comparative economic organization: The analysis of discrete structural alternatives', *Administrative Science Quarterly* 36: 269–96.

—— 1991b. 'Strategizing, economizing and economic organization', *Strategic Management Journal* 12 (Special Issue): 75–94.

—— 1996. *The Mechanisms of Governance.* New York: Oxford University Press.

WINTER, S. 1988. 'On Coase, competence and the corporation', *Journal of Law, Economics and Organization* 4: 163–80.

ZAJAC, E. J., and C. P. OLSEN 1993. 'From transaction cost to transactional value analysis: Implications for the study of interorganizational strategies', *Journal of Management Studies* 30(1): 131–45.

14

Multiple Considerations in Making Governance Choices: Implications of Transaction Cost Economics, Real Options Theory, and Knowledge-Based Theories of the Firm

JAY B. BARNEY AND WOONGHEE LEE

1. Introduction

Consider the following scenario.[1] A small bio-technology firm has developed a product prototype. While this prototype has shown some market potential, it has yet to receive regulatory approval for commercial development. To receive this approval, it must first be tested in a series of clinical trials, and then be produced and marketed to consumers. These activities can take from ten to twelve years to complete. Thus, this firm will not know, with any degree of certainty, if its product prototype is economically viable for at least ten to twelve years.

Despite this uncertainty, this firm must begin to make some critical decisions about how to manufacture its product now. First, it must decide how it will obtain sufficient quantities of this product for clinical trials, and secondly, it must decide how it will obtain sufficient quantities for this product's commercialization if it turns out to be economically viable. In making these manufacturing decisions, this firm has four basic options.

1. It can vertically integrate into manufacturing for both clinical trials and commercial production.
2. It can outsource production for clinical trials and vertically integrate into manufacturing for commercial production.
3. It can vertically integrate into manufacturing for clinical trials and outsource commercial production.
4. It can outsource manufacturing for both clinical trials and commercial production.

There is, in the literature, a well-developed theory that managers can use to

---

[1] This is a common decision-making situation facing many bio-technology firms (Pisano, 1990).

help them make governance decisions of this type. This theory is transaction cost economics (Williamson 1975, 1985). In this context, transaction cost economics would focus the attention of managers in the bio-technology firm on potential hazards associated with outsourcing manufacturing, both for clinical and commercial production. For example, in order for this product to be manufactured by an outside firm for clinical testing, the bio-technology firm may have to reveal a great deal of information about its product prototype. The manufacturing firm could use this information to give it an advantage in obtaining the contract if the bio-technology firm decides to outsource commercial production (Klein, Crawford, and Alchian 1978).[2] More generally, transaction cost economics focuses on the attributes of economic exchanges that can lead to opportunistic behaviour, and suggests that firms should adopt more hierarchical forms of governance when the threat of opportunism is significant.

However, the threat of opportunism is not the only relevant factor for the bio-technology firm making its manufacturing decisions. For example, there is a great deal of uncertainty about the economic viability of this product prototype. This uncertainty may have a significant impact on this firm's manufacturing decision, independent of the threat of opportunism. Moreover, it is likely that this firm's decision about clinical production will have a significant impact on its decision about commercial production. In particular, if this firm does not learn how to manufacture its product during clinical production, it is unlikely that it will possess the resources and capabilities needed to engage in commercial production. Put differently, the decision to outsource clinical production may also be a decision to outsource commercial production.

These additional considerations in making the decisions about how to organize clinical and commercial production do not suggest that minimizing the threat of opportunism is irrelevant. Rather, they only suggest that minimizing the threat of opportunism is just one of several issues that the managers in this bio-technology firm must consider in making their manufacturing choices. The purposes of this chapter are: (1) to describe, in more detail, what these other considerations might be; (2) to suggest what their governance implications are likely to be; (3) to show that they are, in fact, not just special cases of transaction cost economics; and finally, (4) to discuss how firms will choose among these different considerations when they have contradictory implications for governance choices.

2. Non-Opportunism Considerations in Making Governance Choices

The bio-technology scenario discussed above suggests at least two non-opportunism considerations for firms making governance choices: the level of demand

---

[2] This is an example of transaction-specific investment arising because of learning by doing advantages (Williamson 1975).

uncertainty and the extent to which resources and capabilities to be developed through an exchange are tacit and taken for granted. Each of these additional considerations, their governance implications, and their relationship with transaction cost economics and opportunism are discussed below.

2.1. Demand Uncertainty and Governance

The ultimate value of an economic exchange may not be known at the time governance decisions about how to manage that economic exchange are made. This demand uncertainty can exist because there can be significant lags between when governance choices about how to manage a transaction are made and when that transaction yields a product or service that can be sold on the market. In the bio-technology example, there is a long lag between when decisions about how to organize manufacturing must be made and when new products are actually sold on the market.

Of course, the level of demand uncertainty associated with different products or services can vary significantly (Knight 1965). Moreover, parties to an exchange can engage in activities to try to reduce the level of demand uncertainty associated with a particular product or service.[3] Nevertheless, there can still be circumstances in which the ultimate value of a product or service in the marketplace cannot be known with any certainty and important governance choices need to be made about how to develop this product or service.

In these circumstances, firms will be reluctant to invest in hierarchical governance. If the exchange turns out to have no value, then this investment in hierarchical governance will have turned out to be worthless in terms of minimizing the threat of opportunism. Moreover, it will be difficult for parties to this exchange to extract any value from their investments in hierarchical governance, since these investments are typically transaction specific in nature. When demand uncertainty is high, less hierarchical forms of governance, including market and intermediate governance, will be preferred over more hierarchical governance. Applied to the bio-technology firm example, the existence of high demand uncertainty suggests that this firm will want to avoid hierarchical governance in its manufacturing decisions, at least as long as there is some uncertainty about whether or not its product prototype is valuable.

There is some empirical work that supports these conclusions. Building on real options governance theory,[4] Kogut (1991) found that firms operating under conditions of high demand uncertainty prefer intermediate forms of governance

---

[3] This can be done, for example, through the use of various forms of market research.

[4] We distinguish between the real options governance literature—a literature that focuses on making governance choices under conditions of high demand uncertainty—and the financial real options literature—a literature that focuses on estimating the value of a firm's real options. While both of these literatures draw on options logic from finance, their objectives are quite different.

over hierarchical forms of governance. Once demand uncertainty associated with an exchange is reduced, then firms can make governance choices based on other criteria, including, perhaps, the threat of opportunism in an exchange.

Of course, uncertainty also plays an important role in transaction cost logic. However, the type of uncertainty emphasized in this logic is behavioural uncertainty, or the inability to anticipate the future behaviour of an exchange partner. Clearly, the concepts of demand uncertainty and behavioural uncertainty are related. For example, one reason it may be difficult to anticipate the behaviour of an exchange partner is that the value of the exchange in question is not known, and thus all future states of this relationship cannot be anticipated.

However, while these two concepts can be related, they are not identical. It is possible to imagine transactions that are characterized by a great deal of demand uncertainty, but no behavioural uncertainty. Suppose, for example, two firms are contemplating a new business opportunity that they know will evolve in one of three ways. However, they do not know which of these three outcomes will actually obtain. In this setting, it would be possible for these firms to anticipate all future states in this exchange, and thus write a contract that completely protects them from opportunistic behaviour in those different future states. Thus, the threat of opportunism from behavioural uncertainty is quite low. On the other hand, these firms may not be able to predict which of these three states will actually occur. If one of these yields high profits, a second medium profits, and a third losses, there is significant demand uncertainty in this exchange—even though there is virtually no behavioural uncertainty.

Moreover, not only are demand uncertainty and behavioural uncertainty different concepts, they have significantly different governance implications. High behavioural uncertainty suggests that parties to a transaction may face significant threats of opportunism. Transaction cost logic suggests that, in such settings, parties to an exchange should opt for more hierarchical forms of governance to control opportunism. The logic developed here suggests that under conditions of high demand uncertainty, parties to an exchange should opt for less hierarchical forms of governance, to avoid the substantial expense of investing in hierarchical governance that can turn out to have no value.

None of this suggests that opportunism is irrelevant to governance choices under conditions of high demand uncertainty. Indeed, minimizing the threat of opportunism can be a primary motivation for adopting a particular governance structure once demand uncertainty goes away. Thus, for example, a firm may choose intermediate governance when demand uncertainty is high in order to avoid the substantial investments necessary to create hierarchical governance. If, over time, demand uncertainty goes away, this firm may discover that behavioural uncertainty is a substantial problem, and thus replace intermediate governance with hierarchical governance. However, all this occurs after demand uncertainty has been resolved.

It may also be the case that both demand uncertainty and behavioural uncertainty in an exchange are high, and thus the need to minimize the cost of erecting hierarchical governance and the need to minimize the threat of opportunism through the erection of hierarchical governance both exist. How firms make governance choices in this setting is discussed later in this chapter.

2.2. Developing Tacit Resources and Capabilities, and Governance Choices

A second non-opportunism consideration when making governance choices is the desire, by parties to an exchange, to develop new resources and capabilities and the extent to which these resources and capabilities are tacit and taken for granted. To the extent that governance has an impact on the ability of firms to develop these kinds of resources and capabilities, the desire to develop such capabilities will affect governance choices.

Firms can develop new resources and capabilities in a wide variety of ways. For example, a firm can develop such capabilities on its own by simply deciding to engage in new business activities. One of the implications of engaging in new business activities can often be the development of new resources and capabilities. Firms can hire outside consulting firms to help them develop new resources and capabilities, they can benchmark their own organizational skills against the skills of other firms in an attempt to build new resources and capabilities, they can send their employees on advanced training courses, they can develop new resources and capabilities by working closely with suppliers or customers, and so forth. These and other alternatives reflect a firm's choice about what is the most efficient and effective way of building new resources and capabilities. Put differently, these alternatives all reflect governance choices made by firms about how to develop new resources and capabilities. Some of these options (for example, when a firm engages in a new business activity on its own) are more consistent with hierarchical governance, others (for example, working with suppliers or customers to build new capabilities) are more consistent with market governance.

These governance choices may depend on a variety of factors, including some factors normally associated with transaction cost economics. However, one of these other factors may be the extent to which the resources and capabilities a firm wishes to develop are tacit and taken for granted. Several authors have suggested that some of the competitively most important resources and capabilities possessed by a firm are tacit and taken for granted (Polanyi 1962; Barney 1991; Dierickx and Cool 1989). Recent work in the knowledge-based theory of the firm (Conner and Prahalad 1996; Spender 1996) suggests that more hierarchical governance can facilitate the transfer of tacit and taken for granted capabilities, compared to less hierarchical forms of governance. Thus, if the resources and capabilities a firm wants to develop are tacit and taken for granted, it may be necessary for this firm to use hierarchical governance to develop/gain access to these resources and capabilities. In the bio-technology example, because many of the skills needed to manufacture its product prototype are tacit and taken for granted, the desire to develop new resources and capabilities suggests that this firm should use more hierarchical governance to manage its manufacturing.

There is some debate about whether or not the model of governance implied by knowledge-based theories of the firm is actually independent of opportunism considerations (Foss 1996). However, Conner and Prahalad (1996) argue strongly that hierarchical governance can facilitate the transfer of tacit and taken-for-granted knowledge, independent of the threat of opportunism. This is because hierarchical governance enables a party that possesses this knowledge to use it in making business decisions, even if the second party in this exchange does not fully understand the rationale for these decisions.[5] Indeed, in their model, Conner and Prahalad (1996) explicitly adopt the assumption that no opportunism exists in the exchange under consideration. Hierarchy is required, not to reduce the threat of opportunism, but to facilitate the use of valuable, but tacit and taken-for-granted, resources and capabilities. It is the nature of these kinds of resources that makes them very difficult to describe to those individuals or firms that do not possess them.

3. Integrating Multiple Considerations in Making Governance Choices

Examined separately, each of the bases for making governance choices described in this chapter has an internal logic and rationale. As summarized in Table 14.1, transaction cost logic suggests that the threat of opportunism should lead to more hierarchical forms of governance, real options logic suggests that high

TABLE 14.1. Predictions of the main effects, for governance choices, of transaction cost, real options, and knowledge-based theories of the firm

Theory	Prediction of main effect
Transaction cost	Threat of opportunism leads to more hierarchical governance
Real options	Demand uncertainty leads to less hierarchical governance
Knowledge-based theories	Need to learn leads to more hierarchical governance

[5] A good example of the use of hierarchical governance imagined by Conner and Prahalad (1996) is the apprenticeship system of employment. In this system of employment, the master typically has very valuable skills honed over years of practice. However, many of these skills are typically tacit and taken for granted. Many of them cannot be written down. The apprentice recognizes the outcomes associated with those skills, and thus voluntarily puts him/herself under the control of the master so that through direct observation and careful mentoring over several years, the apprentice can develop these skills as well. Notice that hierarchical governance is created, but that minimizing the threat of opportunism does not have to play a significant role.

demand uncertainty should lead to less hierarchical forms of governance, and knowledge-based theories of the firm suggest that the desire to develop tacit and taken-for-granted resources and capabilities should lead to more hierarchical forms of governance. But what governance decisions should be made when all three theories of governance are considered simultaneously?

3.1. Conditions where Conflicts among Perspectives do not Exist

Figure 14.1 examines the situation when these multiple perspectives are considered simultaneously. Figure 14.1 suggests that, in some circumstances, there is no conflict among these different models. For example, in Cell I of Figure 14.1, only the threat of opportunism in an exchange is high, while both demand uncertainty and the need to learn about tacit resources are low. When demand uncertainty is low, real options logic does not make a specific prediction about optimal governance. Rather, real options logic only comes into play when demand uncertainty is high. In settings where demand uncertainty is low, governance choices should be made on the basis of other considerations, besides real options logic. In the same way, when the need to learn about tacit resources and capabilities is low (either because a firm does not need to learn or because what it seeks to learn is not tacit), knowledge-based theories of the firm do not have specific governance predictions, and governance choices should be made on other grounds. In Figure 14.1, those other grounds are transaction cost economics, a logic that suggests that when the threat of opportunism is low, firms should choose the lowest-cost form of governance possible, market governance. Thus, in Cell I of Figure 14.1, firms should choose more market-like forms of governance.[6]

Several cells in Figure 14.1, besides Cell I, have similar unambiguous implications for firms making governance choices. These include Cells II (where more market-like governance is unambiguously preferred), V (where more hierarchical

---

[6] Of course, it is possible to argue that real options logic and knowledge-based theories of the firm do have governance implications when demand uncertainty is low and the need to develop tacit capabilities is low, respectively. This would suggest that the blank lines in Figure 14.1 (suggesting no prediction from a theory) could be replaced by specific predictions. In the case of real options theory, this prediction would be that under conditions of low demand uncertainty, firms should opt for more hierarchical forms of governance. In the case of knowledge-based theories of the firm, this prediction would be that when firms do not need to develop tacit capabilities, the preferred form of governance is market governance. While integrating these perspectives into Figure 14.1 does lead to more conflicts among the perspectives than is currently reflected in the figure, these specific predictions are not included in the figure for two reasons. First, the received real options and knowledge-based literatures do not actually address governance decisions under the conditions described. Secondly, while adding these predictions to the figure adds some information, it does not substantively change the discussion about how to resolve conflicts among the perspectives when they exist. For these reasons, we adopt the less theoretically aggressive assumption that the real options and knowledge-based literatures do not have specific governance predictions in some circumstances.

Need to learn about tacit capabilities

		Low		High	
		Demand uncertainty		Demand uncertainty	
		Low	High	Low	High
Low		I: M	II: M	III: M	IV: M
		—	M	—	M
		—	—	H	H
High		V: H	VI: H	VII: H	VIII: H
		—	M	—	M
		—	—	H	H

(left axis label, rotated: Threat of opportunism)

Note:
In each cell (I–VIII), governance predictions are listed in the following order (from top to bottom): transaction cost, real options, knowledge-based theories.
M = More market-like governance.
H = More hierarchy-like governance.
— = Theory does not make a governance prediction in this setting.

Figure 14.1. Considering simultaneously the effects on governance choices of transaction cost, real options, and knowledge-based theories of the firm

governance is unambiguously preferred), and VII (where more hierarchical governance is unambiguously preferred).

3.2. Conditions where Conflicts among Perspectives do Exist

Of course, the more interesting cells in Figure 14.1 are those where the different models have contradictory implications for governance choices, including Cells III, IV, VI, and VIII. How should firms make governance choices when transaction cost economics suggests, for example, that more hierarchical governance is appropriate, real options logic suggests that more market-like governance is appropriate, and knowledge-based theories of the firm suggest that more hierarchical governance is appropriate (for example, Cell VIII)?

3.2.1. Are these multiple conditions reasonable? A first question to ask about these contradictory cells is: are the exchange conditions they describe reasonable? That is, is it reasonable to expect that some exchanges will be characterized by, for example, high levels of the threat of opportunism, high demand uncertainty, and a high need to learn about tacit capabilities?

It may certainly be the case that some of the combinations of conditions given in Figure 14.1 will be empirically more common than others. However, there is no reason to believe, a priori, that the three relevant attributes of an exchange (that is, the level of the threat of opportunism, the level of demand uncertainty, and the need to learn tacit capabilities) cannot vary independently of each other, and thus may combine in any of the patterns given in Figure 14.1.

For example, it has already been suggested that a transaction can be characterized by low threats of opportunism and high demand uncertainty (that is, when the future states of nature in an exchange are known, but when the probability of these states actually coming to pass is not known). It seems reasonable to assume that in some of these transactions, the need to learn about tacit resources and capabilities could also be high or low. Thus, it does not seem likely that it will be possible to reject conflicting cells in Figure 14.1 on the basis that the conditions described in a cell are unlikely ever to exist.

3.2.2. Weighting different considerations. A second means by which conflicts among these three different perspectives could be resolved would be to weight each criterion by its economic importance in an exchange. For example, a particular exchange may be characterized by low levels of opportunistic threat (suggesting the need only for market-like forms of governance) but high levels of the need to develop tacit resources and capabilities (suggesting the need for more hierarchical governance). However, if the economic consequences of the need to develop new tacit resources are quite substantial, compared to the economic consequences of opportunism, a firm should weight the knowledge-based criterion in making a governance choice over transaction cost considerations, and more hierarchical governance should be chosen. If, on the other hand, the need to learn has only small economic consequences in this exchange, compared to transaction cost concerns, then transaction cost concerns should take on additional weight in decision making, and less hierarchical governance should be chosen.

Unfortunately, it is difficult to specify, a priori, which of these three decision criteria will have the greatest economic consequences in a particular exchange. Overall, because transaction cost economics has received relatively strong and consistent empirical support (Barney and Hesterly 1996), one might be tempted to conclude that transaction cost considerations should take precedence in the making of governance choices. However, this conclusion needs to be qualified in two ways. First, not all empirical research has been consistent with transaction cost predictions. In particular, research on the role of uncertainty in an exchange has yielded some results that are inconsistent with transaction cost considerations (see, for example, Walker and Weber 1984, 1987; Masten, Meehan, and Snyder 1991; Balakrishnan and Wernerfelt 1986). In the settings studied by these authors, some mechanism, besides transaction cost economics, was apparently driving decisions on firm governance. Secondly, even if most empirical research does support transaction costs, since the three perspectives discussed here can, in many circumstances, have the same governance implications, it is not known what percentage of a firm's governance choices are due to transaction cost considerations, and what percentage are due to real options or learning about tacit capabilities. Thus, it is not possible, on the basis of published empirical research, to conclude that transaction cost concerns are the most likely, of the three considerations analysed, here to have the greatest economic impact in an exchange.

While, in general, it may be difficult to specify a weighting of the three decision criteria described here, for particular exchanges it may be quite simple to develop such a weighting. Such transaction-specific weights can be used to make it clear which of the three approaches to governance should take precedence in a particular exchange.

3.2.3. *Minimum required governance.* Another approach to resolving the conflicts among these three perspectives is the 'minimum required governance' approach. This approach assumes that it is in a firm's best interest to adopt the least costly form of governance possible. Then, for any given cell of Figure 14.1, the optimal governance choice becomes the least costly form of governance that addresses the issues identified in all three perspectives. Thus, in Cell II, the least costly form of governance that addresses issues created by all three perspectives is market governance; in Cell IV, the least costly form of governance that addresses issues created by all three perspectives is hierarchical governance.

As presented in Figure 14.1, application of the 'minimum required governance' approach would have the effect of a firm adopting hierarchical governance six out of eight times (for Cells III, IV, V, VI, VII, and VIII). A priori, this seems like too great an emphasis on hierarchical governance. However, this emphasis on hierarchy can be moderated if it is recognized that, in many cases, a particular perspective will suggest only *more* hierarchical governance, rather than strictly hierarchical governance. Thus, intermediate forms of governance, forms that are more hierarchy-like than pure market forms of governance, may often be the 'minimum required governance' for a particular transaction.

3.2.4. *Governance compromises.* A slight modification of the 'minimum required governance' approach to resolving conflicts in Figure 14.1 is the governance compromise approach. In this approach, when one or more of the decision criteria suggest that market governance is appropriate, and the other decision criteria suggest that hierarchical governance is appropriate, firms may well opt for intermediate governance—including strategic alliances and joint ventures. Because intermediate governance has elements of both market and hierarchy, it can represent a governance compromise between these two extremes. And while intermediate governance may not optimize governance with respect to different and conflicting criteria, intermediate governance may provide sufficient elements of hierarchy to address some of the issues that lead to the conclusion that hierarchical governance is needed in an exchange, while providing sufficient elements of market governance to address some of the issues that lead to the conclusion that market governance is necessary.

The advantages of this compromise governance approach to making governance choices may explain why intermediate forms of governance are growing in popularity. In complex economic exchanges, it is unlikely that transaction cost considerations, real options considerations, or knowledge-based considerations will take clear precedence. All three considerations are likely to be important. When they are all likely to be important, and when they have contradictory governance implications, intermediate governance may be the optimal solution.

3.2.5. Governance choices over time.   Finally, Figure 14.1 adopts the simplifying assumption that each of the different perspectives considered here will create governance challenges to exactly the same degree and at exactly the same time. The extent to which different governance problems vary in their economic consequences in an exchange suggests that not all governance challenges create problems to exactly the same degree. Weighting decision criteria by the economic consequences of those criteria can help avoid this problem. However, such a weighting scheme does not address the fact that different governance criteria can become more or less important, for the same transaction, but at different times.

For example, it seems likely that demand uncertainty is more likely to be an important transaction attribute early in a transaction's history and less important later in that transaction's history. This is because, over time, the market responds to new products or services created through a transaction, which, in turn, reduces demand uncertainty. In a similar way, the need to learn about tacit new resources is more likely to be important early in a transaction than later, since, over time, a firm will learn what it wanted to learn. Finally, over time, as parties to an exchange gain experience working with each other, the threat of opportunism in an exchange can be reduced since the behavioural uncertainty that characterizes that exchange can also be reduced (Barney and Hansen 1994).

As these different governance considerations change over the course of an exchange, the optimal form of governance might also change. For example, in the early stages of an exchange, the threat of opportunism may be very significant, and more hierarchical governance may be appropriate. However over time, this threat can be reduced, and the need for hierarchical governance can also be reduced. If, during this same time period, the level of demand uncertainty in an exchange has remained constant, then it would not be unreasonable to see more hierarchical forms of governance replaced with less hierarchical forms of governance.

Indeed, the study of the evolution of governance in a transaction over time has already shown some very distinct patterns. For example, Kogut (1991) has shown that firms facing high demand uncertainty will often adopt intermediate forms of governance. As suggested earlier, intermediate governance represents a compromise between the need, on the one hand, to keep transaction-specific investments in governance low under conditions of high demand uncertainty, and the need, on the other hand, to learn about the tacit resources controlled by other firms. However, Kogut (1991) has shown that once demand uncertainty is reduced and the value of an exchange is known and positive, then intermediate governance is replaced by hierarchical governance. That is, once real options logic is no longer important but the need to learn about the tacit skills of an exchange partner are ongoing, knowledge-based logic takes precedence over real options logic, and governance shifts from the compromise of intermediate governance to the learning-enhancing efficiency of more hierarchical governance. This shift could be described as an 'alliance as a prelude to acquisition'.

Alternatively, Hamel (1991) describes what he calls a 'learning race'. Here, firms adopt intermediate governance, again as a compromise between the need to remain flexible (from real options logic) and the need to enhance learning (from knowledge-based theories of the firm). However, once a firm has learned what it needs to learn in an exchange, the need to learn is no longer important, and real options logic suggests that intermediate governance should be replaced by market governance. And this is what occurs in a 'learning race', as firms co-operate until one of them learns what it is that they wanted to learn from the exchange, then co-operative intermediate governance is replaced by competitive arm's-length market relations. Of course, these 'learning races' have important competitive implications for firms, since the firm that learns first what it wants to learn in an exchange is able to make it difficult for the other firm to learn all that it wanted to learn by shifting governance from intermediate forms (where learning is facilitated) to market forms (where learning is more difficult).

Thus far, 'alliances as preludes to acquisitions' and 'alliances as learning races' have both been characterized as resulting from changes in the extent to which demand uncertainty and the need to learn about tacit capabilities in an exchange vary over time. However, these same governance transitions could be derived from shifts in the real options and transaction cost decision criteria over time, or from shifts in the transaction cost and learning decision criteria over time. In short, governance dynamics may be an important means of resolving what appear to be contradictions in Figure 14.1.

4. Conclusion

This chapter suggests that there are decision-making criteria, beyond opportunism minimization, that firms can use to make governance choices. At least two additional considerations have been identified: real options logic and knowledge-based theories of the firm logic. It has been shown that these theories have predictable governance implications and that they are not just special cases of transactions cost economics.

In some circumstances, transaction cost, real options, and knowledge-based theories of the firm have the same or complementary governance implications for firms. In these settings, the optimal governance a firm should choose is unambiguous. However, in other settings, these three theories have contradictory governance implications.

When these theories have contradictory governance implications, several different approaches can be used to resolve these conflicts to discover what a firm's optimal governance choices should be. These approaches include: weighting the importance of a decision criterion by its economic consequences in an exchange on a transaction by transaction basis; choosing the least costly form of governance that addresses the transaction issues identified by all three decision criteria; using intermediate governance as a form of compromise among conflicting criteria; and recognizing that the importance of governance decision criteria can vary over time. This latter alternative suggests that the evolution of governance in an exchange is an important means whereby apparent conflicts among these models can be resolved.

These different ways of resolving conflicts among the different governance criteria can be used to generate testable hypotheses about how firms actually make governance decisions when multiple criteria conflict. This suggests that the most important conditions under which to study governance choices are conditions where these different theories conflict. At the time of writing we are unaware of empirical research that explicitly examines how firms resolve conflicts among different decision criteria in making governance choices.

We now return briefly to the bio-technology firm with which this chapter began: it would be inappropriate to argue that this firm should make its very difficult manufacturing decision on the basis of a single decision-making criterion, like minimizing the threat of opportunism. While opportunism must, of course, be an important consideration, demand uncertainty and the need to learn about tacit manufacturing skills are also important considerations as well. And, as has been shown in this chapter, these considerations have important governance implications. Indeed, it is very likely that the need to reduce transaction-specific investments in governance and the need to learn about tacit capabilities may, for this firm's manufacturing decision, be just as important as, if not more important than, minimizing the threat of opportunism. It would not be surprising if this firm were to adopt some sort of intermediate governance as a compromise among the rationales for governance of transaction cost, real options, and knowledge-based theories of the firm, and then, over time, to adjust its governance to reflect changes in the relative importance of these different decision-making criteria.

References

BALAKRISHNAN, S., and WERNERFELT, B. 1986. 'Technical change, competition and vertical integration', *Strategic Management Journal* 7: 347–59.

BARNEY, J. 1991. 'Firm resources and sustainable competitive advantage', *Journal of Management* 17: 155–71.

—— and M. HANSEN 1994. 'Trustworthines as a source of competitive advantage', *Strategic Management Journal* 15: 175–90.

—— and W. HESTERLY 1996. 'Organizational economics', in S. Clegg, C. Hardy, and W. Nord, eds. *The Handbook of Organization Studies*. London, Thousand Oaks, and New Delhi: Sage Publications.

CONNER, K., and C. K. PRAHALAD 1996. 'A resource-based theory of the firm: Knowledge versus opportunism', *Organization Science* 7: 477–501.

DIERICKX, I., and K. COOL 1989. 'Asset stock accumulation and the sustainability of competitive advantage', *Management Science* 35: 1504–11.

FOSS, N. 1996. 'More critical comments on knowledge-based theories of the firm', *Organization Science* 7: 519–23.

HAMEL, G. 1991. 'Competition for competence and inter-partner learning within international strategic alliances', *Strategic Management Journal* 12: 83–103.

KLEIN, B., R. G. CRAWFORD, and A. ALCHIEN 1978. 'Vertical integration, appropriable rents, and the competitive contracting process', *Journal of Law and Economics*: 297–326.

—— —— —— 1981. 'The role of market forces in assuring contractual performance', *Journal of Political Economy* 89: 615–41.

KNIGHT, F. 1965. *Risk, Uncertainty, and Profit*. New York: Wiley.

KOGUT, B. 1991. 'Joint ventures and the option to expand and acquire', *Management Science* 37: 19–33.

MASTEN, S., J. MEEHAN, and E. SNYDER 1991. 'The cost of organization', *Journal of Law, Economics, and Organization* 7: 1–25.

POLANYI, M. 1962. *Personal Knowledge*. London: Routledge & Kegan Paul.

PISANO, G. 1990. 'The R&D boundaries of the firm: An empirical analysis', *Administrative Science Quarterly* 35: 153–76.

SPENDER, J. C. 1996. 'Making knowledge the basis of a dynamic theory of the firm', *Strategic Management Journal* 17: 45–62.

WALKER, G., and D. WEBER, 1984. 'A transaction cost approach to make or buy decisions', *Administrative Science Quarterly* 29: 373–91.

—— —— 1987. 'Supplier competition, uncertainty, and make-or-buy decisions', *Academy of Management Journal* 30: 589–96.

WILLIAMSON, O. E. 1975. *Markets and Hierarchies*. New York: Free Press.

—— 1985. *The Economic Institutions of Capitalism*. New York: Free Press.

15

Demand Uncertainty and Asset Flexibility: Incorporating Strategic Options in the Theory of the Firm

RON SANCHEZ

1. Introduction

Since the pioneering paper on the theory of the firm by Ronald Coase (1937), managerial decision making has been the focus of analyses seeking to answer the two closely intertwined questions of economic organization: 'Why do firms exist?' and 'What determines the boundaries of firms?' Like most theorizing about complex phenomena, theorizing about the existence and boundaries of firms has sought to develop insights into these questions by examining in depth certain aspects of managerial decision making, while making some fairly strong simplifying assumptions about other aspects of managerial decision making in an effort to reduce the complexity and facilitate analysis of the problem. Various approaches to developing the theory of the firm put forward over the years can be distinguished by their representations of the nature of managerial decision making, and especially by their (sometimes unstated) simplifying assumptions about what managers consider in their decision making.

Uncertainty in many forms pervades managerial decision making and greatly influences decisions about the boundaries of the firm—that is, about what assets a firm will acquire and use in creating and realizing products. Transaction cost analysis has investigated the impacts of certain forms of 'supply-side' uncertainty on the decisions of managers about which assets to internalize within the firm and which assets will be sourced through market transactions (Williamson 1975, 1985, 1991). A basic argument of transaction cost analysis, discussed more fully below, is that managers' uncertainty about how to define and write complete contracts for the future use of assets sourced through market transactions may expose a firm to unacceptable costs of opportunism in the future and lead to decisions to acquire or 'internalize' certain key assets today. In analysing the influence of this form of supply-side uncertainty on managerial decision making, transaction cost analysis has typically made strong (but often implicit) assumptions of certainty about future market demand for the specific products that would be made by the assets under consideration.

Many observers of product markets have noted, however, that market demand for specific products can be highly uncertain, especially in product markets with rapid changes in market preferences for specific kinds of products or in available technologies for making new products (see, for example, Sanchez 1995). This chapter undertakes to extend the transaction cost perspective on managerial decision making by explicitly incorporating uncertainty about market demand for specific products—and thus about the economic value of specific assets for making those products—into the representation and analysis of managerial decision making. The discussion below draws on options theory to capture and represent two important variables in managerial decision making that are ignored when market demand for specific products is assumed to be certain: (1) the potential benefits of internalizing flexible-use assets rather than specific-use assets, and (2) the potential benefits of the flexibility that comes from using market transactions to source assets in the future rather than internalizing assets today to assure their future availability. This options-theoretic view of managerial decision making under uncertainty leads to a new view of both the kinds of assets that managers will seek to internalize and the extent to which managers will seek to bring various kinds of assets within the boundaries of a firm.

The discussion below is organized in the following way.

Section 2 summarizes the common transaction cost analysis representation of managerial decision making as focused on minimizing the sum of production costs, opportunism costs, and bureaucratic costs. We then consider Riordan and Williamson's (1985) extension of transaction cost analysis to include managers' decisions as to which products the firm should provide to markets, as well as decisions about which production technologies to use and which production assets to internalize for each product selected. We show that this analytic framework commonly leads to the conclusion that managers will seek to internalize specific-use assets that provide greater efficiency and superior quality in offering products to markets.

In section 3, we extend the representations of the Riordan and Williamson model to include some aspects of the demand-side uncertainties and contemporary production technologies that managers commonly consider. The revenues that would be obtained from specific products are represented as uncertain and time dependent. The production costs that must be incurred to offer a product are represented as consisting of both relatively risky initial sunk costs required to acquire a production asset and relatively less risky variable costs that would be incurred only as a product is produced on a production asset. In addition, section 3 extends the representation of the production assets available to managers to include assets with varying degrees of resource flexibility—that is, some assets available to managers may have the flexibility to be used to produce more than one product. We also technologically update the Riordan and

Williamson analysis by characterizing currently available flexible production assets as capable of achieving very nearly the efficiency and quality levels of specific-use production assets.

Section 4 draws on options theory to represent the economic value of a production asset as the value of the strategic options (Sanchez 1993) that it brings to a firm to produce new products. We characterize managerial decision making as being concerned with optimizing the value of the strategic options that various assets make available to a firm. This characterization of managerial decision making makes it possible, in effect, to include in the analysis of economic organizing the *opportunity costs* of internalizing specific-use assets (that is, the economic value of the strategic options that a firm forgoes by acquiring specific-use assets rather than flexible-use assets), as well as the *opportunism costs* that firms can avoid by internalizing specific-use assets.

Section 5 explores the interrelationships of strategic options, sunk costs, and governance modes associated with flexible-use versus specific-use assets. Analysis of these interrelationships leads to some predictions about prevalent forms of economic organization:

- 'Static economizing', achieved through internalization of specific-use assets, will be prevalent when market demand for specific products is stable and when specific-use assets offer significant cost and quality benefits.
- 'Dynamic internal economizing', achieved through internalization of flexible assets, will prevail when demand for specific products is highly uncertain and when assets with desired levels of flexibility must be specially designed and built.
- 'Dynamic market economizing,' achieved through market sourcing of flexible assets, will prevail when demand for specific products is highly uncertain and when general-purpose assets are readily obtainable from markets and offer desired levels of flexibility.

Section 6 offers concluding comments.

2. A Transaction Cost Representation of Managerial Decision Making

The transaction cost framework introduced by Coase (1937, 1988) and developed most extensively by Williamson (1975, 1985, 1991) analyses transactions for the exchange of goods to understand the factors that may lead managers to decide to internalize an asset or to rely on market transactions to obtain the use of an asset. Transaction cost analysis recognizes that 'supply-side' uncertainties may limit the ability of managers to write a complete contract—or more realistically, a contract judged to be adequate by managers—to secure the use of an asset at acceptable costs in the future. When a firm's future exchanges would depend on the continued availability (at reasonable cost) of a specific asset, the inability to write or enforce a complete contract for the use of the asset may lead managers to decide that there is an unacceptable threat of *ex post* opportunistic behaviour by the owner of the asset. When an essential asset is a specialized or specific-use asset for which substitute assets would be too costly or impossible to arrange (*ex post* small numbers bargaining), transaction cost analysis suggests that the potential costs of opportunism resulting from supply-side contracting uncertainty will often lead managers to decide to internalize an asset to bring it under the hierarchical control of the firm.

In transaction cost analysis, the basis for management decisions to internalize or source an asset from the market is the desire to achieve economic efficiency by organizing transactions so as to minimize the sum of production costs and governance costs for each transaction. Governance costs consist of both the costs of opportunistic behaviour to which the firm is exposed when it uses market transactions and the bureaucratic costs of administering internal transactions that are sheltered from market discipline. Thus, in transaction cost analysis the objective of managerial decision making may be stated as

Minimize [*Production costs + Bureaucratic costs + Opportunism costs*]   (1)

In the usual transaction cost analysis, both the product to be produced by the firm and the revenue to be derived from producing the product are exogenously determined. Riordan and Williamson (1985) propose an expanded, more strategic statement of the objective of managerial decision making. They include in this objective decision making about which product designs a firm should provide to markets and which production technology and related assets to use for each product design the firm offers. In the Riordan and Williamson model, a specific-use production asset is characterized as having lower unit costs and/or producing a higher-quality product than a general-use production asset. Further, the revenue to be derived from a product is characterized as increasing with product quality. Thus, the Riordan and Williamson model both endogenizes managerial choice of products and makes product revenues dependent on the production technologies and assets chosen.

In this more complete representation of managerial decision making, the objective of managers becomes maximizing the net present value of the revenues obtainable from each of the product designs the firm can offer, less costs associated with the production technologies and governance modes selected for each product design. Thus, managerial decision making becomes a process of making profit-maximizing choices about production modes for alternative product designs $1 \ldots n$:

Maximize [*Revenues − (Production costs + Bureaucratic costs*
    + Opportunism costs)]$_{1 \ldots n}$ (2)

In the general transaction cost framework, costs of opportunism increase with

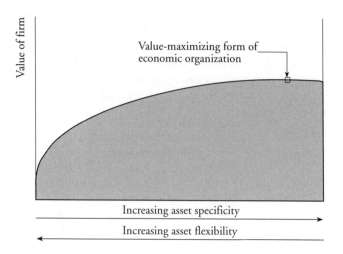

Figure 15.1. Value-maximizing form of economic organization under the Riordan and Williamson (1985) model

asset specificity, and in the Riordan and Williamson model, net revenues (revenues minus costs) obtainable from each product also increase with asset specificity. Given these assumptions, an analysis of managerial decision making based on this model will tend to suggest that managers will maximize net revenues by choosing and internalizing specific-use assets for each of its product opportunities, as indicated in Figure 15.1. Of course, as the concave curve in Figure 15.1 suggests, for some asset classes the potential increases in product quality or reductions in product costs obtainable from a specialized asset would be minimal or non-existent, and the bureaucratic costs of internalizing all assets a firm might ever use would become very high. For example, it usually is not net-revenue maximizing for a firm to own the assets needed to make its own paper or pens, or even its own computers. Thus, for each firm it will still be optimal to have less than total internalization of all assets the firm might ever use, though under the assumptions of the Riordan and Williamson model, a high level of internalization of specific-use assets that can increase quality and lower costs will generally be indicated.

3. Recognizing Demand-Side Uncertainties and the Characteristics of Contemporary Production Technologies

We now consider some important aspects of contemporary product markets and production technologies that suggest four important extensions to the Riordan and Williamson model that it would be desirable to incorporate in a more complete model of managerial decision making.

1. *'Demand-side' uncertainty about future revenues.* In recent years, the heightened intensity of competition in a growing number of product markets has led to increased uncertainty about the revenues that can be obtained from new products. In addition, the longer it takes the firm to acquire and start to use an asset to supply a given product to its markets, the lower the present value of the future revenues to be derived from producing that product (due simply to discounting by the risk-adjusted discount rate applicable to future revenues). Further, in many product markets prices are subject to rapid erosion as more firms become capable of bringing competing products to market, suggesting that both market demand and prices (and therefore total revenues generated from use of a production asset) may decrease over time due to competition between firms. To incorporate these aspects of demand-side uncertainty in contemporary product markets, the representations of the Riordan and Williamson model need to be extended to recognize that the revenues that can be obtained from specific products are uncertain and time dependent.

2. Relative riskiness of sunk versus variable costs. The Riordan and Williamson model characterizes alternative production assets as differing in their relative cost efficiencies, suggesting that specific-use assets may lead to lower overall costs of production. This representation of production assets, however, does not distinguish differences in the relative riskiness of alternative production assets with differing sunk versus variable cost characteristics. Sunk costs that must be incurred before a product can be brought to market (such as investments in production machines) are inherently more risky than variable costs (such as those for materials and labour) that are incurred in providing each unit sold in a market. In this regard, specific-use assets that may lead to lower variable costs of materials and labour may none the less incur considerable financial risk, because they often cost more than general flexible-use assets and thus represent a larger sunk cost. An extended model of managerial decision making should allow the greater riskiness of assets with high sunk costs to be weighed against the potential benefits of any reductions in variable costs they may make possible.

3. Resource flexibility. In modelling managers' decisions about which assets to internalize, transaction cost analysis generally does not recognize the economic value of resource flexibility (Sanchez 1995)—that is, the value of being able to switch flexible assets from the production of one product to another as uncertain future demand for specific products evolves. Typically, however, assets with varying degrees of flexibility are available to managers, and the flexibilities of production assets available for many product markets are increasing rapidly. For example, flexible manufacturing systems now make it possible for Motorola to produce any of twenty

million variations of pager products in its pager factories. Thus, it would be very desirable to represent the value of resource flexibility in contemporary managerial decision making.

4. Improved efficiency and quality of flexible production assets. The assumption made in the Riordan and Williamson model that product quality levels increase and production costs decrease with increasing specialization of production assets more or less accurately represented the production technologies available in the early 1980s. However, the production efficiencies obtainable today from flexible manufacturing technologies increasingly make possible an economic order quantity (EOQ) approaching 1—that is, production costs are becoming as low for a single unit of a product as for large numbers of the same product. Thus the cost efficiency of many flexible production systems is approaching that of dedicated, specific-use production systems. The quality levels obtainable from flexible production systems are also increasingly comparable to quality levels obtainable from specialized equipment.

4. An Options-Theoretic Representation of Managerial Decisions about Economic Organizing

We now incorporate the demand-side uncertainties and technology characteristics considered in section 2 in an options-theoretic model of managerial decision making.

To begin, we add four important representations to the Riordan and Williamson model in order to represent more realistically the decision environments commonly faced by managers:

1. Revenues from specific products are represented as uncertain because market demand for specific products is uncertain, and the present value of expected revenues to be derived from specific products is represented as decreasing with the increasing time required to put a production asset in place and to begin production of a new product.

2. Production costs are represented as consisting of both relatively high-risk sunk costs, which must be invested to acquire a production asset, and relatively low-risk variable costs, which are incurred only as an asset is used in production to meet actual demand.

3. Production assets are represented as including a spectrum of possible assets with varying flexibilities to be used in the production of other products.

4. Flexible-use production assets are represented as offering cost efficiencies and quality levels approaching those obtainable from specific-use assets.

Extending the Riordan and Williamson model in this way restates the problem of economic organizing as an optimization problem, because adding the flexibility to switch production assets from one product to another creates inter-dependences among alternative products and production assets. Given significant uncertainties about demand for specific products, significant differences in possible sunk costs and variable costs of alternative production assets, and a significant range of production asset flexibilities and efficiencies, choosing the value-maximizing form of economic organization requires selecting the optimal set of products, production assets, and governance modes for each product possibility the firm can identify. This extended statement of the problem of economic organizing leads to the following optimization problem for decision makers evaluating a set of n identified product possibilities:

Optimize f[*Revenues*(t)$_{1 \ldots n}$ – (Sunk costs of production assets
+ *Variable costs* of using production assets + Bureaucratic costs
+ Opportunism costs)$_{1 \ldots n}$] $\hspace{2cm}$ (3)

In equation (3), *Revenues*(t)$_{1 \ldots n}$ and *Variable costs* of using production assets are regarded as uncertain at the time the economic organizing decision is made about each of the product opportunities $1 \ldots n$, while the Sunk costs of production assets, the Bureaucratic costs, and the Opportunism costs associated with each production asset are assumed to be determinate and estimatable at the time of the decision.

We now relate the terms in equation (3) to the concepts used in options theory (Black and Scholes 1973; Merton 1973, 1982; Myers 1979) and to options approaches to evaluating a firm's alternative choices of product designs and production technologies as strategic options (Sanchez 1993, 1995; Sanchez and Thomas 1996).

In an options approach to interpreting equation (3), an investment of sunk costs in acquiring the use of a production asset can be characterized as creating an option to produce a new product. The product option created by the availability of a production asset may be exercised by paying the variable costs of producing products to serve the realized market demand for that product. When a firm exercises one of its available product options (that is, it incurs the variable costs of producing a specific product), it receives a revenue stream generated by the sales of the new product. Thus, a simplified statement[1] of the value of the option to offer a new product P$_i$ created by acquiring a production asset is given by the expression

Option P$_i$ = f{*Revenues(t)*$_i$ – (*Variable costs of using production assets*)$_i$} $\hspace{1cm}$ (4)

Recalling equation (3) and its assumptions that the Sunk costs, the Bureaucratic costs, and the Opportunism costs associated with each product opportunity P$_i$ and its associated production assets are assumed to be determinate and estimatable at

---

[1] For a complete statement of the options pricing model, see Sanchez (1999). Note that the functional form f {. . .} in equation (4) denotes the need to interpret Revenues and Variable costs in accordance with an appropriate options pricing model.

the time of the decision, equations (3) and (4) can be combined to yield the following options-theoretic representation of the objective of managerial decision making about economic organizing:

$$\text{Optimize } [\textit{Options } P_{1 \ldots n} - (\textit{Sunk costs of production assets}$$
$$+ \textit{Bureaucratic costs} + \textit{Opportunism costs})_{1 \ldots n}] \qquad (5)$$

or more conveniently for the following discussion:

$$\text{Optimize } [\textit{Options } P_{1 \ldots n} - \textit{Sunk costs of production}$$
$$\textit{assets}_{1 \ldots n} + \textit{Governance costs}_{1 \ldots n}] \qquad (6)$$

In various ways that are explained in the next section, using flexible assets may improve the speed with which a firm may bring new products to market, may help to reduce the risk inherent in the sunk costs of production assets, and may enable a firm to switch production assets from one product to another. All of these benefits of flexible assets may create significant economic value by increasing the value of a firm's strategic options, by reducing sunk costs, and by reducing the costs of governance. In the next section, we use equation (6) to investigate in greater detail how the availability of flexible assets can affect managers' decisions about economic organizing.

5. Impacts of Flexible Assets on Economic Organizing

We now consider some specific ways in which using flexible assets may create greater economic value by improving the speed with which a firm may bring new products to market, by helping to reduce the risk inherent in the sunk costs of production assets, and by enabling a firm to switch production assets from one product to another.

1. *Value of greater speed to market.* A flexible-use asset like general-purpose production machinery may generally be sourced more quickly in the market-place than specific-use production equipment, which often must be custom designed and built. In addition, contracting for production services based on general-purpose machines is also likely to be more readily available than contracting for production services based on machines that are specifically designed for a given product. Thus, it will often be possible to arrange and begin the use of either internalized or market-sourced flexible (general-purpose) machines more quickly than the use of specific-use production assets.

   The economic value that can be created by using flexible-use assets to speed a new product to market will depend on the specific values of all terms in equation (6). However, in general terms, when the value of a new product opportunity decreases sharply with increasing time to market, the

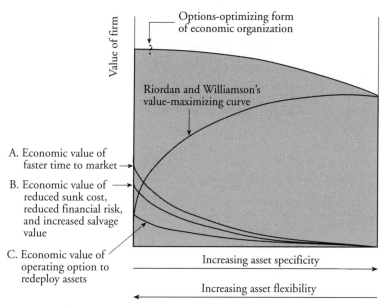

Figure 15.2. Options-optimizing form of economic organization

ability to extract any net revenues from a product opportunity may depend on a firm being one of the first two or three firms to reach the market with a new product. In such cases, the value of a firm's product options may be substantially greater when it can use readily available flexible production assets to increase the speed with which it brings its products to market. This increased value of the firm's product options is suggested in Figure 15.2 by curve A which shows the additional 'economic value of faster time to market' that is possible as the flexibility of the assets available for producing a product increases.

2. *Value of reducing sunk costs.* Although specific-use assets may lead to lower variable costs of production than flexible general-purpose production assets, flexible assets are likely to have lower initial purchase costs than costs for custom-designed and built, specific-use production assets. Reducing initial sunk costs by using flexible general-purpose assets reduces the financial risk of creating a new product option. Using flexible, general-use assets that can be sourced through markets is also likely to lower governance costs for transactions to supply such assets (that is, compared with the bureaucratic costs of internal sourcing of the assets). In addition, flexible assets may have greater salvage value than specific-use assets, so that actual sunk costs of (that is, the non-recoverable investment in) flexible assets may be quite low compared with non-recoverable investments in

specific-use equipment. The reduction of sunk costs and financial risk and the likelihood of a significant salvage value may all add economic value to a firm's product options when it can use flexible assets. This additional economic value is suggested by curve B in Figure 15.2, indicating the additional 'economic value of reduced sunk costs, reduced financial risk, and increased salvage value'.

3. *Value of production flexibility.* Flexible production assets may also be switched from production of one product to another. The economic value of this flexibility is easy to recognize intuitively as the net gain in profits that are possible when a flexible asset may be switched to production of the most profitable product among the set of products that it is feasible to produce with that asset. Thus, a flexible production asset brings a firm a potentially valuable operating option to switch production to the most profitable among a portfolio of n possible products.[2] The additional 'economic value of the operating option to redeploy flexible assets' to their most profitable uses is shown by curve C in Figure 15.2.

As the foregoing discussion and the curves in Figure 15.2 suggest, the total opportunity costs of using specific-use assets instead of flexible-use assets may be significant compared with the economic value of production cost efficiencies and improved product quality that may be available from use of specific-use assets, although these opportunity costs have generally not been considered in the transaction cost framework.

4. *Impacts on economic organizing.* The additional economic value that may be created by the use of flexible assets rather than specific-use assets can be combined with the value-maximizing 'Riordan and Williamson' curve from Figure 15.1, which does not consider these potential sources of economic value. Adding curves A, B, and C to the Riordan and Williamson value-maximizing curve in Figure 15.2 creates a new 'economic value optimizing curve' based on the options formulation of equation (6) that suggests that:

(a) the economic value of a firm's product opportunities may be greatest when the firm can use production assets with high levels of flexibility;

(b) the economic value of a firm's product opportunities increases with increasing flexibilities of the assets available to the firm for realizing its product opportunities.

If the combined transaction cost and options-theoretic representation in equation (6) and Figure 15.2 more fully captures the essential features of the problem of economic organizing, equation (6) should enable improved

---

[2] Stulz (1982), Johnson (1987), and Sanchez (1991) developed options pricing models for valuing this kind of operating option.

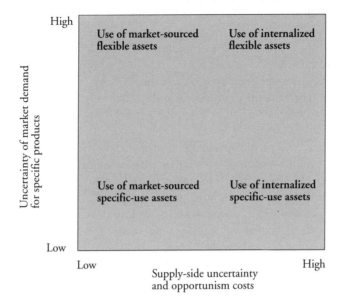

Figure 15.3. Predictions of options-optimizing forms of economic organization under demand-side and supply-side uncertainties

predictions of the approaches managers will actually take to selecting products, production technologies, and modes of governance. Since the value of flexible assets increases under conditions of demand-side uncertainty, for example, equation (6) may be used to predict the efficient (and thus dominant) forms of economic organization managers will decide to adopt under differing levels of supply-side and demand-side uncertainty. These predictions are summarized in Figure 15.3 and explained below.

In a stable market environment with low levels of demand uncertainty, low demand uncertainty lowers the value of speed to market, reduces the financial risk of incurring large sunk costs, and diminishes the value of the flexibility to switch a production asset among products. Under these conditions, the additional value to be derived by using readily obtainable, low sunk-cost, flexible assets may not be significant compared with the value of the production cost reductions and quality improvements that may be obtainable from specific-use assets. Thus, when market demand is predictable and stable, managerial decision making should favour (a) the use of specific-use assets and (b) the internalization of specific-use assets to economize on governance costs (that is, to minimize costs of opportunism). In effect, when demand uncertainty is low, the additional options value created by flexible assets is low, and the predictions of the Riordan and Williamson model are likely to be supported.

In a dynamic market environment with high levels of demand uncertainty, the economic value of greater speed to market, reduced financial risk of incurring large sunk costs, and the flexibility to switch a production asset among various products may be significant compared with the value of the cost reductions and quality enhancements obtainable from specific-use assets. Under these conditions, managerial decision making should generally favour the use of flexible assets. Whether managers will favour internalization or market sourcing of flexible-use assets will depend on the governance costs associated with each supply alternative. When high levels of production flexibility in a given product market context are offered by general-purpose assets that are readily available in markets, supply-side uncertainty and resulting opportunism costs will be low, and governance costs will be minimized by sourcing flexible-use assets through market transactions. However, when assets must be custom-designed and built to achieve desired levels of flexibility, the potential opportunism costs of market transactions to source or use the production assets may be significant, and internalization of the flexible assets to minimize governance costs may be the most common approach to organizing production.

In the case of low market uncertainty and low supply uncertainty, the prediction of an expected form of economic organizing would depend on more precise analysis of product options, sunk costs, and transaction costs, although use of market-sourced specific-use assets would generally be indicated.

6. Conclusions

This chapter has proposed a more complete model of managerial decision making about economic organizing by combining: (1) usual transaction cost representations of the opportunism costs of contracting for specific-use assets and the bureaucratic costs of internalizing assets; (2) characterizations of production cost reductions and quality enhancement benefits of specific-use assets suggested by Riordan and Williamson (1985); and (3) options-theoretic representations of several potential forms of economic value obtainable from flexible-use assets. In this more complete model, decisions about economic organizing are characterized as motivated not by an objective of simply minimizing the sum of production costs and transaction costs (as in some transaction cost analyses), or by the desire to maximize the value of product design, production technology, or governance mode possibilities (as in the Riordan and Williamson model), but rather by an objective to optimize the value of a set of product options that may be realized on production assets with varying time-to-market characteristics, that have differing ratios of sunk costs to variable costs, that offer varying flexibilities to switch among products, and that are subject to varying costs of governance.

This approach to the problem of economic organizing suggests that in product markets subject to high demand uncertainty, the preferred forms of economic organization may be ones that allow high levels of dynamic optimizing, achieved through the use of either internalized or market-sourced flexible assets to produce a changing array of profit-maximizing product options. When demand in product markets is stable, however, the preferred forms of economic organization may be ones that allow high levels of static economizing to be achieved through internalization of specific-use assets for low-cost, high-quality production of a stable offering of products.

References

BLACK, FISCHER, and MYRON SCHOLES 1973. 'The pricing of options and corporate liabilities', *Journal of Political Economy* 81(3): 637–54.

COASE, RONALD H. 1937. 'The nature of the firm', *Economica* (NS) 4: 386–405.

—— 1988. 'The nature of the firm: Origin, meaning, influence', *Journal of Law, Economics and Organization* 4(1): 3–47.

JOHNSON, HERB 1987. 'Options on the maximum or the minimum of several assets', *Journal of Financial and Quantitative Analysis* 22(2): 277–83.

MERTON, ROBERT 1973. 'Theory of rational option pricing', *Bell Journal of Economics and Management Science* 4(1): 141–83.

—— 1982. 'On the microeconomic theory of investment under uncertainty', in Kenneth J. Arrow and Michael D. Intriligator, eds., *Handbook of Mathematical Economics* Amsterdam: North-Holland Publishing Company, vol. 2: 601–69.

MYERS, STEWART C. 1977. 'Determinants of corporate borrowing', *Journal of Financial Economics* 5: 147–75.

RIORDAN, MICHAEL, and OLIVER WILLIAMSON 1985. 'Asset specificity and economic organization', *International Journal of Industrial Organization* 3: 365–78.

SANCHEZ, RON 1991. 'Strategic flexibility, real options, and product-based strategy', Ph.D. dissertation, Massachusetts Institute of Technology, Cambridge, MA.

—— 1993. 'Strategic flexibility, firm organization, and managerial work in dynamic markets: A strategic options perspective', *Advances in Strategic Management* 9: 251–91.

—— 1995. 'Strategic flexibility in product competition', *Strategic Management Journal* 16 (Summer special issue): 135–59.

—— 1999. 'Uncertainty, flexibility, and economic organization: Foundations for an options theory of the firm', Working Paper No. 1999-5, Department of Strategy and Industrial Economics, Copenhagen Business School.

—— and HOWARD THOMAS 1996. 'Strategic goals', in R. Sanchez, A. Heene, and H. Thomas, eds., *Dynamics of Competence-Based Competition*, Oxford: Elsevier Pergamon, 63–84.

STULZ, RENE M. 1982. 'Options on the minimum or the maximum of two risky assets', *Journal of Financial Economics* 10: 161–85.

WILLIAMSON, OLIVER E. 1975. *Markets and Hierarchies: Analysis and Antitrust Implications*. New York: Free Press.

—— 1985. *The Economic Institutions of Capitalism*. New York: Free Press.

—— 1991. 'Strategizing, economizing, and economic organization', *Strategic Management Journal* 12: 75–94.

Index